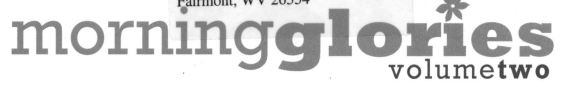

morningglories

volumetwo

all will be free

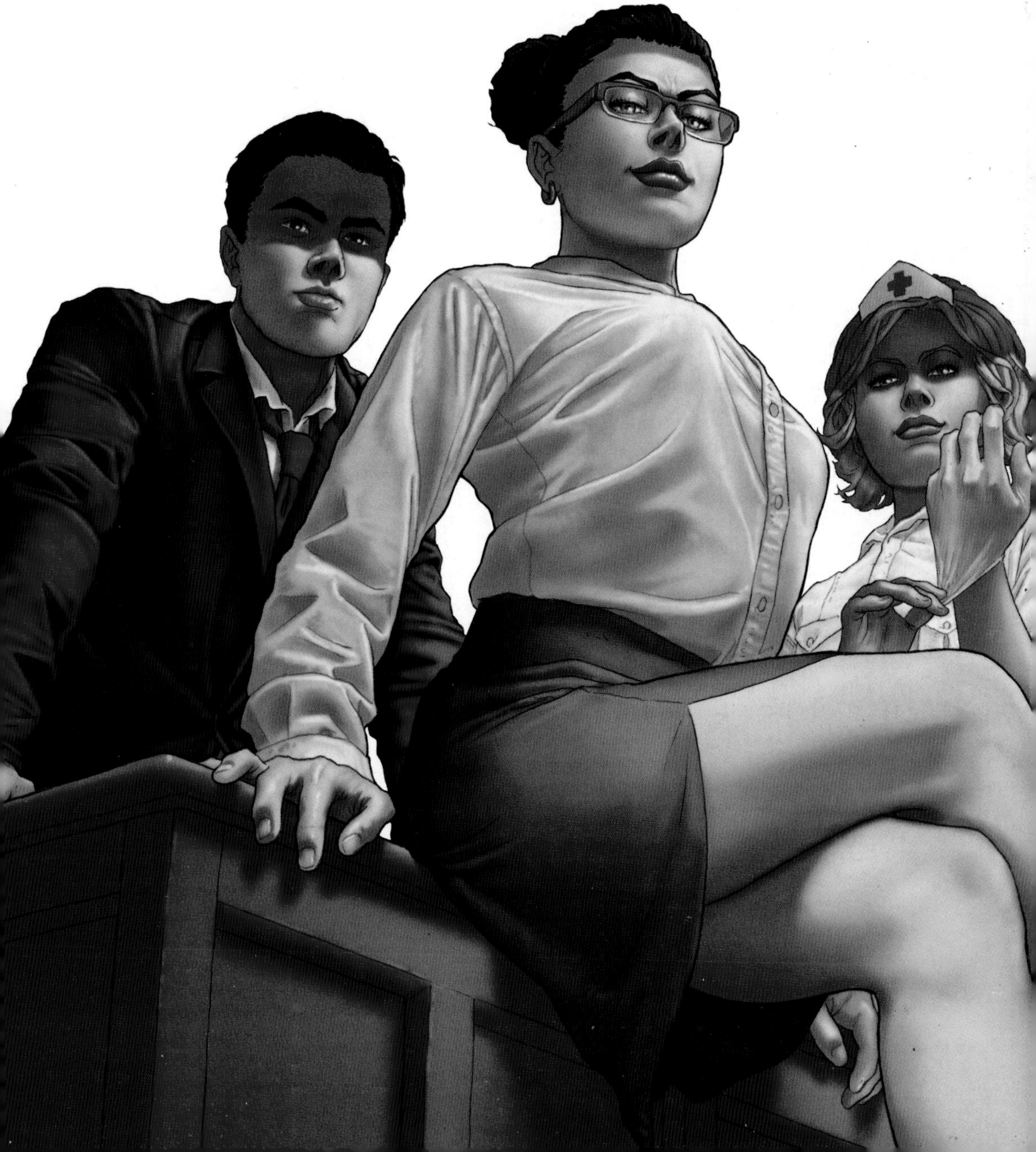

WORDS
NICK SPENCER

ART
JOE EISMA

RODIN ESQUEJO
COVERS

ALEX SOLLAZZO - JOHNNY LOWE - TIM DANIEL
COLORS · LETTERS · DESIGN

IMAGE COMICS, INC.
Robert Kirkman - chief operating officer
Erik Larsen - chief financial officer
Todd McFarlane - president
Marc Silvestri - chief executive officer
Jim Valentino - vice-president

Eric Stephenson - publisher
Ron Richards - director of business development
Jennifer de Guzman - pr & marketing director
Branwyn Bigglestone - accounts manager
Emily Miller - accounting assistant
Jamie Parreno - marketing assistant
Emilio Bautista - sales assistant
Susie Giroux - administrative assistant
Kevin Yuen - digital rights coordinator
Tyler Shainline - events coordinator
David Brothers - content manager
Jonathan Chan - production manager
Drew Gill - art director
Jana Cook - print manager
Monica Garcia - senior production artist
Vincent Kukua - production artist
Jenna Savage - production artist
www.imagecomics.com

seven

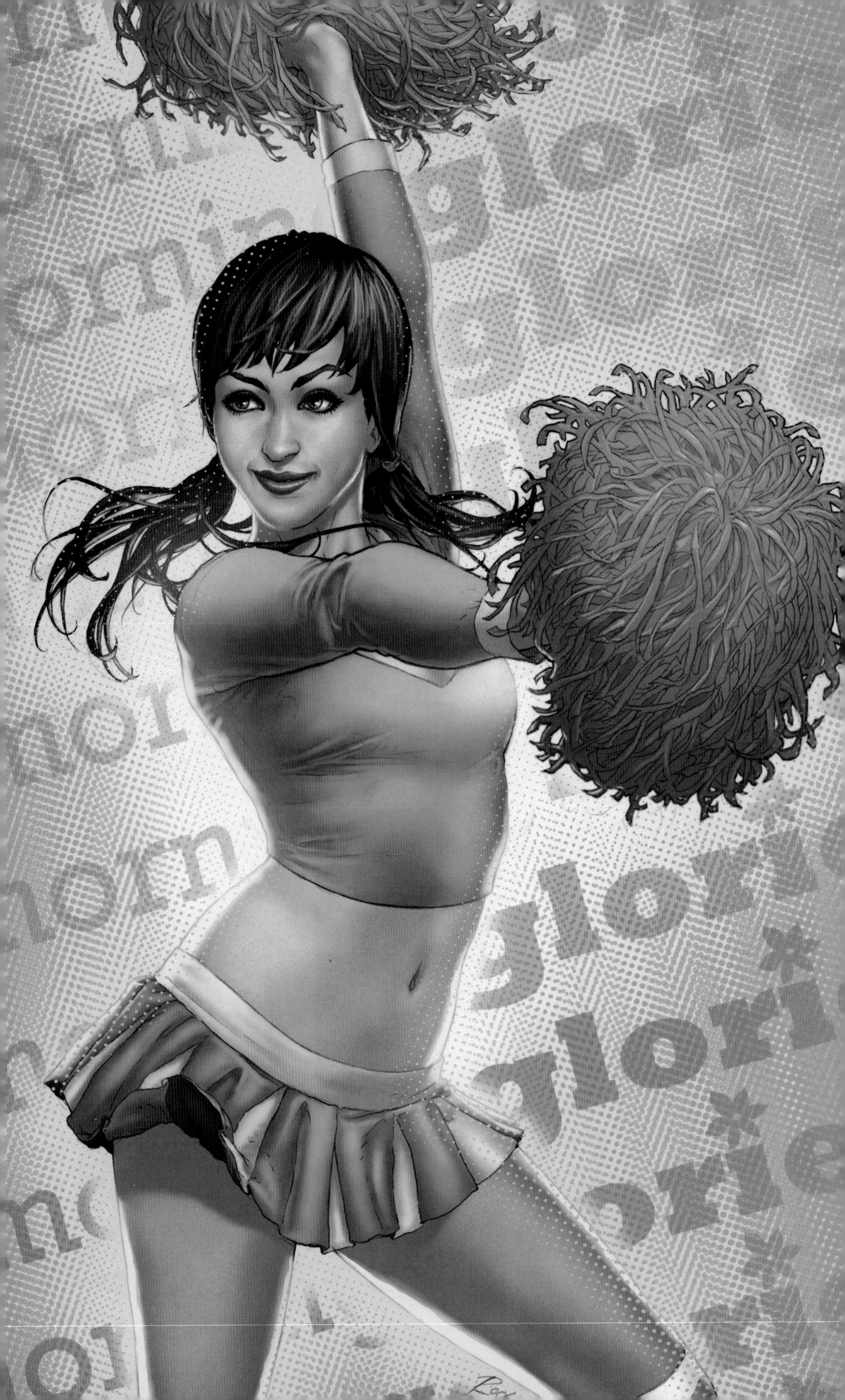

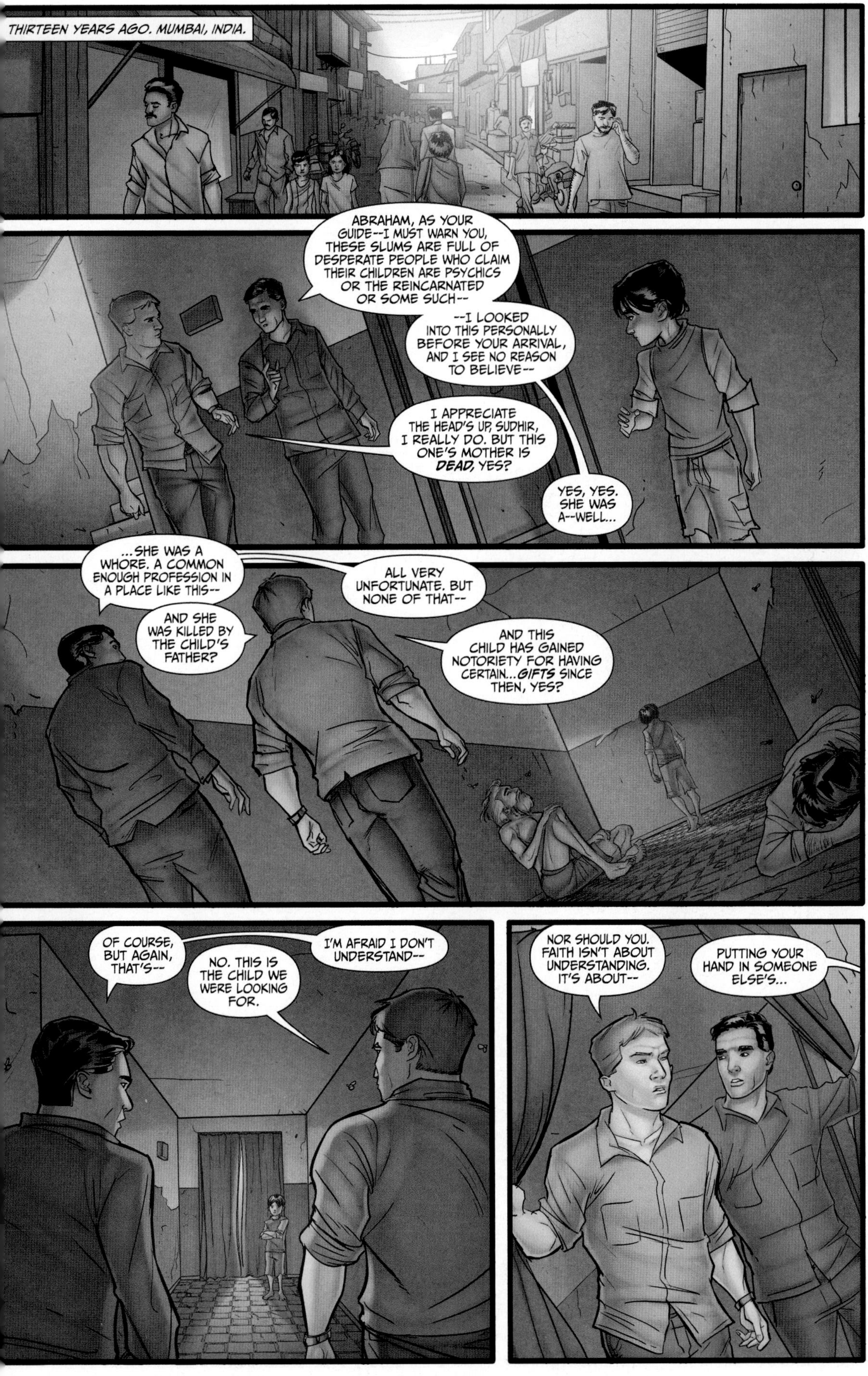
THIRTEEN YEARS AGO. MUMBAI, INDIA.
ABRAHAM, AS YOUR GUIDE--I MUST WARN YOU, THESE SLUMS ARE FULL OF DESPERATE PEOPLE WHO CLAIM THEIR CHILDREN ARE PSYCHICS OR THE REINCARNATED OR SOME SUCH--
--I LOOKED INTO THIS PERSONALLY BEFORE YOUR ARRIVAL, AND I SEE NO REASON TO BELIEVE--
I APPRECIATE THE HEAD'S UP, SUDHIR, I REALLY DO. BUT THIS ONE'S MOTHER IS DEAD, YES?
YES, YES. SHE WAS A--WELL...
...SHE WAS A WHORE. A COMMON ENOUGH PROFESSION IN A PLACE LIKE THIS--
ALL VERY UNFORTUNATE. BUT NONE OF THAT--
AND SHE WAS KILLED BY THE CHILD'S FATHER?
AND THIS CHILD HAS GAINED NOTORIETY FOR HAVING CERTAIN...GIFTS SINCE THEN, YES?
OF COURSE, BUT AGAIN, THAT'S--
I'M AFRAID I DON'T UNDERSTAND--
NO. THIS IS THE CHILD WE WERE LOOKING FOR.
NOR SHOULD YOU. FAITH ISN'T ABOUT UNDERSTANDING. IT'S ABOUT--
PUTTING YOUR HAND IN SOMEONE ELSE'S...

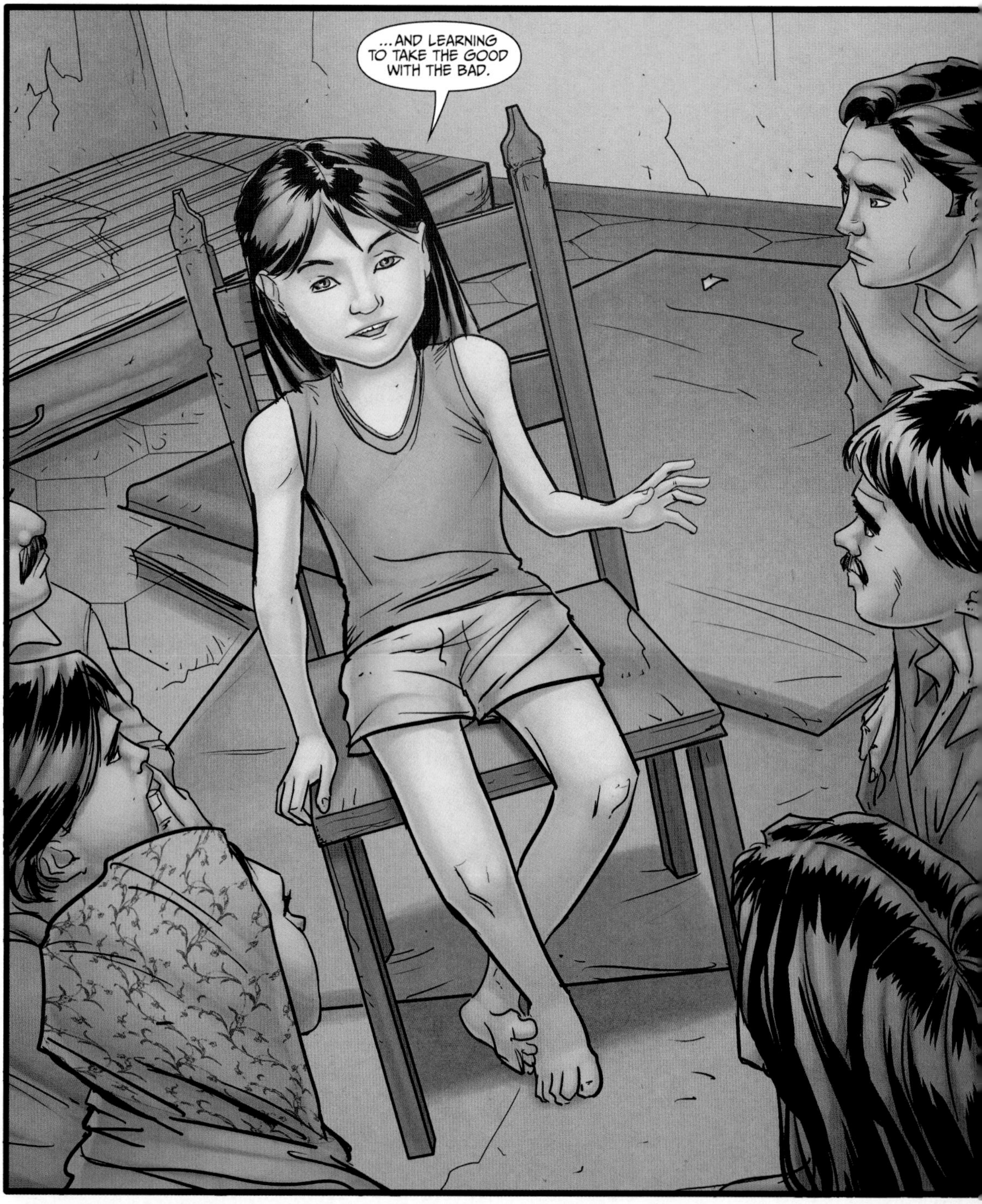
...AND LEARNING TO TAKE THE GOOD WITH THE BAD.

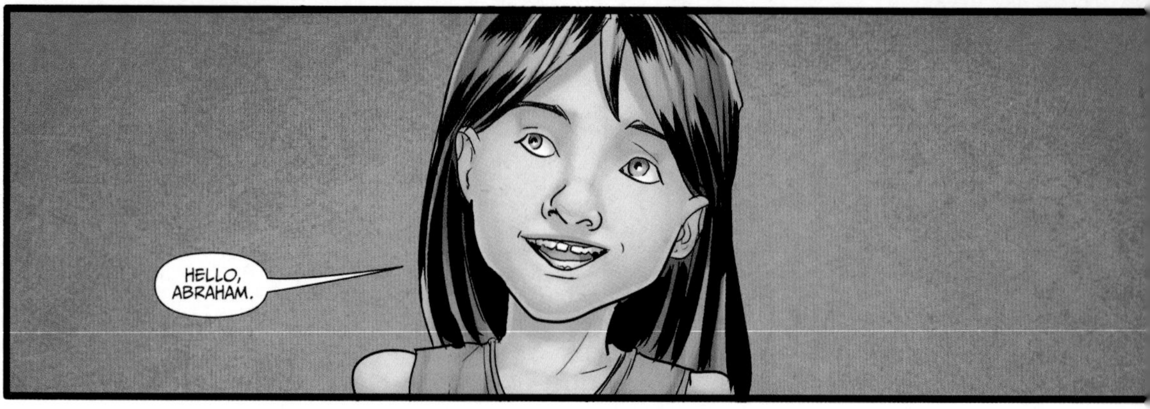
HELLO, ABRAHAM.

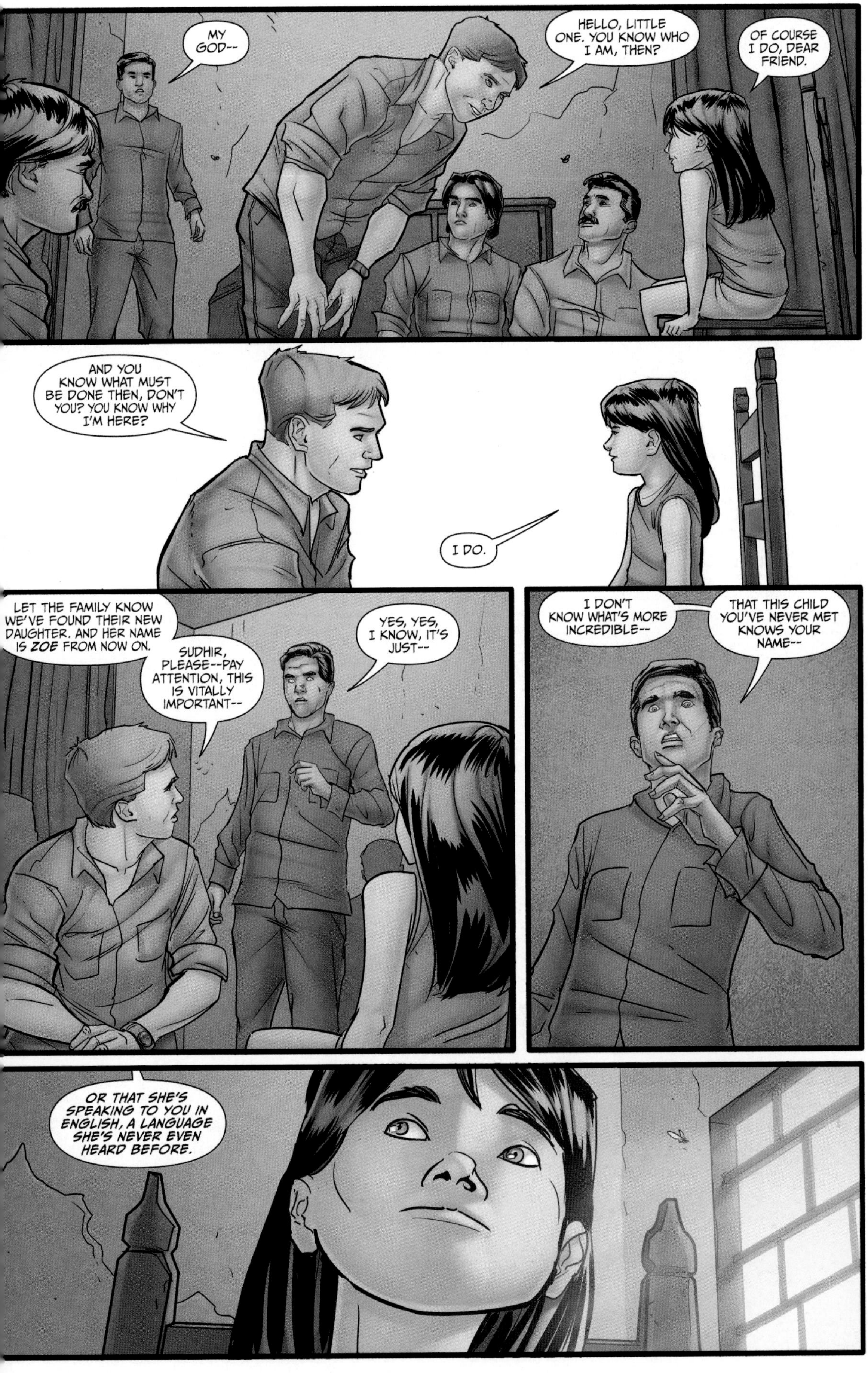
MY GOD--
HELLO, LITTLE ONE. YOU KNOW WHO I AM, THEN?
OF COURSE I DO, DEAR FRIEND.
AND YOU KNOW WHAT MUST BE DONE THEN, DON'T YOU? YOU KNOW WHY I'M HERE?
I DO.
LET THE FAMILY KNOW WE'VE FOUND THEIR NEW DAUGHTER. AND HER NAME IS *ZOE* FROM NOW ON.
SUDHIR, PLEASE--PAY ATTENTION, THIS IS VITALLY IMPORTANT--
YES, YES, I KNOW, IT'S JUST--
I DON'T KNOW WHAT'S MORE INCREDIBLE--
THAT THIS CHILD YOU'VE NEVER MET KNOWS YOUR NAME--
OR THAT SHE'S SPEAKING TO YOU IN ENGLISH, A LANGUAGE SHE'S NEVER EVEN HEARD BEFORE.

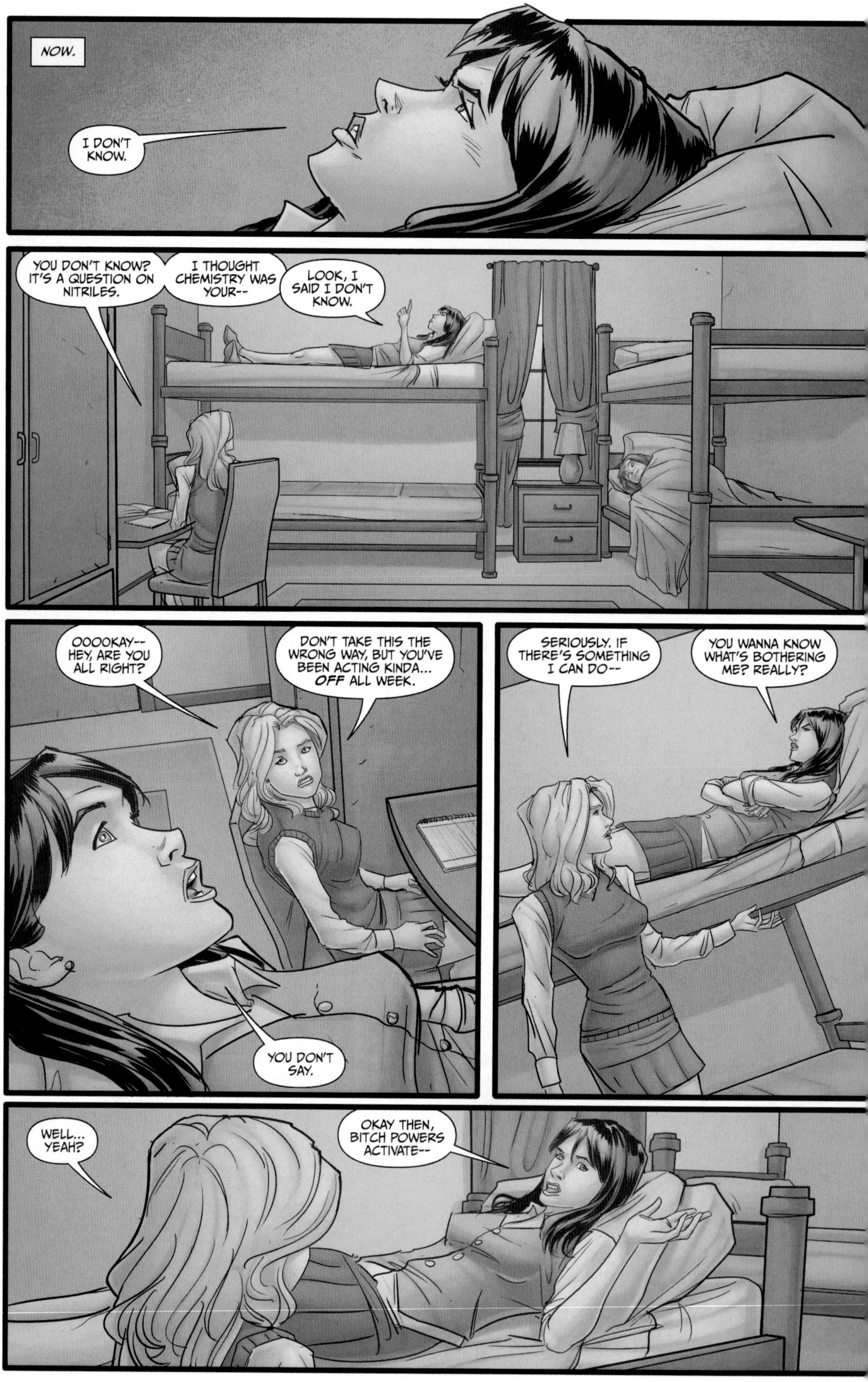
NOW.
I DON'T KNOW.
YOU DON'T KNOW? IT'S A QUESTION ON NITRILES.
I THOUGHT CHEMISTRY WAS YOUR--
LOOK, I SAID I DON'T KNOW.
OOOOKAY-- HEY, ARE YOU ALL RIGHT?
DON'T TAKE THIS THE WRONG WAY, BUT YOU'VE BEEN ACTING KINDA... OFF ALL WEEK.
YOU DON'T SAY.
SERIOUSLY. IF THERE'S SOMETHING I CAN DO--
YOU WANNA KNOW WHAT'S BOTHERING ME? REALLY?
WELL... YEAH?
OKAY THEN, BITCH POWERS ACTIVATE--

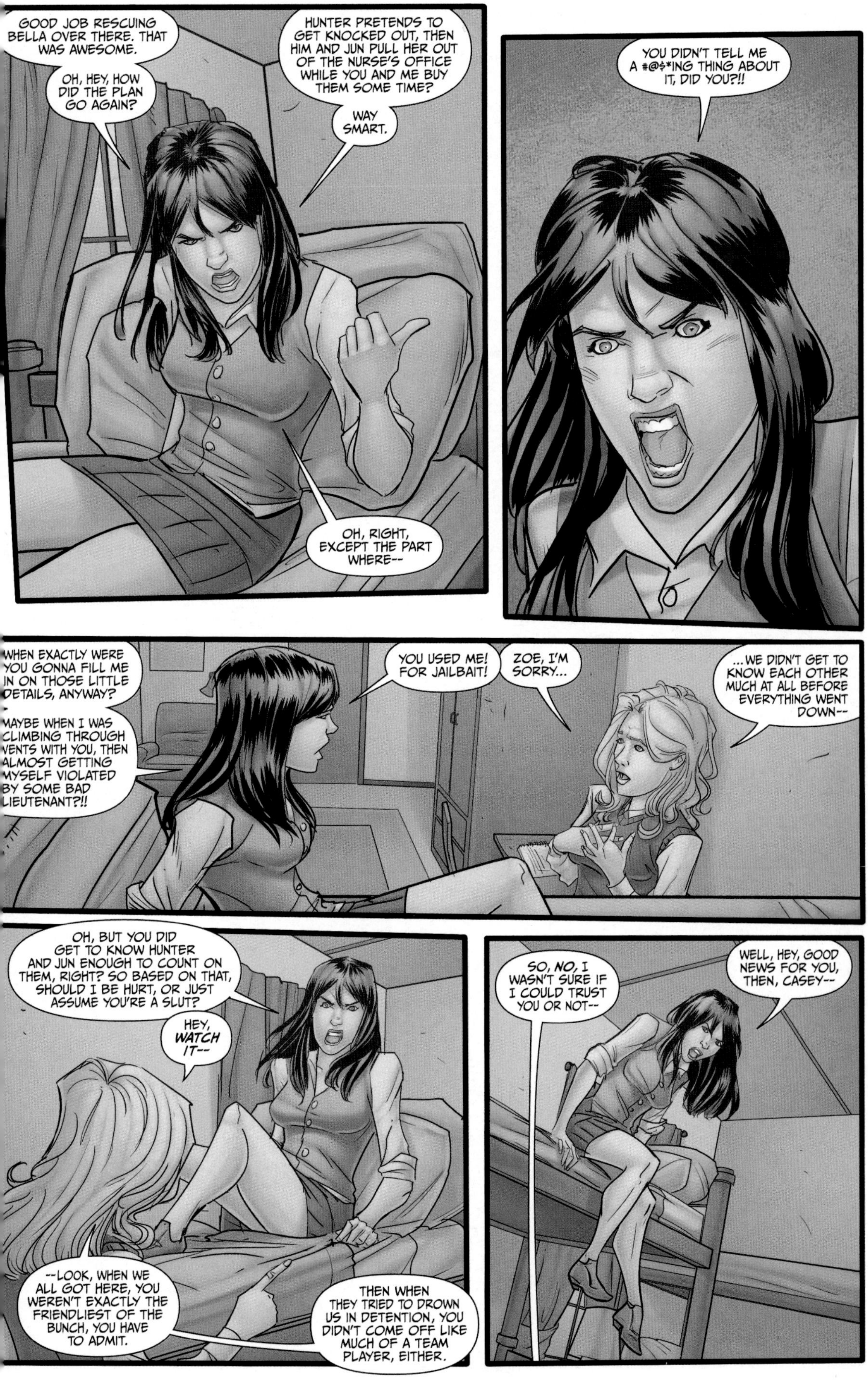
GOOD JOB RESCUING BELLA OVER THERE. THAT WAS AWESOME.
OH, HEY, HOW DID THE PLAN GO AGAIN?
HUNTER PRETENDS TO GET KNOCKED OUT, THEN HIM AND JUN PULL HER OUT OF THE NURSE'S OFFICE WHILE YOU AND ME BUY THEM SOME TIME?
WAY SMART.
OH, RIGHT, EXCEPT THE PART WHERE--
YOU DIDN'T TELL ME A #@$*ING THING ABOUT IT, DID YOU?!!
WHEN EXACTLY WERE YOU GONNA FILL ME IN ON THOSE LITTLE DETAILS, ANYWAY?
MAYBE WHEN I WAS CLIMBING THROUGH VENTS WITH YOU, THEN ALMOST GETTING MYSELF VIOLATED BY SOME BAD LIEUTENANT?!!
YOU USED ME! FOR JAILBAIT!
ZOE, I'M SORRY...
...WE DIDN'T GET TO KNOW EACH OTHER MUCH AT ALL BEFORE EVERYTHING WENT DOWN--
OH, BUT YOU DID GET TO KNOW HUNTER AND JUN ENOUGH TO COUNT ON THEM, RIGHT? SO BASED ON THAT, SHOULD I BE HURT, OR JUST ASSUME YOU'RE A SLUT?
HEY, *WATCH* IT--
--LOOK, WHEN WE ALL GOT HERE, YOU WEREN'T EXACTLY THE FRIENDLIEST OF THE BUNCH, YOU HAVE TO ADMIT.
THEN WHEN THEY TRIED TO DROWN US IN DETENTION, YOU DIDN'T COME OFF LIKE MUCH OF A TEAM PLAYER, EITHER.
SO, *NO*, I WASN'T SURE IF I COULD TRUST YOU OR NOT--
WELL, HEY, GOOD NEWS FOR YOU, THEN, CASEY--

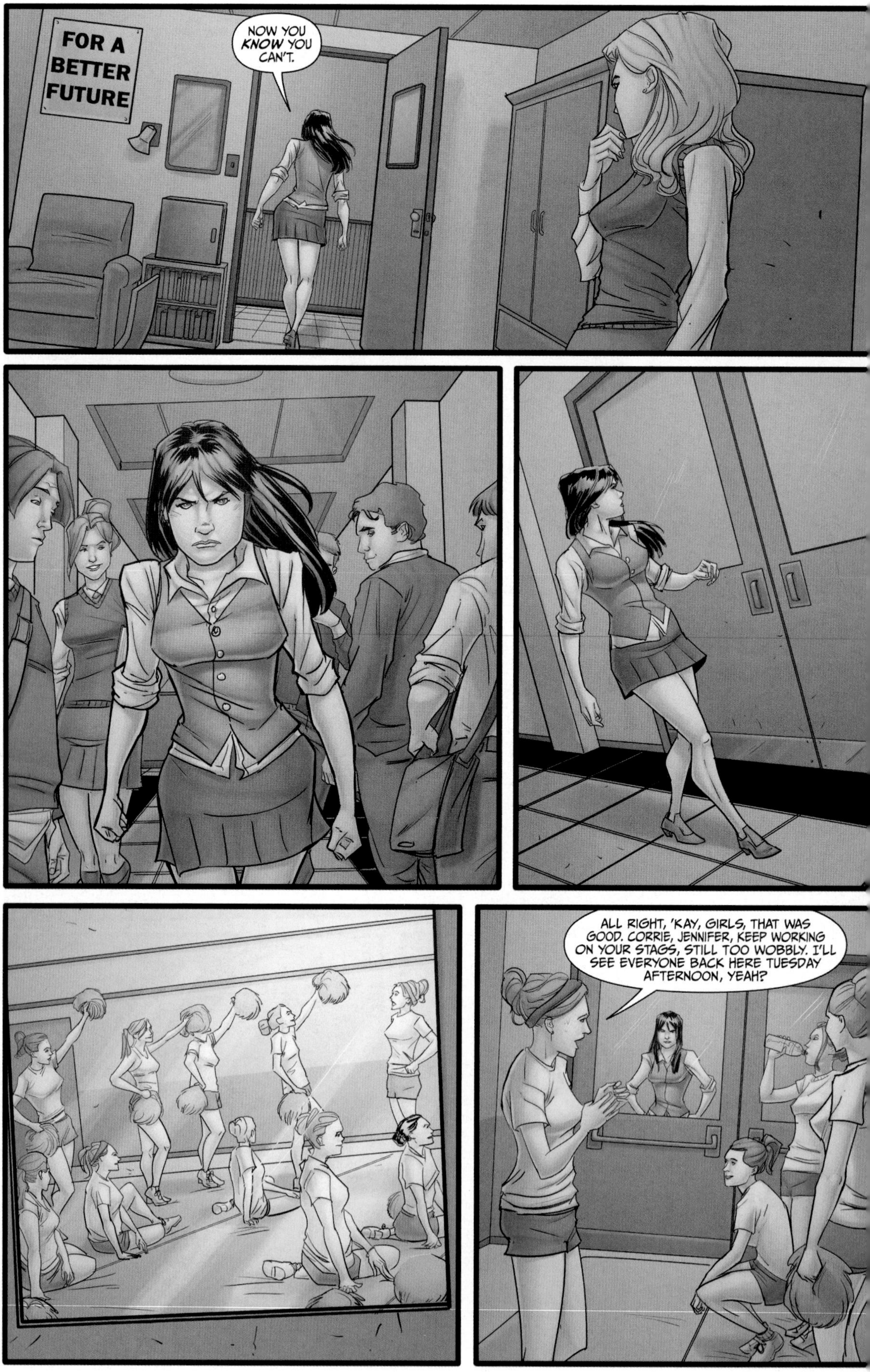
FOR A BETTER FUTURE
NOW YOU *KNOW* YOU CAN'T.
ALL RIGHT, 'KAY, GIRLS, THAT WAS GOOD. CORRIE, JENNIFER, KEEP WORKING ON YOUR STAGS, STILL TOO WOBBLY. I'LL SEE EVERYONE BACK HERE TUESDAY AFTERNOON, YEAH?

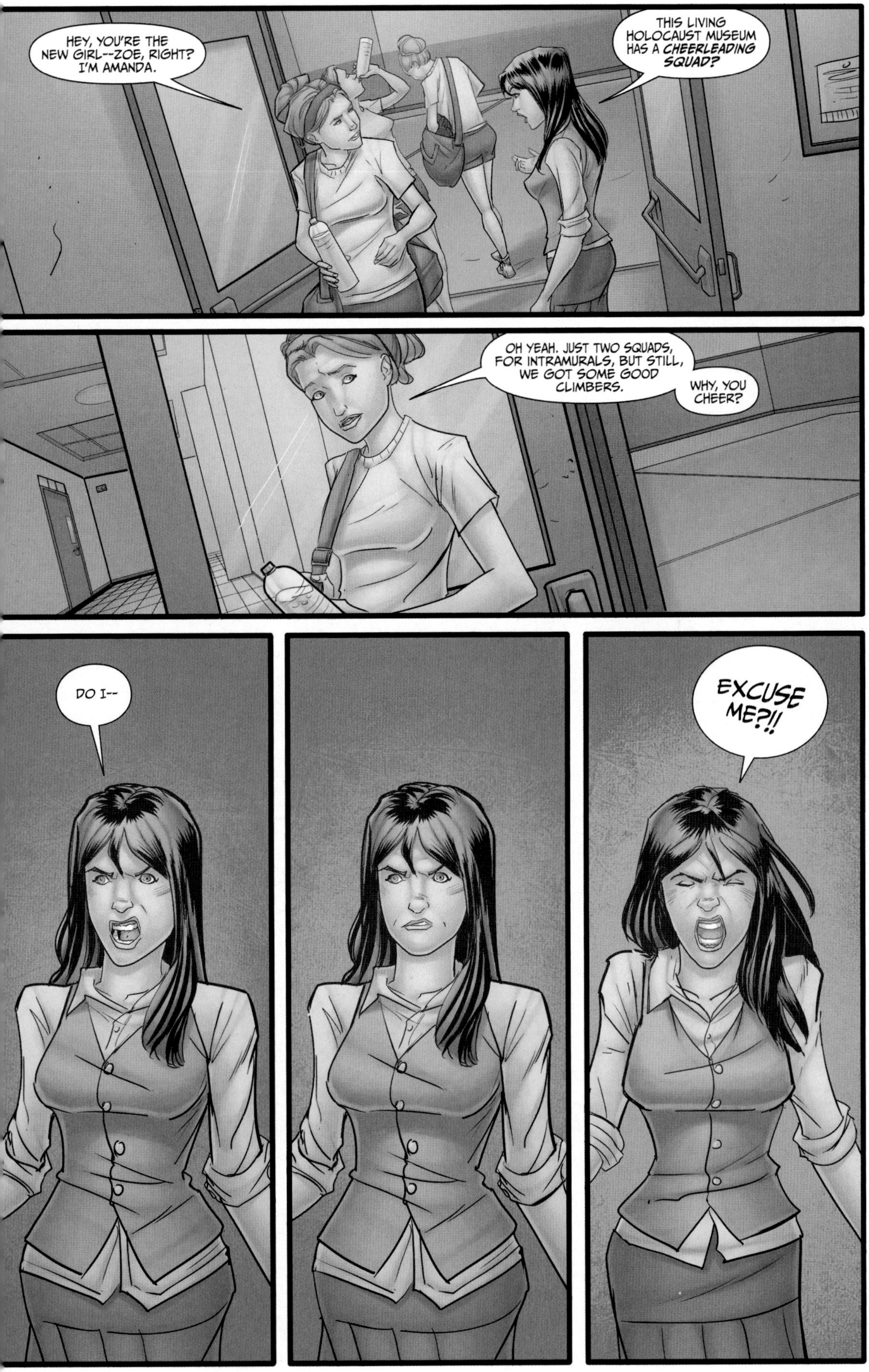
HEY, YOU'RE THE NEW GIRL--ZOE, RIGHT? I'M AMANDA.
THIS LIVING HOLOCAUST MUSEUM HAS A *CHEERLEADING SQUAD?*
OH YEAH. JUST TWO SQUADS, FOR INTRAMURALS, BUT STILL, WE GOT SOME GOOD CLIMBERS.
WHY, YOU CHEER?
DO I--
EXCUSE ME?!!

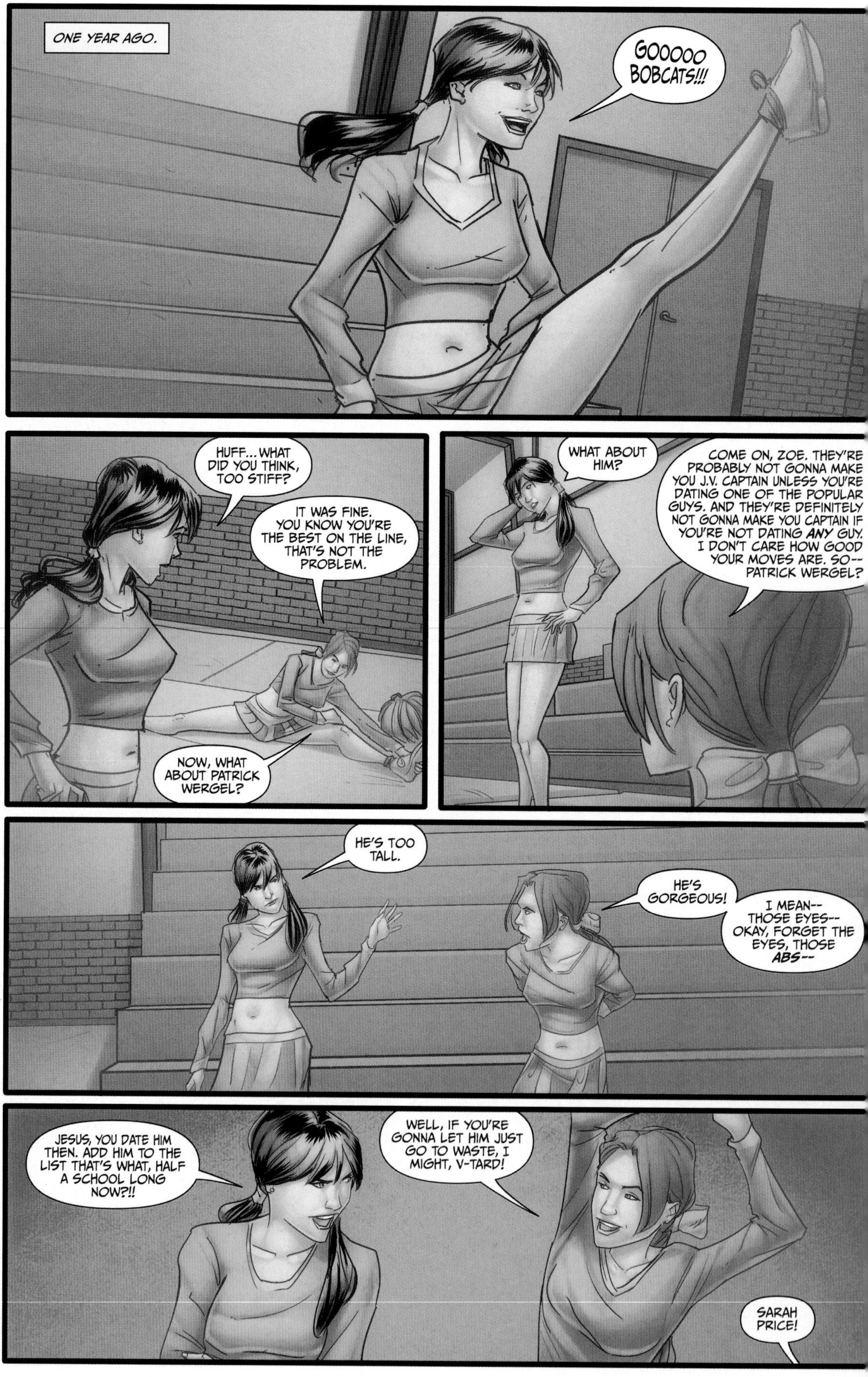
ONE YEAR AGO.
GOOOOO BOBCATS!!!
HUFF... WHAT DID YOU THINK, TOO STIFF?
IT WAS FINE. YOU KNOW YOU'RE THE BEST ON THE LINE, THAT'S NOT THE PROBLEM.
NOW, WHAT ABOUT PATRICK WERGEL?
WHAT ABOUT HIM?
COME ON, ZOE. THEY'RE PROBABLY NOT GONNA MAKE YOU J.V. CAPTAIN UNLESS YOU'RE DATING ONE OF THE POPULAR GUYS. AND THEY'RE DEFINITELY NOT GONNA MAKE YOU CAPTAIN IF YOU'RE NOT DATING ANY GUY. I DON'T CARE HOW GOOD YOUR MOVES ARE. SO-- PATRICK WERGEL?
HE'S TOO TALL.
HE'S GORGEOUS!
I MEAN-- THOSE EYES-- OKAY, FORGET THE EYES, THOSE ABS--
JESUS, YOU DATE HIM THEN. ADD HIM TO THE LIST THAT'S WHAT, HALF A SCHOOL LONG NOW?!!
WELL, IF YOU'RE GONNA LET HIM JUST GO TO WASTE, I MIGHT, V-TARD!
SARAH PRICE!

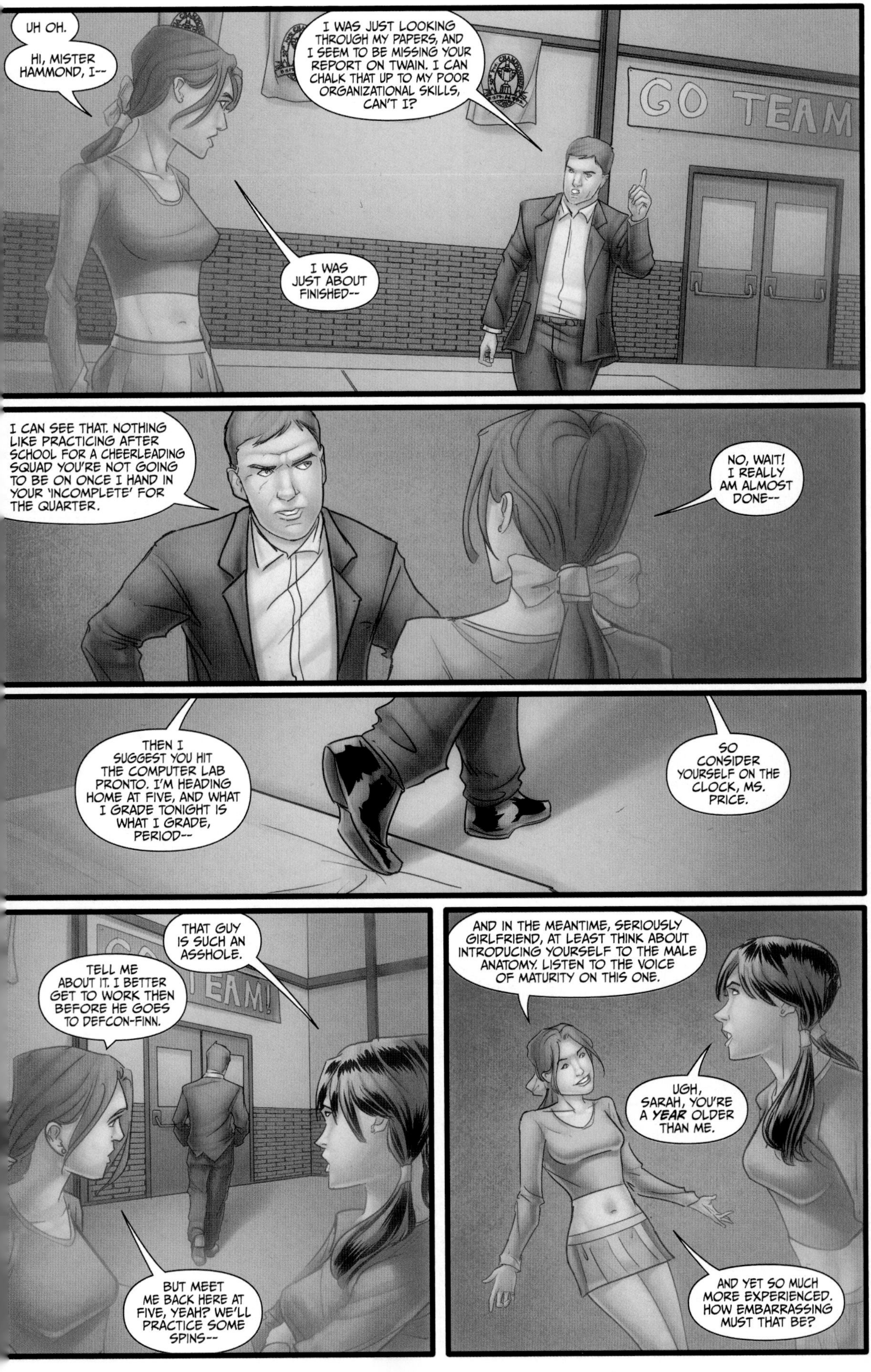
UH OH.
HI, MISTER HAMMOND, I--
I WAS JUST LOOKING THROUGH MY PAPERS, AND I SEEM TO BE MISSING YOUR REPORT ON TWAIN. I CAN CHALK THAT UP TO MY POOR ORGANIZATIONAL SKILLS, CAN'T I?
GO TEAM
I WAS JUST ABOUT FINISHED--
I CAN SEE THAT. NOTHING LIKE PRACTICING AFTER SCHOOL FOR A CHEERLEADING SQUAD YOU'RE NOT GOING TO BE ON ONCE I HAND IN YOUR 'INCOMPLETE' FOR THE QUARTER.
NO, WAIT! I REALLY AM ALMOST DONE--
THEN I SUGGEST YOU HIT THE COMPUTER LAB PRONTO. I'M HEADING HOME AT FIVE, AND WHAT I GRADE TONIGHT IS WHAT I GRADE, PERIOD--
SO CONSIDER YOURSELF ON THE CLOCK, MS. PRICE.
THAT GUY IS SUCH AN ASSHOLE.
TELL ME ABOUT IT. I BETTER GET TO WORK THEN BEFORE HE GOES TO DEFCON-FINN.
BUT MEET ME BACK HERE AT FIVE, YEAH? WE'LL PRACTICE SOME SPINS--
AND IN THE MEANTIME, SERIOUSLY GIRLFRIEND, AT LEAST THINK ABOUT INTRODUCING YOURSELF TO THE MALE ANATOMY. LISTEN TO THE VOICE OF MATURITY ON THIS ONE.
UGH, SARAH, YOU'RE A *YEAR* OLDER THAN ME.
AND YET SO MUCH MORE EXPERIENCED. HOW EMBARRASSING MUST THAT BE?

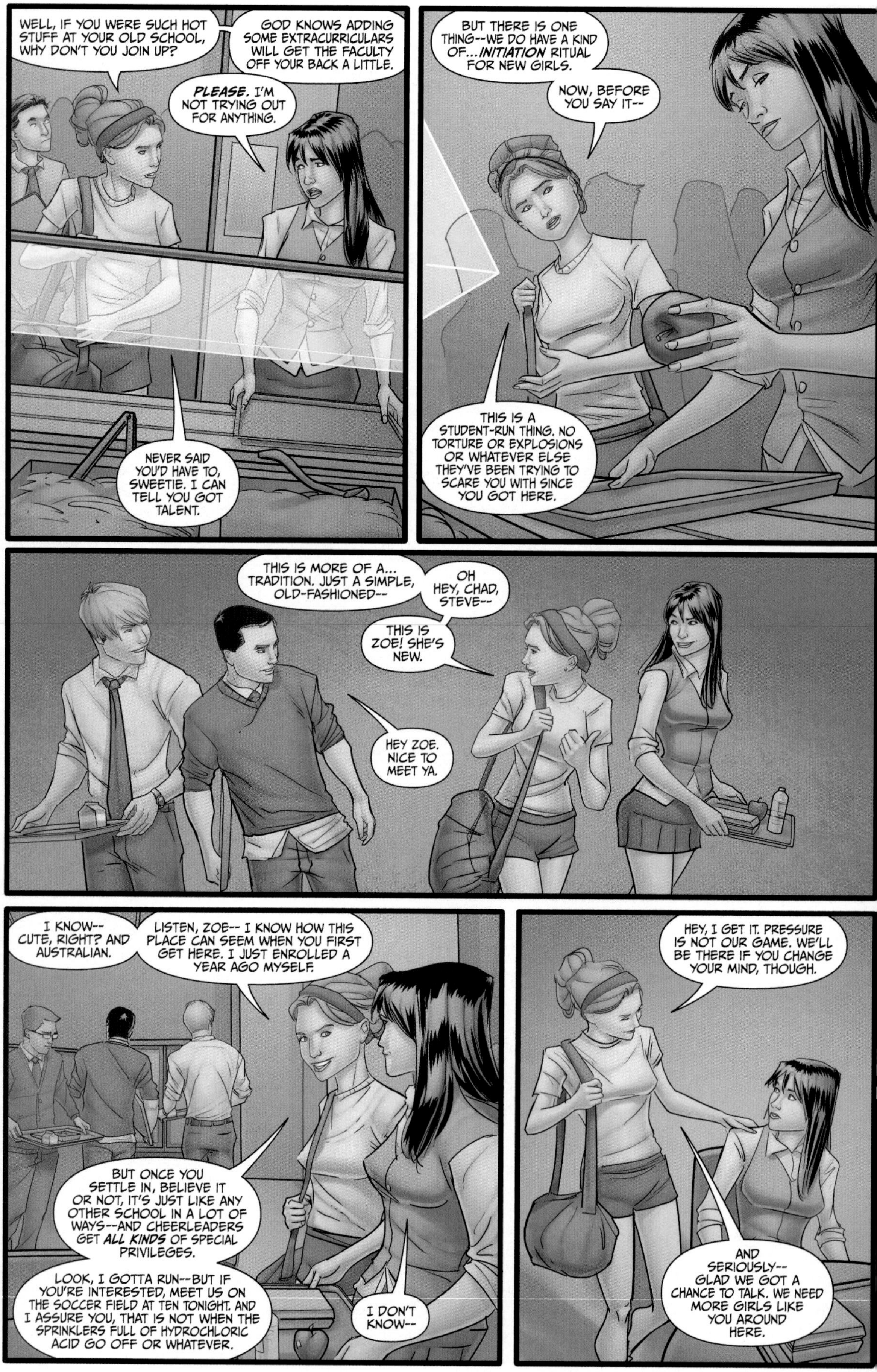

WELL, IF YOU WERE SUCH HOT STUFF AT YOUR OLD SCHOOL, WHY DON'T YOU JOIN UP?
GOD KNOWS ADDING SOME EXTRACURRICULARS WILL GET THE FACULTY OFF YOUR BACK A LITTLE.
PLEASE. I'M NOT TRYING OUT FOR ANYTHING.
NEVER SAID YOU'D HAVE TO, SWEETIE. I CAN TELL YOU GOT TALENT.
BUT THERE IS ONE THING--WE DO HAVE A KIND OF...INITIATION RITUAL FOR NEW GIRLS.
NOW, BEFORE YOU SAY IT--
THIS IS A STUDENT-RUN THING. NO TORTURE OR EXPLOSIONS OR WHATEVER ELSE THEY'VE BEEN TRYING TO SCARE YOU WITH SINCE YOU GOT HERE.
THIS IS MORE OF A... TRADITION. JUST A SIMPLE, OLD-FASHIONED--
OH HEY, CHAD, STEVE--
THIS IS ZOE! SHE'S NEW.
HEY ZOE. NICE TO MEET YA.
I KNOW-- CUTE, RIGHT? AND AUSTRALIAN.
LISTEN, ZOE-- I KNOW HOW THIS PLACE CAN SEEM WHEN YOU FIRST GET HERE. I JUST ENROLLED A YEAR AGO MYSELF.
BUT ONCE YOU SETTLE IN, BELIEVE IT OR NOT, IT'S JUST LIKE ANY OTHER SCHOOL IN A LOT OF WAYS--AND CHEERLEADERS GET ALL KINDS OF SPECIAL PRIVILEGES.
LOOK, I GOTTA RUN--BUT IF YOU'RE INTERESTED, MEET US ON THE SOCCER FIELD AT TEN TONIGHT. AND I ASSURE YOU, THAT IS NOT WHEN THE SPRINKLERS FULL OF HYDROCHLORIC ACID GO OFF OR WHATEVER.
I DON'T KNOW--
HEY, I GET IT. PRESSURE IS NOT OUR GAME. WE'LL BE THERE IF YOU CHANGE YOUR MIND, THOUGH.
AND SERIOUSLY-- GLAD WE GOT A CHANCE TO TALK. WE NEED MORE GIRLS LIKE YOU AROUND HERE.

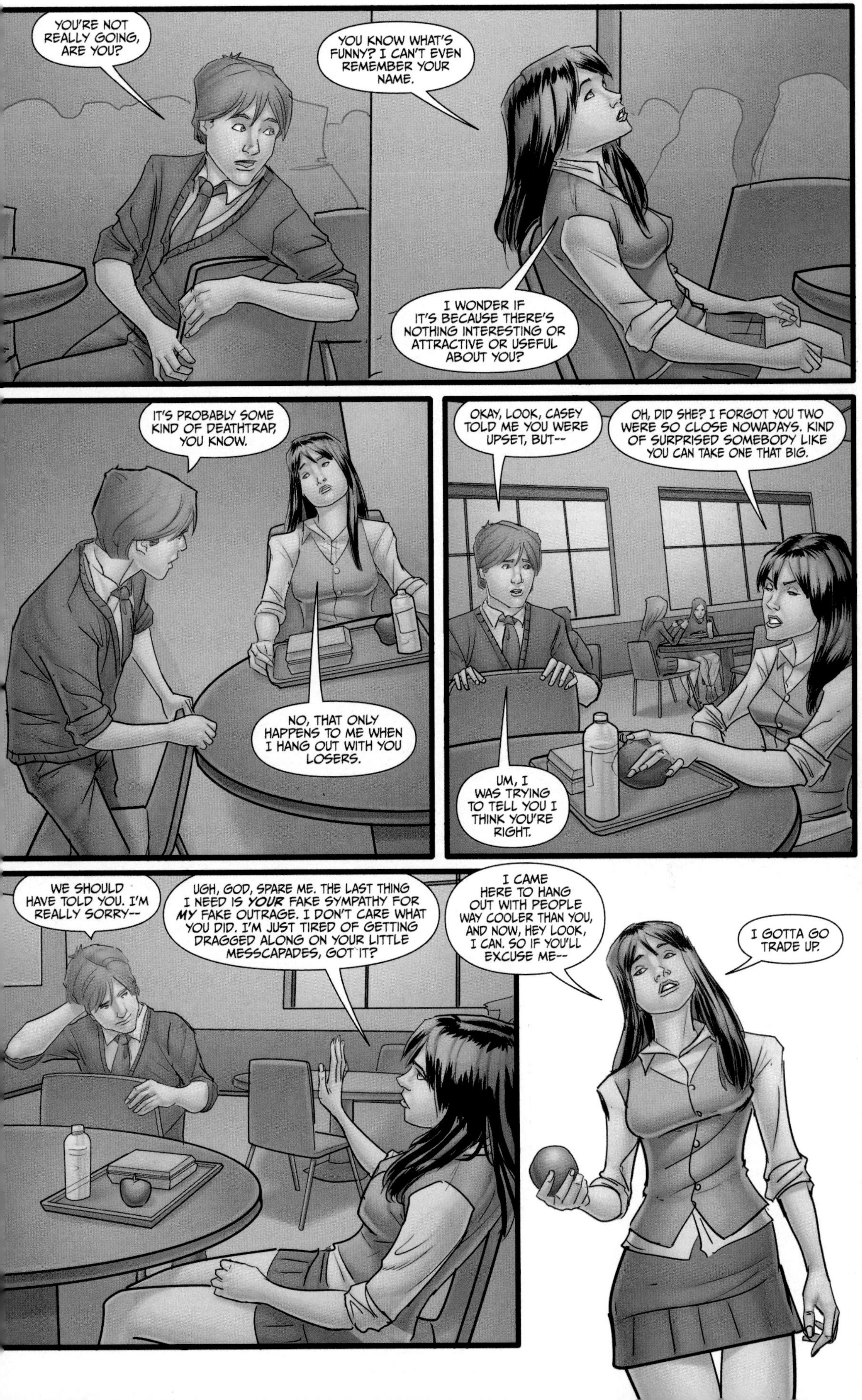
YOU'RE NOT REALLY GOING, ARE YOU?
YOU KNOW WHAT'S FUNNY? I CAN'T EVEN REMEMBER YOUR NAME.
I WONDER IF IT'S BECAUSE THERE'S NOTHING INTERESTING OR ATTRACTIVE OR USEFUL ABOUT YOU?
IT'S PROBABLY SOME KIND OF DEATHTRAP, YOU KNOW.
NO, THAT ONLY HAPPENS TO ME WHEN I HANG OUT WITH YOU LOSERS.
OKAY, LOOK, CASEY TOLD ME YOU WERE UPSET, BUT--
OH, DID SHE? I FORGOT YOU TWO WERE SO CLOSE NOWADAYS. KIND OF SURPRISED SOMEBODY LIKE YOU CAN TAKE ONE THAT BIG.
UM, I WAS TRYING TO TELL YOU I THINK YOU'RE RIGHT.
WE SHOULD HAVE TOLD YOU. I'M REALLY SORRY--
UGH, GOD, SPARE ME. THE LAST THING I NEED IS YOUR FAKE SYMPATHY FOR MY FAKE OUTRAGE. I DON'T CARE WHAT YOU DID. I'M JUST TIRED OF GETTING DRAGGED ALONG ON YOUR LITTLE MESSCAPADES, GOT IT?
I CAME HERE TO HANG OUT WITH PEOPLE WAY COOLER THAN YOU, AND NOW, HEY LOOK, I CAN. SO IF YOU'LL EXCUSE ME--
I GOTTA GO TRADE UP.

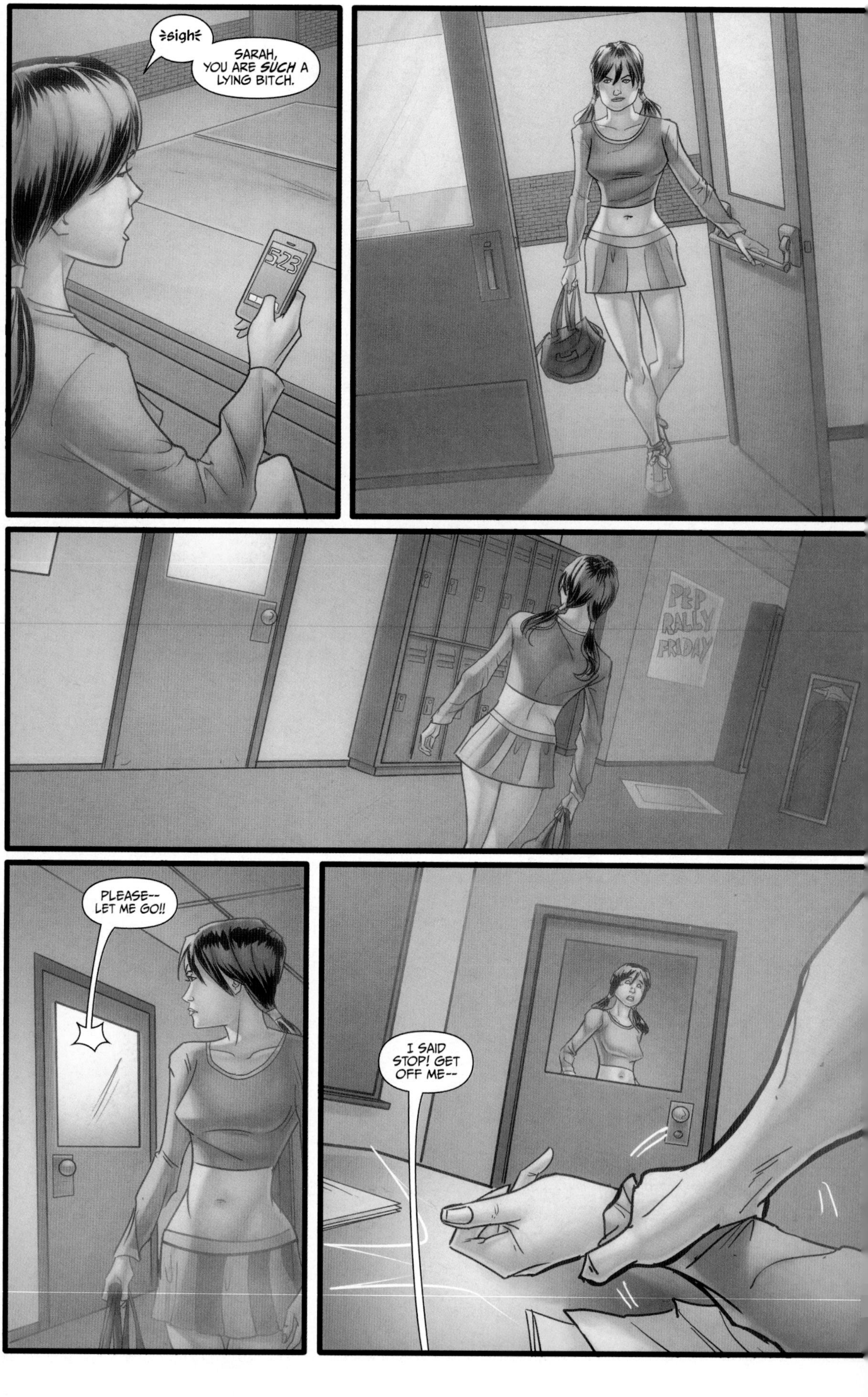

≈sigh≈
SARAH, YOU ARE SUCH A LYING BITCH.
523
PEP RALLY FRIDAY
PLEASE-- LET ME GO!!
I SAID STOP! GET OFF ME--

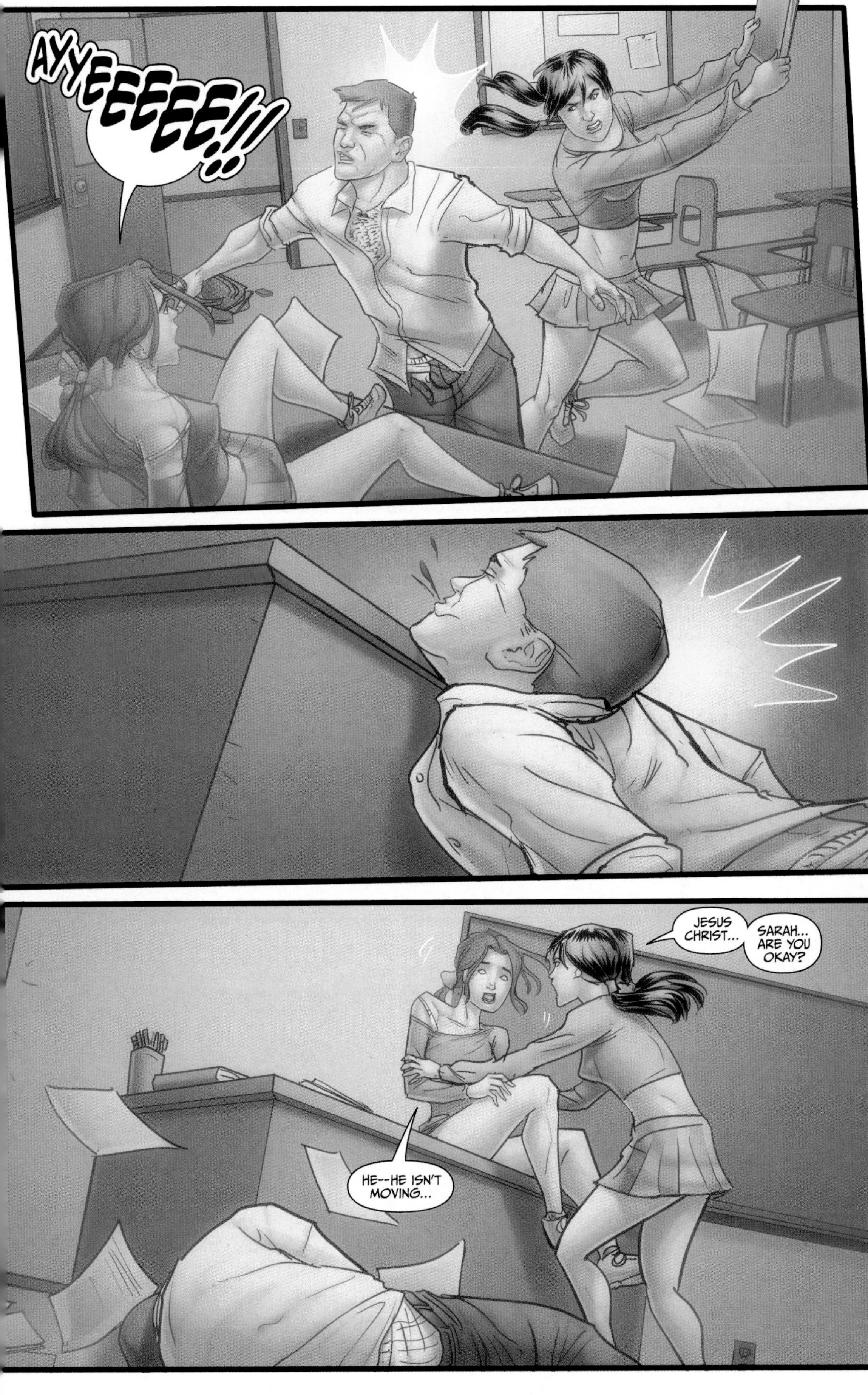
AYYEEEEEE!!!
JESUS CHRIST...
SARAH... ARE YOU OKAY?
HE--HE ISN'T MOVING...

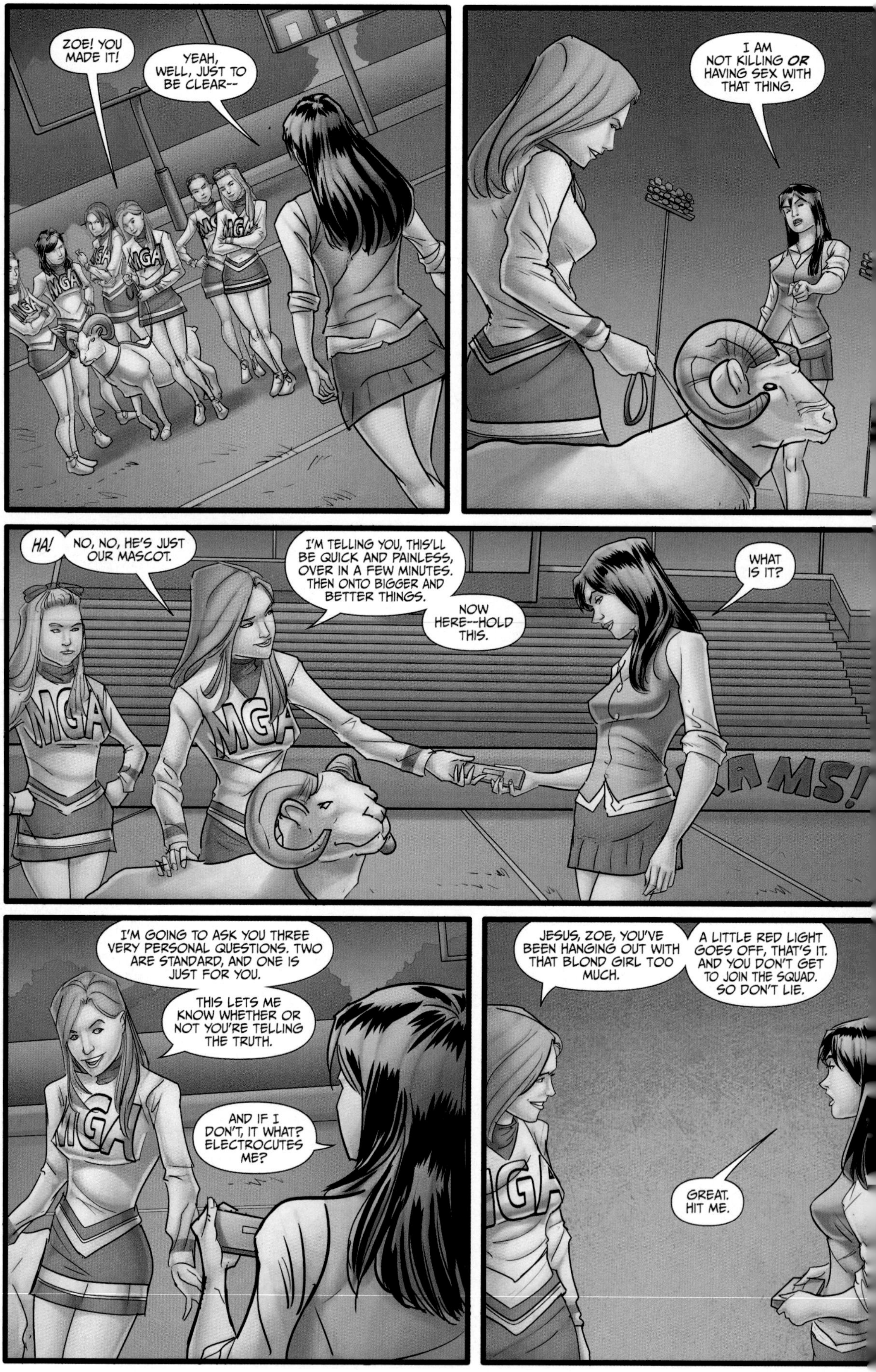
ZOE! YOU MADE IT!
YEAH, WELL, JUST TO BE CLEAR--
I AM NOT KILLING *OR* HAVING SEX WITH THAT THING.
HA!
NO, NO, HE'S JUST OUR MASCOT.
I'M TELLING YOU, THIS'LL BE QUICK AND PAINLESS, OVER IN A FEW MINUTES. THEN ONTO BIGGER AND BETTER THINGS.
NOW HERE--HOLD THIS.
WHAT IS IT?
I'M GOING TO ASK YOU THREE VERY PERSONAL QUESTIONS. TWO ARE STANDARD, AND ONE IS JUST FOR YOU.
THIS LETS ME KNOW WHETHER OR NOT YOU'RE TELLING THE TRUTH.
AND IF I DON'T, IT WHAT? ELECTROCUTES ME?
JESUS, ZOE, YOU'VE BEEN HANGING OUT WITH THAT BLOND GIRL TOO MUCH.
A LITTLE RED LIGHT GOES OFF, THAT'S IT. AND YOU DON'T GET TO JOIN THE SQUAD. SO DON'T LIE.
GREAT. HIT ME.

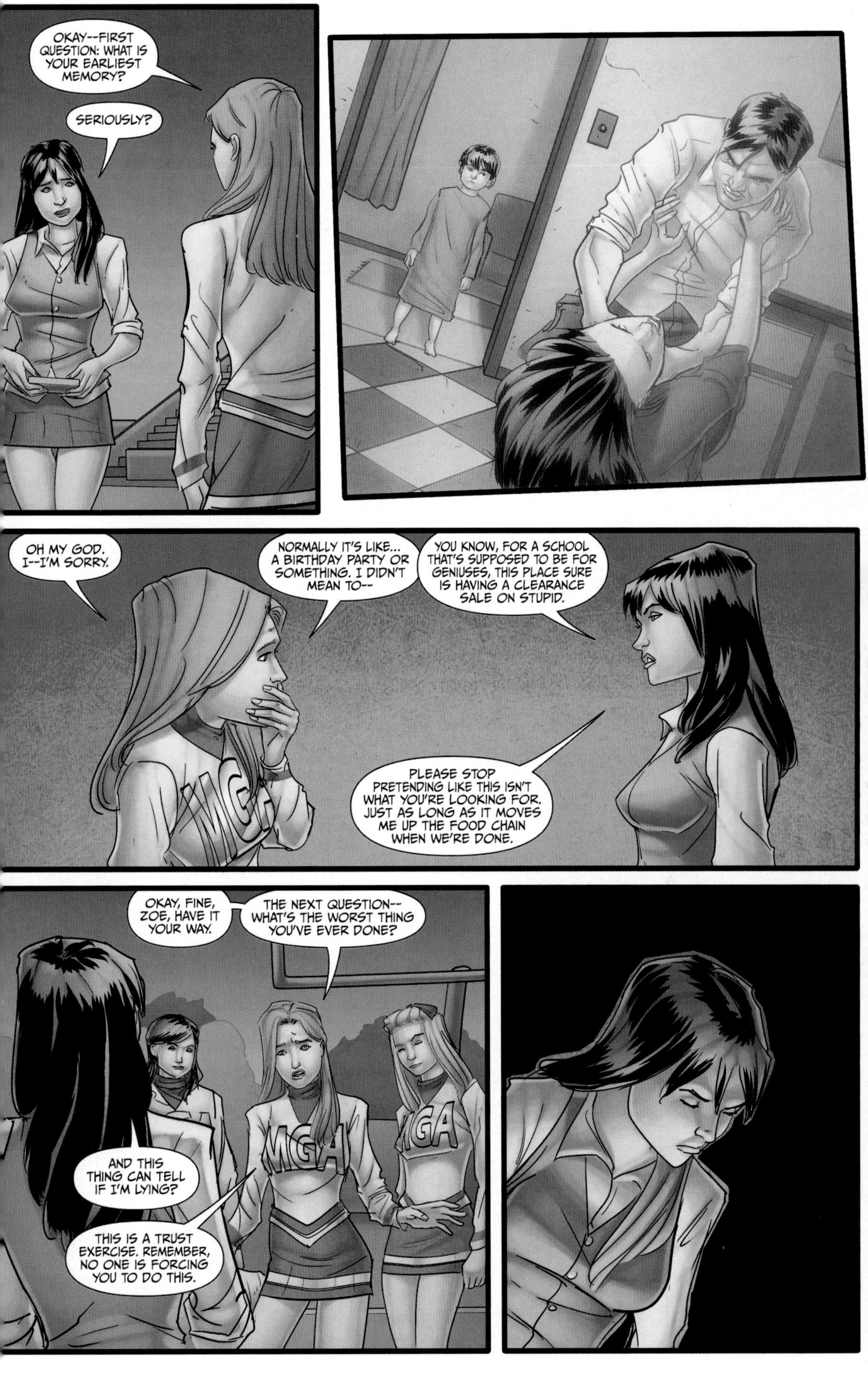
OKAY--FIRST QUESTION: WHAT IS YOUR EARLIEST MEMORY?
SERIOUSLY?
OH MY GOD. I--I'M SORRY.
NORMALLY IT'S LIKE... A BIRTHDAY PARTY OR SOMETHING. I DIDN'T MEAN TO--
YOU KNOW, FOR A SCHOOL THAT'S SUPPOSED TO BE FOR GENIUSES, THIS PLACE SURE IS HAVING A CLEARANCE SALE ON STUPID.
PLEASE STOP PRETENDING LIKE THIS ISN'T WHAT YOU'RE LOOKING FOR. JUST AS LONG AS IT MOVES ME UP THE FOOD CHAIN WHEN WE'RE DONE.
OKAY, FINE, ZOE, HAVE IT YOUR WAY.
THE NEXT QUESTION-- WHAT'S THE WORST THING YOU'VE EVER DONE?
AND THIS THING CAN TELL IF I'M LYING?
THIS IS A TRUST EXERCISE. REMEMBER, NO ONE IS FORCING YOU TO DO THIS.
MGA
MGA

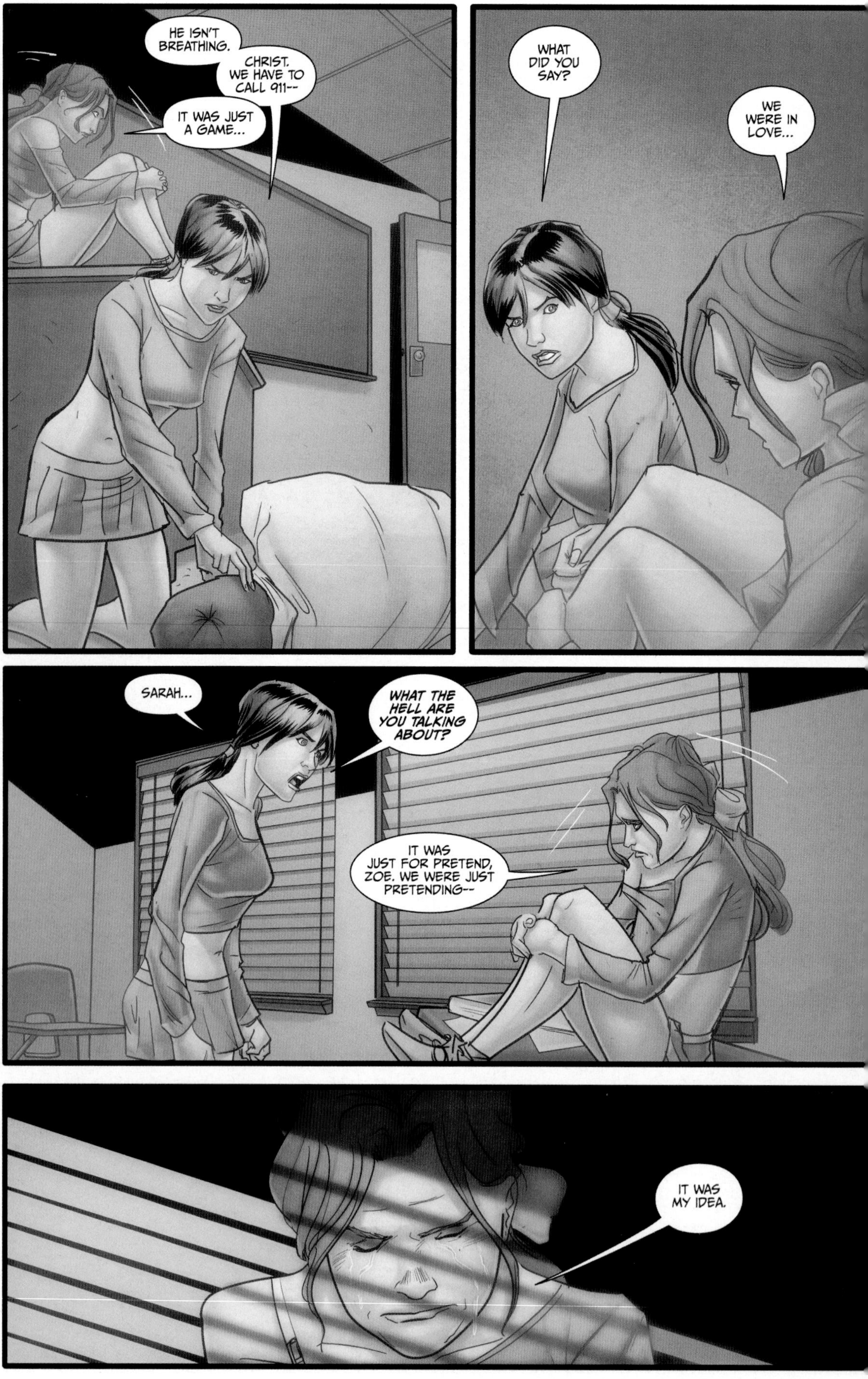
HE ISN'T BREATHING.
CHRIST. WE HAVE TO CALL 911--
IT WAS JUST A GAME...
WHAT DID YOU SAY?
WE WERE IN LOVE...
SARAH...
WHAT THE HELL ARE YOU TALKING ABOUT?
IT WAS JUST FOR PRETEND, ZOE. WE WERE JUST PRETENDING--
IT WAS MY IDEA.

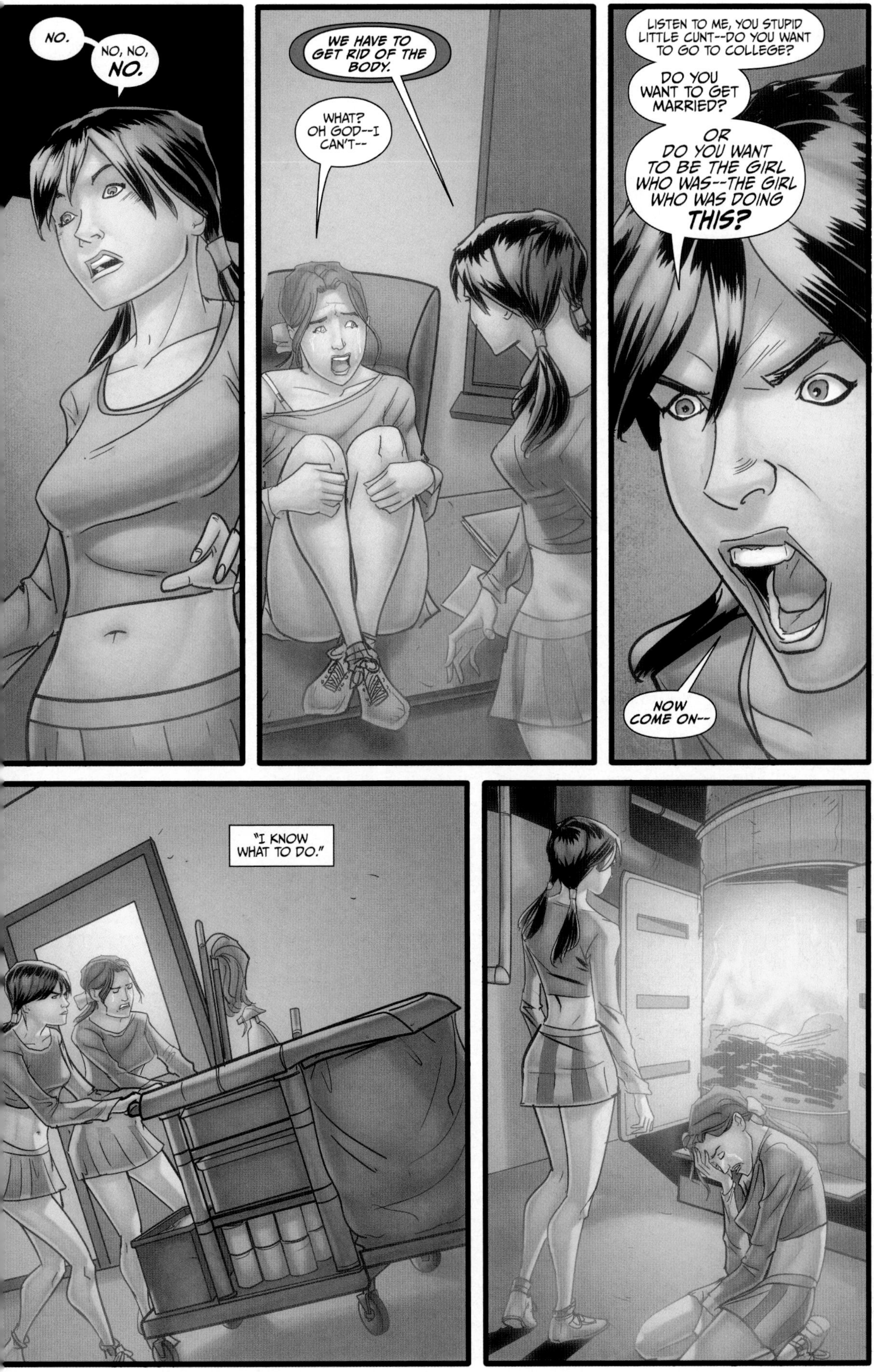
NO.
NO, NO, NO.
WE HAVE TO GET RID OF THE BODY.
WHAT? OH GOD--I CAN'T--
LISTEN TO ME, YOU STUPID LITTLE CUNT--DO YOU WANT TO GO TO COLLEGE?
DO YOU WANT TO GET MARRIED?
OR DO YOU WANT TO BE THE GIRL WHO WAS--THE GIRL WHO WAS DOING THIS?
NOW COME ON--
"I KNOW WHAT TO DO."

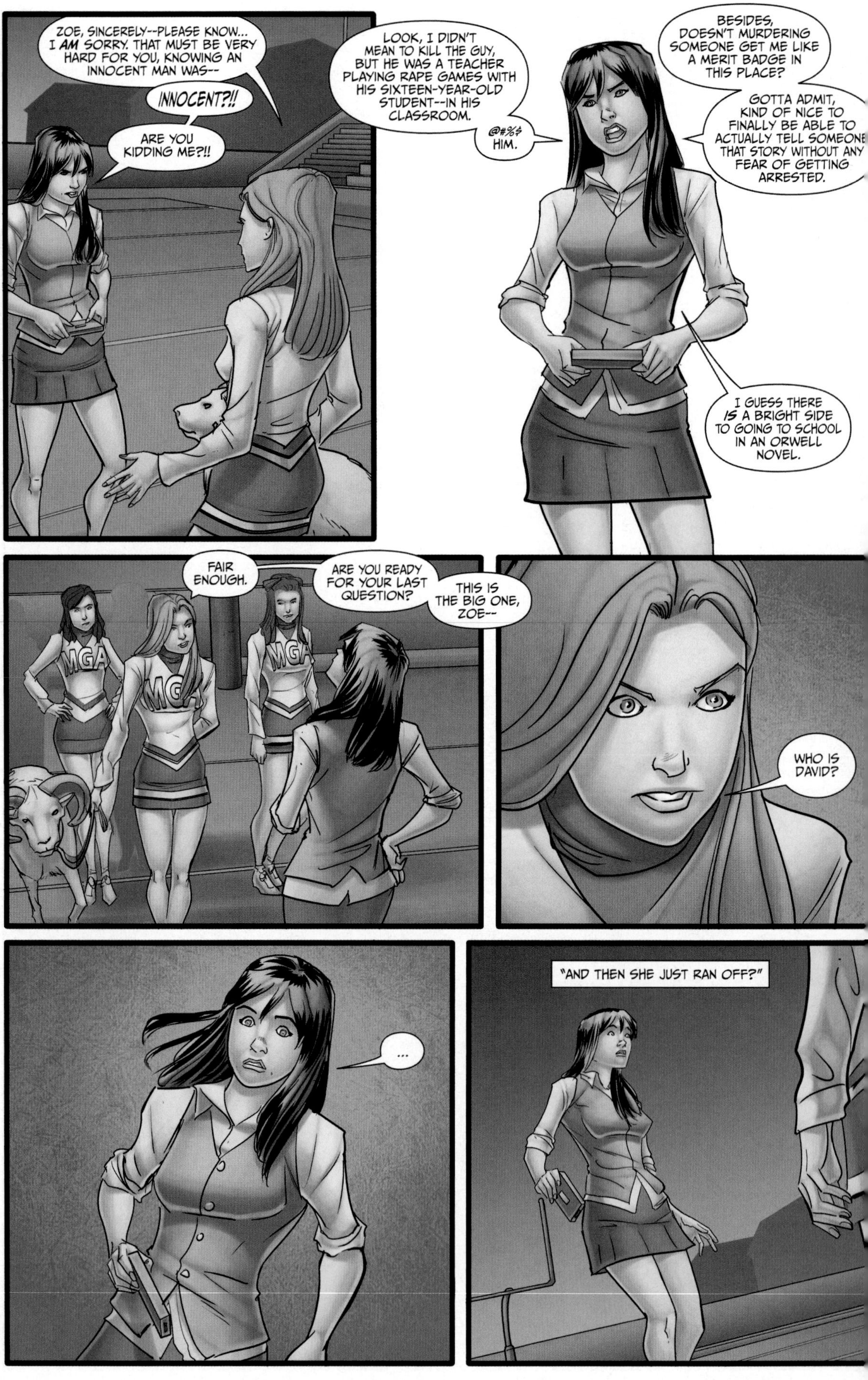
ZOE, SINCERELY--PLEASE KNOW... I AM SORRY. THAT MUST BE VERY HARD FOR YOU, KNOWING AN INNOCENT MAN WAS--
INNOCENT?!!
ARE YOU KIDDING ME?!!
LOOK, I DIDN'T MEAN TO KILL THE GUY, BUT HE WAS A TEACHER PLAYING RAPE GAMES WITH HIS SIXTEEN-YEAR-OLD STUDENT--IN HIS CLASSROOM.
@#%$ HIM.
BESIDES, DOESN'T MURDERING SOMEONE GET ME LIKE A MERIT BADGE IN THIS PLACE?
GOTTA ADMIT, KIND OF NICE TO FINALLY BE ABLE TO ACTUALLY TELL SOMEONE THAT STORY WITHOUT ANY FEAR OF GETTING ARRESTED.
I GUESS THERE IS A BRIGHT SIDE TO GOING TO SCHOOL IN AN ORWELL NOVEL.
FAIR ENOUGH.
ARE YOU READY FOR YOUR LAST QUESTION?
THIS IS THE BIG ONE, ZOE--
MGA
MGA
MGA
WHO IS DAVID?
...
"AND THEN SHE JUST RAN OFF?"

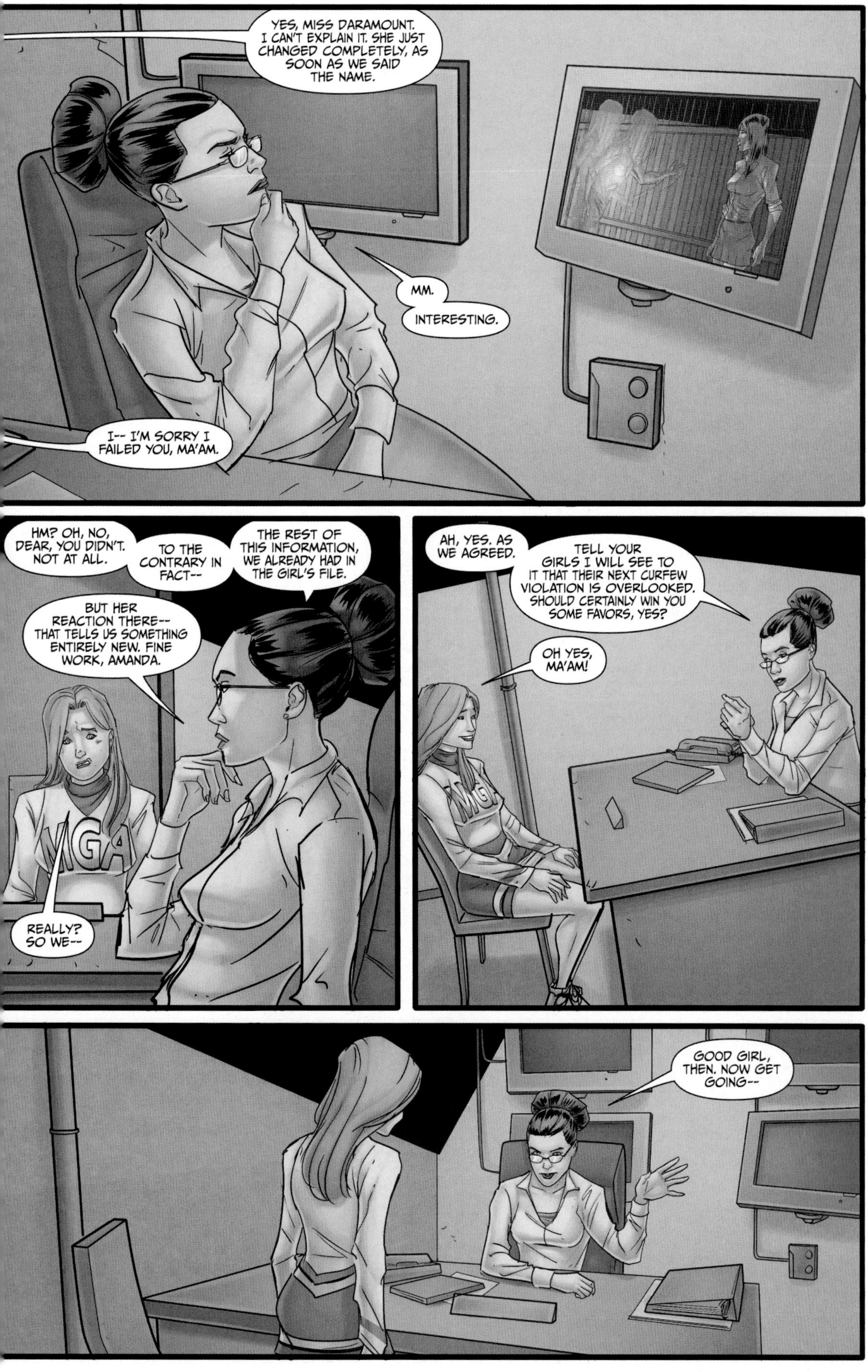
YES, MISS DARAMOUNT. I CAN'T EXPLAIN IT. SHE JUST CHANGED COMPLETELY, AS SOON AS WE SAID THE NAME.
MM.
INTERESTING.
I-- I'M SORRY I FAILED YOU, MA'AM.
HM? OH, NO, DEAR, YOU DIDN'T. NOT AT ALL.
TO THE CONTRARY IN FACT--
THE REST OF THIS INFORMATION, WE ALREADY HAD IN THE GIRL'S FILE.
BUT HER REACTION THERE-- THAT TELLS US SOMETHING ENTIRELY NEW. FINE WORK, AMANDA.
REALLY? SO WE--
AH, YES. AS WE AGREED.
TELL YOUR GIRLS I WILL SEE TO IT THAT THEIR NEXT CURFEW VIOLATION IS OVERLOOKED. SHOULD CERTAINLY WIN YOU SOME FAVORS, YES?
OH YES, MA'AM!
GOOD GIRL, THEN. NOW GET GOING--

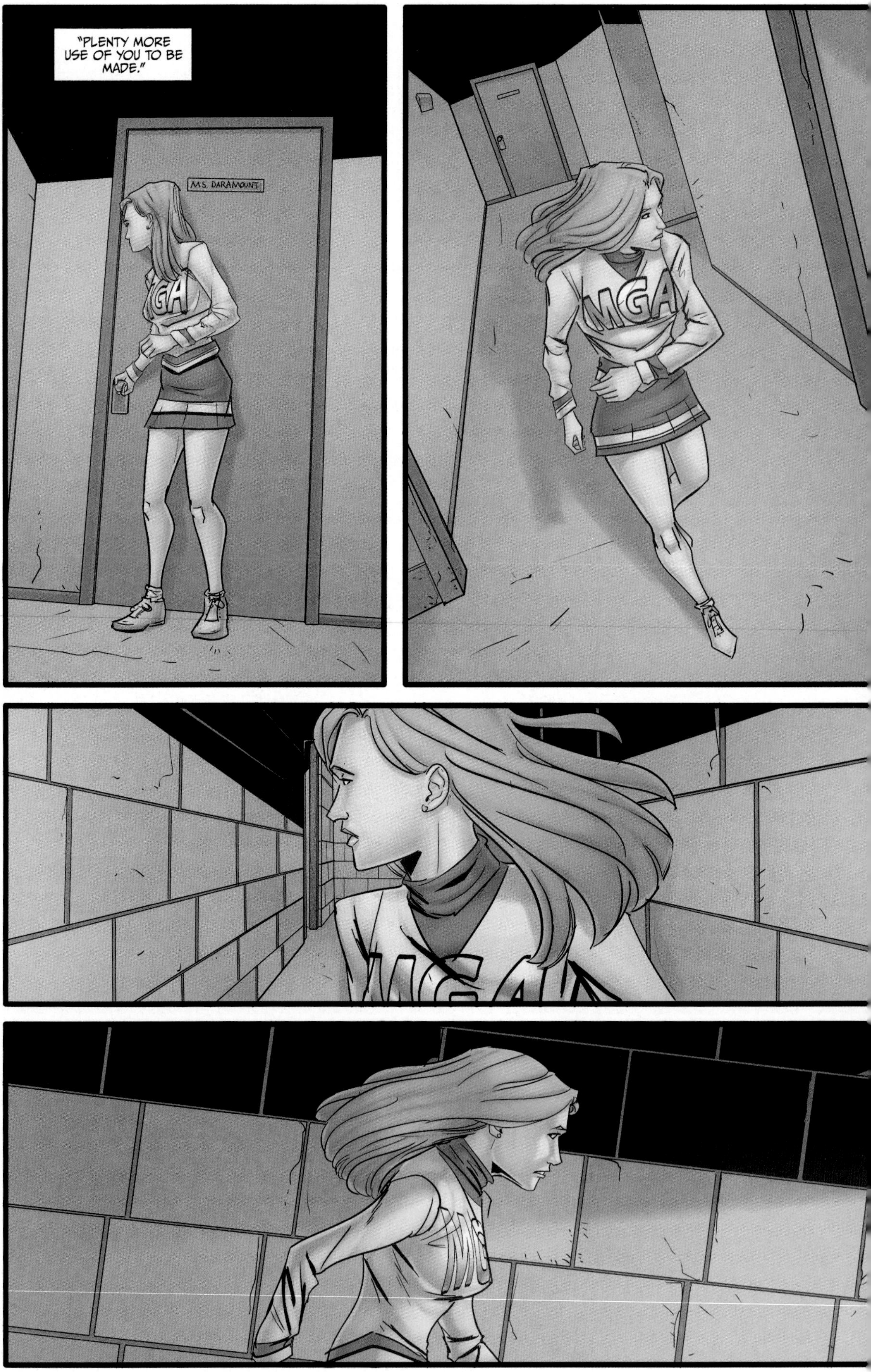
"PLENTY MORE USE OF YOU TO BE MADE."
MS. DARAMOUNT
MGA

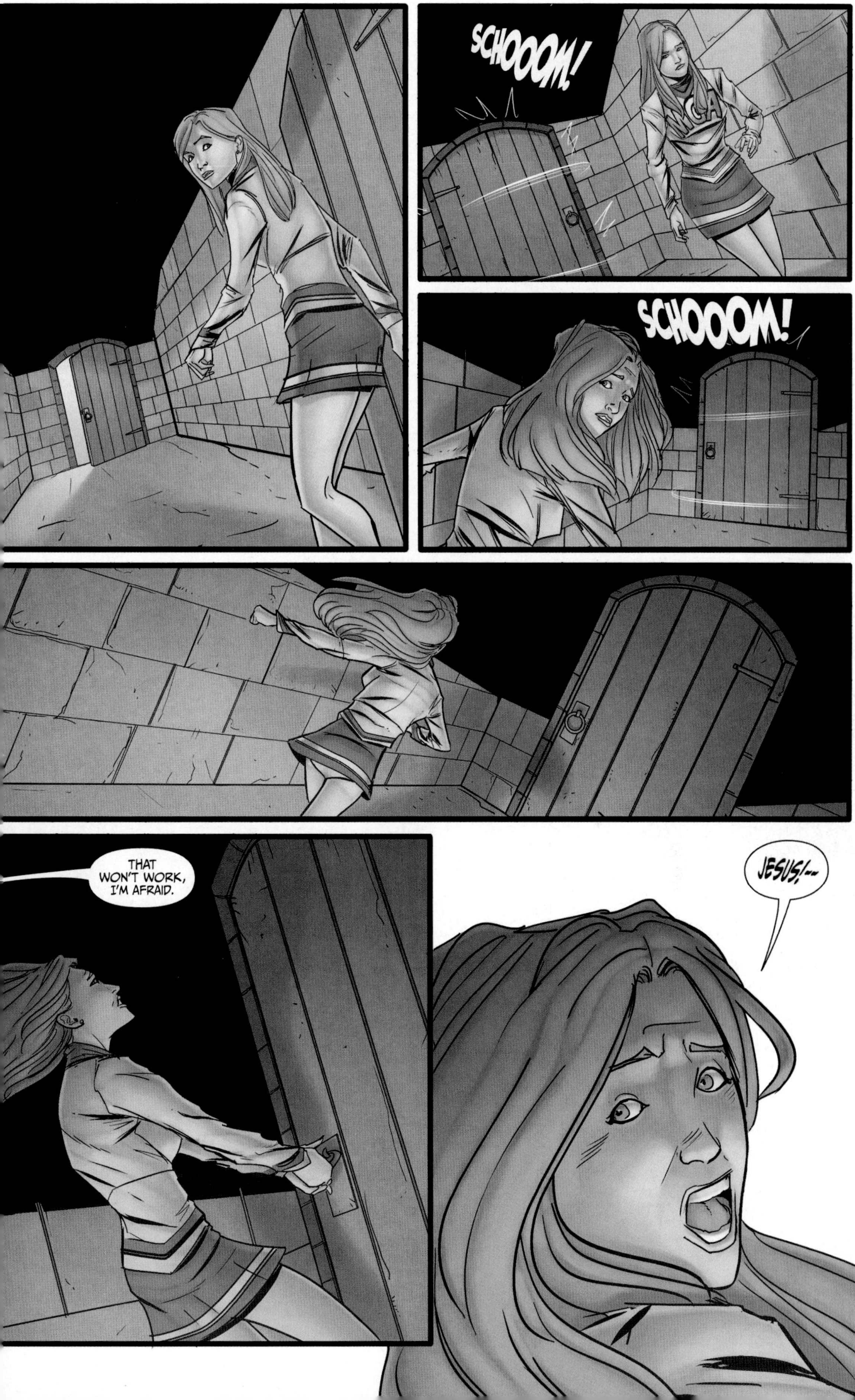
SCHOOOM!
SCHOOOM!
THAT WON'T WORK, I'M AFRAID.
JESUS!--

WHAT ARE *YOU* DOING DOWN HERE?!!

SHOULD BE OBVIOUS. I CAME TO SEE YOU.

OKAY...LISTEN TO ME--I DIDN'T HAVE A CHOICE-- SHE--SHE MADE ME DO IT--

I KNOW. TRUST ME--

I'M NOT ANGRY.

OH GOD.

OH GOD, PLEASE... NO--

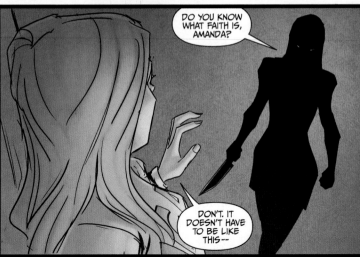

DO YOU KNOW WHAT FAITH IS, AMANDA?

DON'T. IT DOESN'T HAVE TO BE LIKE THIS--

I USED TO STRUGGLE WITH IT. AS A CONCEPT, I MEAN.

BUT THEN, A LONG TIME AGO, I HEARD A WISE MAN PUT IT SO SIMPLY, I'VE NEVER HAD A HARD TIME BELIEVING SINCE.

DO YOU KNOW HOW HE EXPLAINED IT?

I CAN'T--

I CAN'T--

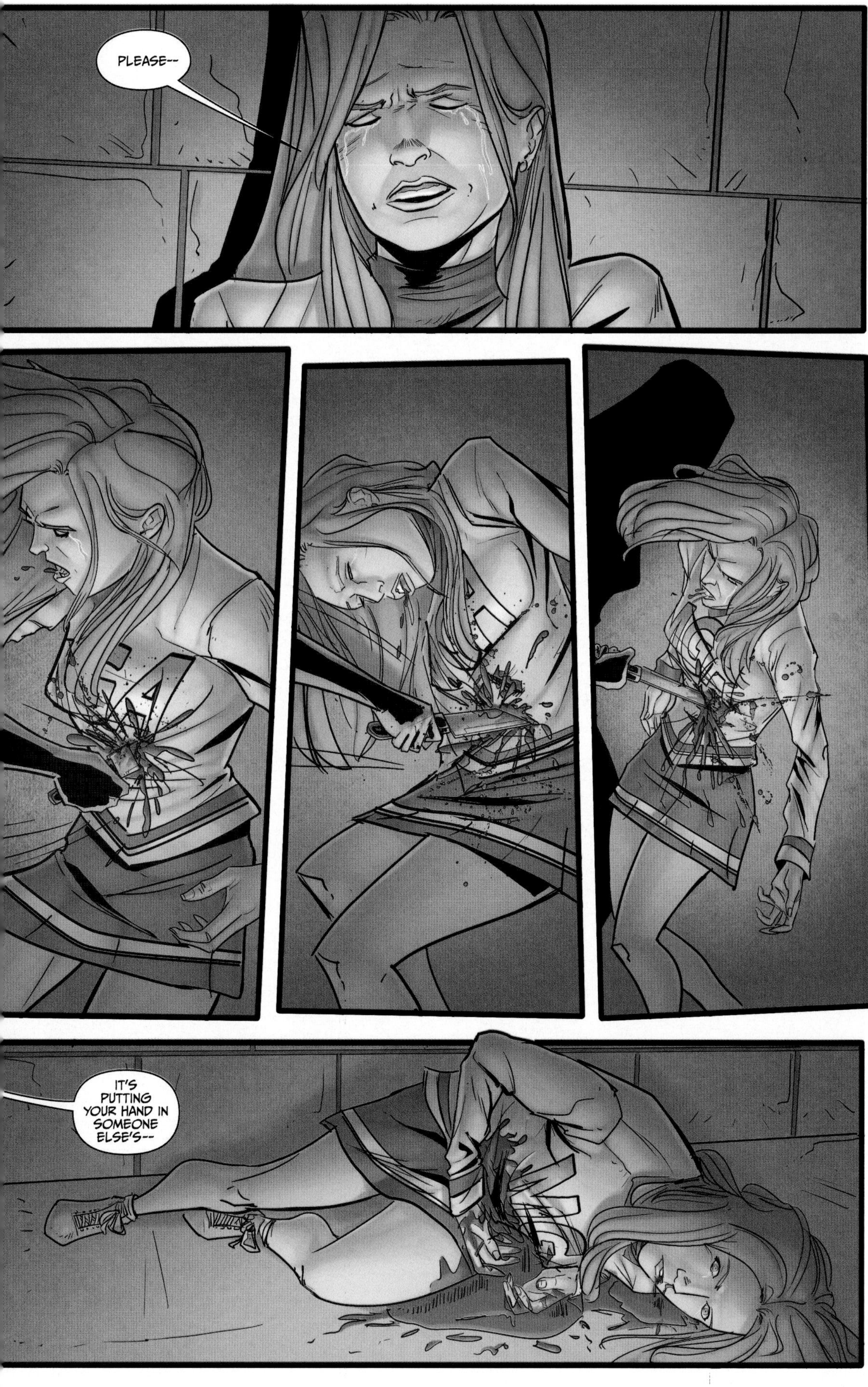
PLEASE--
IT'S PUTTING YOUR HAND IN SOMEONE ELSE'S--

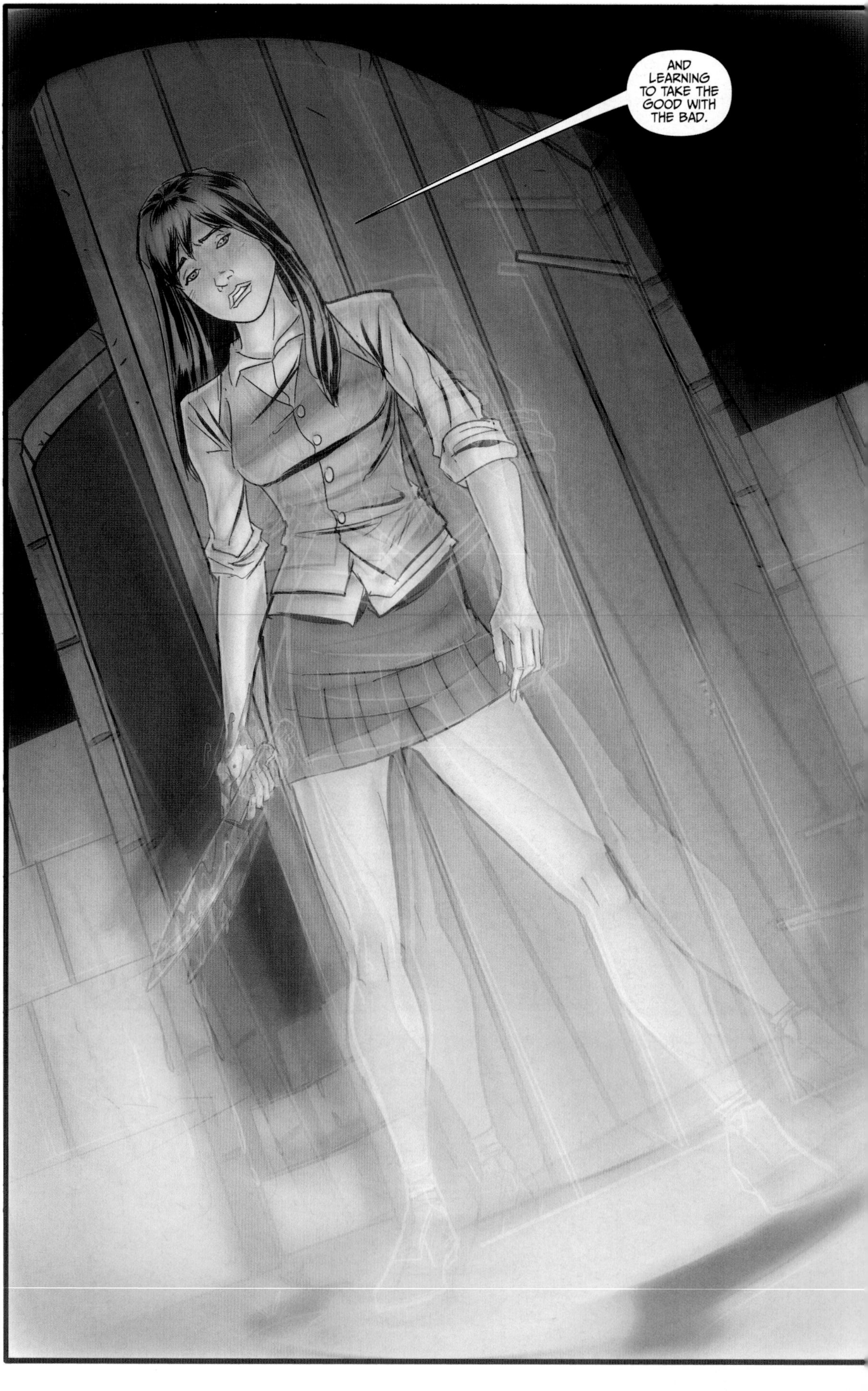
AND LEARNING TO TAKE THE GOOD WITH THE BAD.

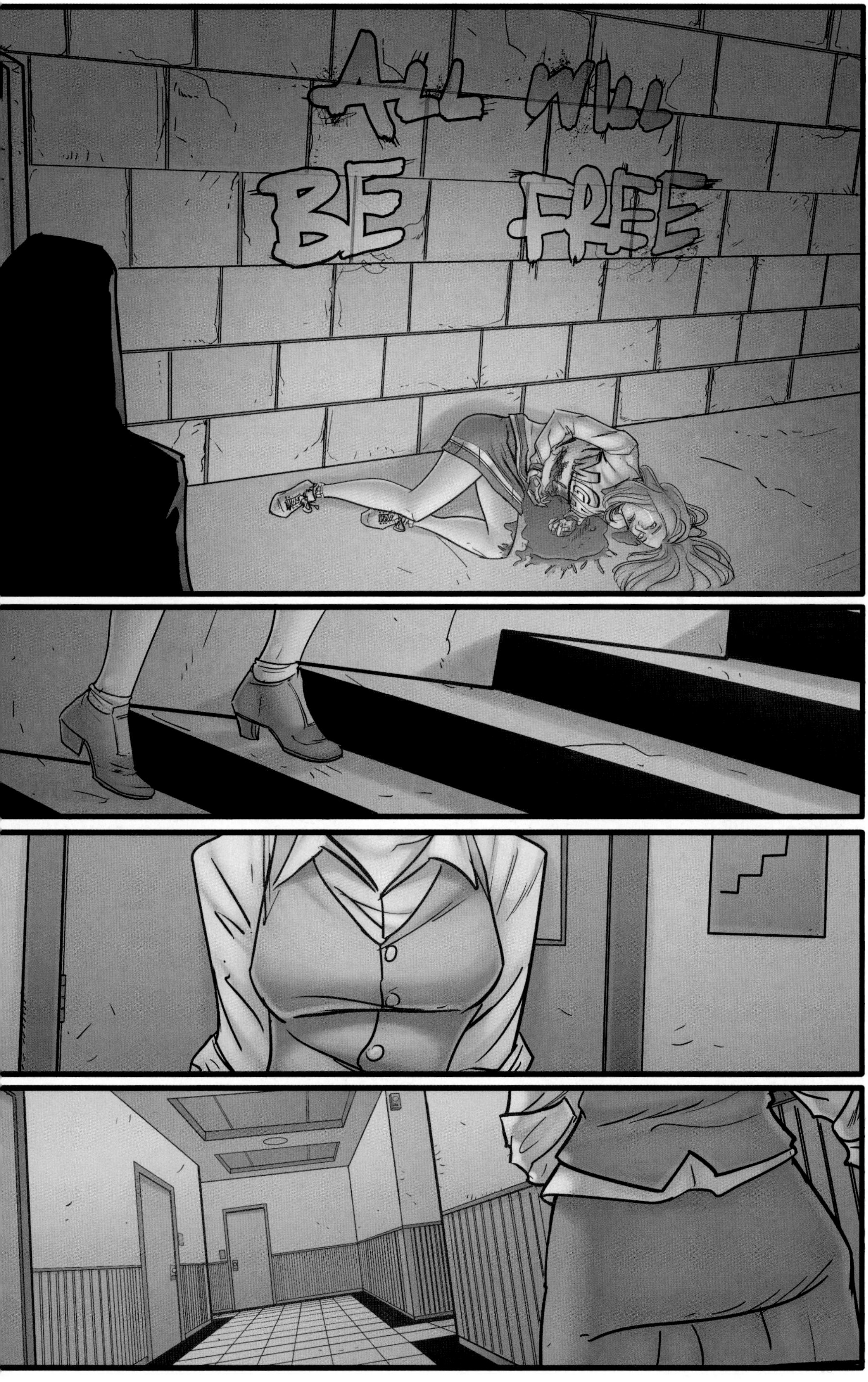
ALL WILL
BE FREE

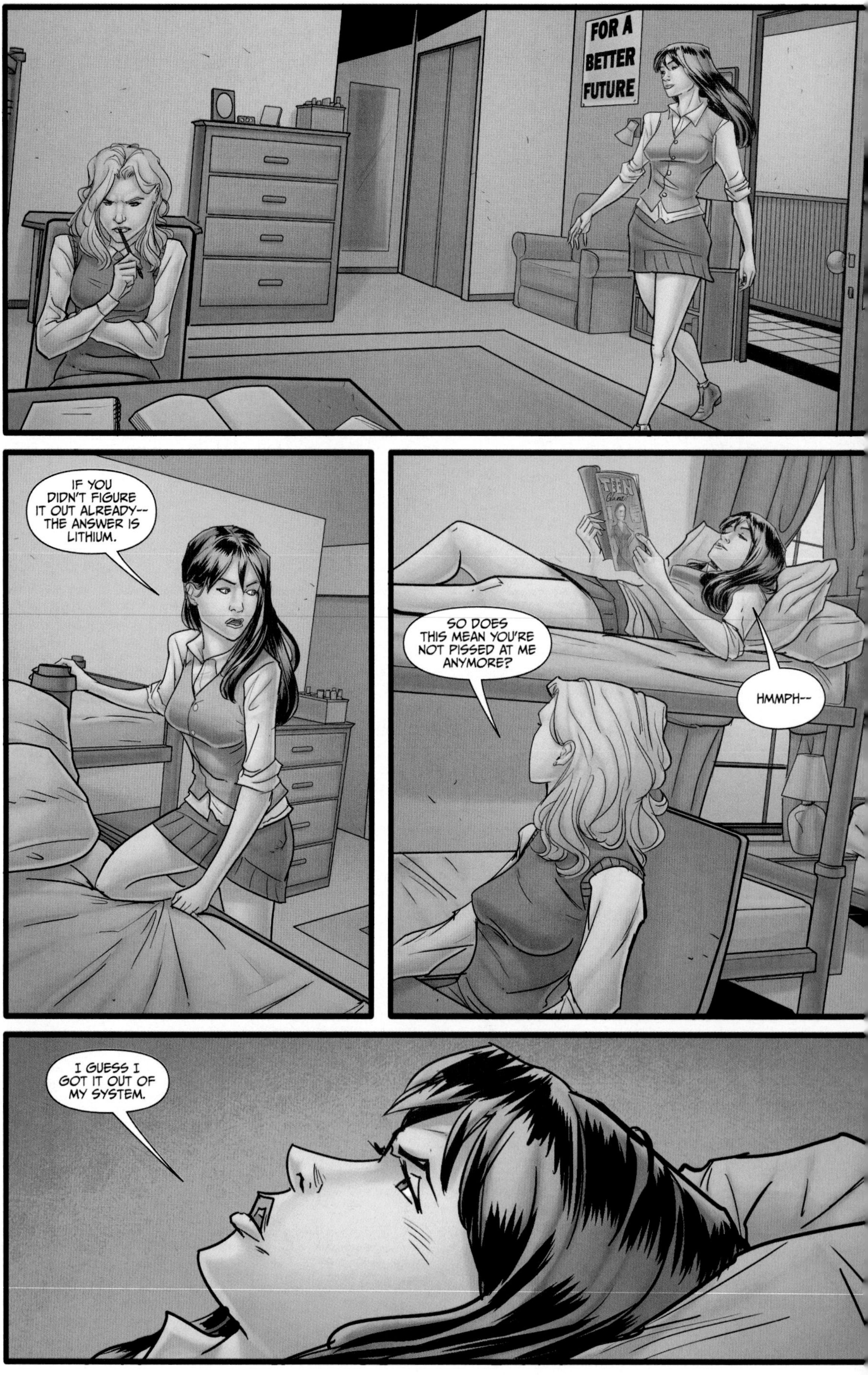
FOR A BETTER FUTURE
IF YOU DIDN'T FIGURE IT OUT ALREADY-- THE ANSWER IS LITHIUM.
TEEN
SO DOES THIS MEAN YOU'RE NOT PISSED AT ME ANYMORE?
HMMPH--
I GUESS I GOT IT OUT OF MY SYSTEM.

eight

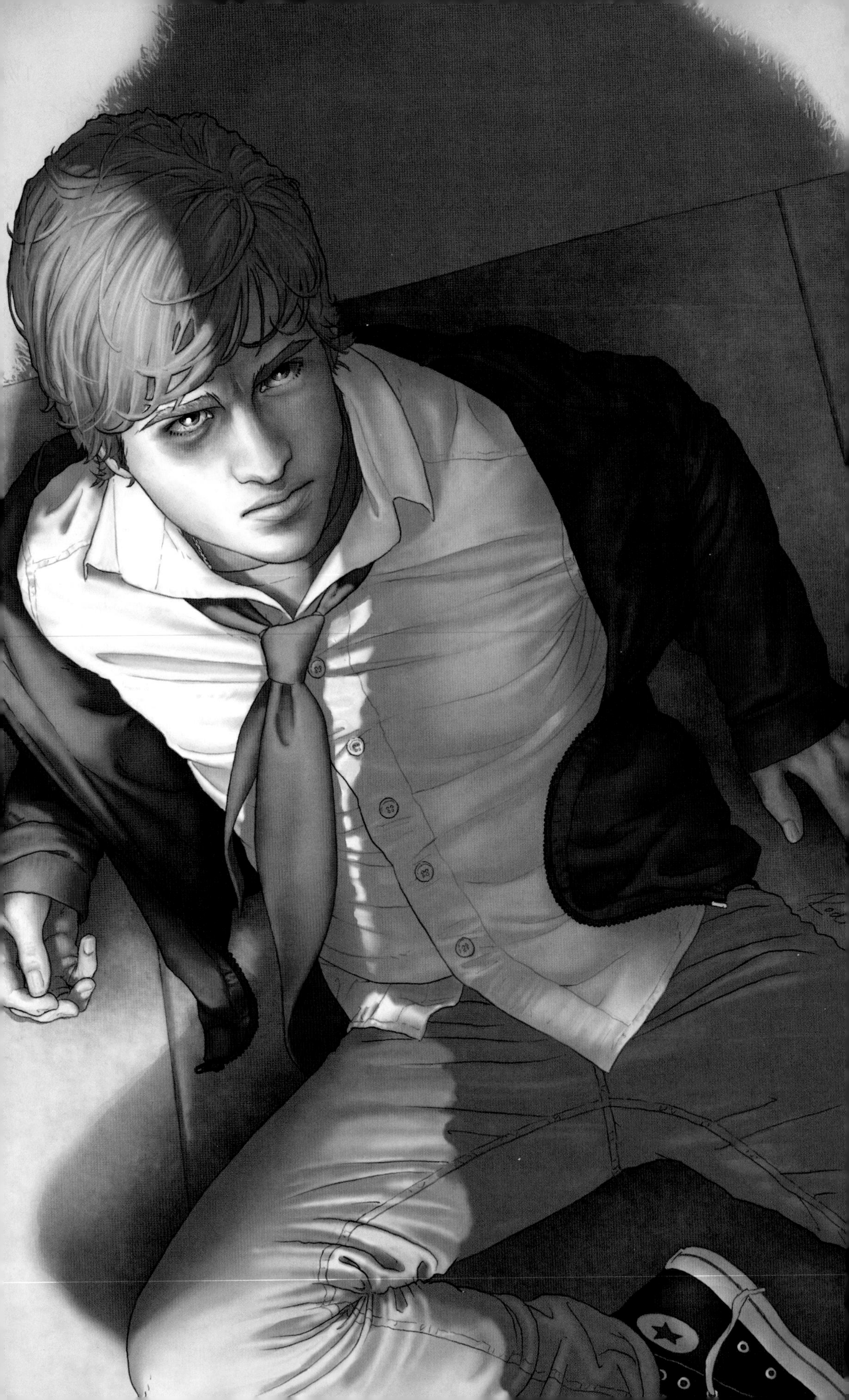

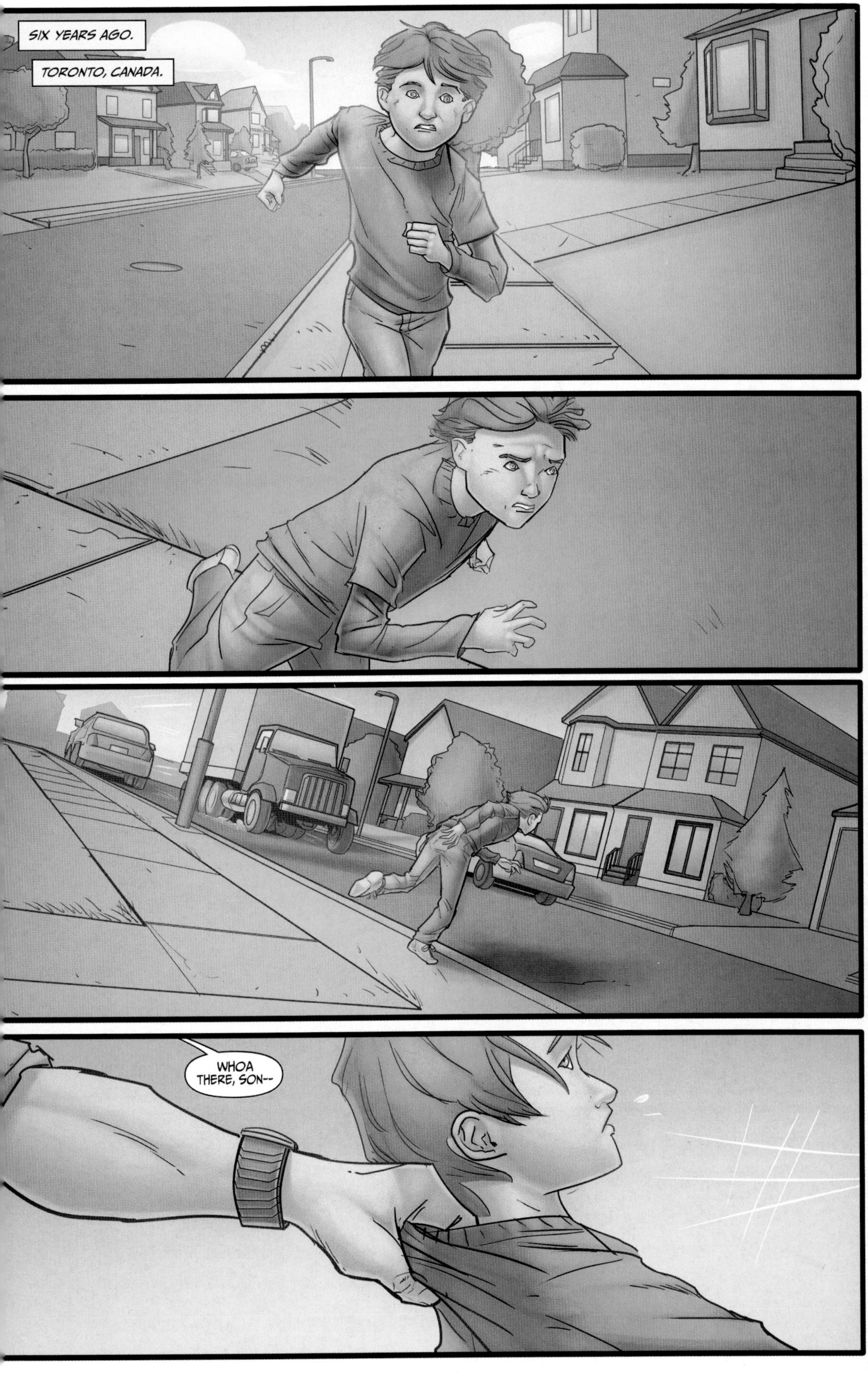
SIX YEARS AGO.
TORONTO, CANADA.
WHOA THERE, SON--

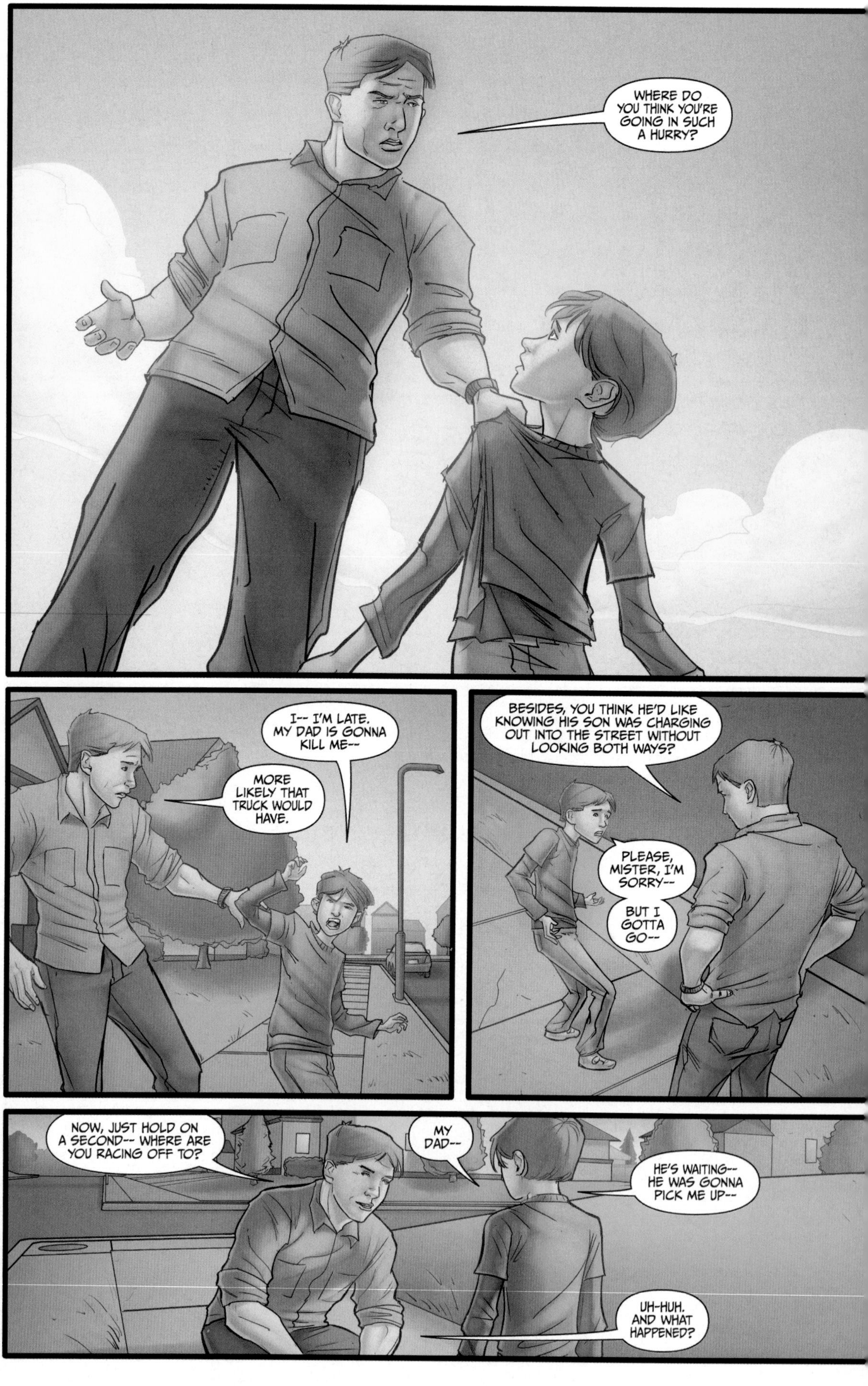
WHERE DO YOU THINK YOU'RE GOING IN SUCH A HURRY?
I-- I'M LATE. MY DAD IS GONNA KILL ME--
MORE LIKELY THAT TRUCK WOULD HAVE.
BESIDES, YOU THINK HE'D LIKE KNOWING HIS SON WAS CHARGING OUT INTO THE STREET WITHOUT LOOKING BOTH WAYS?
PLEASE, MISTER, I'M SORRY--
BUT I GOTTA GO--
NOW, JUST HOLD ON A SECOND-- WHERE ARE YOU RACING OFF TO?
MY DAD--
HE'S WAITING-- HE WAS GONNA PICK ME UP--
UH-HUH. AND WHAT HAPPENED?

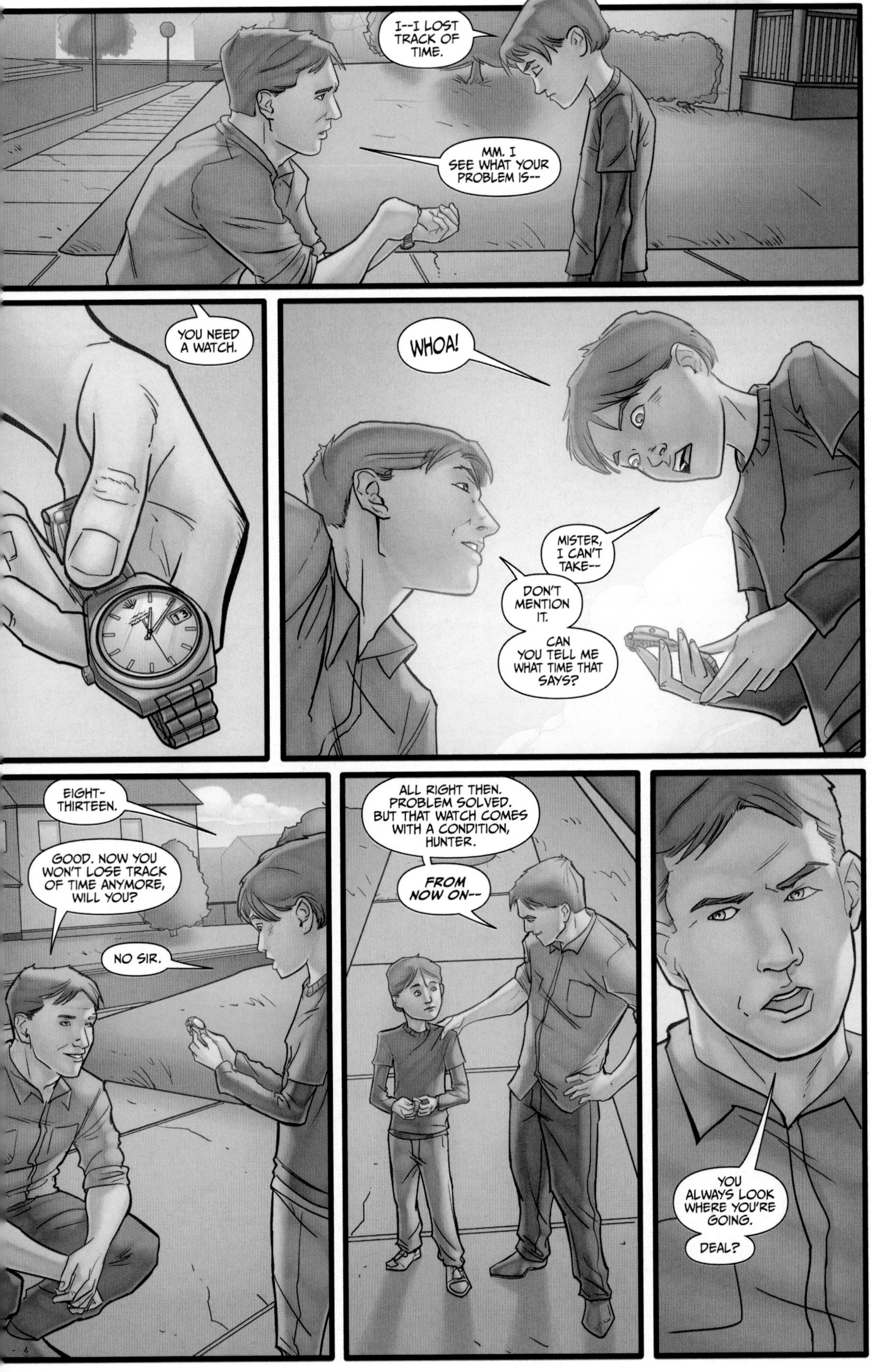
I--I LOST TRACK OF TIME.
MM. I SEE WHAT YOUR PROBLEM IS--
YOU NEED A WATCH.
WHOA!
MISTER, I CAN'T TAKE--
DON'T MENTION IT.
CAN YOU TELL ME WHAT TIME THAT SAYS?
EIGHT-THIRTEEN.
GOOD. NOW YOU WON'T LOSE TRACK OF TIME ANYMORE, WILL YOU?
NO SIR.
ALL RIGHT THEN. PROBLEM SOLVED. BUT THAT WATCH COMES WITH A CONDITION, HUNTER.
FROM NOW ON--
YOU ALWAYS LOOK WHERE YOU'RE GOING.
DEAL?

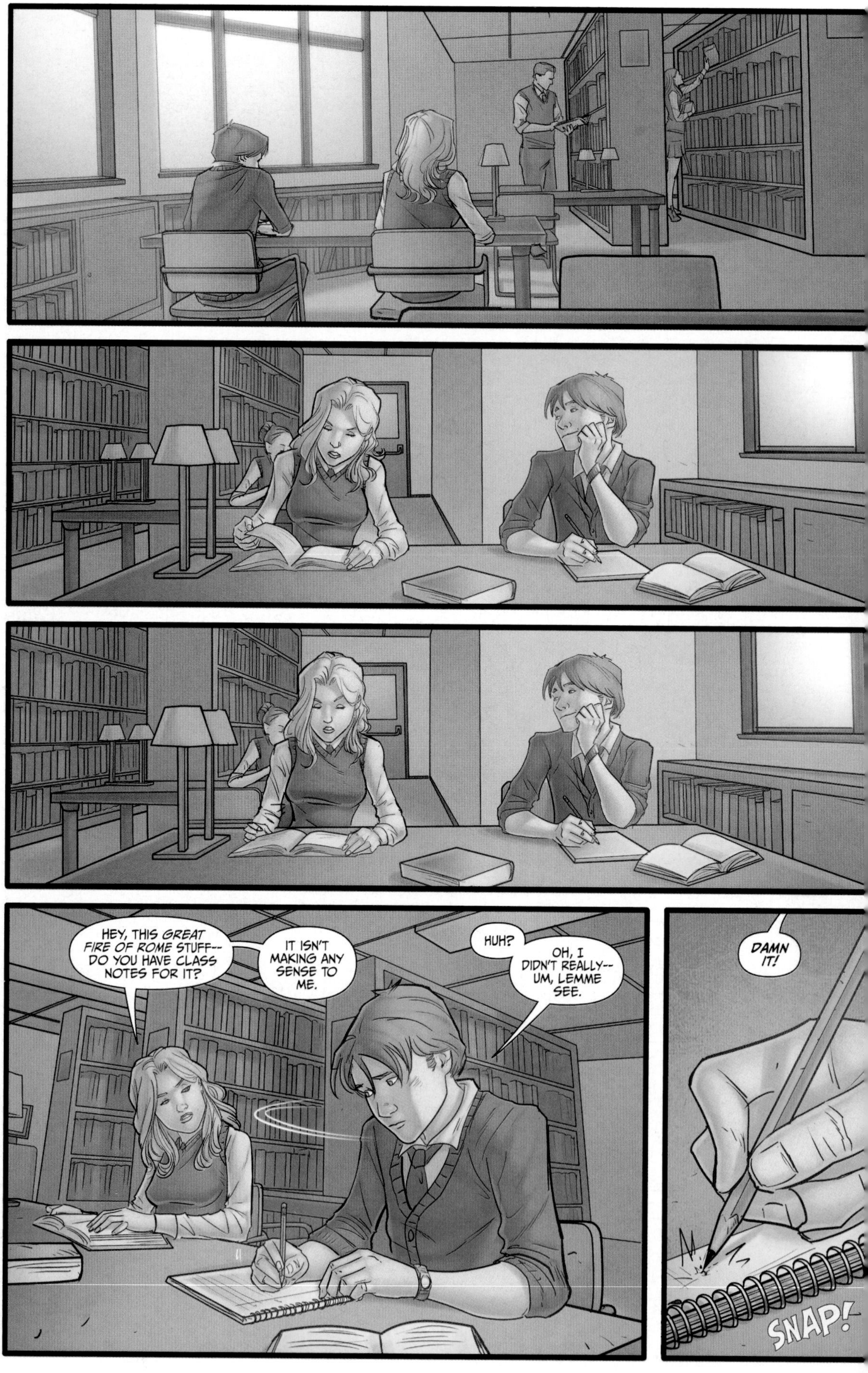
HEY, THIS GREAT FIRE OF ROME STUFF-- DO YOU HAVE CLASS NOTES FOR IT?
IT ISN'T MAKING ANY SENSE TO ME.
HUH?
OH, I DIDN'T REALLY-- UM, LEMME SEE.
DAMN IT!
SNAP!

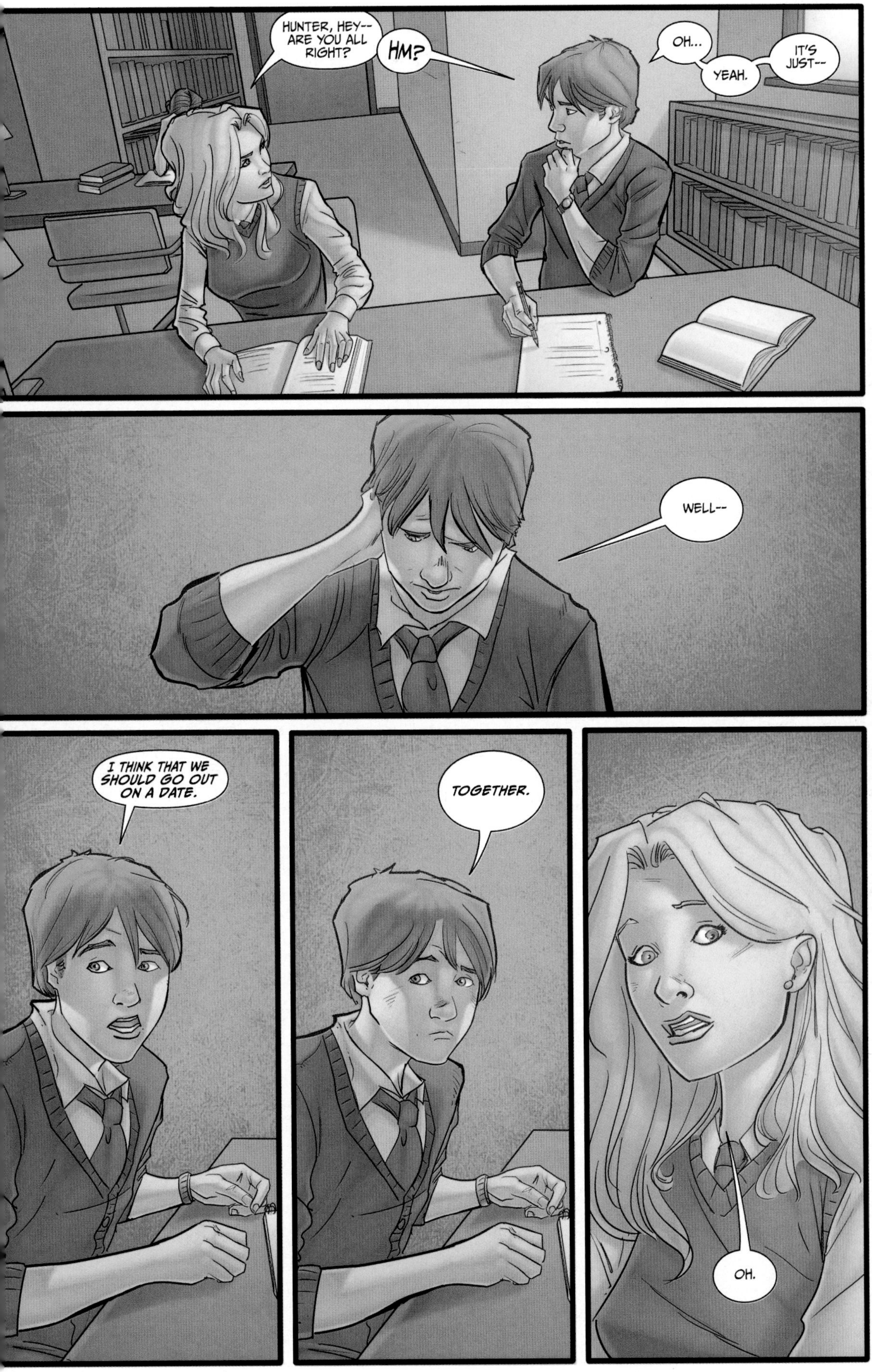
HUNTER, HEY-- ARE YOU ALL RIGHT?
HM?
OH...
YEAH.
IT'S JUST--
WELL--
I THINK THAT WE SHOULD GO OUT ON A DATE.
TOGETHER.
OH.

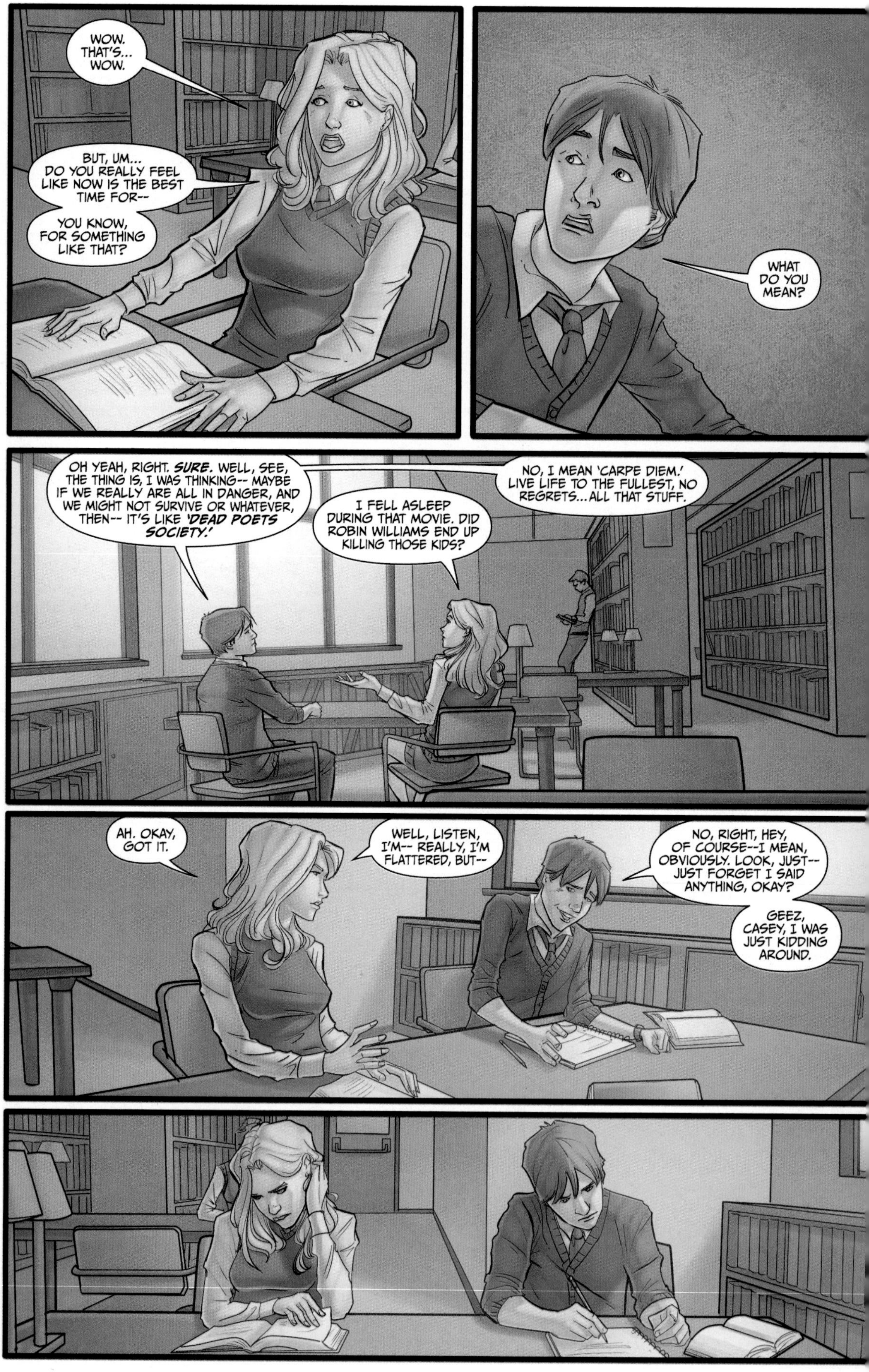
WOW. THAT'S... WOW.
BUT, UM... DO YOU REALLY FEEL LIKE NOW IS THE BEST TIME FOR--
YOU KNOW, FOR SOMETHING LIKE THAT?
WHAT DO YOU MEAN?
OH YEAH, RIGHT. SURE. WELL, SEE, THE THING IS, I WAS THINKING-- MAYBE IF WE REALLY ARE ALL IN DANGER, AND WE MIGHT NOT SURVIVE OR WHATEVER, THEN-- IT'S LIKE 'DEAD POETS SOCIETY.'
I FELL ASLEEP DURING THAT MOVIE. DID ROBIN WILLIAMS END UP KILLING THOSE KIDS?
NO, I MEAN 'CARPE DIEM.' LIVE LIFE TO THE FULLEST, NO REGRETS...ALL THAT STUFF.
AH. OKAY, GOT IT.
WELL, LISTEN, I'M-- REALLY, I'M FLATTERED, BUT--
NO, RIGHT, HEY, OF COURSE--I MEAN, OBVIOUSLY. LOOK, JUST-- JUST FORGET I SAID ANYTHING, OKAY?
GEEZ, CASEY, I WAS JUST KIDDING AROUND.

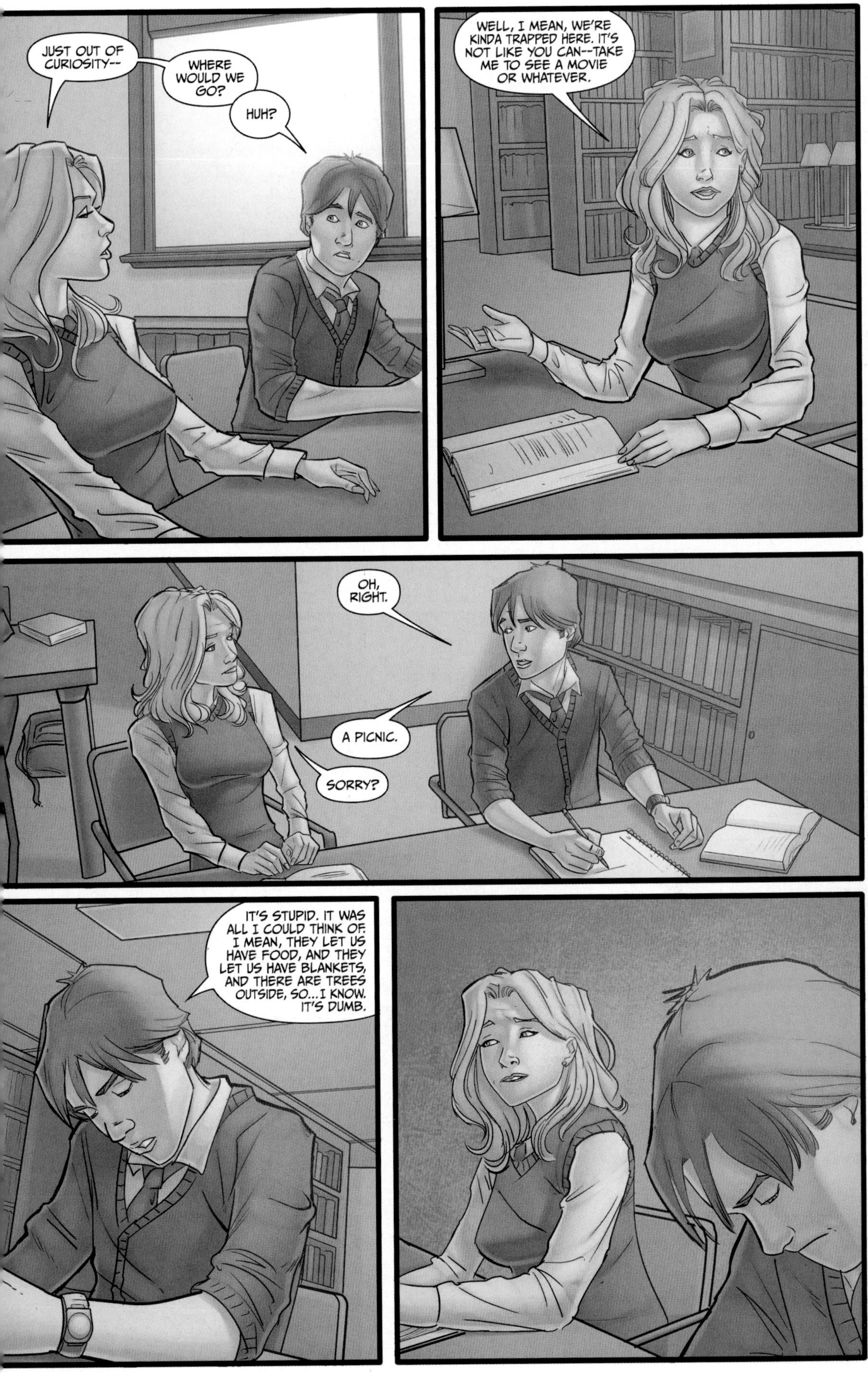
JUST OUT OF CURIOSITY--
WHERE WOULD WE GO?
HUH?
WELL, I MEAN, WE'RE KINDA TRAPPED HERE. IT'S NOT LIKE YOU CAN--TAKE ME TO SEE A MOVIE OR WHATEVER.
OH, RIGHT.
A PICNIC.
SORRY?
IT'S STUPID. IT WAS ALL I COULD THINK OF. I MEAN, THEY LET US HAVE FOOD, AND THEY LET US HAVE BLANKETS, AND THERE ARE TREES OUTSIDE, SO...I KNOW. IT'S DUMB.

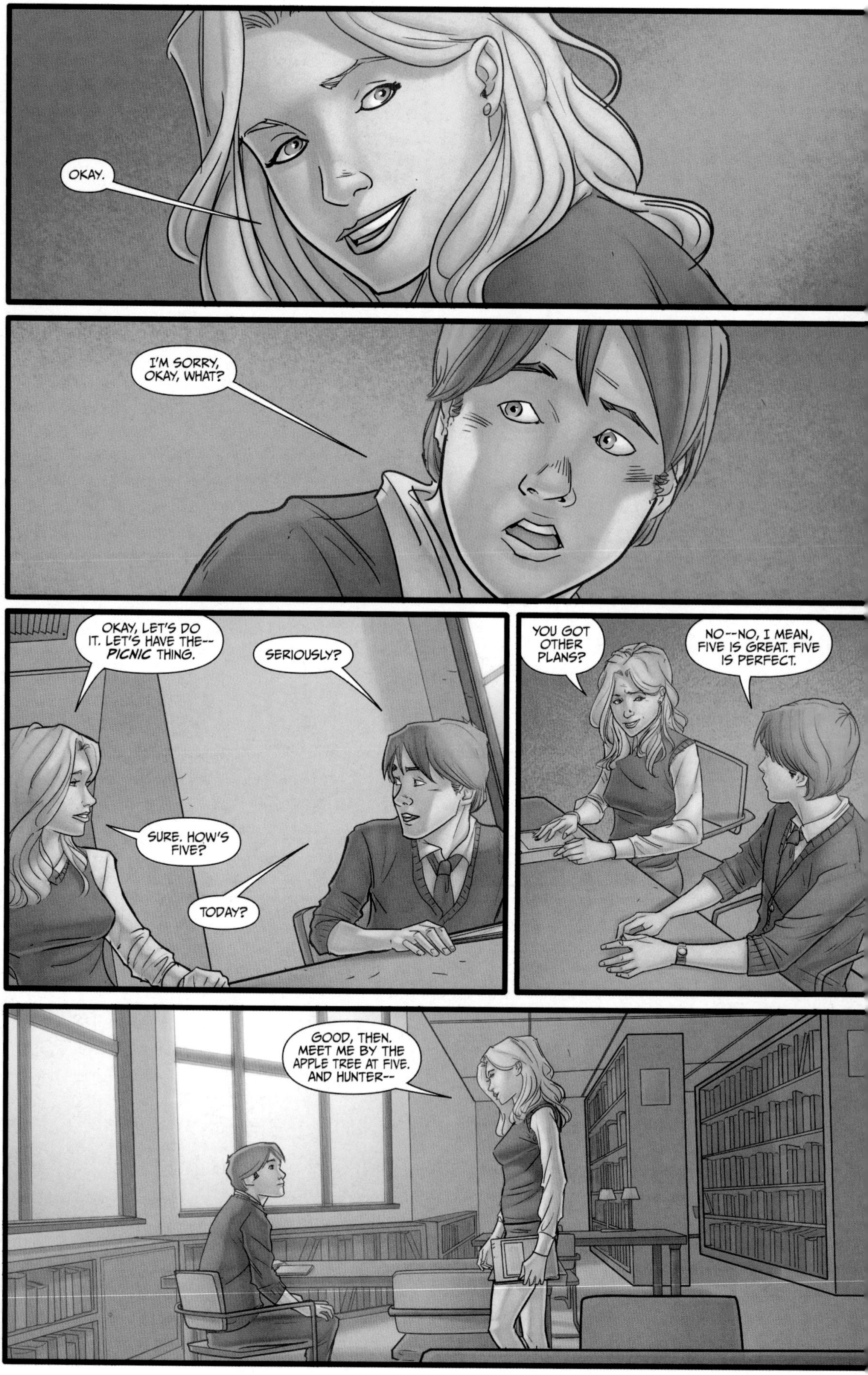
OKAY.
I'M SORRY, OKAY, WHAT?
OKAY, LET'S DO IT. LET'S HAVE THE-- PICNIC THING.
SERIOUSLY?
SURE. HOW'S FIVE?
TODAY?
YOU GOT OTHER PLANS?
NO--NO, I MEAN, FIVE IS GREAT. FIVE IS PERFECT.
GOOD, THEN. MEET ME BY THE APPLE TREE AT FIVE. AND HUNTER--

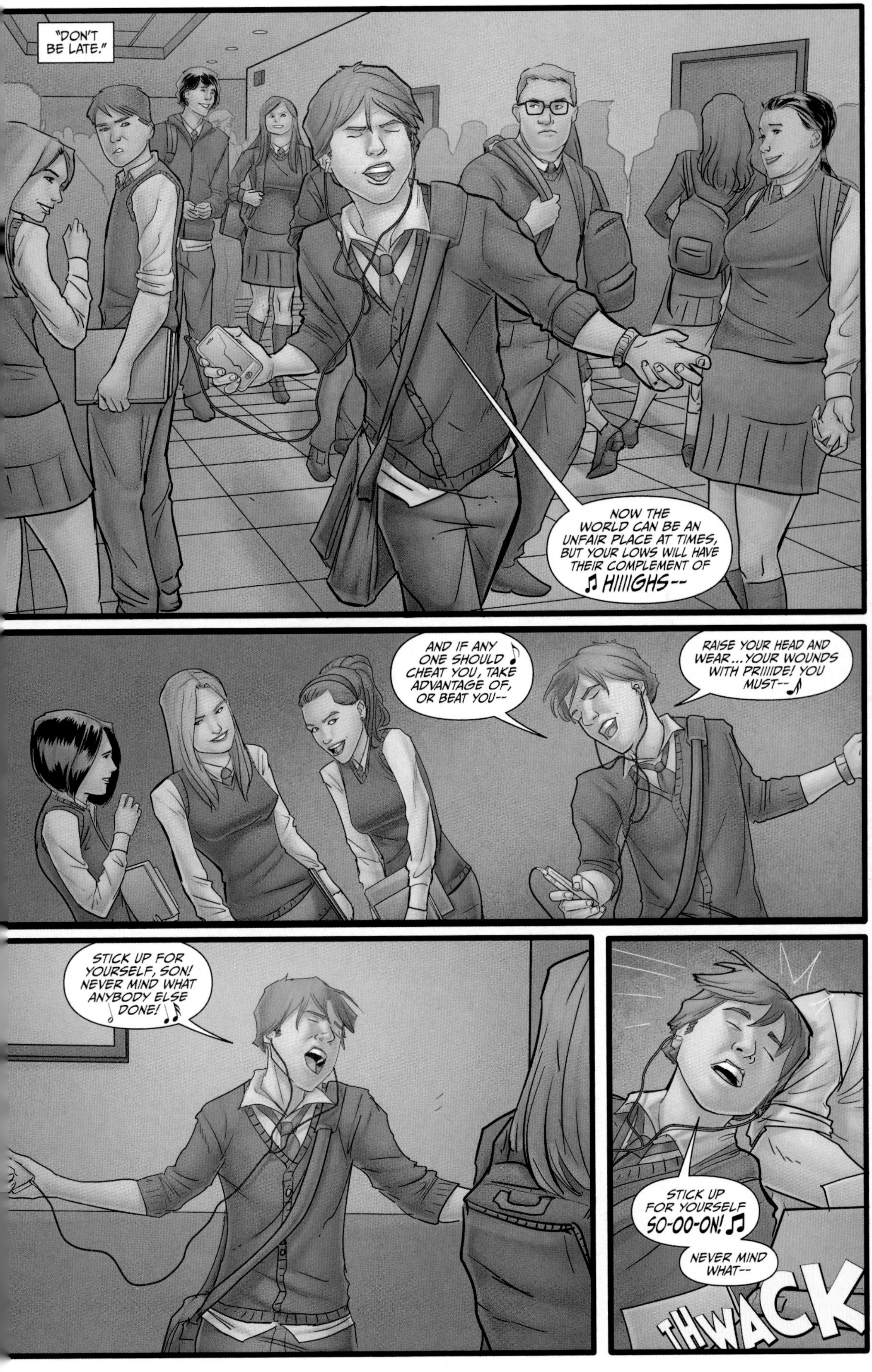
"DON'T BE LATE."
NOW THE WORLD CAN BE AN UNFAIR PLACE AT TIMES, BUT YOUR LOWS WILL HAVE THEIR COMPLEMENT OF ♫ HIIIIGHS--
AND IF ANY ONE SHOULD CHEAT YOU, TAKE ADVANTAGE OF, OR BEAT YOU--
RAISE YOUR HEAD AND WEAR...YOUR WOUNDS WITH PRIIIIDE! YOU MUST--
STICK UP FOR YOURSELF, SON! NEVER MIND WHAT ANYBODY ELSE DONE!
STICK UP FOR YOURSELF SO-OO-ON! ♫
NEVER MIND WHAT--
THWACK

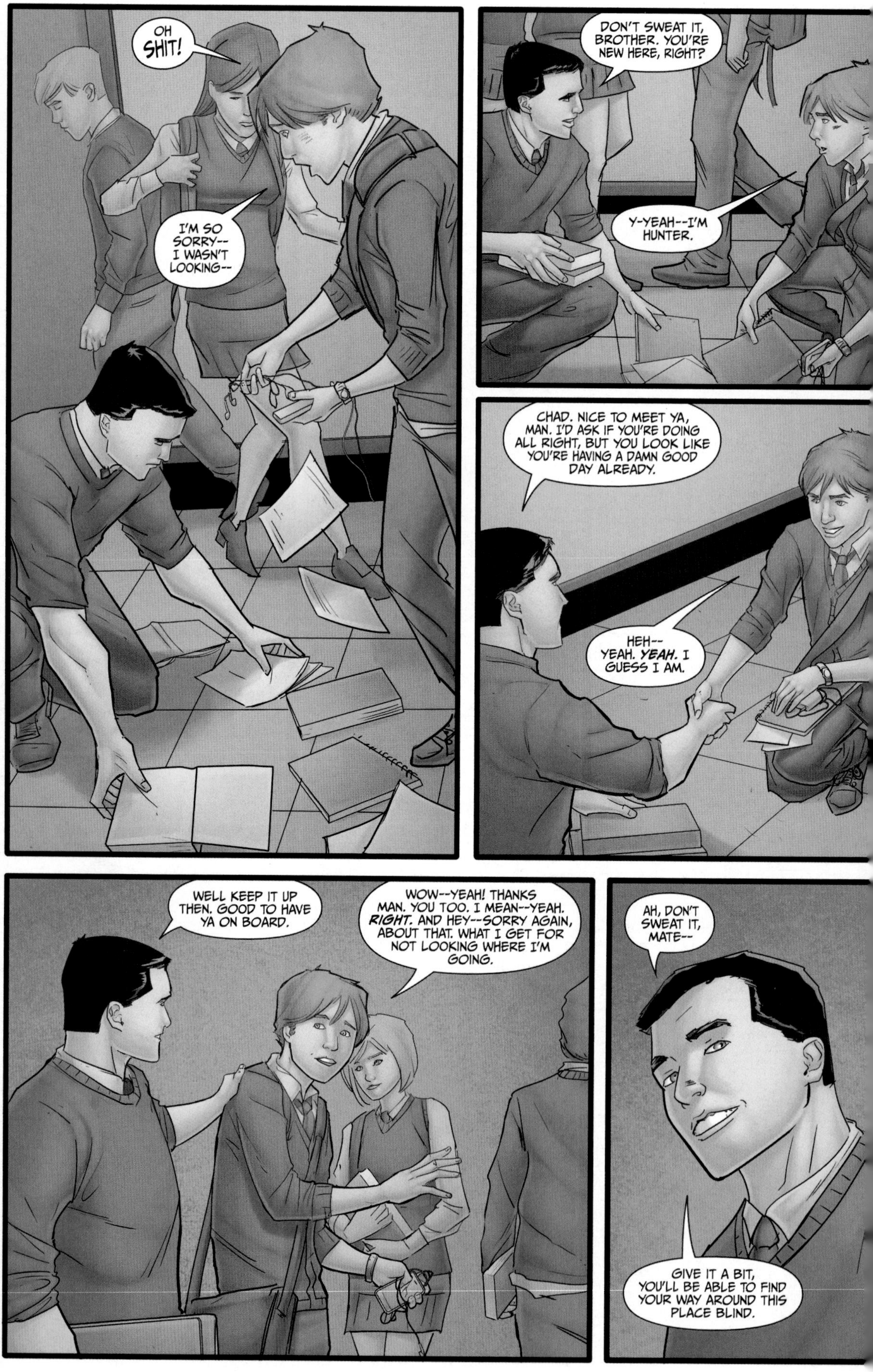
OH SHIT!
I'M SO SORRY--I WASN'T LOOKING--
DON'T SWEAT IT, BROTHER. YOU'RE NEW HERE, RIGHT?
Y-YEAH--I'M HUNTER.
CHAD. NICE TO MEET YA, MAN. I'D ASK IF YOU'RE DOING ALL RIGHT, BUT YOU LOOK LIKE YOU'RE HAVING A DAMN GOOD DAY ALREADY.
HEH--YEAH. *YEAH.* I GUESS I AM.
WELL KEEP IT UP THEN. GOOD TO HAVE YA ON BOARD.
WOW--YEAH! THANKS MAN. YOU TOO. I MEAN--YEAH. *RIGHT.* AND HEY--SORRY AGAIN, ABOUT THAT. WHAT I GET FOR NOT LOOKING WHERE I'M GOING.
AH, DON'T SWEAT IT, MATE--
GIVE IT A BIT, YOU'LL BE ABLE TO FIND YOUR WAY AROUND THIS PLACE BLIND.

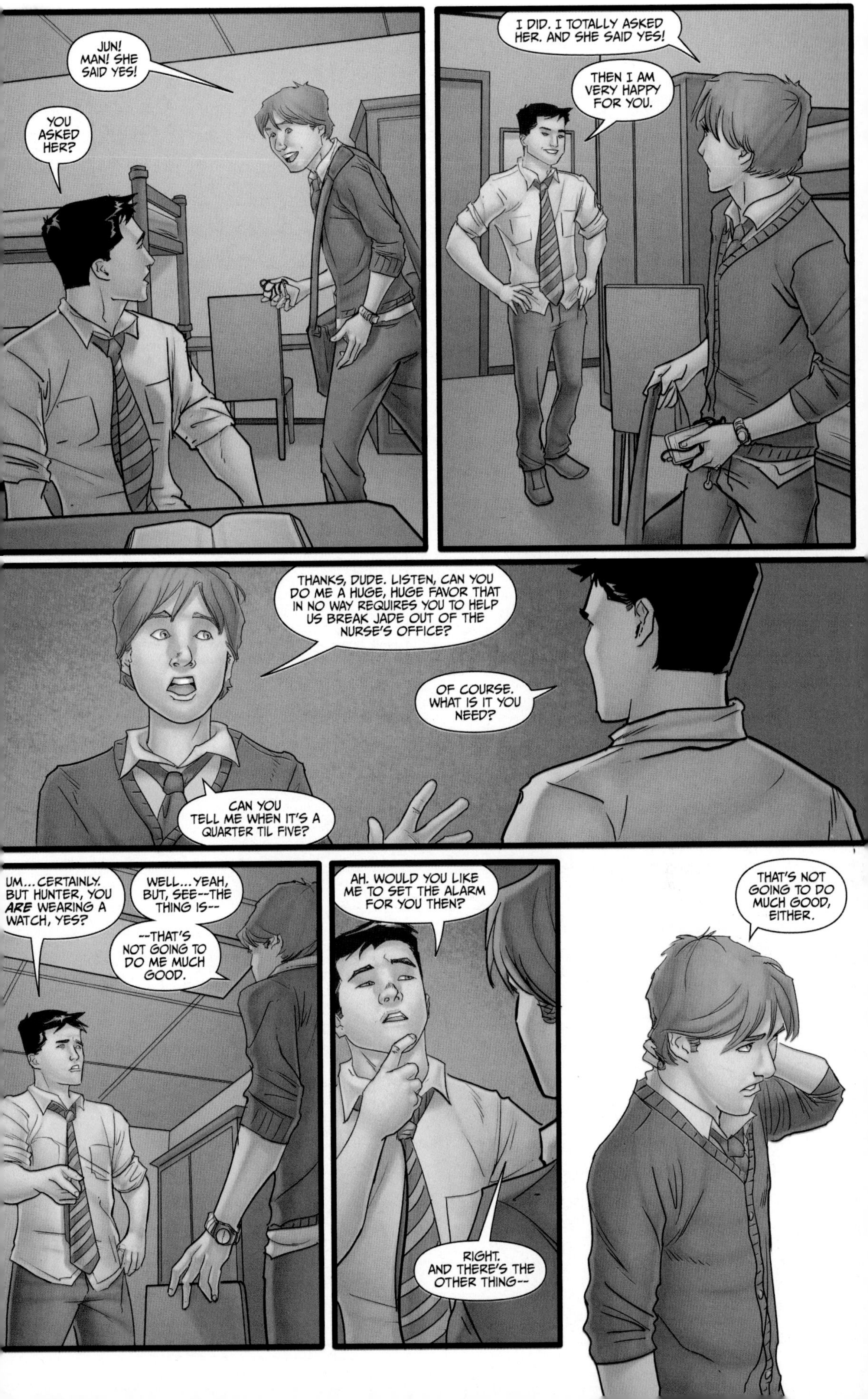
JUN! MAN! SHE SAID YES!
YOU ASKED HER?
I DID. I TOTALLY ASKED HER. AND SHE SAID YES!
THEN I AM VERY HAPPY FOR YOU.
THANKS, DUDE. LISTEN, CAN YOU DO ME A HUGE, HUGE FAVOR THAT IN NO WAY REQUIRES YOU TO HELP US BREAK JADE OUT OF THE NURSE'S OFFICE?
OF COURSE. WHAT IS IT YOU NEED?
CAN YOU TELL ME WHEN IT'S A QUARTER TIL FIVE?
UM... CERTAINLY. BUT HUNTER, YOU *ARE* WEARING A WATCH, YES?
WELL... YEAH, BUT, SEE--THE THING IS--
--THAT'S NOT GOING TO DO ME MUCH GOOD.
AH. WOULD YOU LIKE ME TO SET THE ALARM FOR YOU THEN?
RIGHT. AND THERE'S THE OTHER THING--
THAT'S NOT GOING TO DO MUCH GOOD, EITHER.

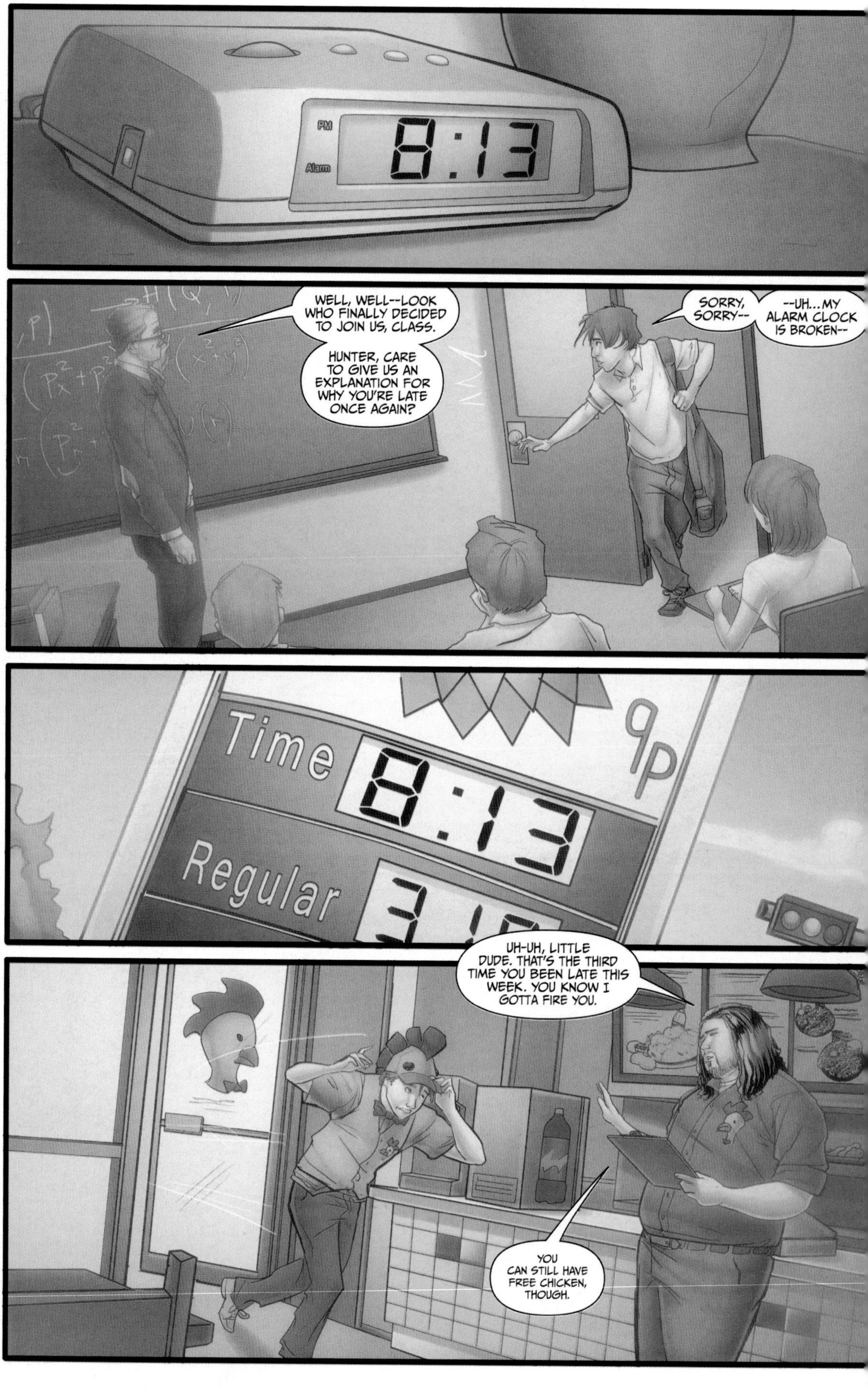
PM
Alarm
8:13
WELL, WELL--LOOK WHO FINALLY DECIDED TO JOIN US, CLASS.
HUNTER, CARE TO GIVE US AN EXPLANATION FOR WHY YOU'RE LATE ONCE AGAIN?
SORRY, SORRY--
--UH...MY ALARM CLOCK IS BROKEN--
Time
8:13
Regular
UH-UH, LITTLE DUDE. THAT'S THE THIRD TIME YOU BEEN LATE THIS WEEK. YOU KNOW I GOTTA FIRE YOU.
YOU CAN STILL HAVE FREE CHICKEN, THOUGH.

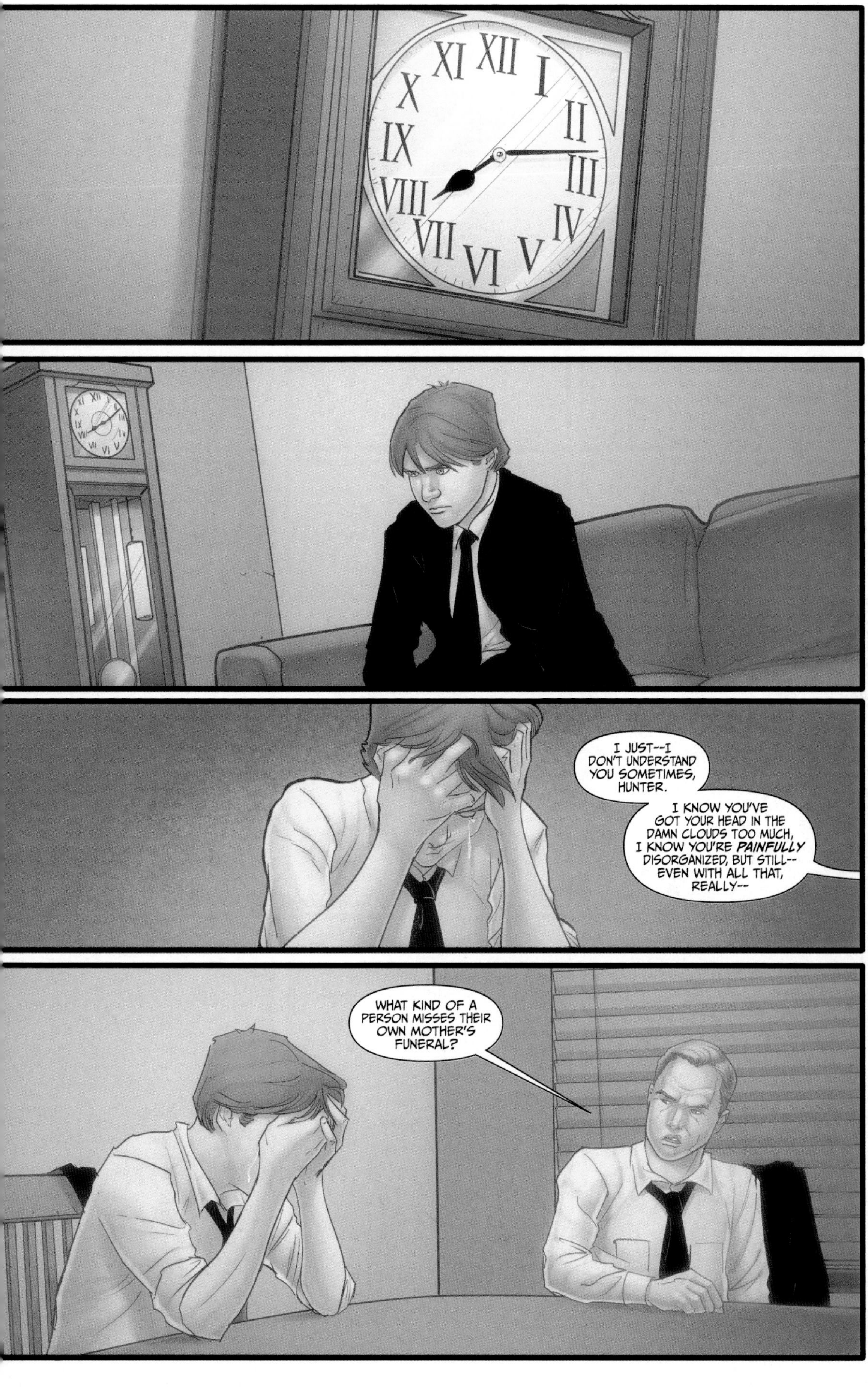

I JUST--I DON'T UNDERSTAND YOU SOMETIMES, HUNTER.
I KNOW YOU'VE GOT YOUR HEAD IN THE DAMN CLOUDS TOO MUCH, I KNOW YOU'RE ***PAINFULLY*** DISORGANIZED, BUT STILL-- EVEN WITH ALL THAT, REALLY--
WHAT KIND OF A PERSON MISSES THEIR OWN MOTHER'S FUNERAL?

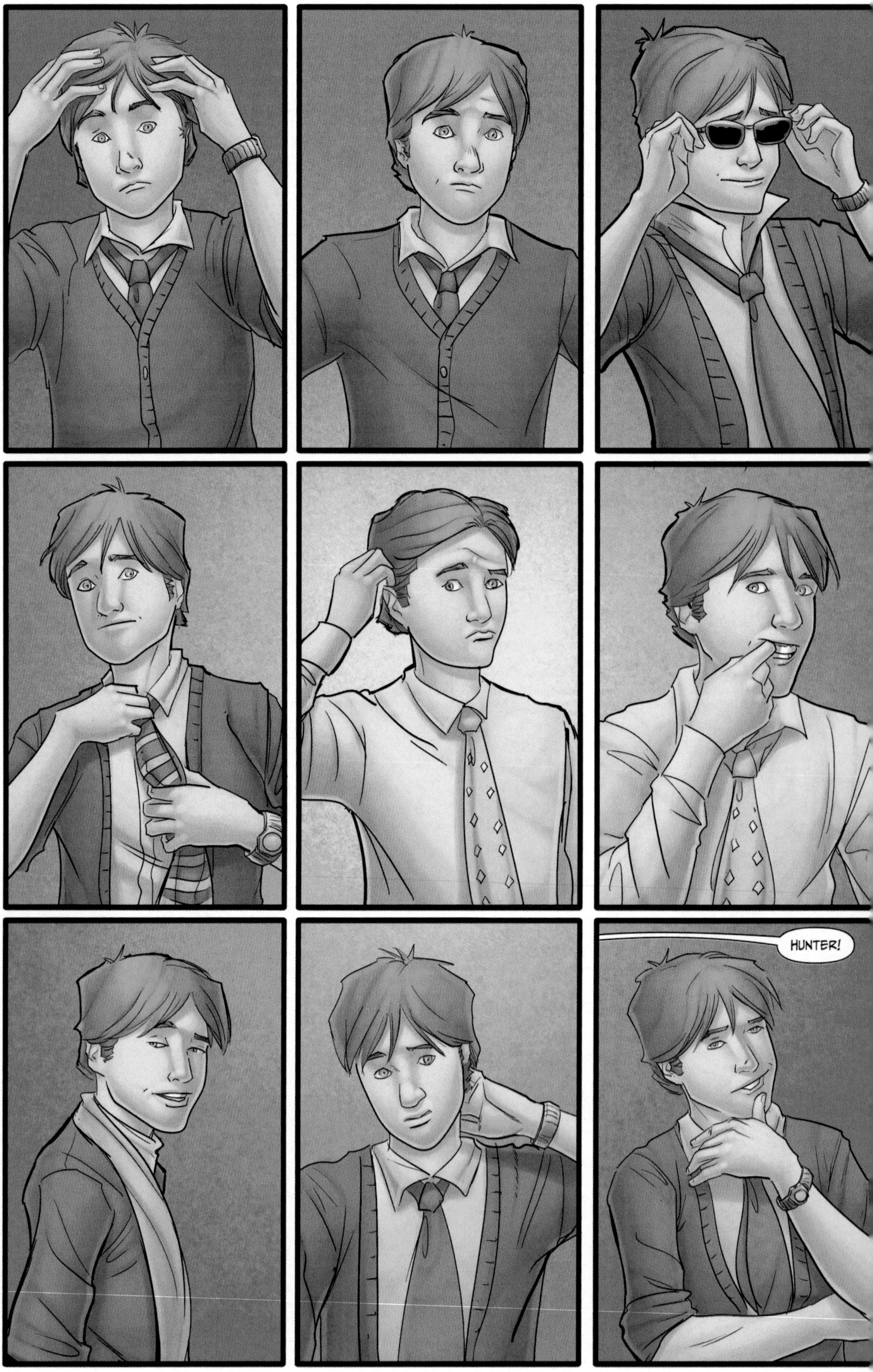
HUNTER!

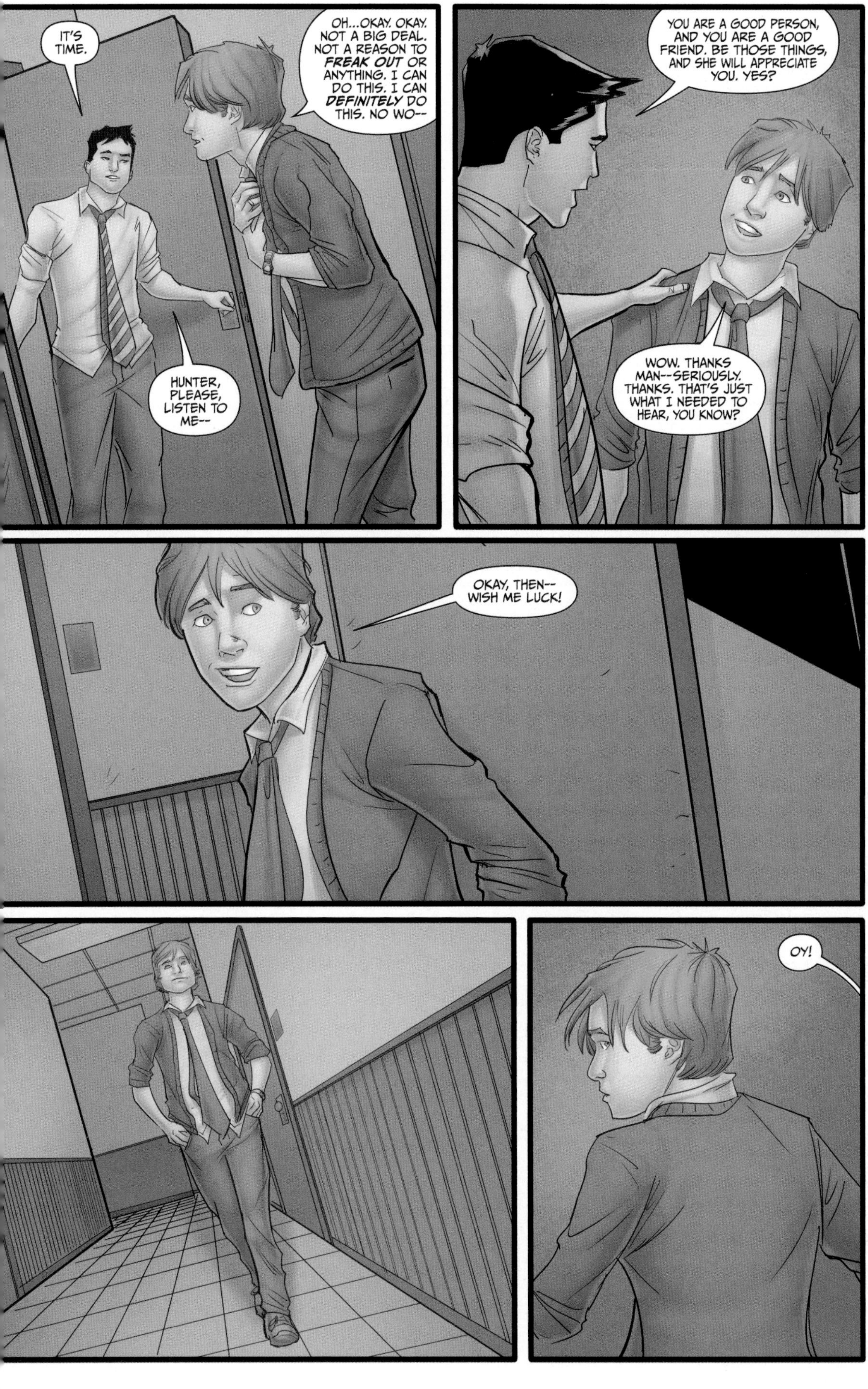
IT'S TIME.
OH...OKAY. OKAY. NOT A BIG DEAL. NOT A REASON TO FREAK OUT OR ANYTHING. I CAN DO THIS. I CAN DEFINITELY DO THIS. NO WO--
HUNTER, PLEASE, LISTEN TO ME--
YOU ARE A GOOD PERSON, AND YOU ARE A GOOD FRIEND. BE THOSE THINGS, AND SHE WILL APPRECIATE YOU. YES?
WOW. THANKS MAN--SERIOUSLY. THANKS. THAT'S JUST WHAT I NEEDED TO HEAR, YOU KNOW?
OKAY, THEN--WISH ME LUCK!
OY!

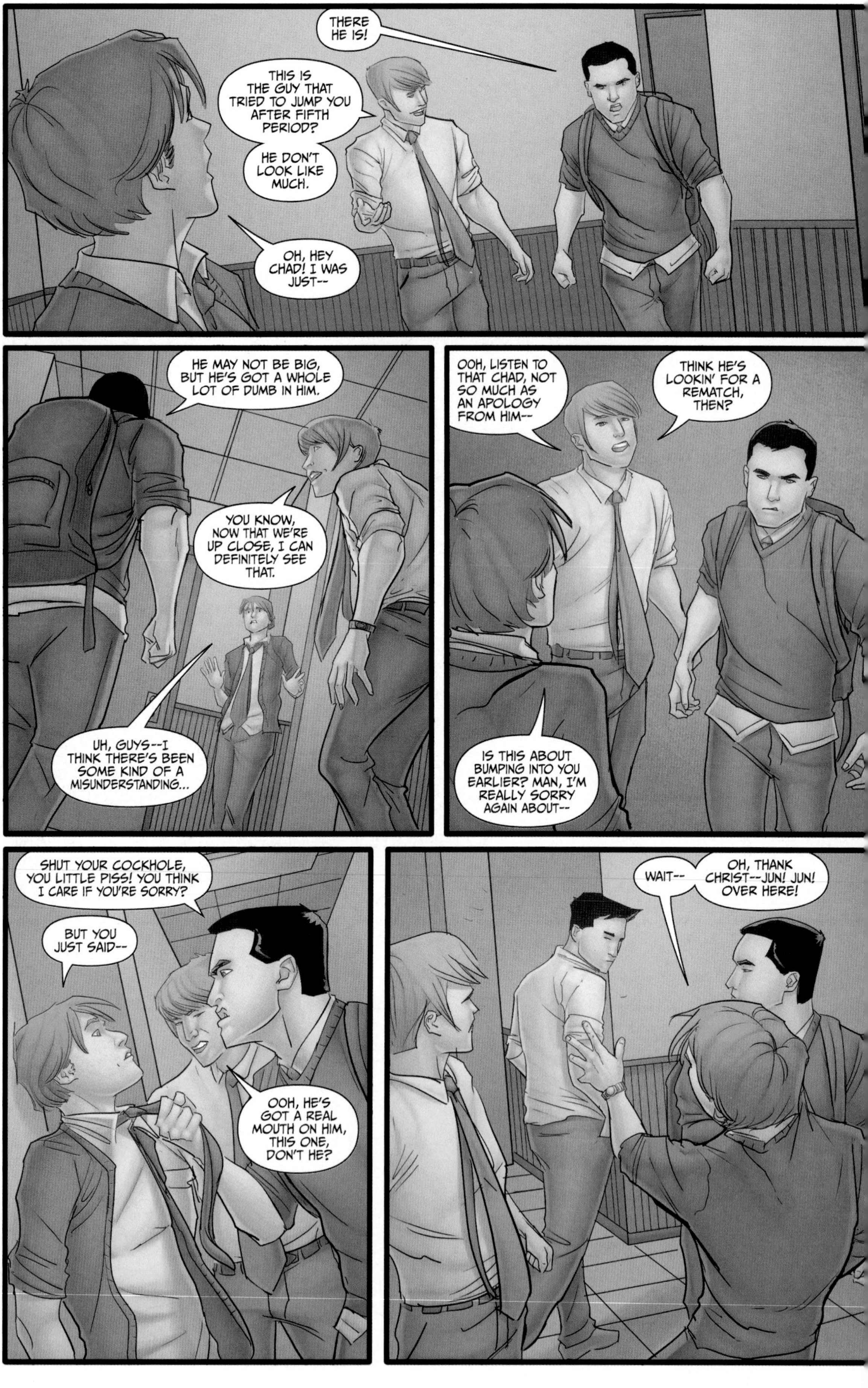
THERE HE IS!
THIS IS THE GUY THAT TRIED TO JUMP YOU AFTER FIFTH PERIOD?
HE DON'T LOOK LIKE MUCH.
OH, HEY CHAD! I WAS JUST--
HE MAY NOT BE BIG, BUT HE'S GOT A WHOLE LOT OF DUMB IN HIM.
YOU KNOW, NOW THAT WE'RE UP CLOSE, I CAN DEFINITELY SEE THAT.
UH, GUYS--I THINK THERE'S BEEN SOME KIND OF A MISUNDERSTANDING...
OOH, LISTEN TO THAT CHAD, NOT SO MUCH AS AN APOLOGY FROM HIM--
THINK HE'S LOOKIN' FOR A REMATCH, THEN?
IS THIS ABOUT BUMPING INTO YOU EARLIER? MAN, I'M REALLY SORRY AGAIN ABOUT--
SHUT YOUR COCKHOLE, YOU LITTLE PISS! YOU THINK I CARE IF YOU'RE SORRY?
BUT YOU JUST SAID--
OOH, HE'S GOT A REAL MOUTH ON HIM, THIS ONE, DON'T HE?
OH, THANK CHRIST--JUN! JUN! OVER HERE!
WAIT--

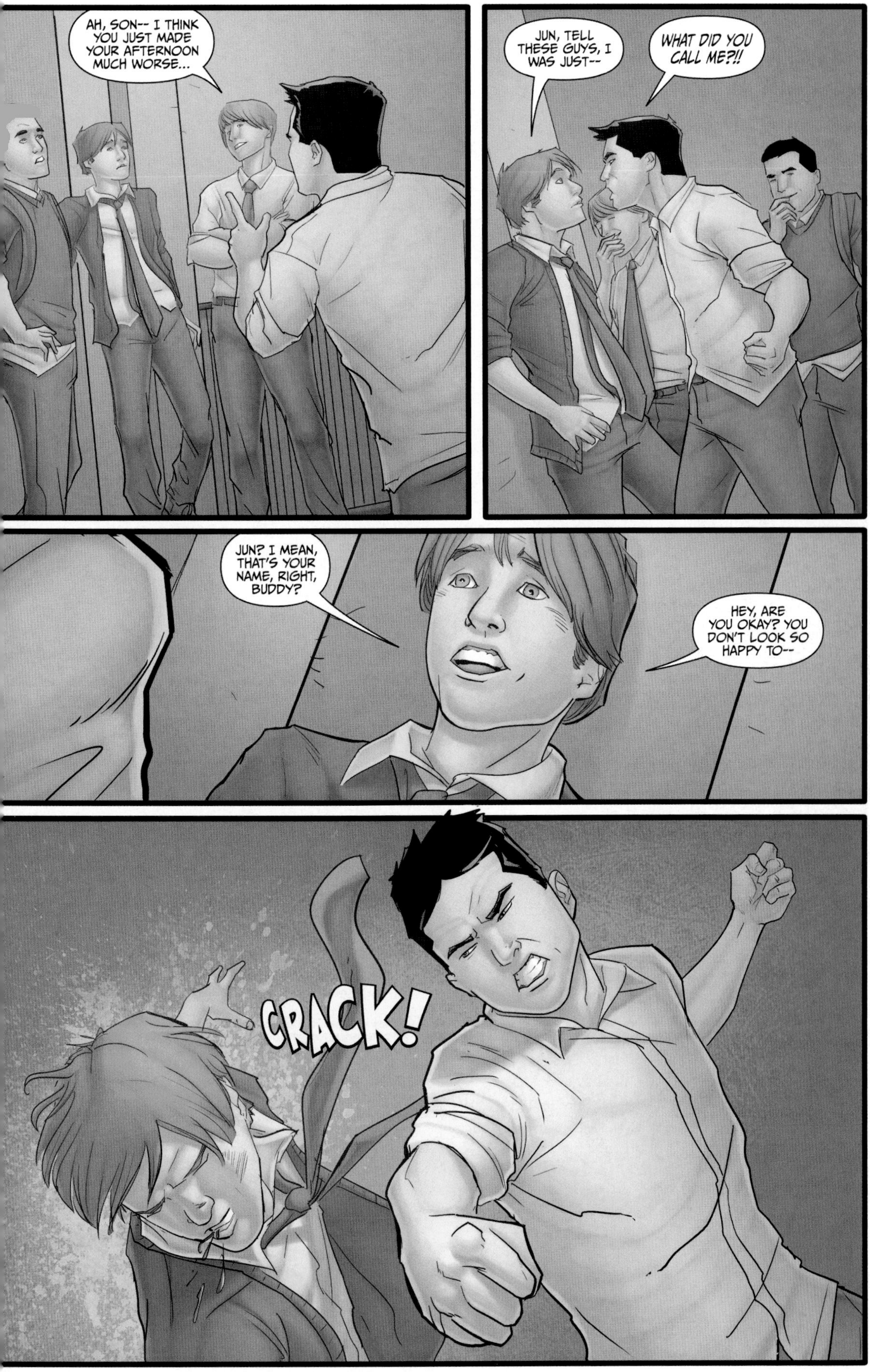
AH, SON-- I THINK YOU JUST MADE YOUR AFTERNOON MUCH WORSE...
JUN, TELL THESE GUYS, I WAS JUST--
WHAT DID YOU CALL ME?!!
JUN? I MEAN, THAT'S YOUR NAME, RIGHT, BUDDY?
HEY, ARE YOU OKAY? YOU DON'T LOOK SO HAPPY TO--
CRACK!

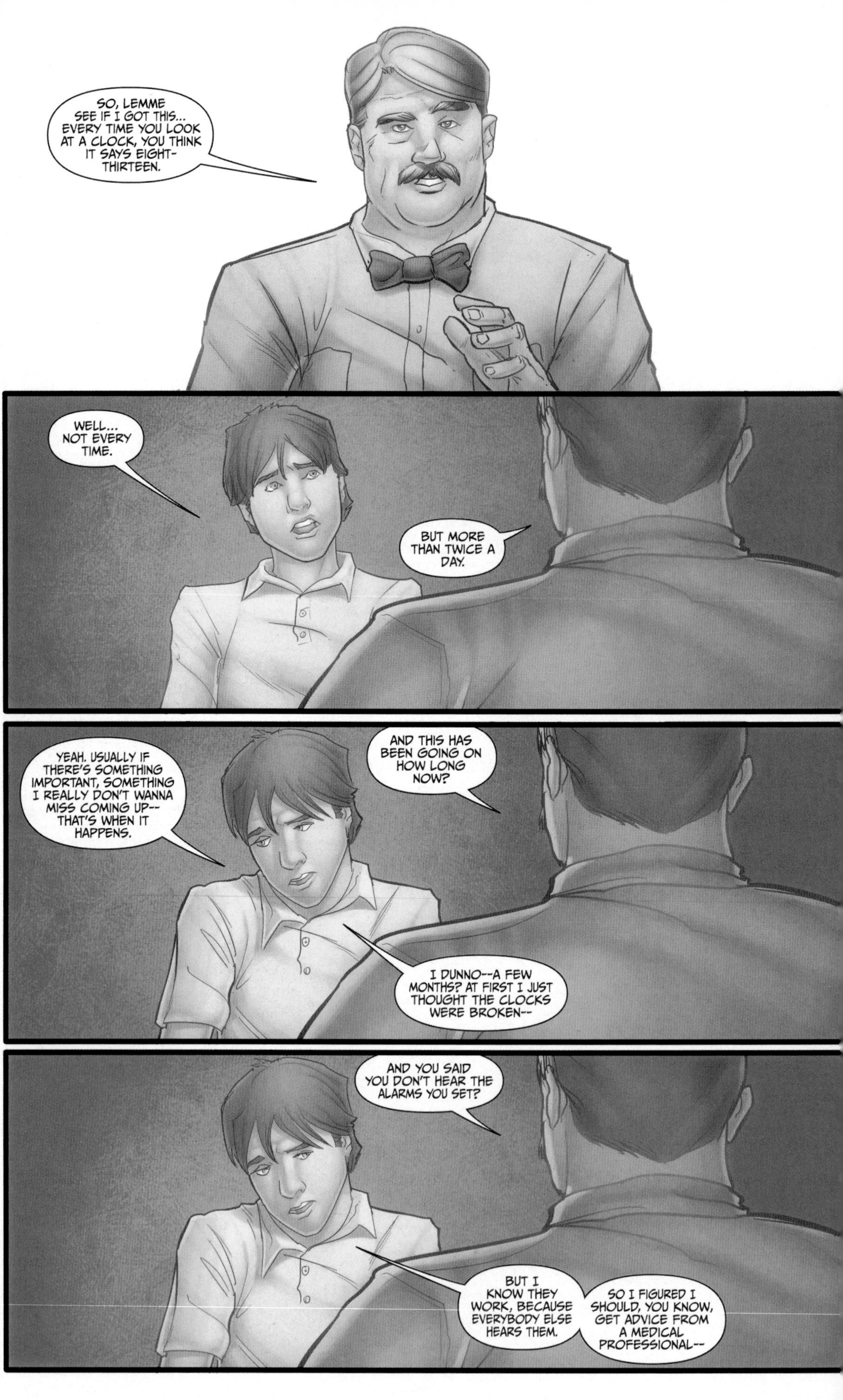
SO, LEMME SEE IF I GOT THIS... EVERY TIME YOU LOOK AT A CLOCK, YOU THINK IT SAYS EIGHT-THIRTEEN.
WELL... NOT EVERY TIME.
BUT MORE THAN TWICE A DAY.
YEAH. USUALLY IF THERE'S SOMETHING IMPORTANT, SOMETHING I REALLY DON'T WANNA MISS COMING UP-- THAT'S WHEN IT HAPPENS.
AND THIS HAS BEEN GOING ON HOW LONG NOW?
I DUNNO--A FEW MONTHS? AT FIRST I JUST THOUGHT THE CLOCKS WERE BROKEN--
AND YOU SAID YOU DON'T HEAR THE ALARMS YOU SET?
BUT I KNOW THEY WORK, BECAUSE EVERYBODY ELSE HEARS THEM.
SO I FIGURED I SHOULD, YOU KNOW, GET ADVICE FROM A MEDICAL PROFESSIONAL--

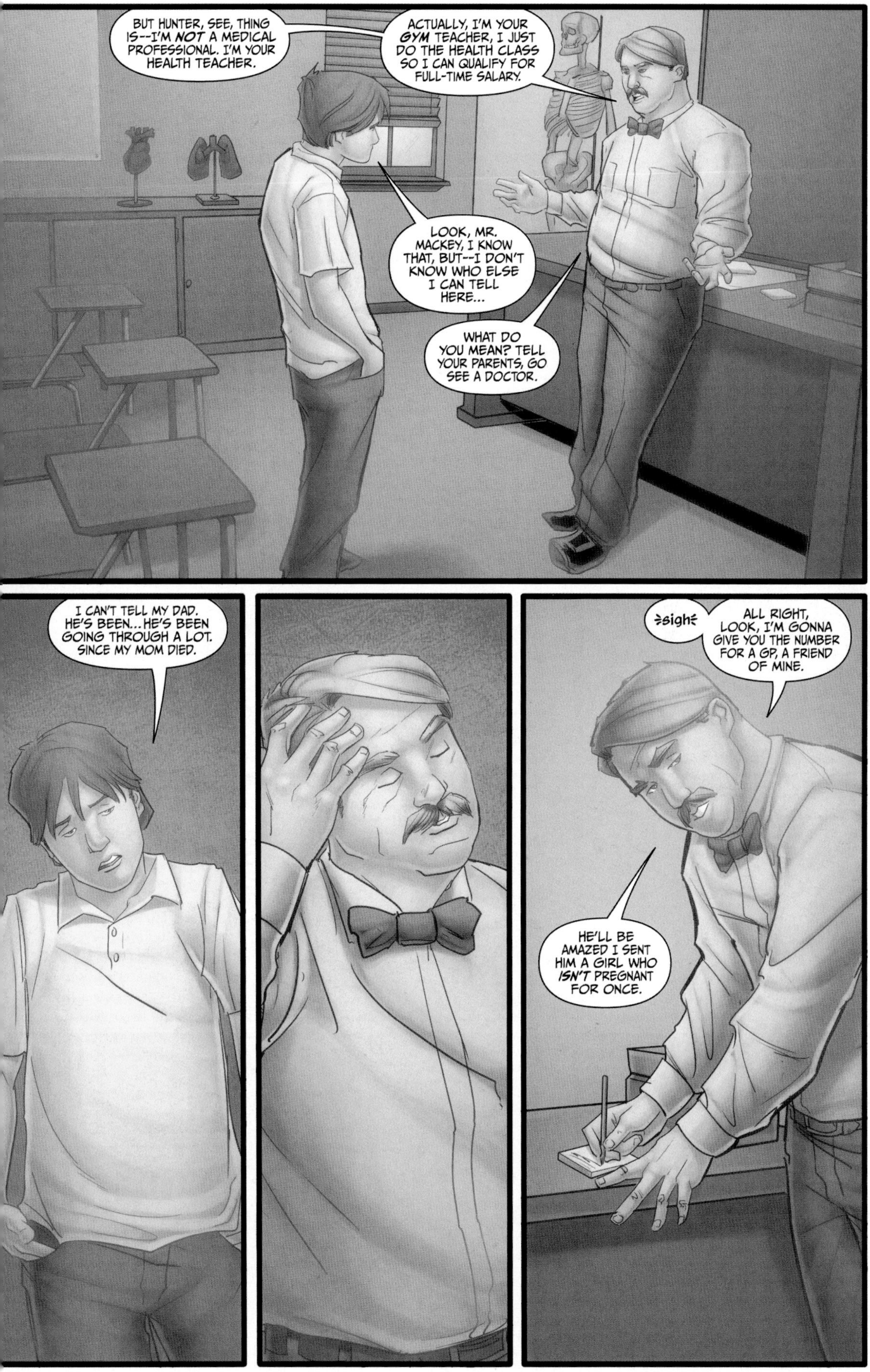
BUT HUNTER, SEE, THING IS--I'M NOT A MEDICAL PROFESSIONAL. I'M YOUR HEALTH TEACHER.
ACTUALLY, I'M YOUR GYM TEACHER, I JUST DO THE HEALTH CLASS SO I CAN QUALIFY FOR FULL-TIME SALARY.
LOOK, MR. MACKEY, I KNOW THAT, BUT--I DON'T KNOW WHO ELSE I CAN TELL HERE...
WHAT DO YOU MEAN? TELL YOUR PARENTS, GO SEE A DOCTOR.
I CAN'T TELL MY DAD. HE'S BEEN...HE'S BEEN GOING THROUGH A LOT. SINCE MY MOM DIED.
sigh
ALL RIGHT, LOOK, I'M GONNA GIVE YOU THE NUMBER FOR A GP, A FRIEND OF MINE.
HE'LL BE AMAZED I SENT HIM A GIRL WHO ISN'T PREGNANT FOR ONCE.

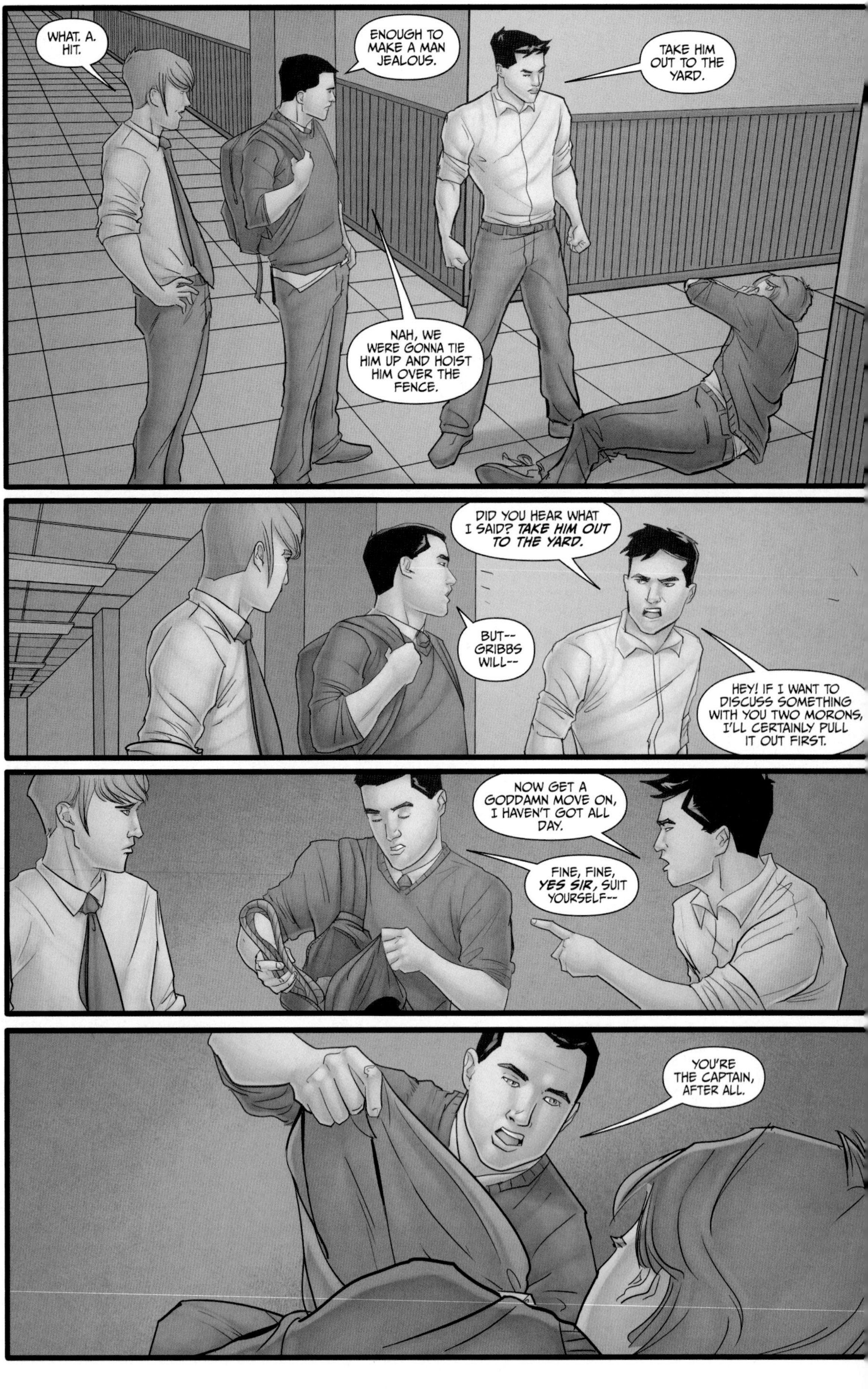
WHAT. A. HIT.
ENOUGH TO MAKE A MAN JEALOUS.
TAKE HIM OUT TO THE YARD.
NAH, WE WERE GONNA TIE HIM UP AND HOIST HIM OVER THE FENCE.
DID YOU HEAR WHAT I SAID? TAKE HIM OUT TO THE YARD.
BUT-- GRIBBS WILL--
HEY! IF I WANT TO DISCUSS SOMETHING WITH YOU TWO MORONS, I'LL CERTAINLY PULL IT OUT FIRST.
NOW GET A GODDAMN MOVE ON, I HAVEN'T GOT ALL DAY.
FINE, FINE, YES SIR, SUIT YOURSELF--
YOU'RE THE CAPTAIN, AFTER ALL.

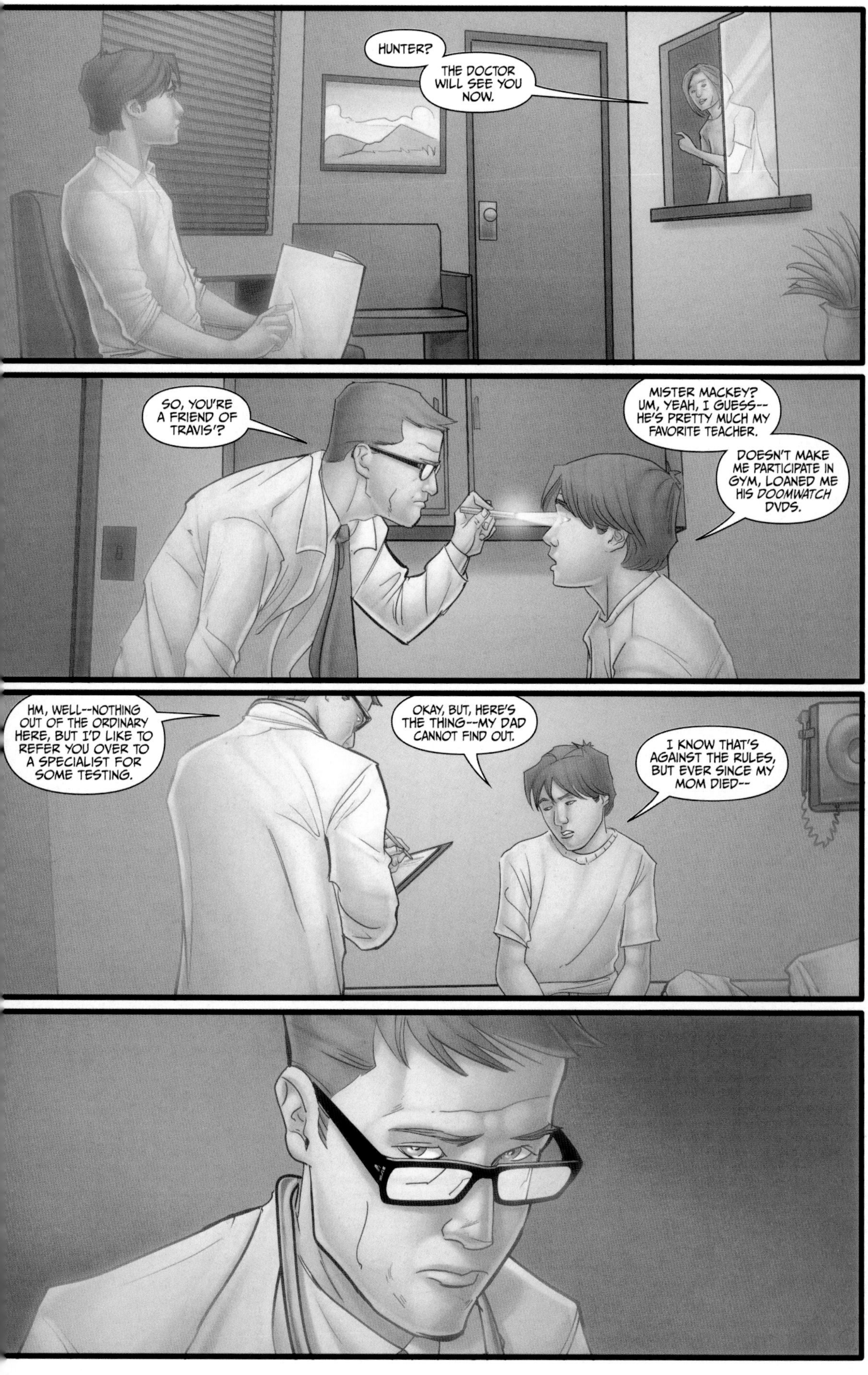
HUNTER?
THE DOCTOR WILL SEE YOU NOW.
SO, YOU'RE A FRIEND OF TRAVIS'?
MISTER MACKEY? UM, YEAH, I GUESS-- HE'S PRETTY MUCH MY FAVORITE TEACHER.
DOESN'T MAKE ME PARTICIPATE IN GYM, LOANED ME HIS *DOOMWATCH* DVDS.
HM, WELL--NOTHING OUT OF THE ORDINARY HERE, BUT I'D LIKE TO REFER YOU OVER TO A SPECIALIST FOR SOME TESTING.
OKAY, BUT, HERE'S THE THING--MY DAD CANNOT FIND OUT.
I KNOW THAT'S AGAINST THE RULES, BUT EVER SINCE MY MOM DIED--

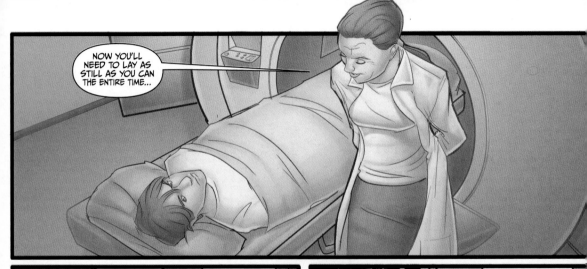

NOW YOU'LL NEED TO LAY AS STILL AS YOU CAN THE ENTIRE TIME...

OH--DOCTOR INGRAM, THE RESULTS FROM YOUR 9:30 ARE WAITING IN YOUR OFFICE.

THANK YOU, ANDY. I'LL NEED A FEW MINUTES--

MY GOD--INCREDIBLE. JUST *INCREDIBLE*. I'VE NEVER SEEN ANYTHING LIKE THIS BEFORE IN MY LIFE--

CLICK

WELL, IF YOU DON'T DO WHAT I SAY--YOU NEVER WILL AGAIN.

CALL THE BOY AND TELL HIM THE RESULTS ARE NORMAL, AND THAT HIS PROBLEM IS PSYCHOSOMATIC.

REFER HIM TO A THERAPIST.

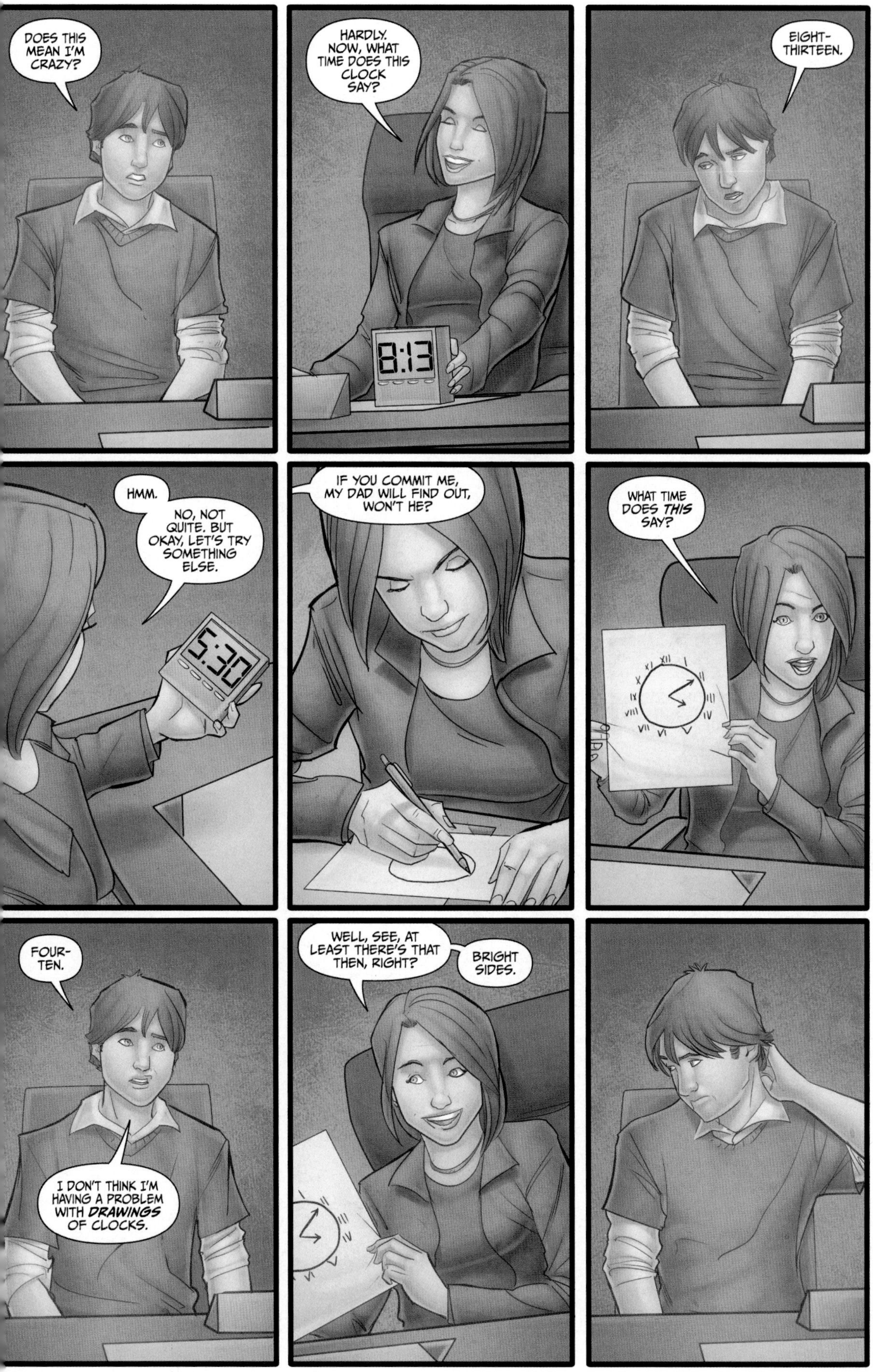
DOES THIS MEAN I'M CRAZY?
HARDLY. NOW, WHAT TIME DOES THIS CLOCK SAY?
8:13
EIGHT-THIRTEEN.
HMM.
NO, NOT QUITE. BUT OKAY, LET'S TRY SOMETHING ELSE.
5:30
IF YOU COMMIT ME, MY DAD WILL FIND OUT, WON'T HE?
WHAT TIME DOES *THIS* SAY?
FOUR-TEN.
I DON'T THINK I'M HAVING A PROBLEM WITH *DRAWINGS* OF CLOCKS.
WELL, SEE, AT LEAST THERE'S THAT THEN, RIGHT?
BRIGHT SIDES.

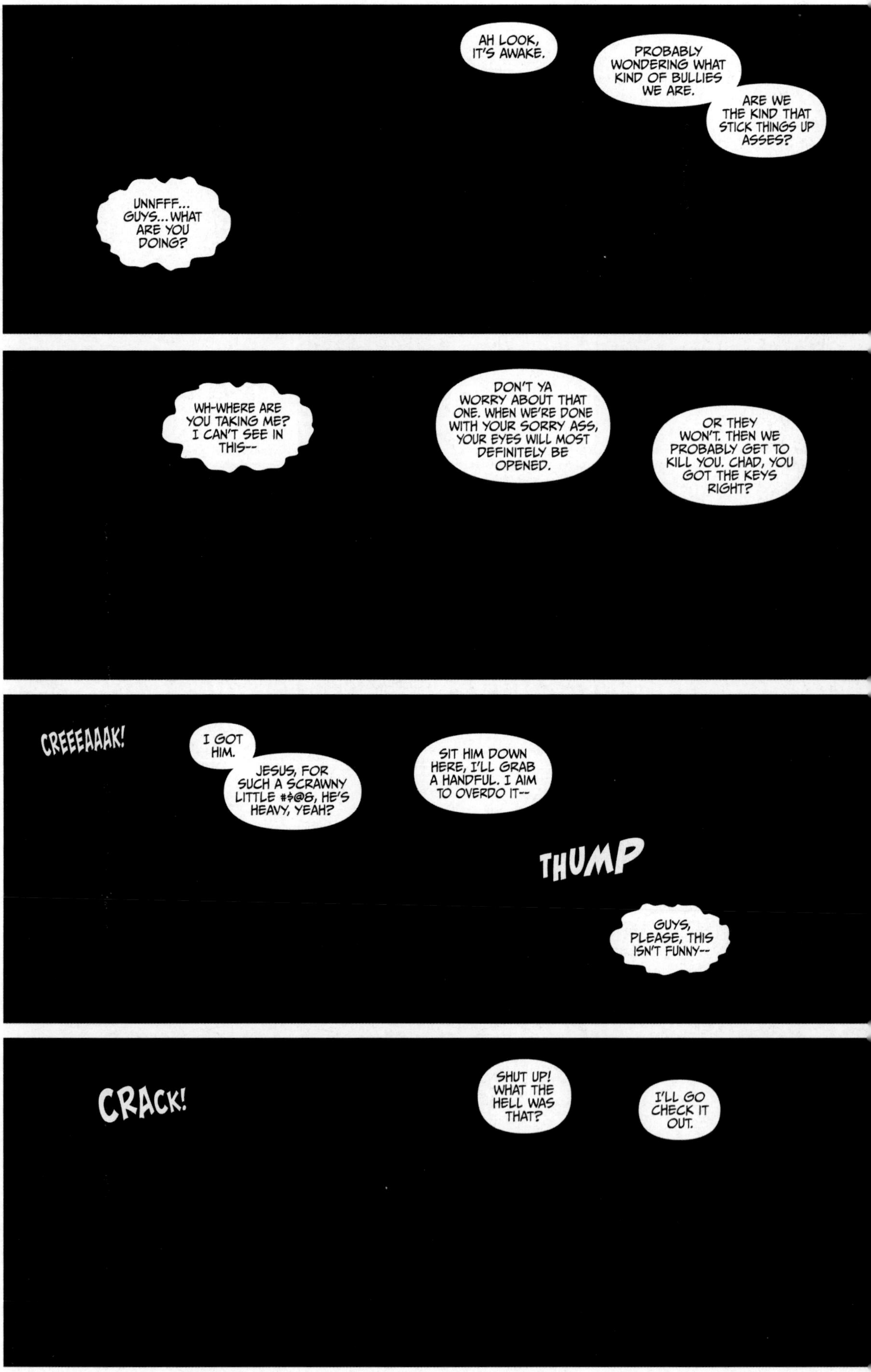
AH LOOK, IT'S AWAKE.
PROBABLY WONDERING WHAT KIND OF BULLIES WE ARE.
ARE WE THE KIND THAT STICK THINGS UP ASSES?
UNNFFF... GUYS... WHAT ARE YOU DOING?
WH-WHERE ARE YOU TAKING ME? I CAN'T SEE IN THIS--
DON'T YA WORRY ABOUT THAT ONE. WHEN WE'RE DONE WITH YOUR SORRY ASS, YOUR EYES WILL MOST DEFINITELY BE OPENED.
OR THEY WON'T. THEN WE PROBABLY GET TO KILL YOU. CHAD, YOU GOT THE KEYS RIGHT?
CREEEAAAK!
I GOT HIM.
JESUS, FOR SUCH A SCRAWNY LITTLE #$@&, HE'S HEAVY, YEAH?
SIT HIM DOWN HERE, I'LL GRAB A HANDFUL. I AIM TO OVERDO IT--
THUMP
GUYS, PLEASE, THIS ISN'T FUNNY--
CRACK!
SHUT UP! WHAT THE HELL WAS THAT?
I'LL GO CHECK IT OUT.

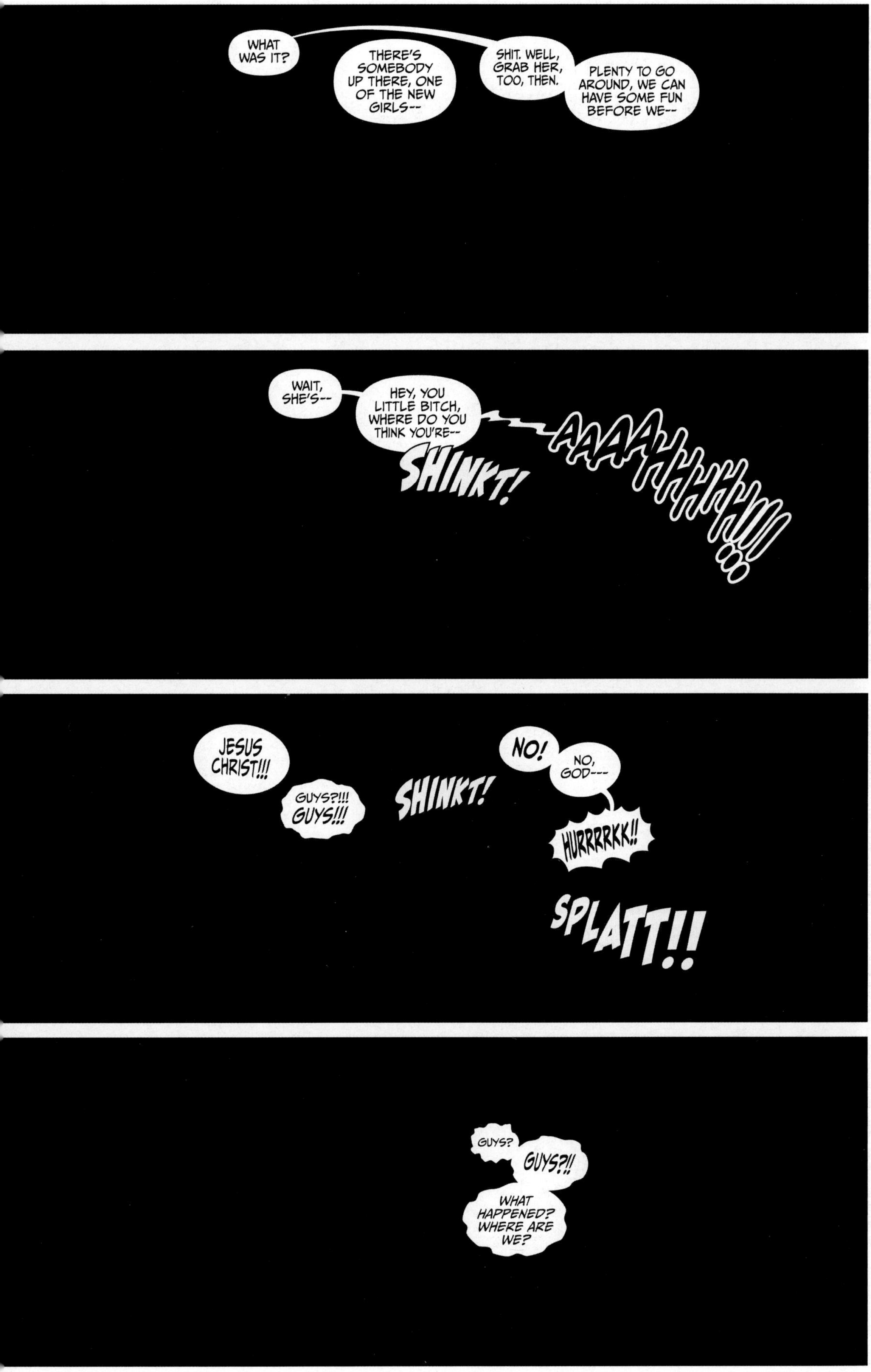
WHAT WAS IT?
THERE'S SOMEBODY UP THERE, ONE OF THE NEW GIRLS--
SHIT. WELL, GRAB HER, TOO, THEN.
PLENTY TO GO AROUND, WE CAN HAVE SOME FUN BEFORE WE--
WAIT, SHE'S--
HEY, YOU LITTLE BITCH, WHERE DO YOU THINK YOU'RE--
SHINKT!
AAAAHHHH!!!...
JESUS CHRIST!!!
GUYS?!!! GUYS!!!
SHINKT!
NO!
NO, GOD---
HURRRRKK!!
SPLATT!!
GUYS?
GUYS?!!
WHAT HAPPENED? WHERE ARE WE?

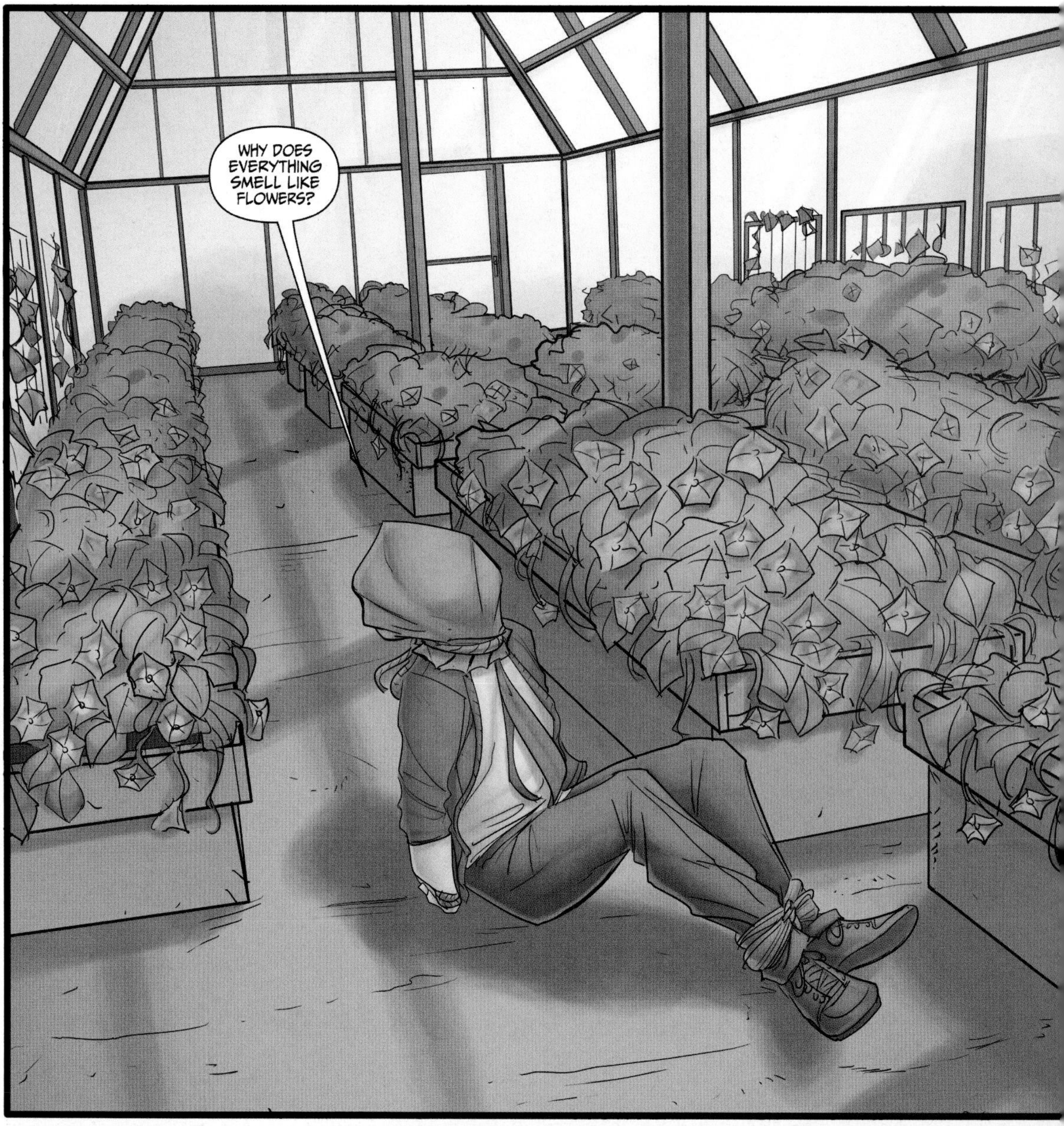
WHY DOES EVERYTHING SMELL LIKE FLOWERS?

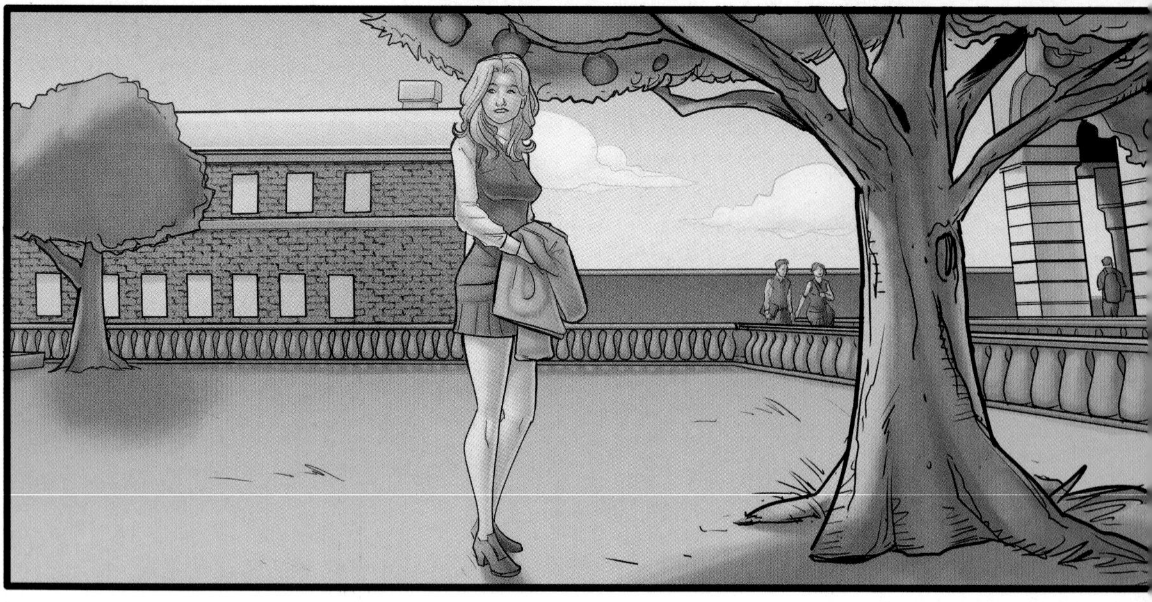

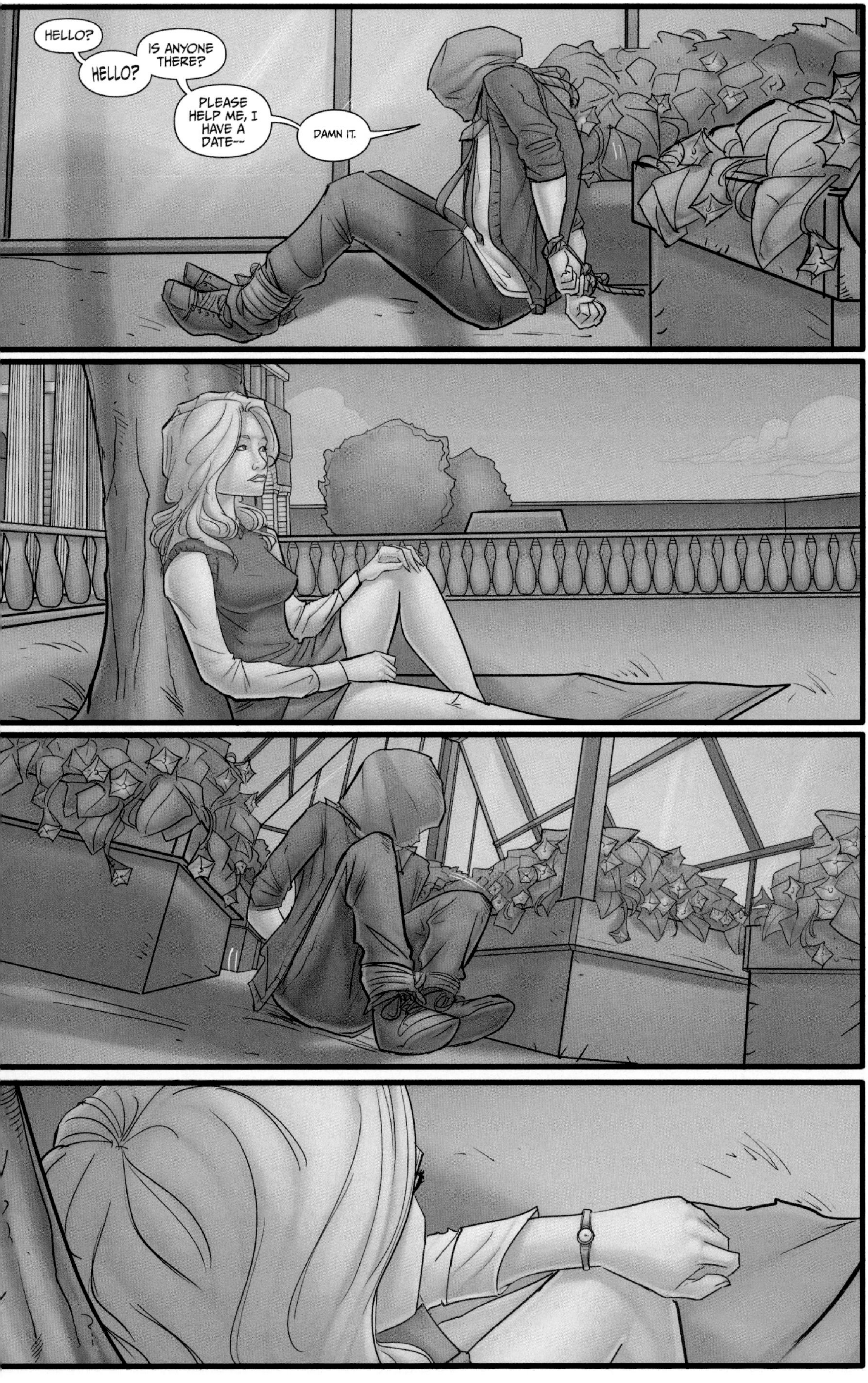
HELLO?
HELLO?
IS ANYONE THERE?
PLEASE HELP ME, I HAVE A DATE--
DAMN IT.

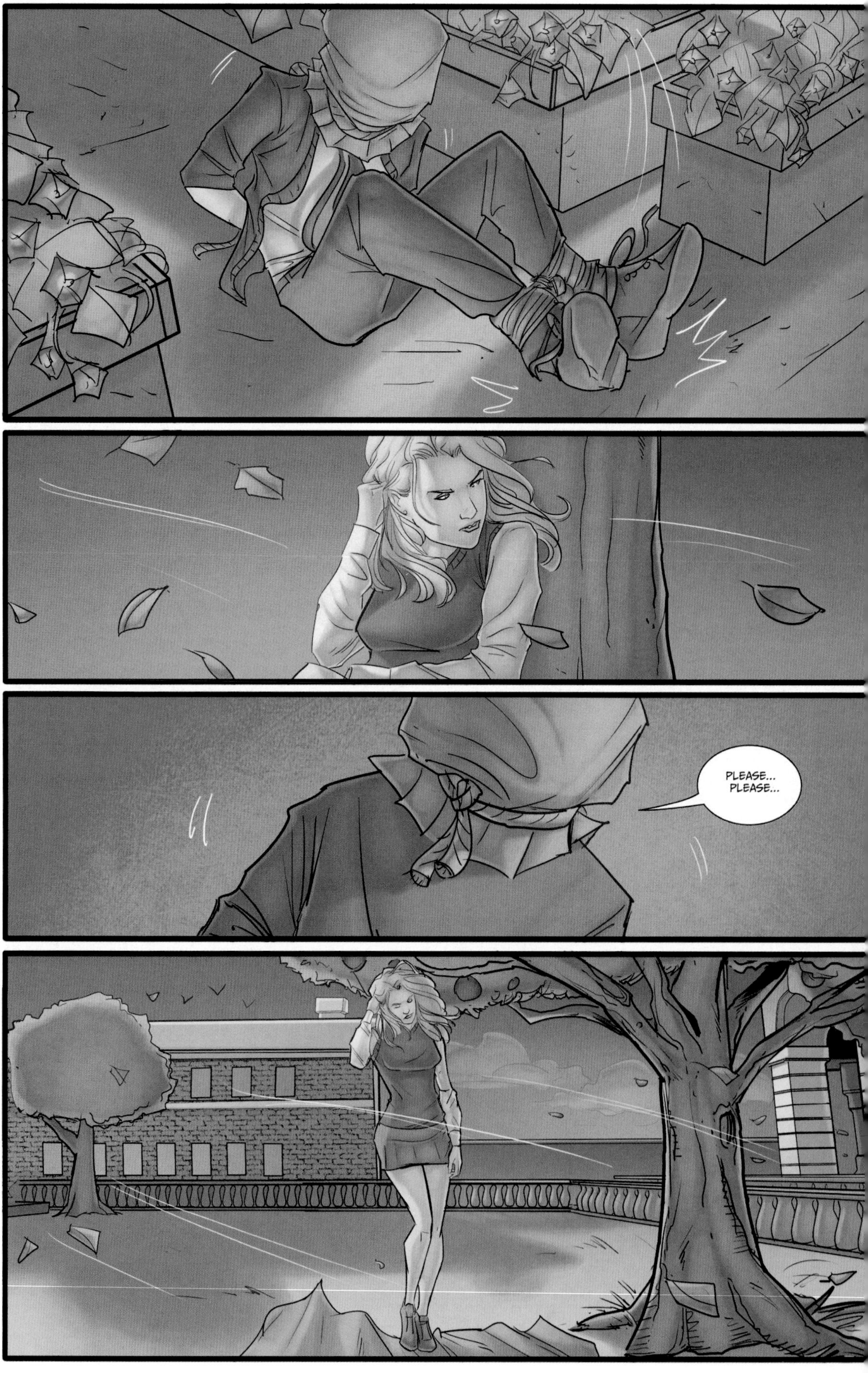
PLEASE...
PLEASE...

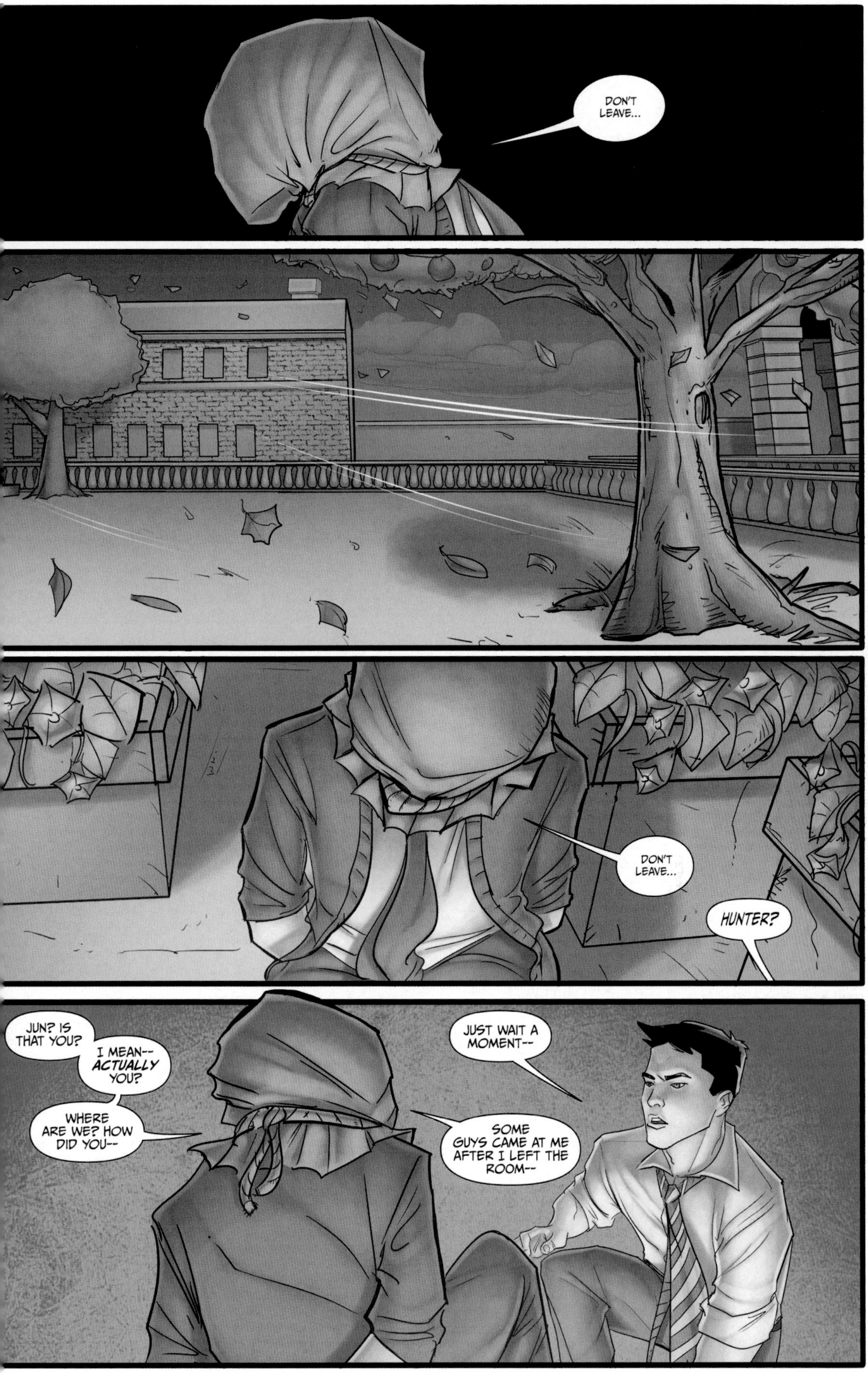
DON'T LEAVE...
DON'T LEAVE...
HUNTER?
JUN? IS THAT YOU?
I MEAN-- ACTUALLY YOU?
WHERE ARE WE? HOW DID YOU--
JUST WAIT A MOMENT--
SOME GUYS CAME AT ME AFTER I LEFT THE ROOM--

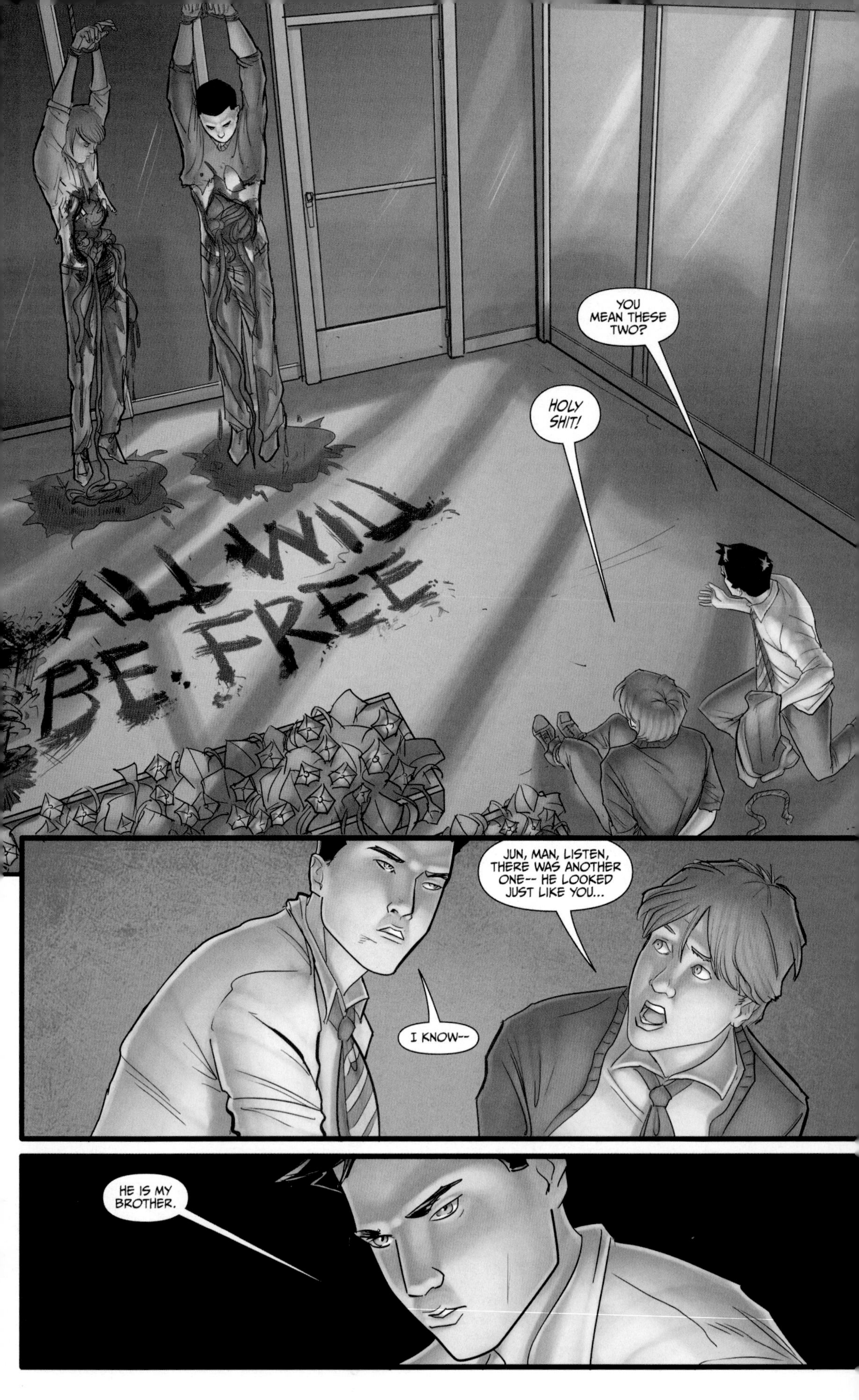
ALL WILL BE FREE
YOU MEAN THESE TWO?
HOLY SHIT!
JUN, MAN, LISTEN, THERE WAS ANOTHER ONE-- HE LOOKED JUST LIKE YOU...
I KNOW--
HE IS MY BROTHER.

nine

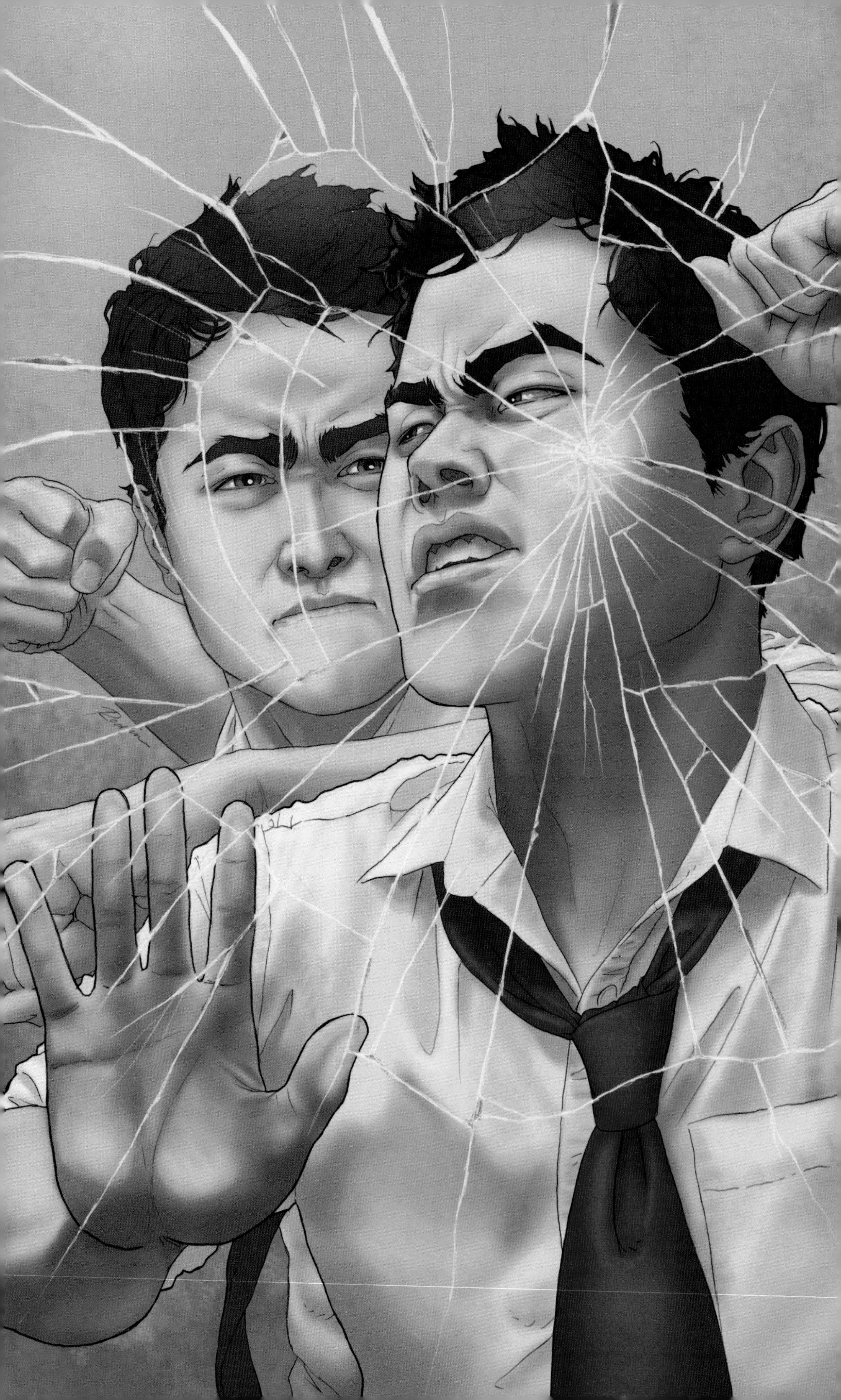

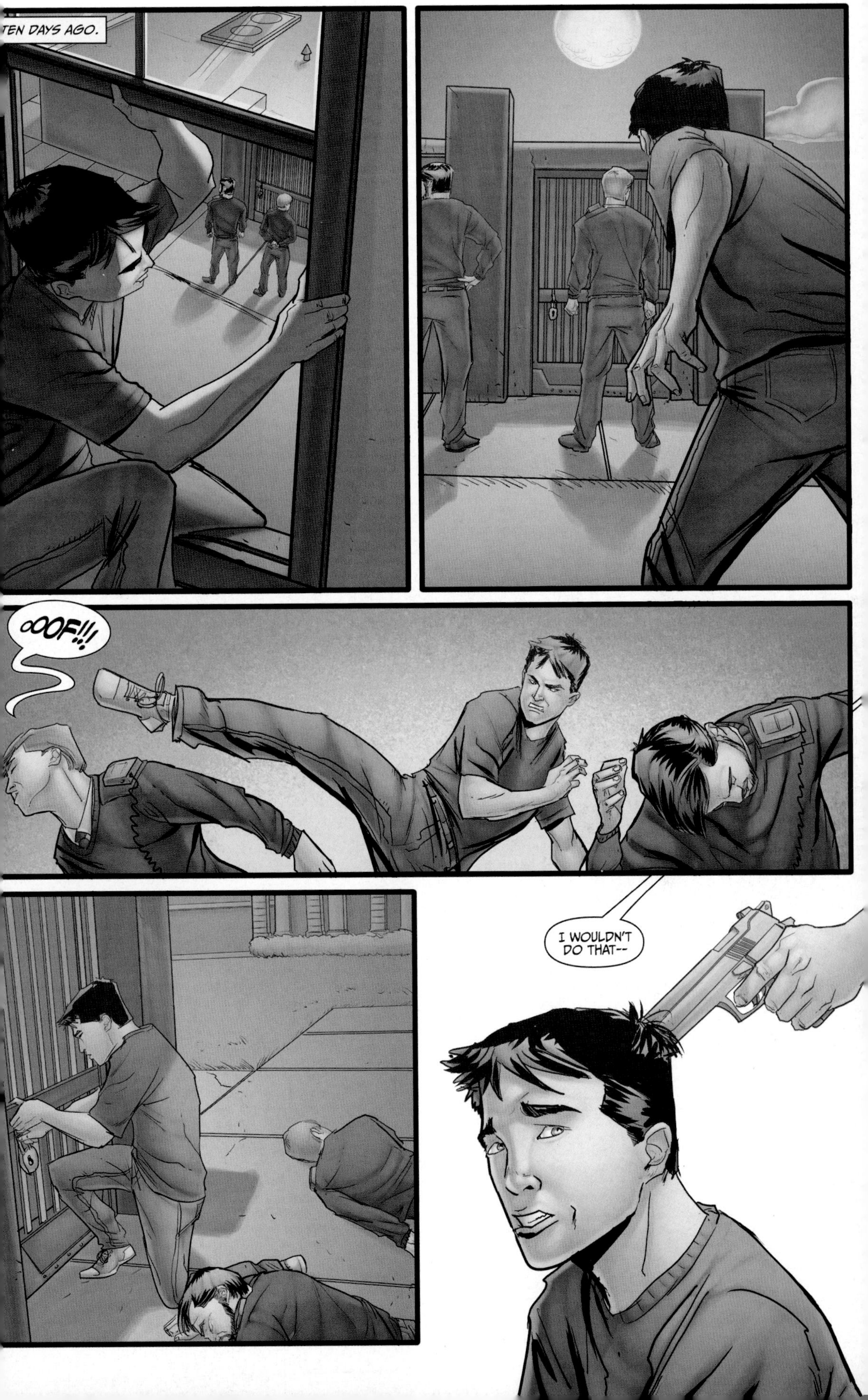

TEN DAYS AGO.
OOOF!!!
I WOULDN'T DO THAT--

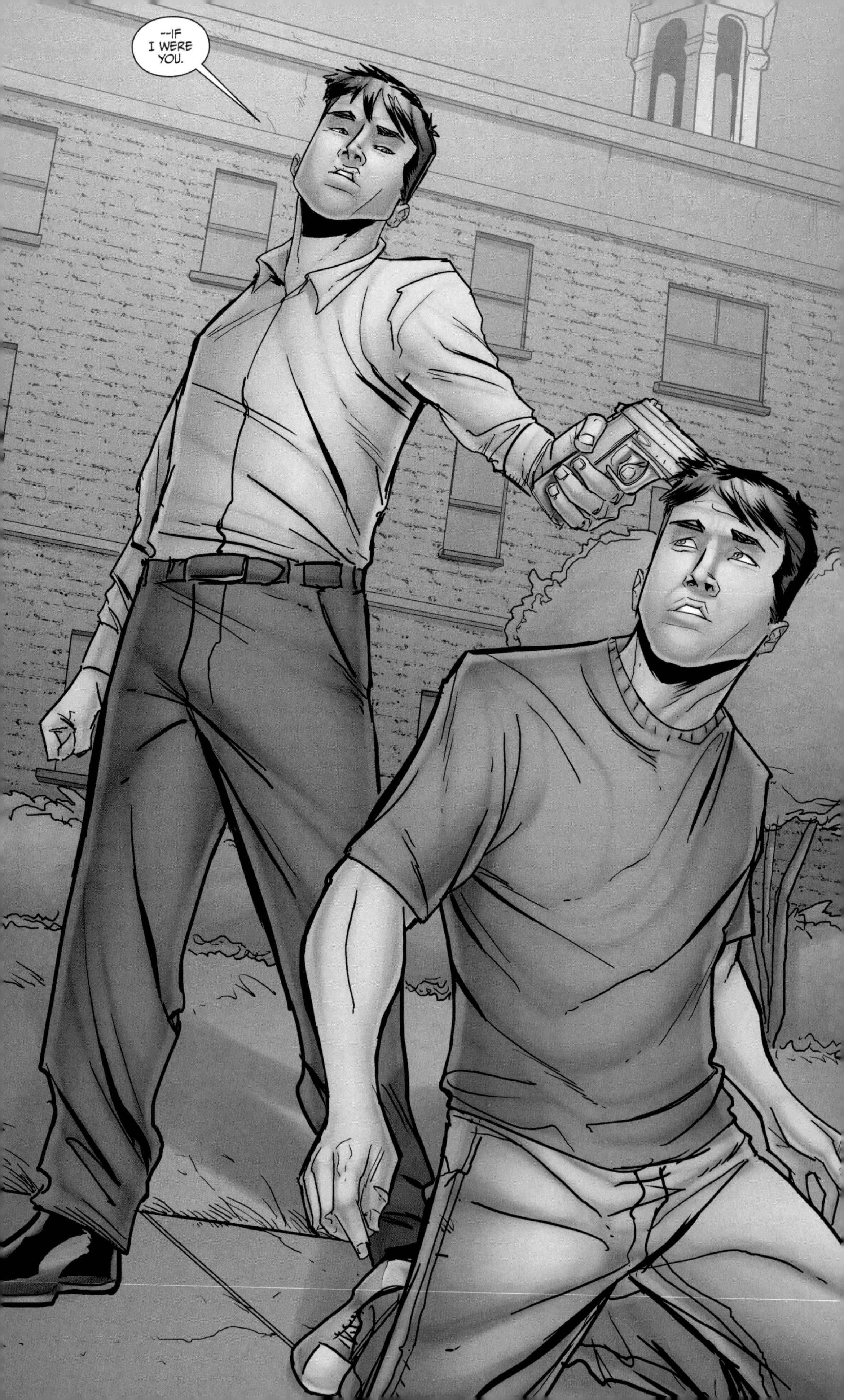
--IF I WERE YOU.

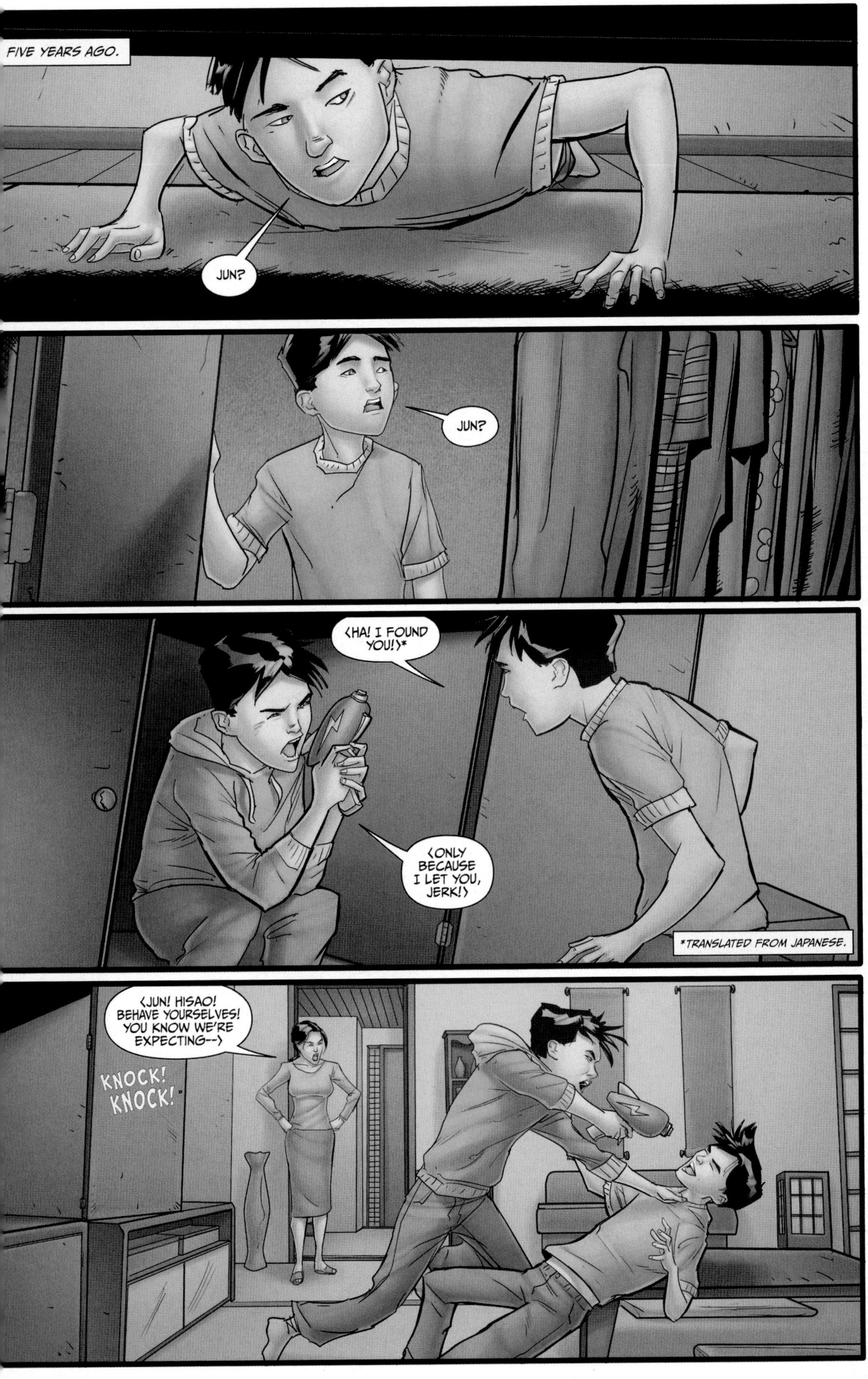

FIVE YEARS AGO.
JUN?
JUN?
<HA! I FOUND YOU!>*
<ONLY BECAUSE I LET YOU, JERK!>
*TRANSLATED FROM JAPANESE.
<JUN! HISAO! BEHAVE YOURSELVES! YOU KNOW WE'RE EXPECTING-->
KNOCK! KNOCK!

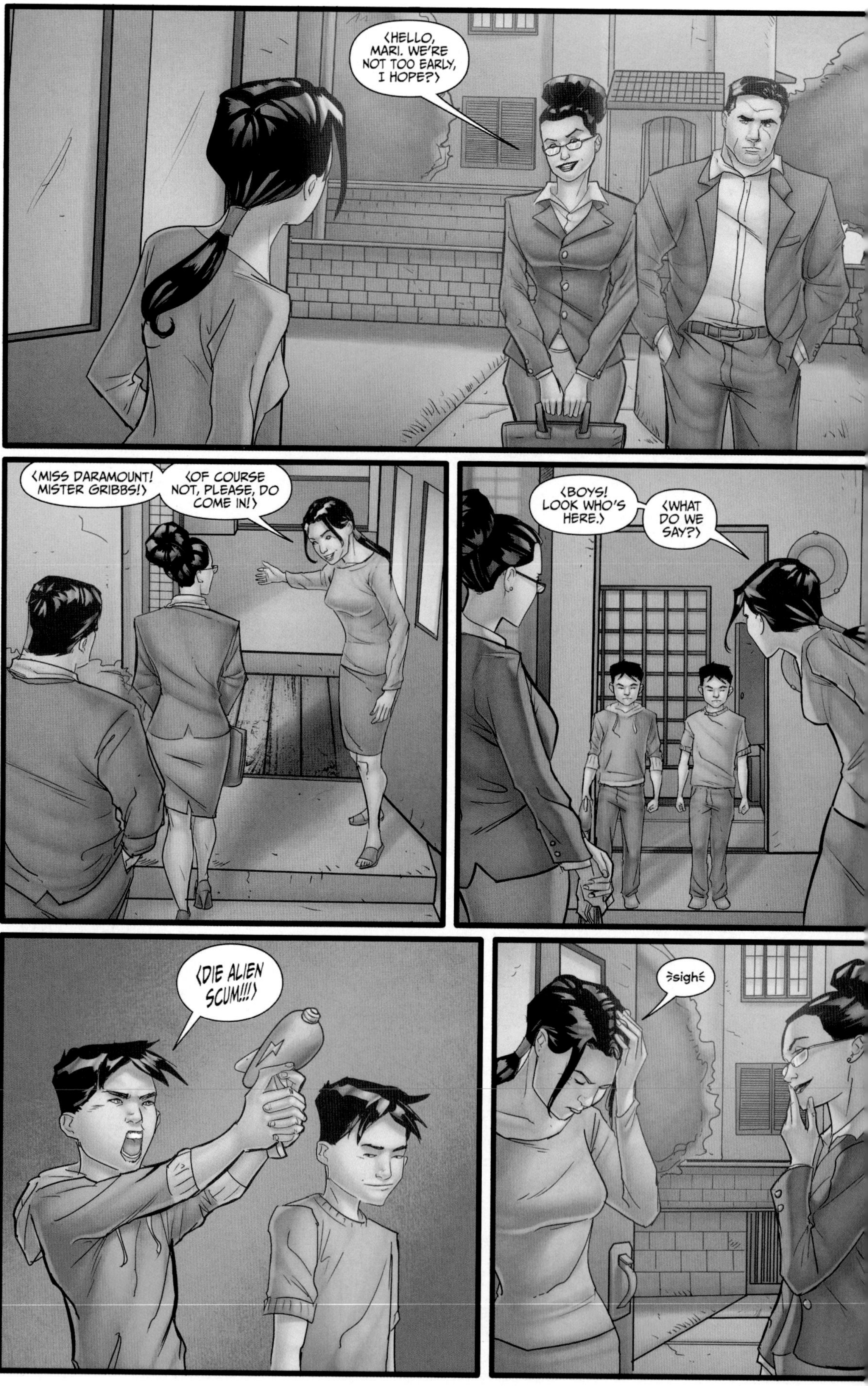

‹HELLO, MARI. WE'RE NOT TOO EARLY, I HOPE?›
‹MISS DARAMOUNT! MISTER GRIBBS!›
‹OF COURSE NOT, PLEASE, DO COME IN!›
‹BOYS! LOOK WHO'S HERE.›
‹WHAT DO WE SAY?›
‹DIE ALIEN SCUM!!!›
sigh

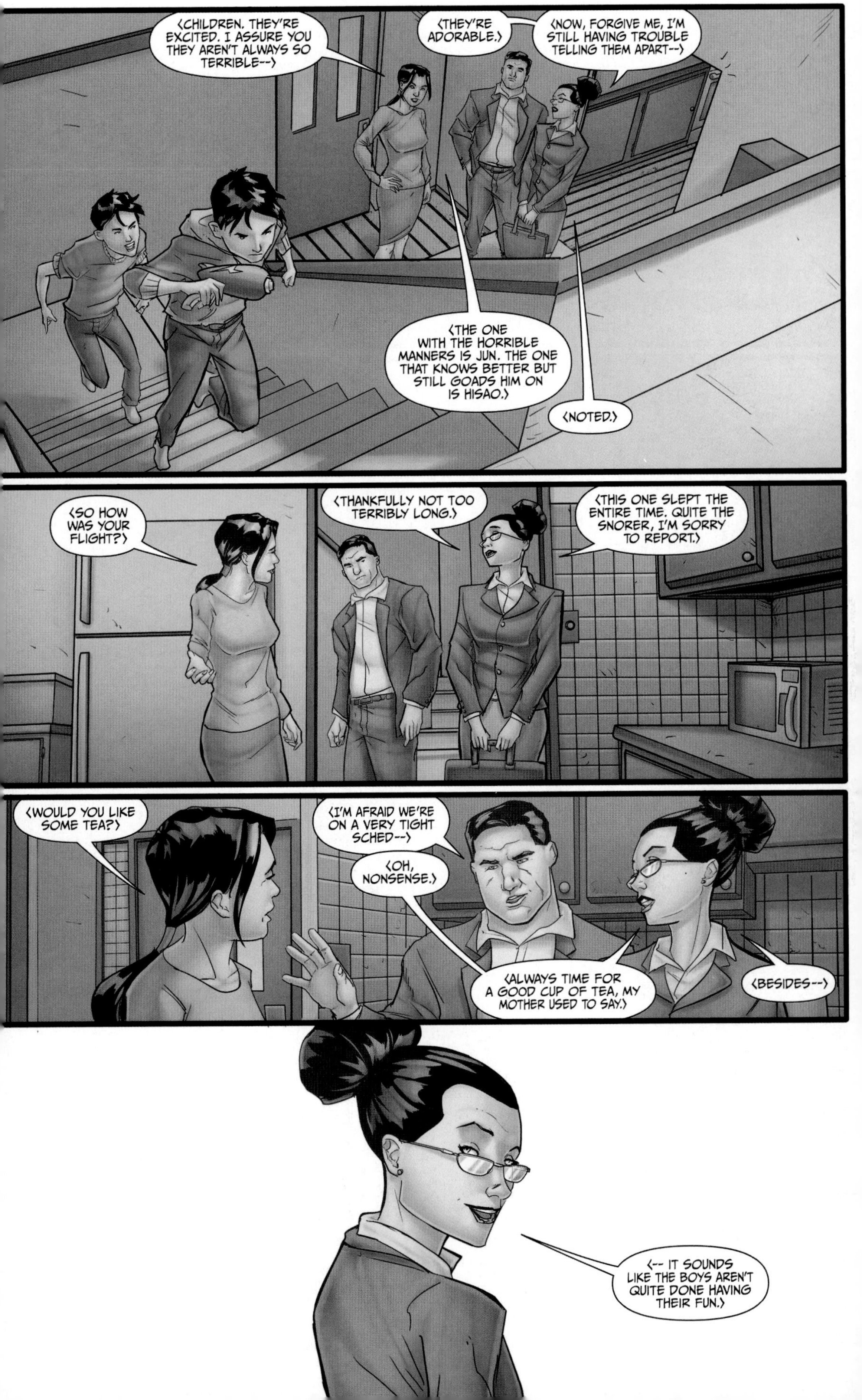

‹CHILDREN. THEY'RE EXCITED. I ASSURE YOU THEY AREN'T ALWAYS SO TERRIBLE--›
‹THEY'RE ADORABLE.›
‹NOW, FORGIVE ME, I'M STILL HAVING TROUBLE TELLING THEM APART--›
‹THE ONE WITH THE HORRIBLE MANNERS IS JUN. THE ONE THAT KNOWS BETTER BUT STILL GOADS HIM ON IS HISAO.›
‹NOTED.›
‹SO HOW WAS YOUR FLIGHT?›
‹THANKFULLY NOT TOO TERRIBLY LONG.›
‹THIS ONE SLEPT THE ENTIRE TIME. QUITE THE SNORER, I'M SORRY TO REPORT.›
‹WOULD YOU LIKE SOME TEA?›
‹I'M AFRAID WE'RE ON A VERY TIGHT SCHED--›
‹OH, NONSENSE.›
‹ALWAYS TIME FOR A GOOD CUP OF TEA, MY MOTHER USED TO SAY.›
‹BESIDES--›
‹-- IT SOUNDS LIKE THE BOYS AREN'T QUITE DONE HAVING THEIR FUN.›

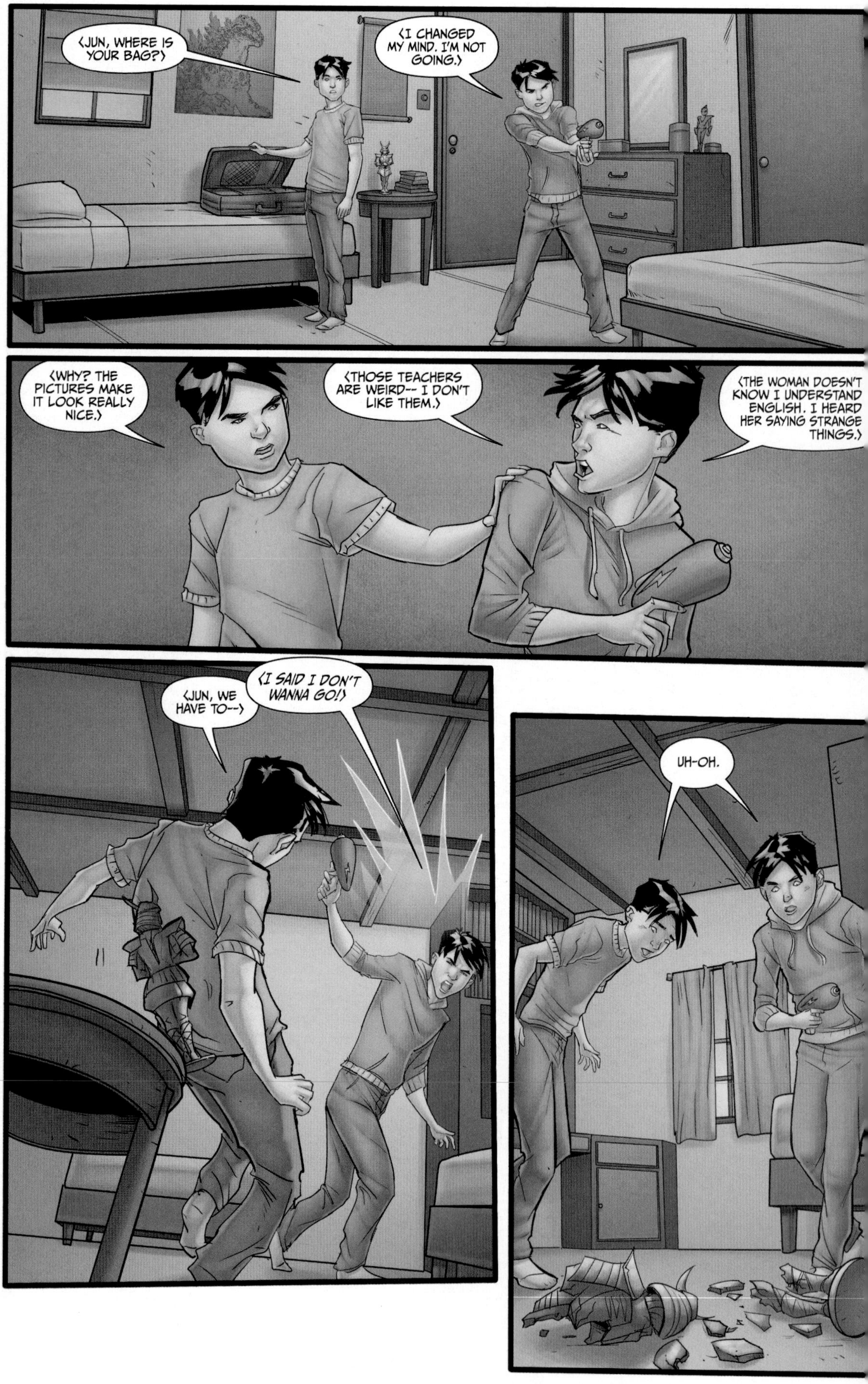

‹JUN, WHERE IS YOUR BAG?›
‹I CHANGED MY MIND. I'M NOT GOING.›
‹WHY? THE PICTURES MAKE IT LOOK REALLY NICE.›
‹THOSE TEACHERS ARE WEIRD-- I DON'T LIKE THEM.›
‹THE WOMAN DOESN'T KNOW I UNDERSTAND ENGLISH. I HEARD HER SAYING STRANGE THINGS.›
‹JUN, WE HAVE TO--›
‹I SAID I DON'T WANNA GO!›
UH-OH.

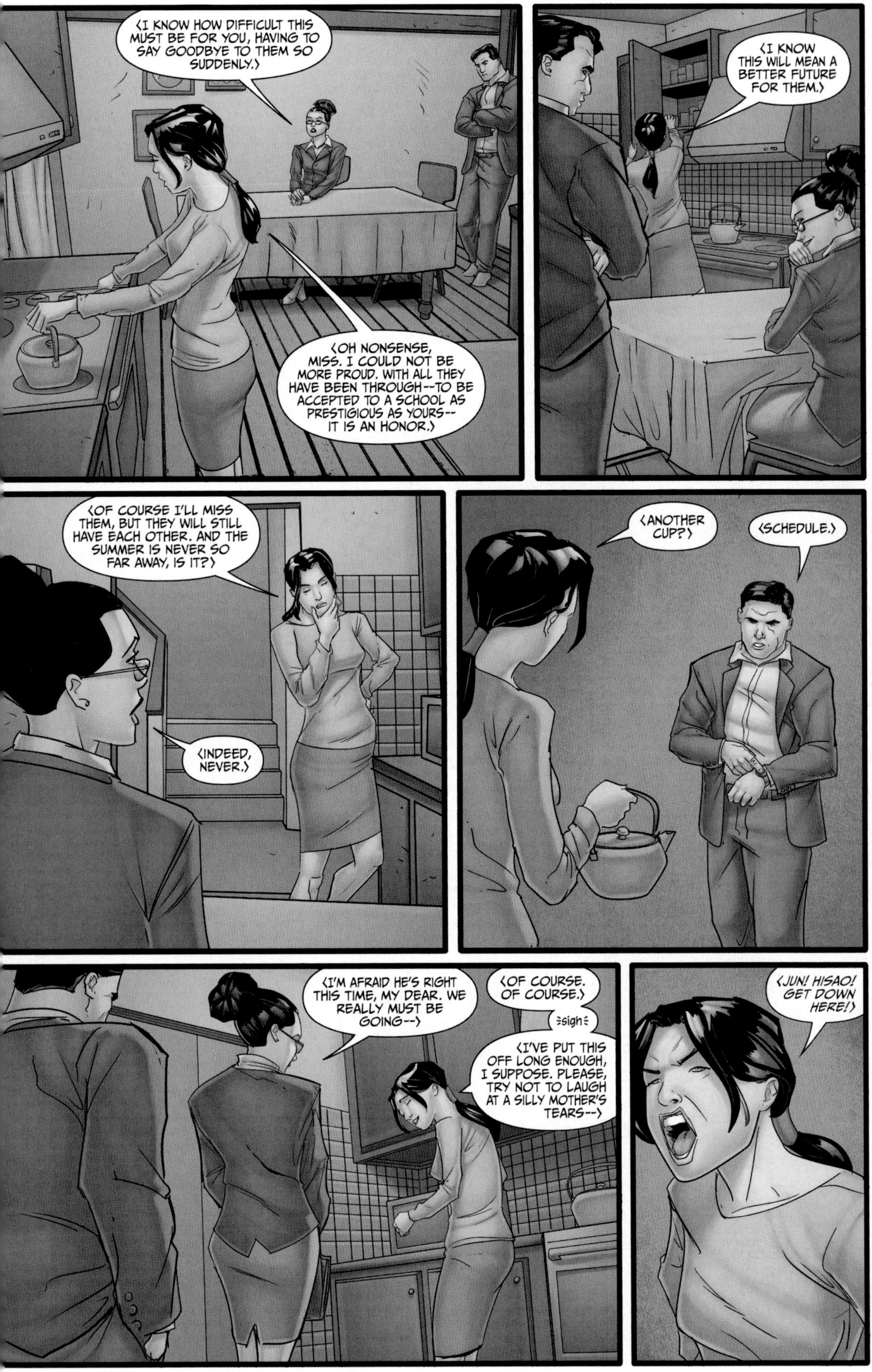
〈I KNOW HOW DIFFICULT THIS MUST BE FOR YOU, HAVING TO SAY GOODBYE TO THEM SO SUDDENLY.〉
〈OH NONSENSE, MISS. I COULD NOT BE MORE PROUD. WITH ALL THEY HAVE BEEN THROUGH--TO BE ACCEPTED TO A SCHOOL AS PRESTIGIOUS AS YOURS--IT IS AN HONOR.〉
〈I KNOW THIS WILL MEAN A BETTER FUTURE FOR THEM.〉
〈OF COURSE I'LL MISS THEM, BUT THEY WILL STILL HAVE EACH OTHER. AND THE SUMMER IS NEVER SO FAR AWAY, IS IT?〉
〈INDEED, NEVER.〉
〈ANOTHER CUP?〉
〈SCHEDULE.〉
〈I'M AFRAID HE'S RIGHT THIS TIME, MY DEAR. WE REALLY MUST BE GOING--〉
〈OF COURSE. OF COURSE.〉
sigh
〈I'VE PUT THIS OFF LONG ENOUGH, I SUPPOSE. PLEASE, TRY NOT TO LAUGH AT A SILLY MOTHER'S TEARS--〉
〈JUN! HISAO! GET DOWN HERE!〉

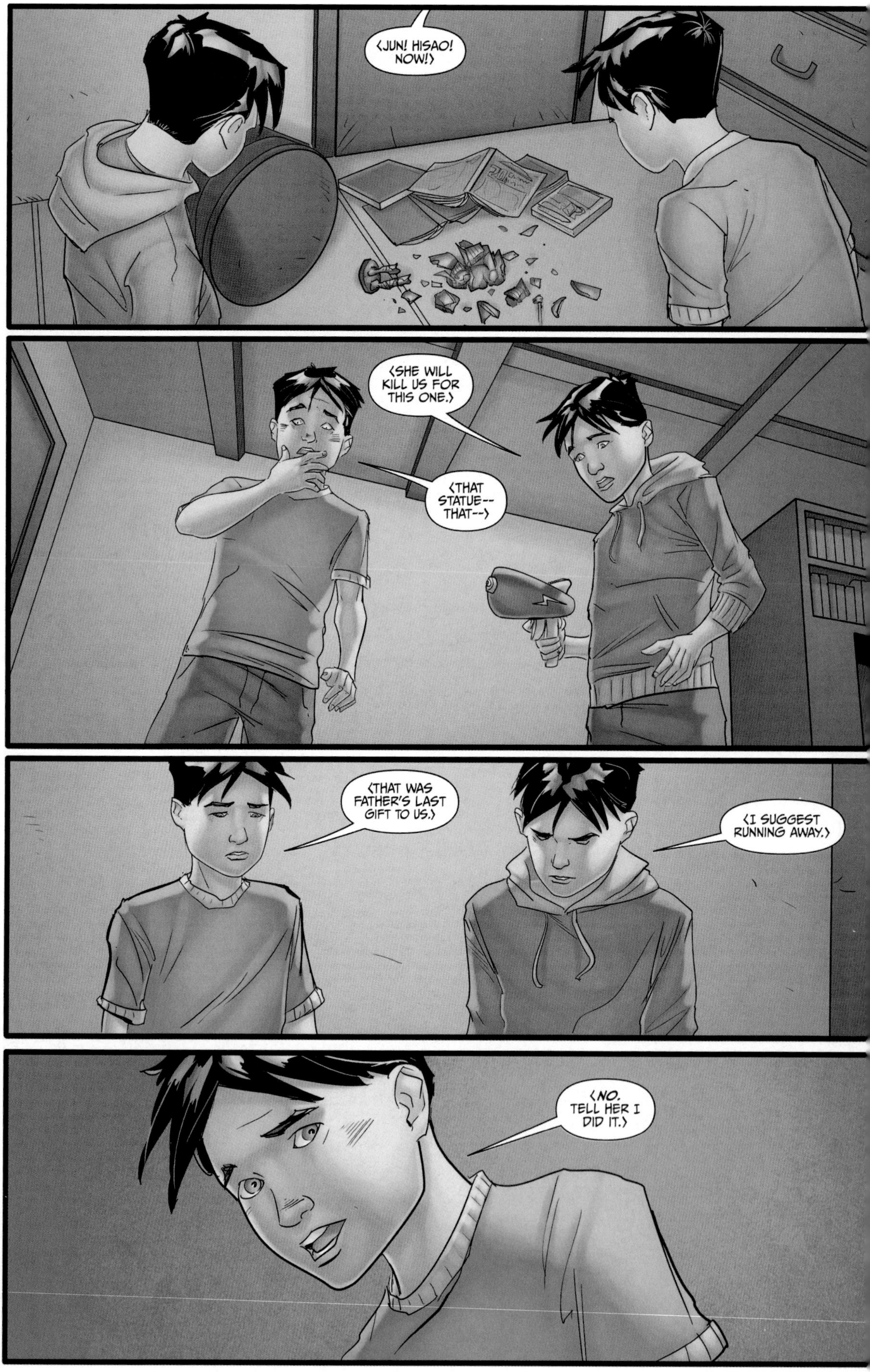
<JUN! HISAO! NOW!>
<SHE WILL KILL US FOR THIS ONE.>
<THAT STATUE-- THAT-->
<THAT WAS FATHER'S LAST GIFT TO US.>
<I SUGGEST RUNNING AWAY.>
<*NO.* TELL HER I DID IT.>

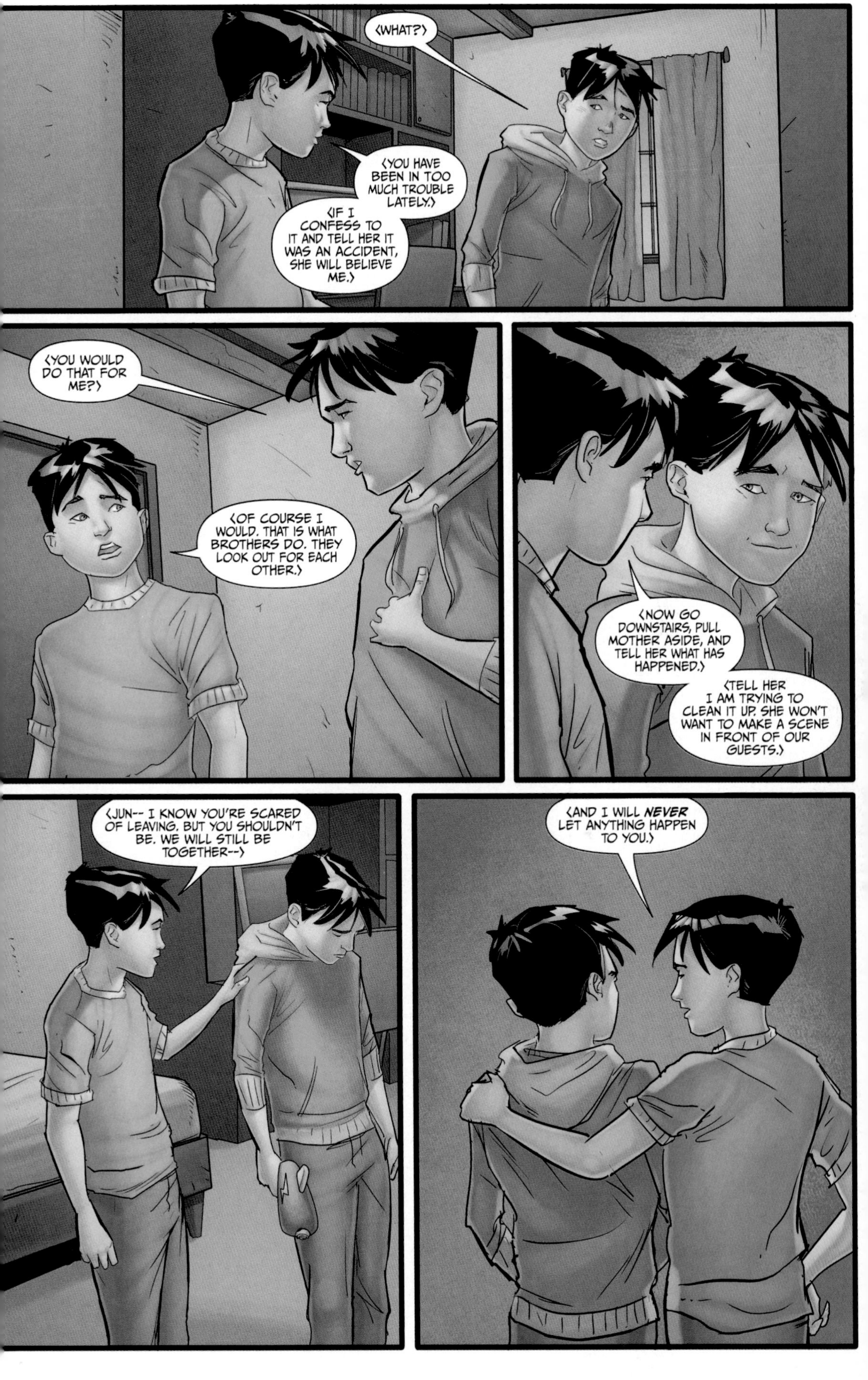
‹WHAT?›
‹YOU HAVE BEEN IN TOO MUCH TROUBLE LATELY.›
‹IF I CONFESS TO IT AND TELL HER IT WAS AN ACCIDENT, SHE WILL BELIEVE ME.›
‹YOU WOULD DO THAT FOR ME?›
‹OF COURSE I WOULD. THAT IS WHAT BROTHERS DO. THEY LOOK OUT FOR EACH OTHER.›
‹NOW GO DOWNSTAIRS, PULL MOTHER ASIDE, AND TELL HER WHAT HAS HAPPENED.›
‹TELL HER I AM TRYING TO CLEAN IT UP. SHE WON'T WANT TO MAKE A SCENE IN FRONT OF OUR GUESTS.›
‹JUN-- I KNOW YOU'RE SCARED OF LEAVING. BUT YOU SHOULDN'T BE. WE WILL STILL BE TOGETHER--›
‹AND I WILL ***NEVER*** LET ANYTHING HAPPEN TO YOU.›

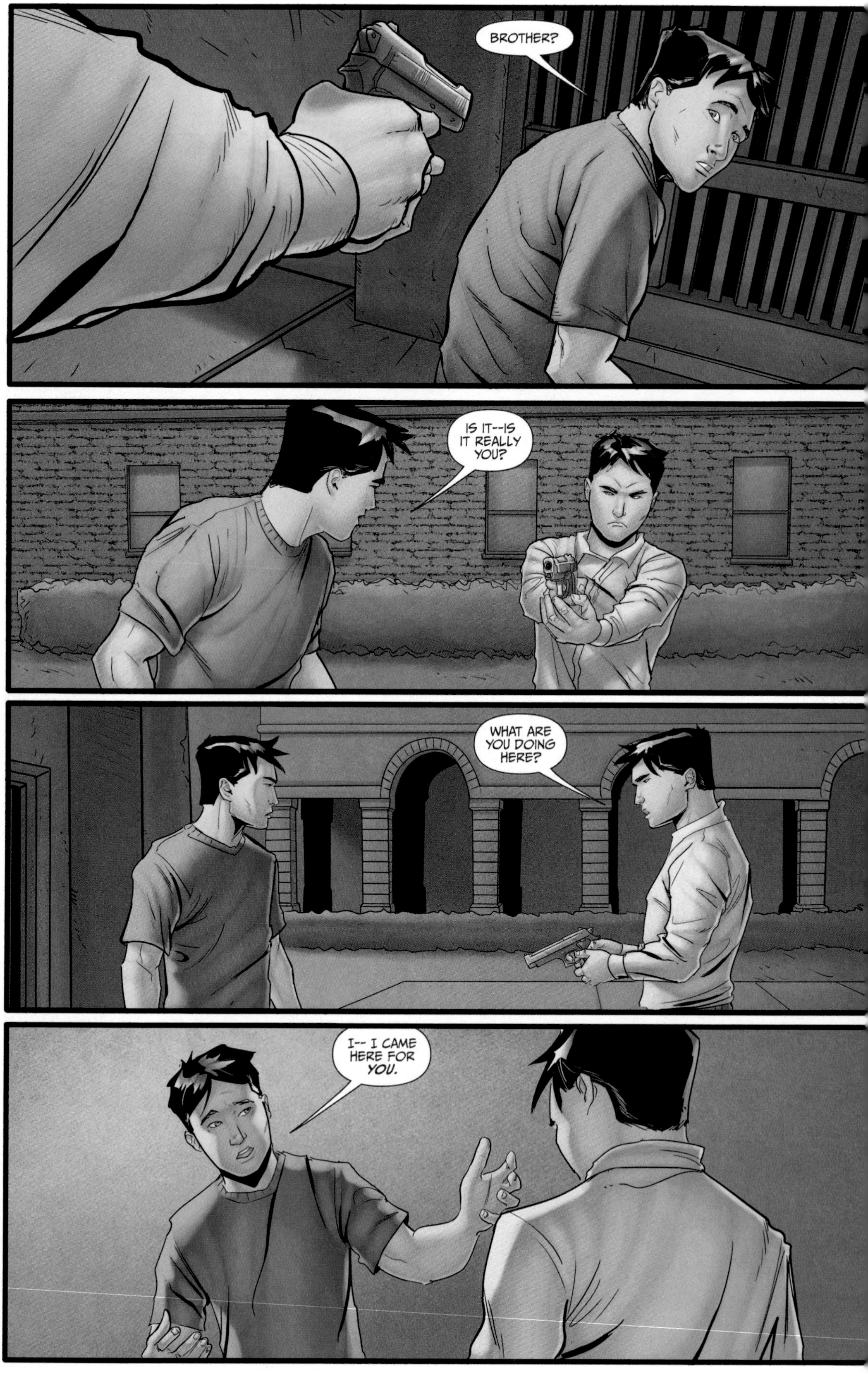
BROTHER?
IS IT--IS IT REALLY YOU?
WHAT ARE YOU DOING HERE?
I-- I CAME HERE FOR *YOU.*

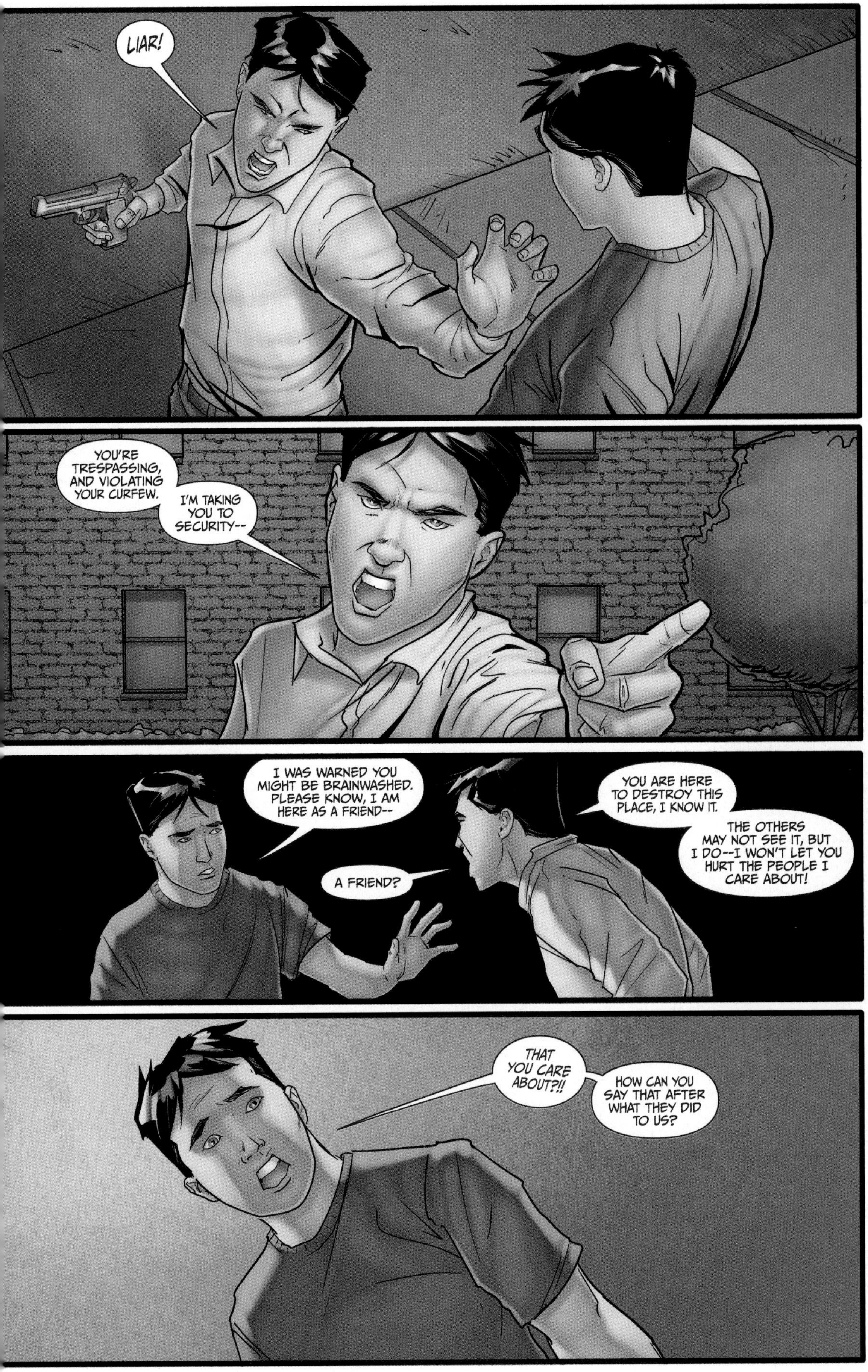
LIAR!
YOU'RE TRESPASSING, AND VIOLATING YOUR CURFEW.
I'M TAKING YOU TO SECURITY--
I WAS WARNED YOU MIGHT BE BRAINWASHED. PLEASE KNOW, I AM HERE AS A FRIEND--
A FRIEND?
YOU ARE HERE TO DESTROY THIS PLACE, I KNOW IT.
THE OTHERS MAY NOT SEE IT, BUT I DO--I WON'T LET YOU HURT THE PEOPLE I CARE ABOUT!
THAT YOU CARE ABOUT?!!
HOW CAN YOU SAY THAT AFTER WHAT THEY DID TO US?

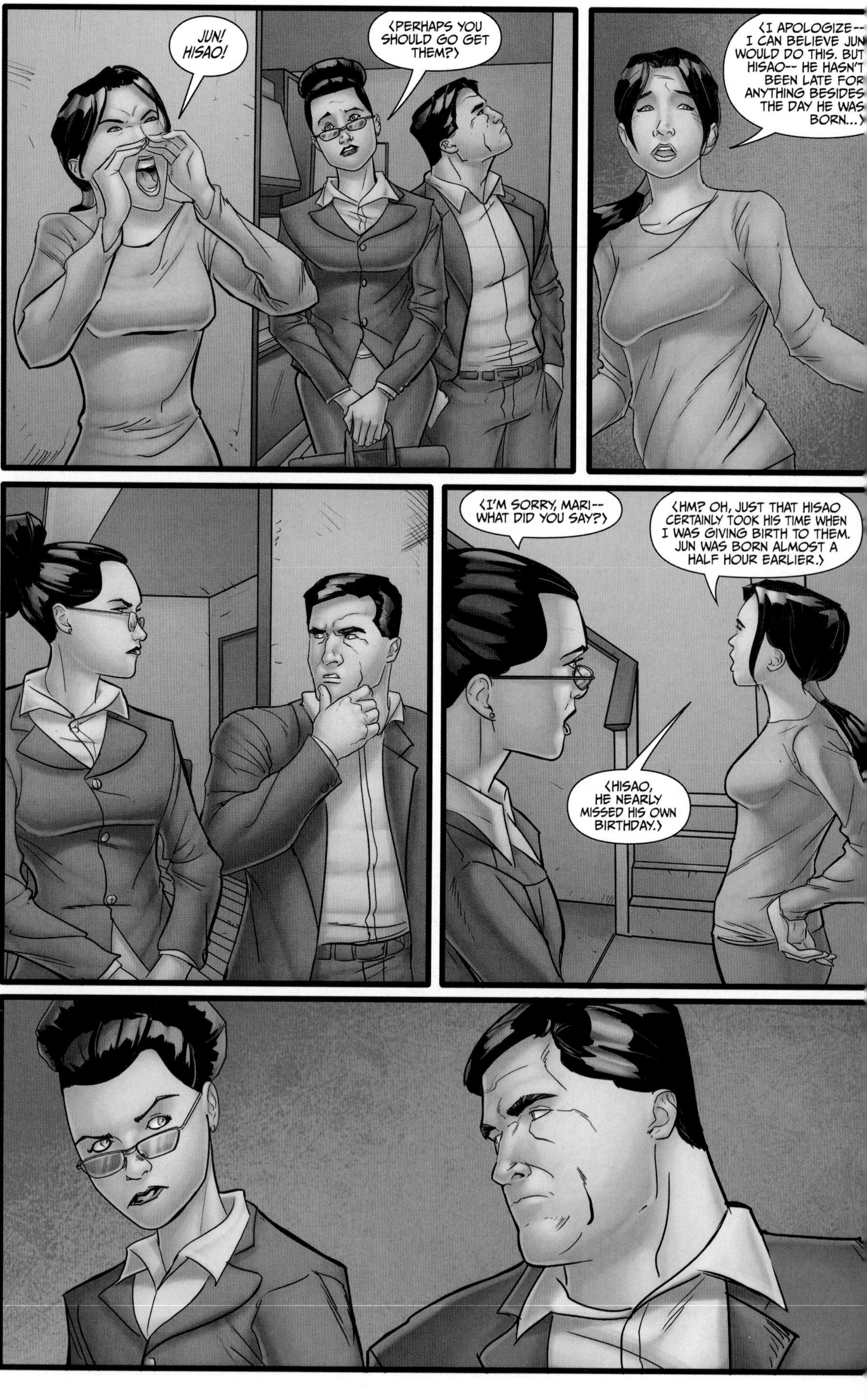
JUN! HISAO!
⟨PERHAPS YOU SHOULD GO GET THEM?⟩
⟨I APOLOGIZE-- I CAN BELIEVE JUN WOULD DO THIS. BUT HISAO-- HE HASN'T BEEN LATE FOR ANYTHING BESIDES THE DAY HE WAS BORN...⟩
⟨I'M SORRY, MARI-- WHAT DID YOU SAY?⟩
⟨HM? OH, JUST THAT HISAO CERTAINLY TOOK HIS TIME WHEN I WAS GIVING BIRTH TO THEM. JUN WAS BORN ALMOST A HALF HOUR EARLIER.⟩
⟨HISAO, HE NEARLY MISSED HIS OWN BIRTHDAY.⟩

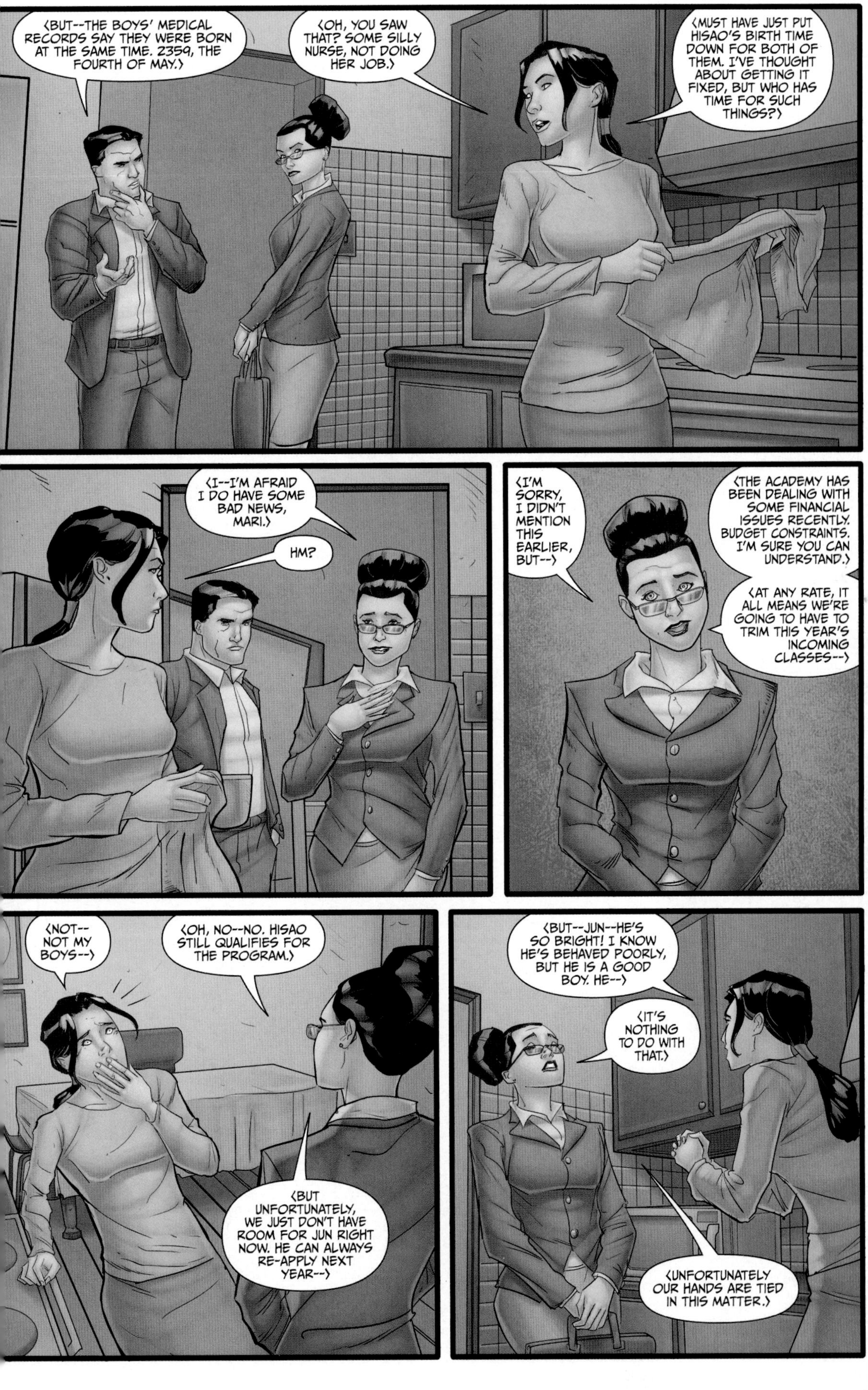
‹BUT--THE BOYS' MEDICAL RECORDS SAY THEY WERE BORN AT THE SAME TIME. 2359, THE FOURTH OF MAY.›
‹OH, YOU SAW THAT? SOME SILLY NURSE, NOT DOING HER JOB.›
‹MUST HAVE JUST PUT HISAO'S BIRTH TIME DOWN FOR BOTH OF THEM. I'VE THOUGHT ABOUT GETTING IT FIXED, BUT WHO HAS TIME FOR SUCH THINGS?›
‹I--I'M AFRAID I DO HAVE SOME BAD NEWS, MARI.›
HM?
‹I'M SORRY, I DIDN'T MENTION THIS EARLIER, BUT--›
‹THE ACADEMY HAS BEEN DEALING WITH SOME FINANCIAL ISSUES RECENTLY. BUDGET CONSTRAINTS. I'M SURE YOU CAN UNDERSTAND.›
‹AT ANY RATE, IT ALL MEANS WE'RE GOING TO HAVE TO TRIM THIS YEAR'S INCOMING CLASSES--›
‹NOT--NOT MY BOYS--›
‹OH, NO--NO. HISAO STILL QUALIFIES FOR THE PROGRAM.›
‹BUT UNFORTUNATELY, WE JUST DON'T HAVE ROOM FOR JUN RIGHT NOW. HE CAN ALWAYS RE-APPLY NEXT YEAR--›
‹BUT--JUN--HE'S SO BRIGHT! I KNOW HE'S BEHAVED POORLY, BUT HE IS A GOOD BOY. HE--›
‹IT'S NOTHING TO DO WITH THAT.›
‹UNFORTUNATELY OUR HANDS ARE TIED IN THIS MATTER.›

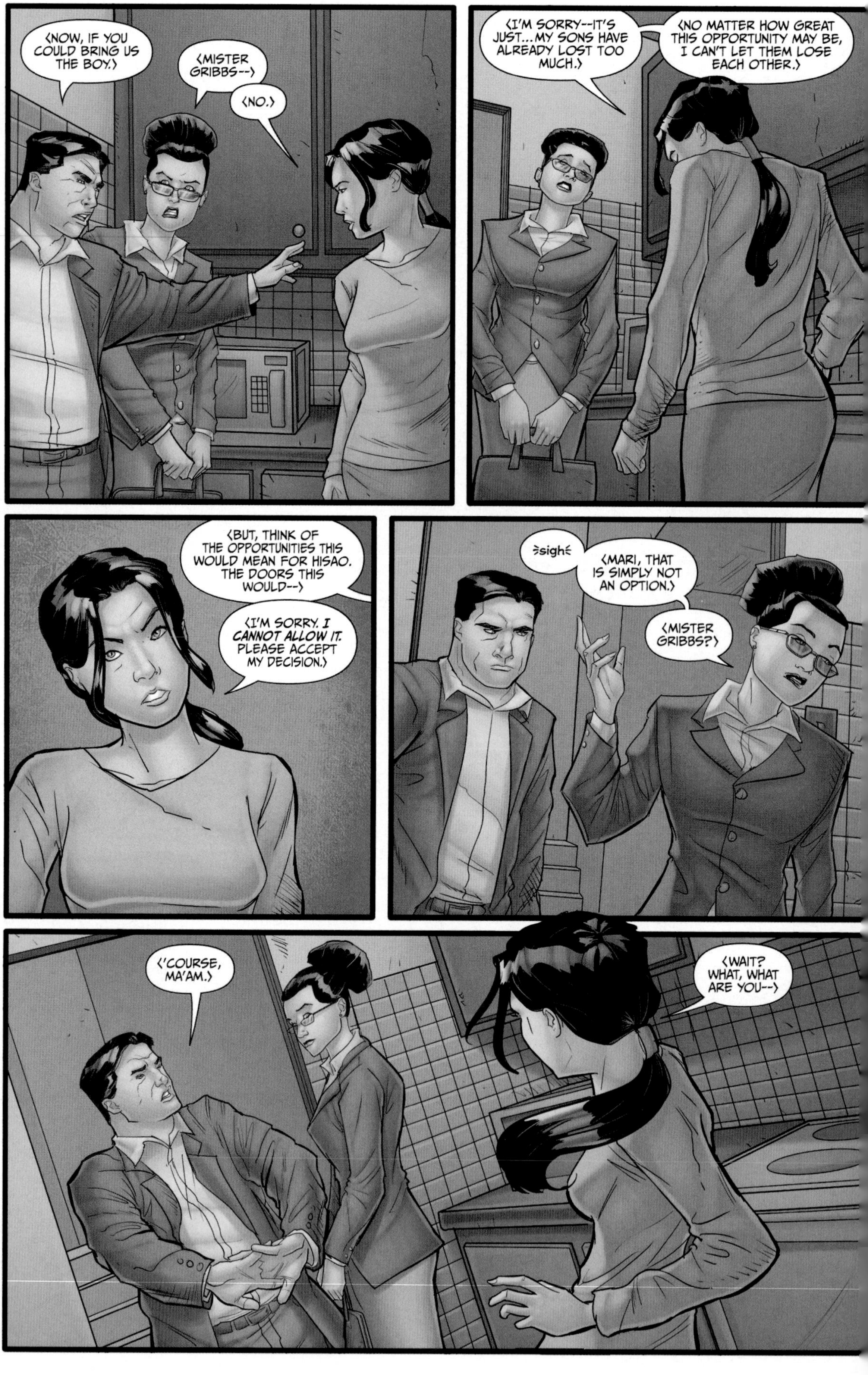
‹NOW, IF YOU COULD BRING US THE BOY.›
‹MISTER GRIBBS--›
‹NO.›
‹I'M SORRY--IT'S JUST... MY SONS HAVE ALREADY LOST TOO MUCH.›
‹NO MATTER HOW GREAT THIS OPPORTUNITY MAY BE, I CAN'T LET THEM LOSE EACH OTHER.›
‹BUT, THINK OF THE OPPORTUNITIES THIS WOULD MEAN FOR HISAO. THE DOORS THIS WOULD--›
‹I'M SORRY. *I CANNOT ALLOW IT.* PLEASE ACCEPT MY DECISION.›
›sigh‹
‹MARI, THAT IS SIMPLY NOT AN OPTION.›
‹MISTER GRIBBS?›
‹'COURSE, MA'AM.›
‹WAIT? WHAT, WHAT ARE YOU--›

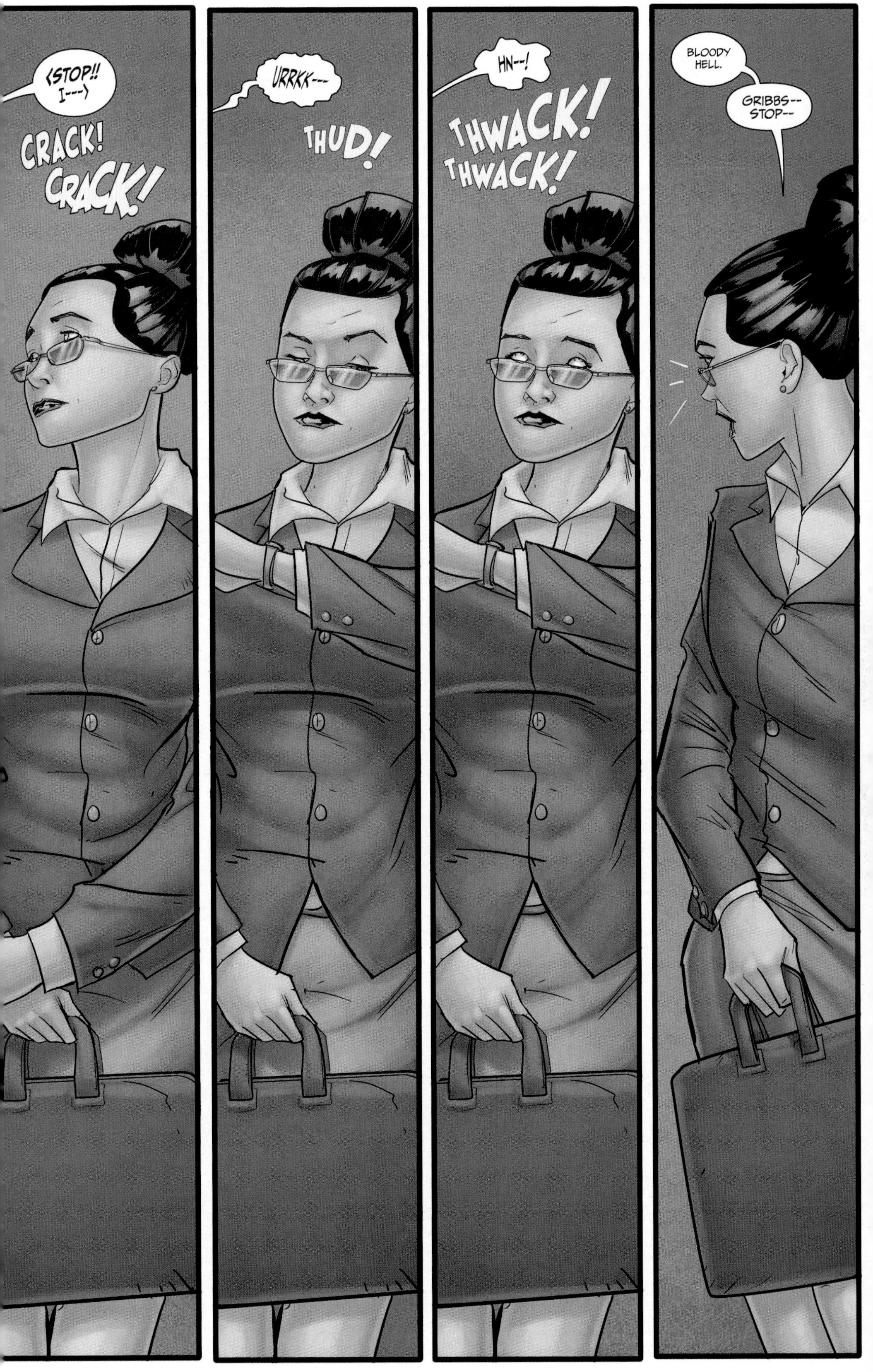

⟨STOP!! I---⟩
CRACK!
CRACK!
URRKK---
THUD!
HN--!
THWACK!
THWACK!
BLOODY HELL.
GRIBBS-- STOP--

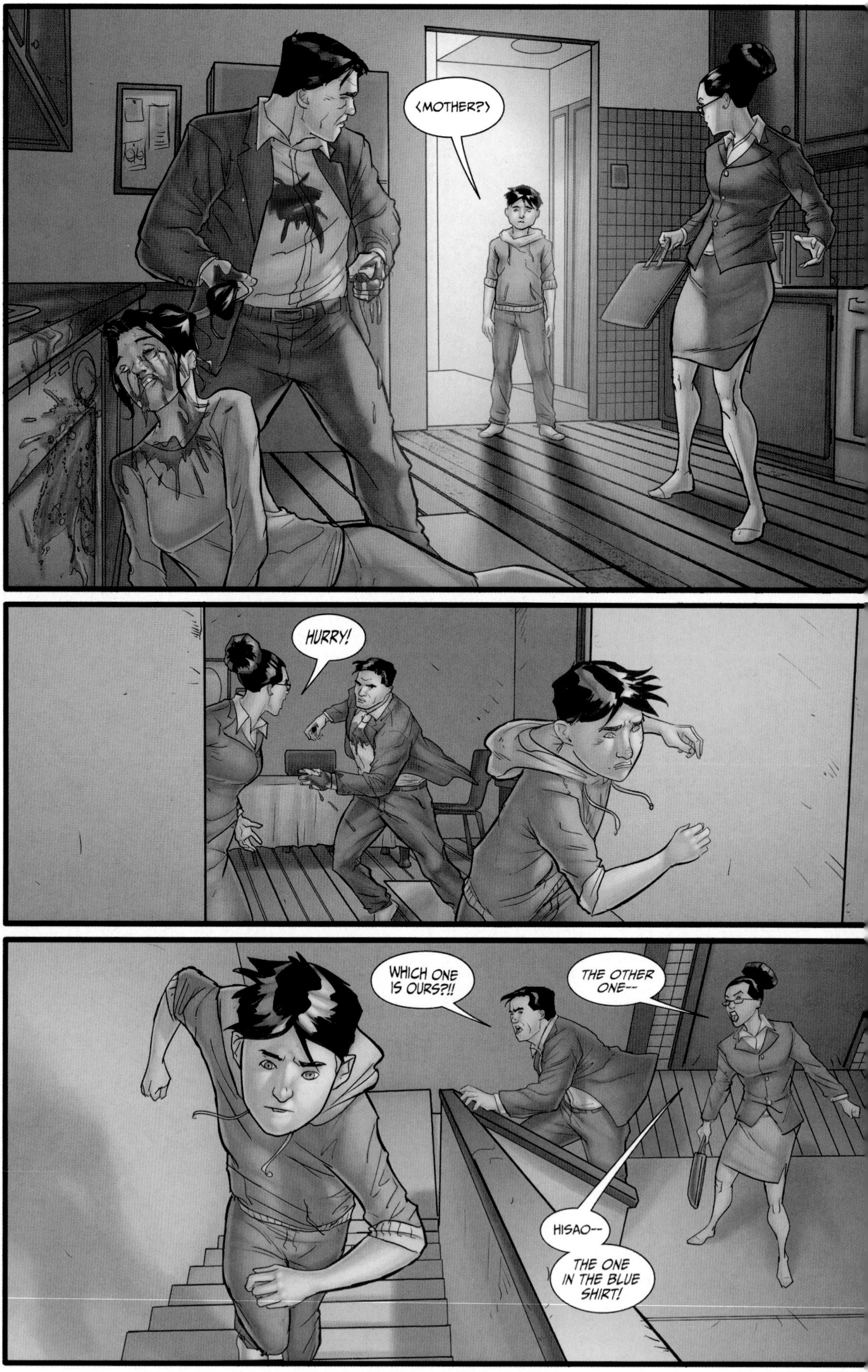

<MOTHER?>
HURRY!
WHICH ONE IS OURS?!!
THE OTHER ONE--
HISAO--
THE ONE IN THE BLUE SHIRT!

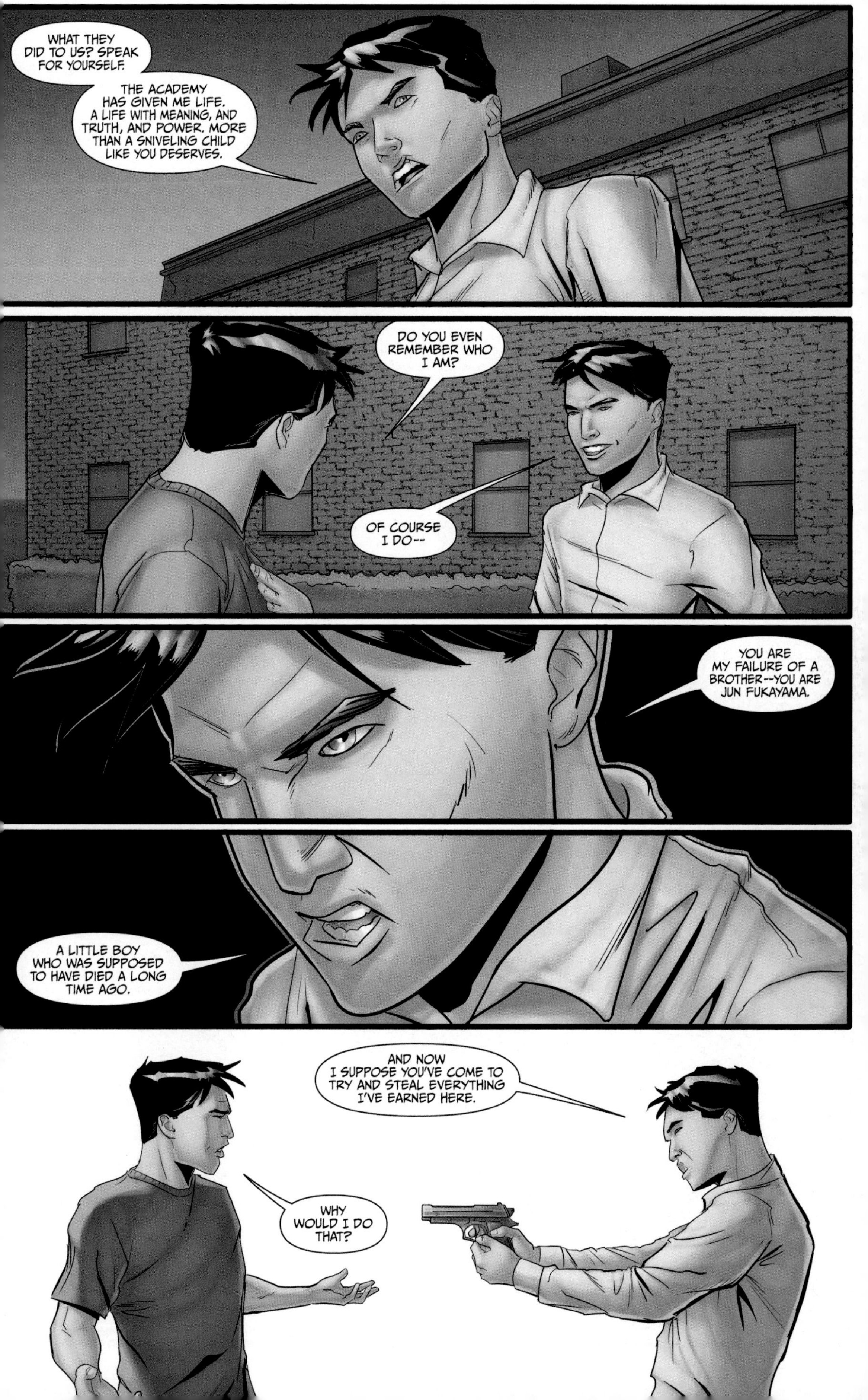
WHAT THEY DID TO US? SPEAK FOR YOURSELF.
THE ACADEMY HAS GIVEN ME LIFE. A LIFE WITH MEANING, AND TRUTH, AND POWER. MORE THAN A SNIVELING CHILD LIKE YOU DESERVES.
DO YOU EVEN REMEMBER WHO I AM?
OF COURSE I DO--
YOU ARE MY FAILURE OF A BROTHER--YOU ARE JUN FUKAYAMA.
A LITTLE BOY WHO WAS SUPPOSED TO HAVE DIED A LONG TIME AGO.
AND NOW I SUPPOSE YOU'VE COME TO TRY AND STEAL EVERYTHING I'VE EARNED HERE.
WHY WOULD I DO THAT?

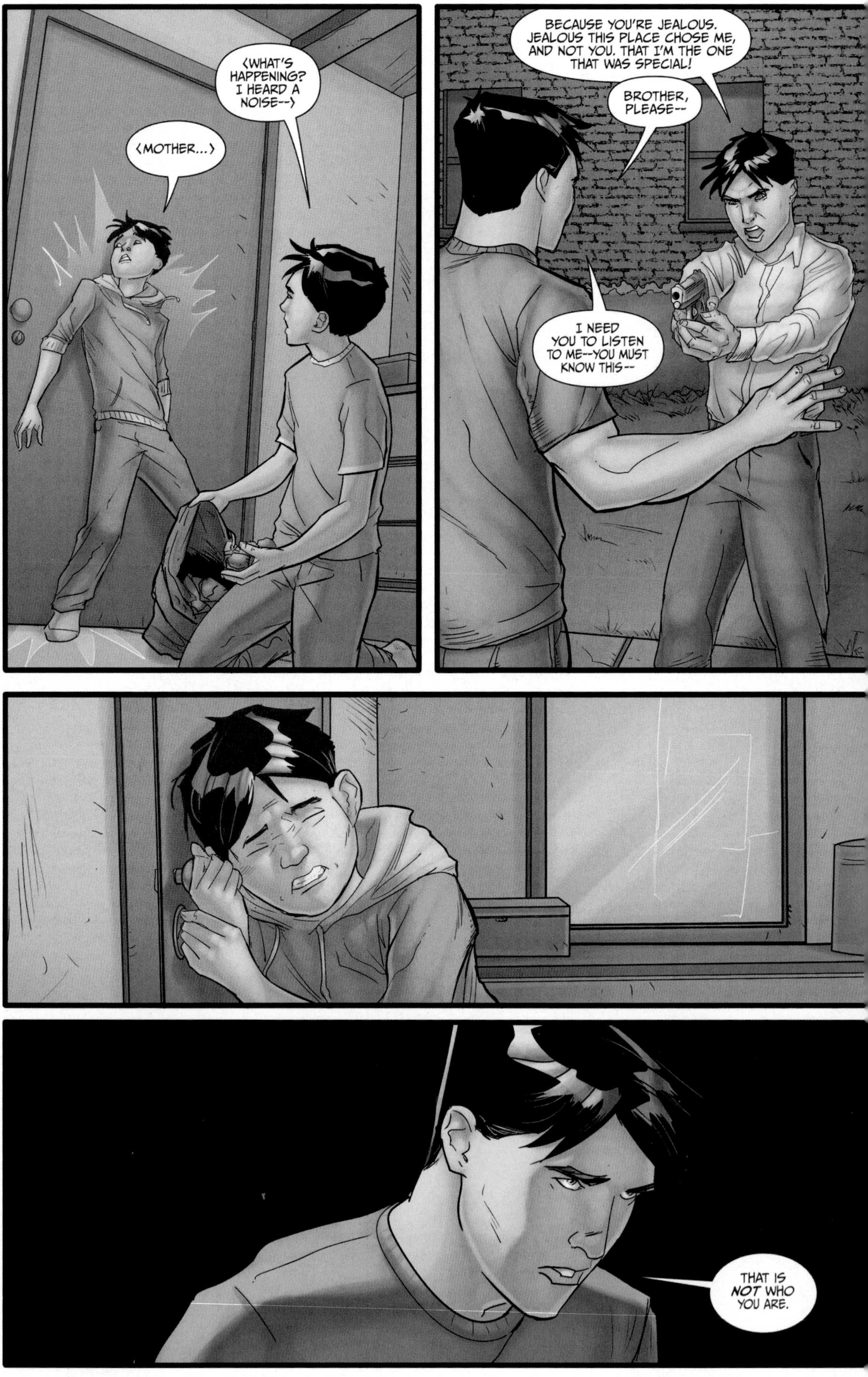

‹MOTHER...›
‹WHAT'S HAPPENING? I HEARD A NOISE--›
BECAUSE YOU'RE JEALOUS. JEALOUS THIS PLACE CHOSE ME, AND NOT YOU. THAT I'M THE ONE THAT WAS SPECIAL!
BROTHER, PLEASE--
I NEED YOU TO LISTEN TO ME--YOU MUST KNOW THIS--
THAT IS *NOT* WHO YOU ARE.

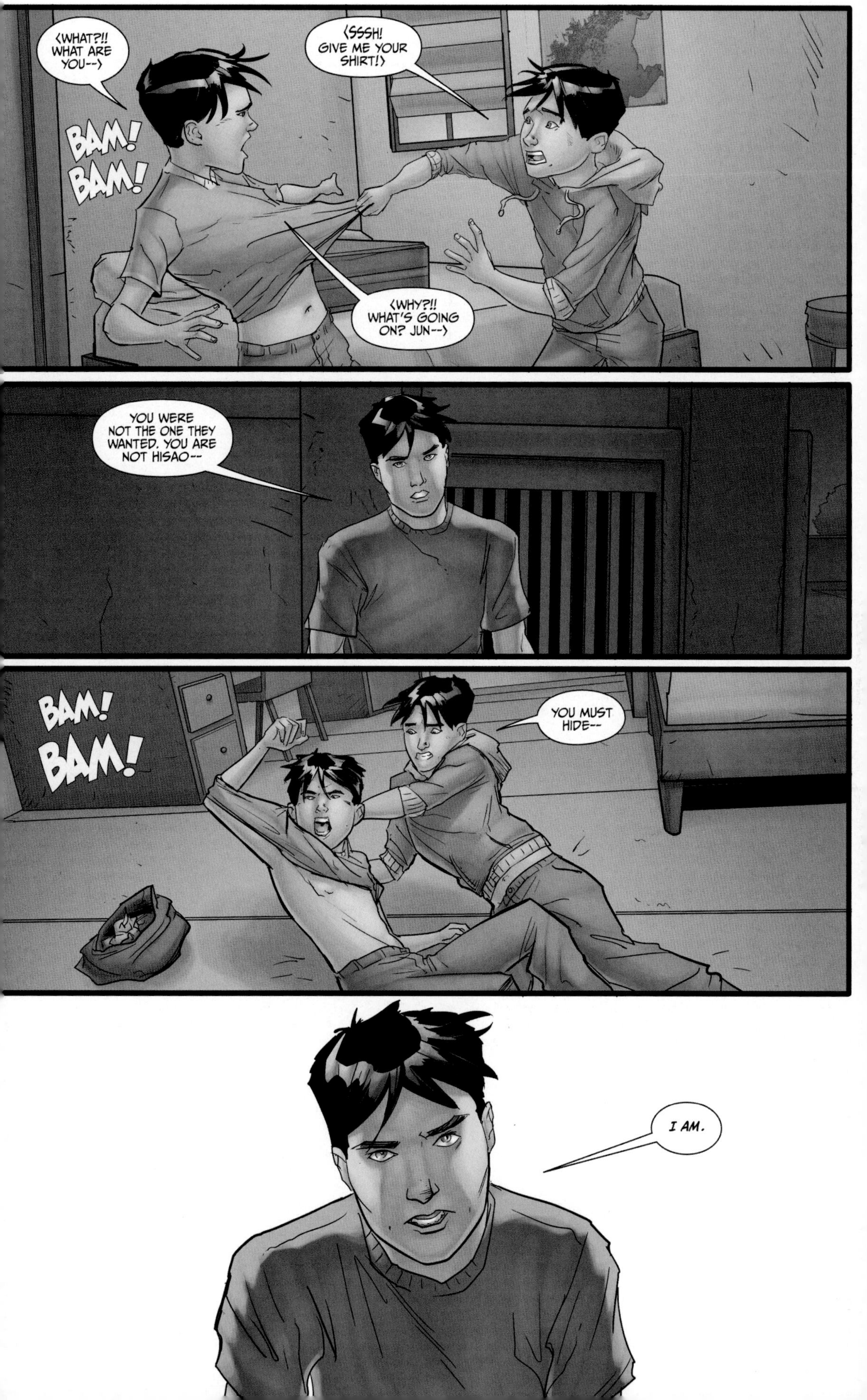

⟨WHAT?!! WHAT ARE YOU--⟩
BAM! BAM!
⟨SSSH! GIVE ME YOUR SHIRT!⟩
⟨WHY?!! WHAT'S GOING ON? JUN--⟩
YOU WERE NOT THE ONE THEY WANTED. YOU ARE NOT HISAO--
BAM! BAM!
YOU MUST HIDE--
I AM.

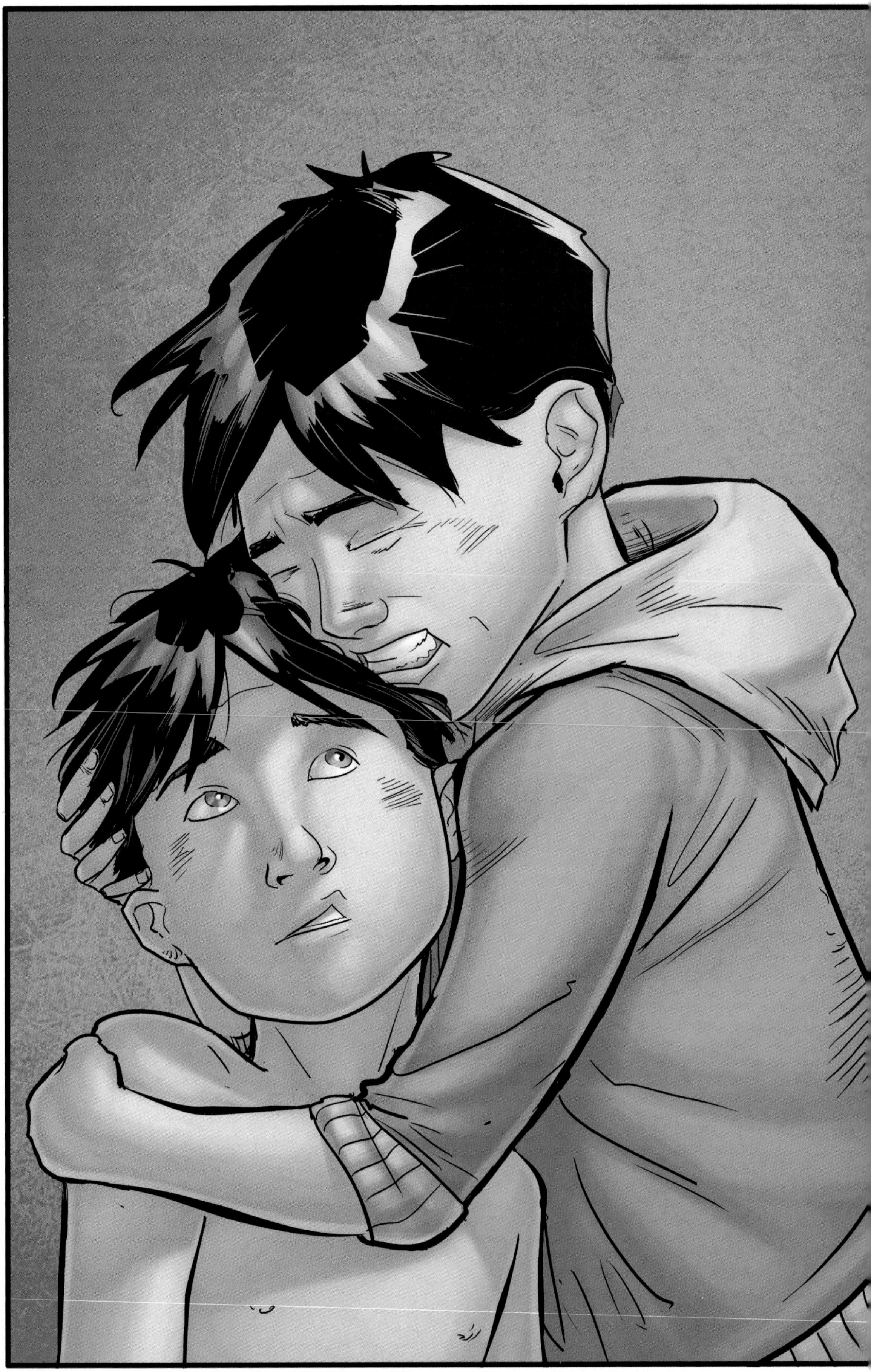

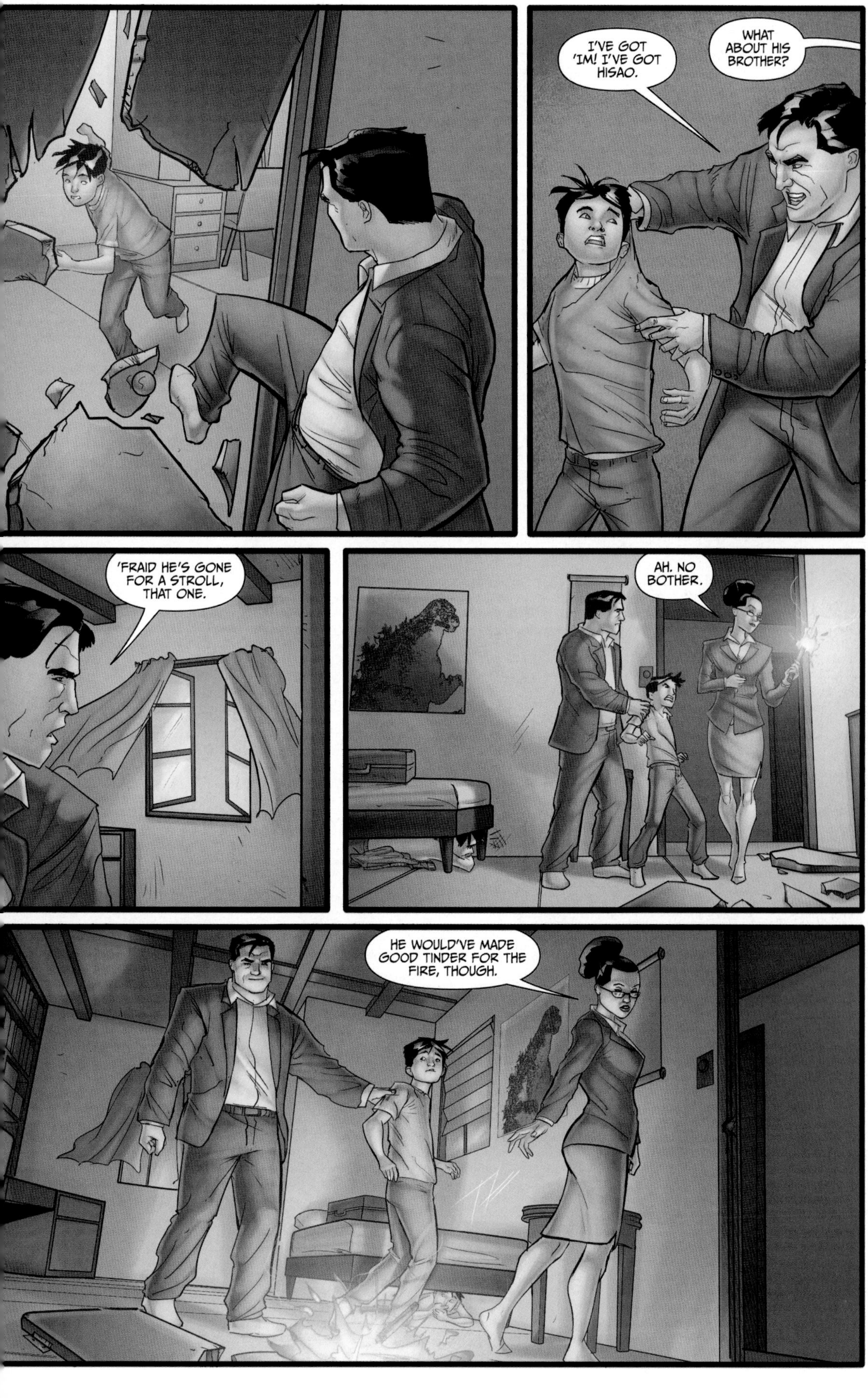
I'VE GOT 'IM! I'VE GOT HISAO.
WHAT ABOUT HIS BROTHER?
'FRAID HE'S GONE FOR A STROLL, THAT ONE.
AH. NO BOTHER.
HE WOULD'VE MADE GOOD TINDER FOR THE FIRE, THOUGH.

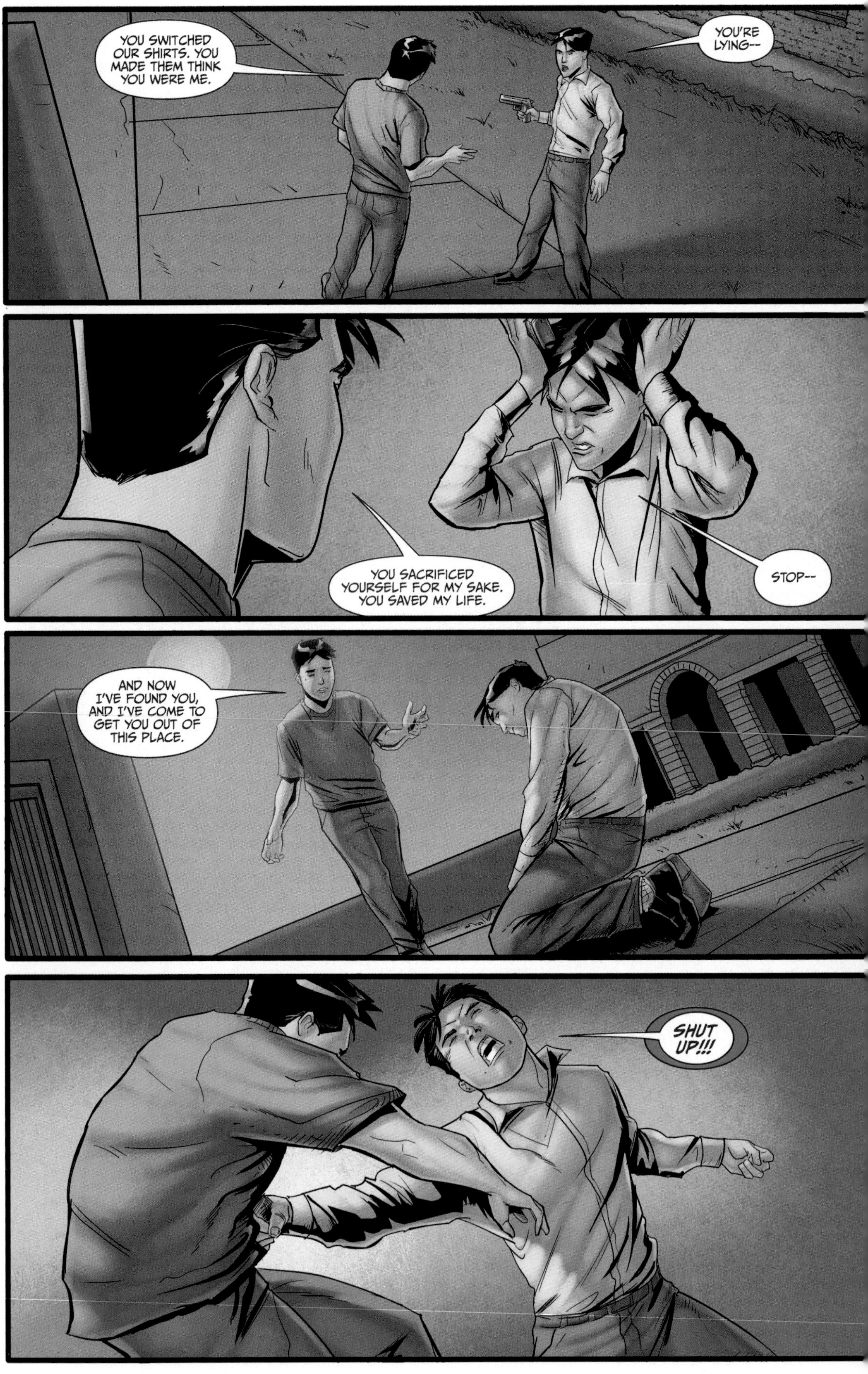
YOU SWITCHED OUR SHIRTS. YOU MADE THEM THINK YOU WERE ME.
YOU'RE LYING--
YOU SACRIFICED YOURSELF FOR MY SAKE. YOU SAVED MY LIFE.
STOP--
AND NOW I'VE FOUND YOU, AND I'VE COME TO GET YOU OUT OF THIS PLACE.
SHUT UP!!!

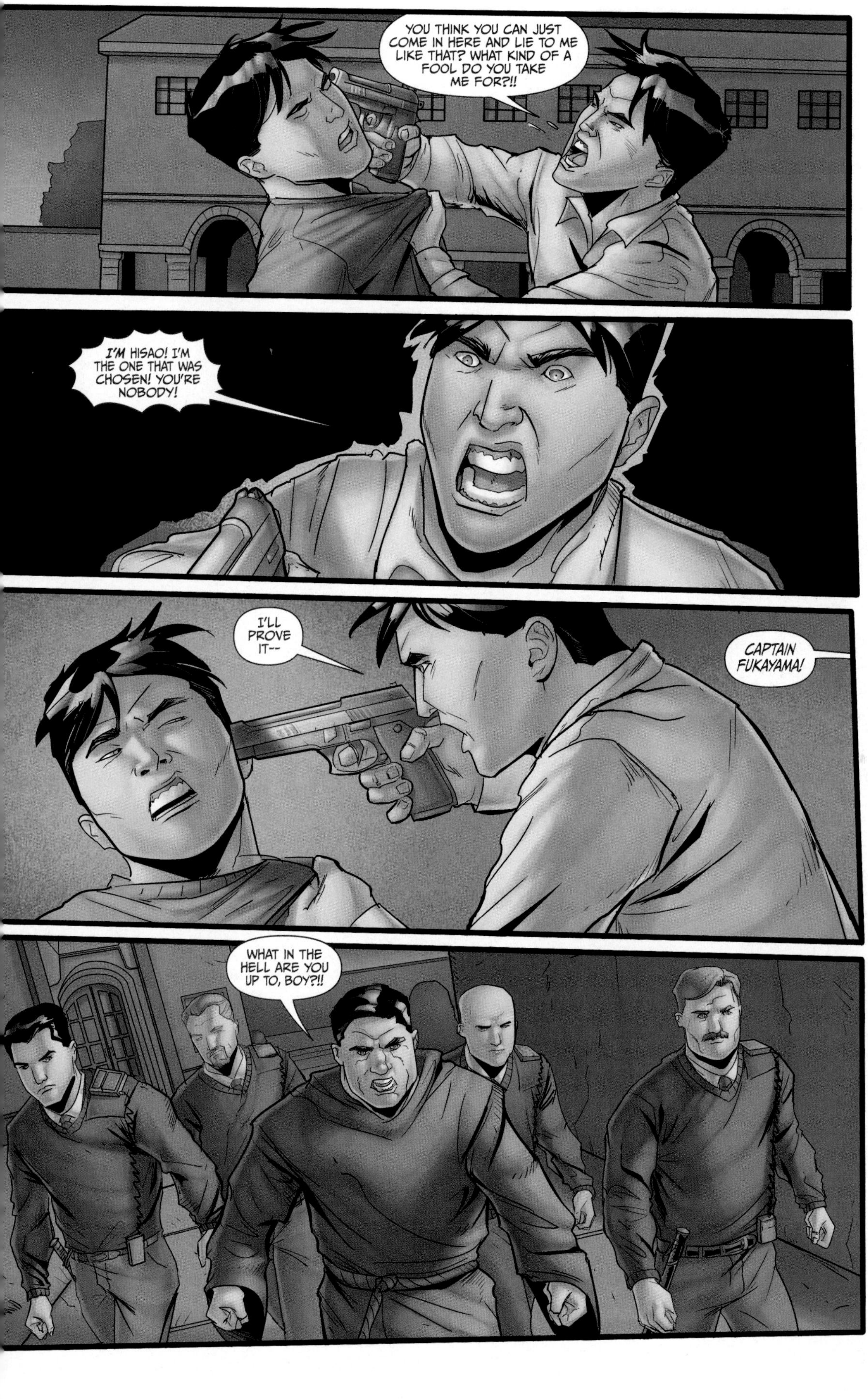
YOU THINK YOU CAN JUST COME IN HERE AND LIE TO ME LIKE THAT? WHAT KIND OF A FOOL DO YOU TAKE ME FOR?!!
I'M HISAO! I'M THE ONE THAT WAS CHOSEN! YOU'RE NOBODY!
I'LL PROVE IT--
CAPTAIN FUKAYAMA!
WHAT IN THE HELL ARE YOU UP TO, BOY?!!

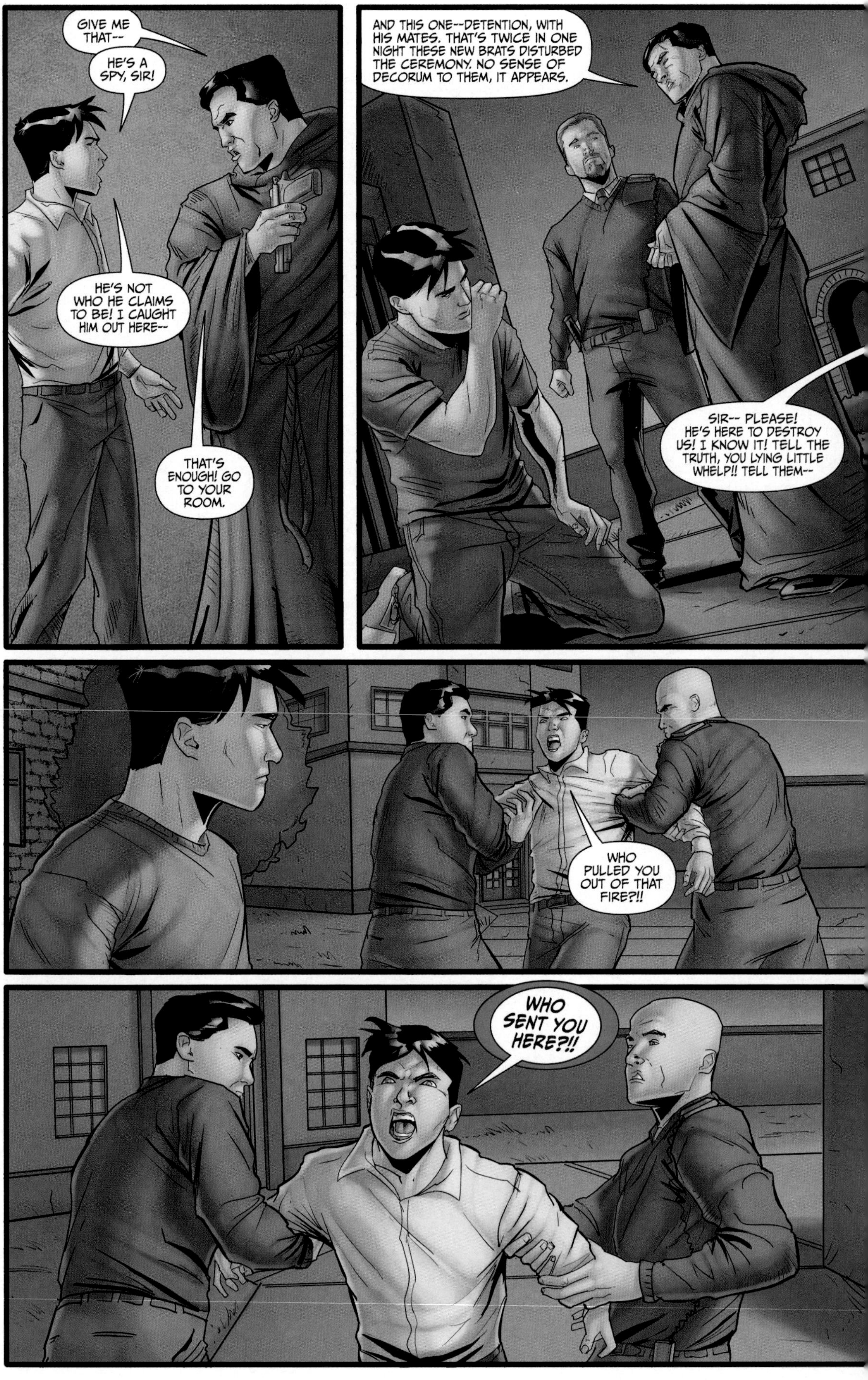
GIVE ME THAT--
HE'S A SPY, SIR!
HE'S NOT WHO HE CLAIMS TO BE! I CAUGHT HIM OUT HERE--
THAT'S ENOUGH! GO TO YOUR ROOM.
AND THIS ONE--DETENTION, WITH HIS MATES. THAT'S TWICE IN ONE NIGHT THESE NEW BRATS DISTURBED THE CEREMONY. NO SENSE OF DECORUM TO THEM, IT APPEARS.
SIR-- PLEASE! HE'S HERE TO DESTROY US! I KNOW IT! TELL THE TRUTH, YOU LYING LITTLE WHELP!! TELL THEM--
WHO PULLED YOU OUT OF THAT FIRE?!!
WHO SENT YOU HERE?!!

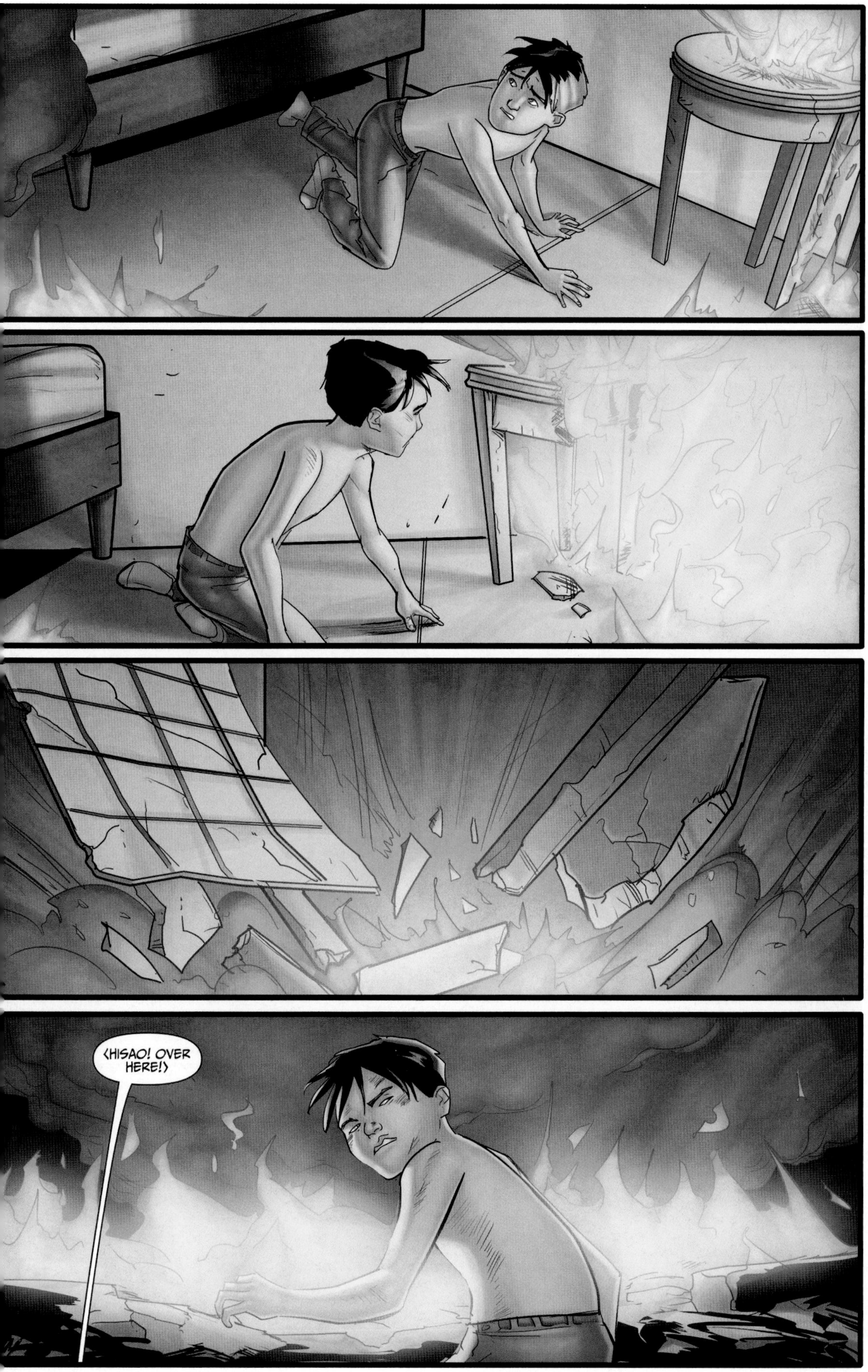

‹HISAO! OVER HERE!›

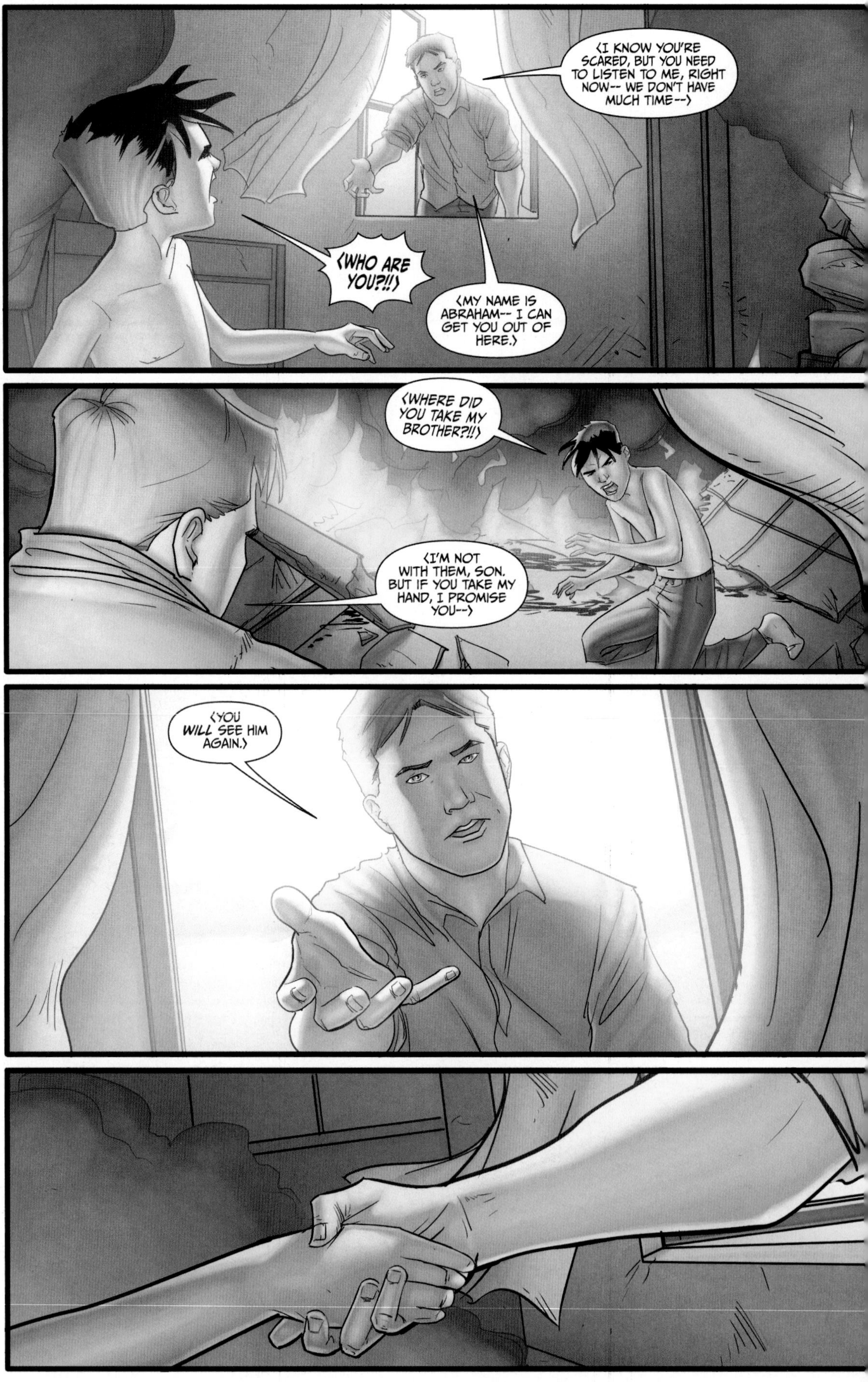

‹I KNOW YOU'RE SCARED, BUT YOU NEED TO LISTEN TO ME, RIGHT NOW-- WE DON'T HAVE MUCH TIME--›
‹WHO ARE YOU?!!›
‹MY NAME IS ABRAHAM-- I CAN GET YOU OUT OF HERE.›
‹WHERE DID YOU TAKE MY BROTHER?!!›
‹I'M NOT WITH THEM, SON. BUT IF YOU TAKE MY HAND, I PROMISE YOU--›
‹YOU WILL SEE HIM AGAIN.›

ten

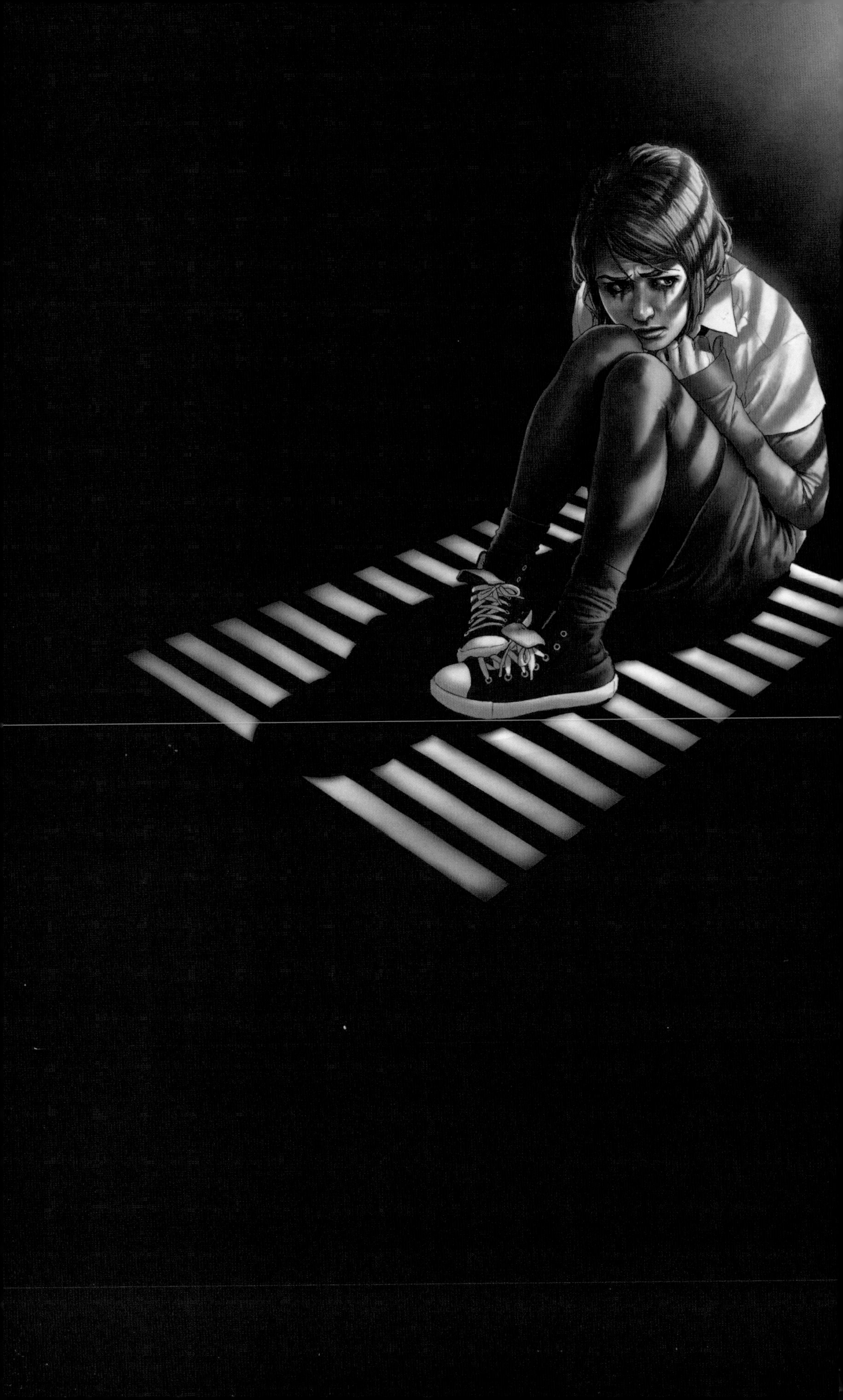

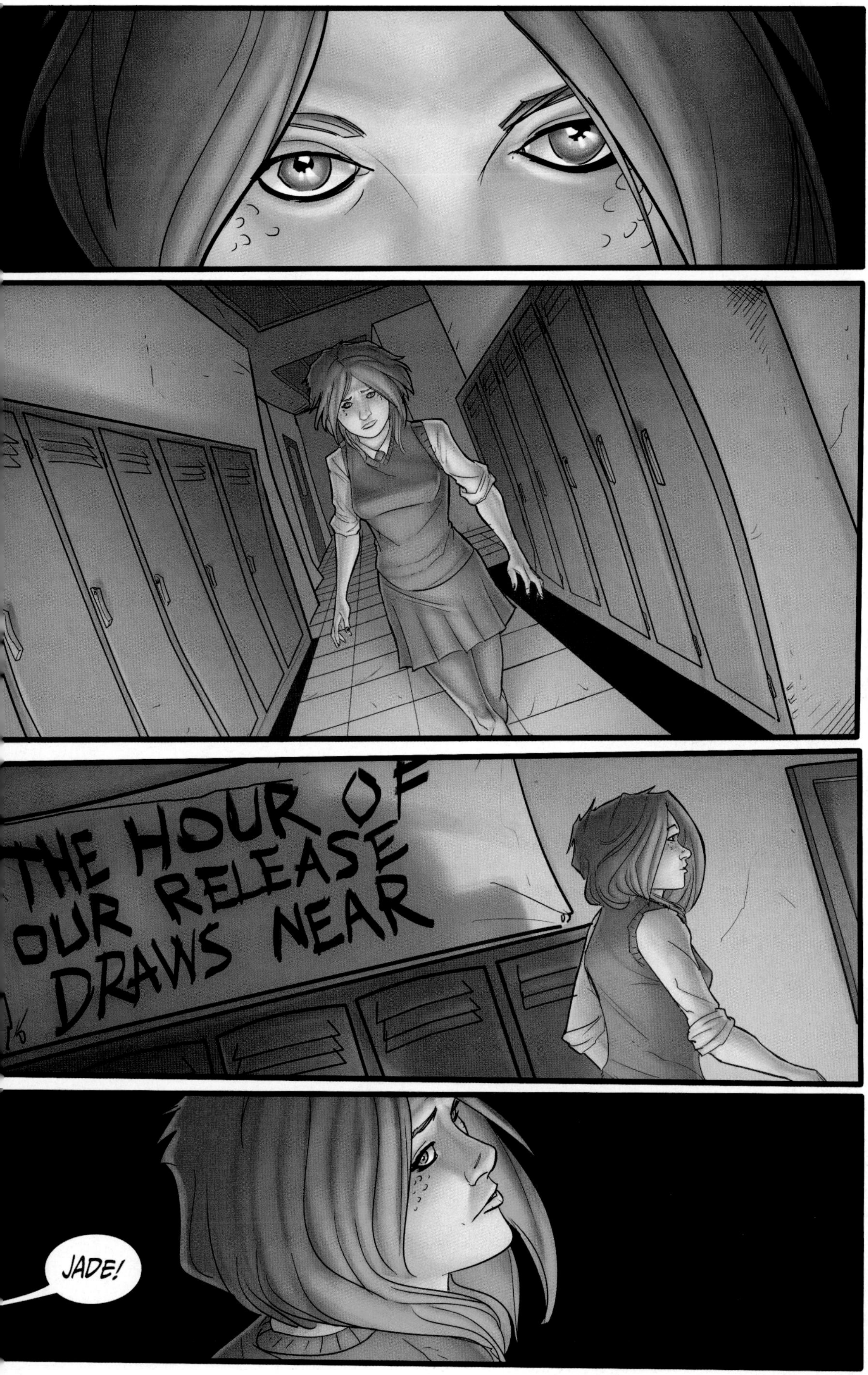
THE HOUR OF
OUR RELEASE
DRAWS NEAR
JADE!

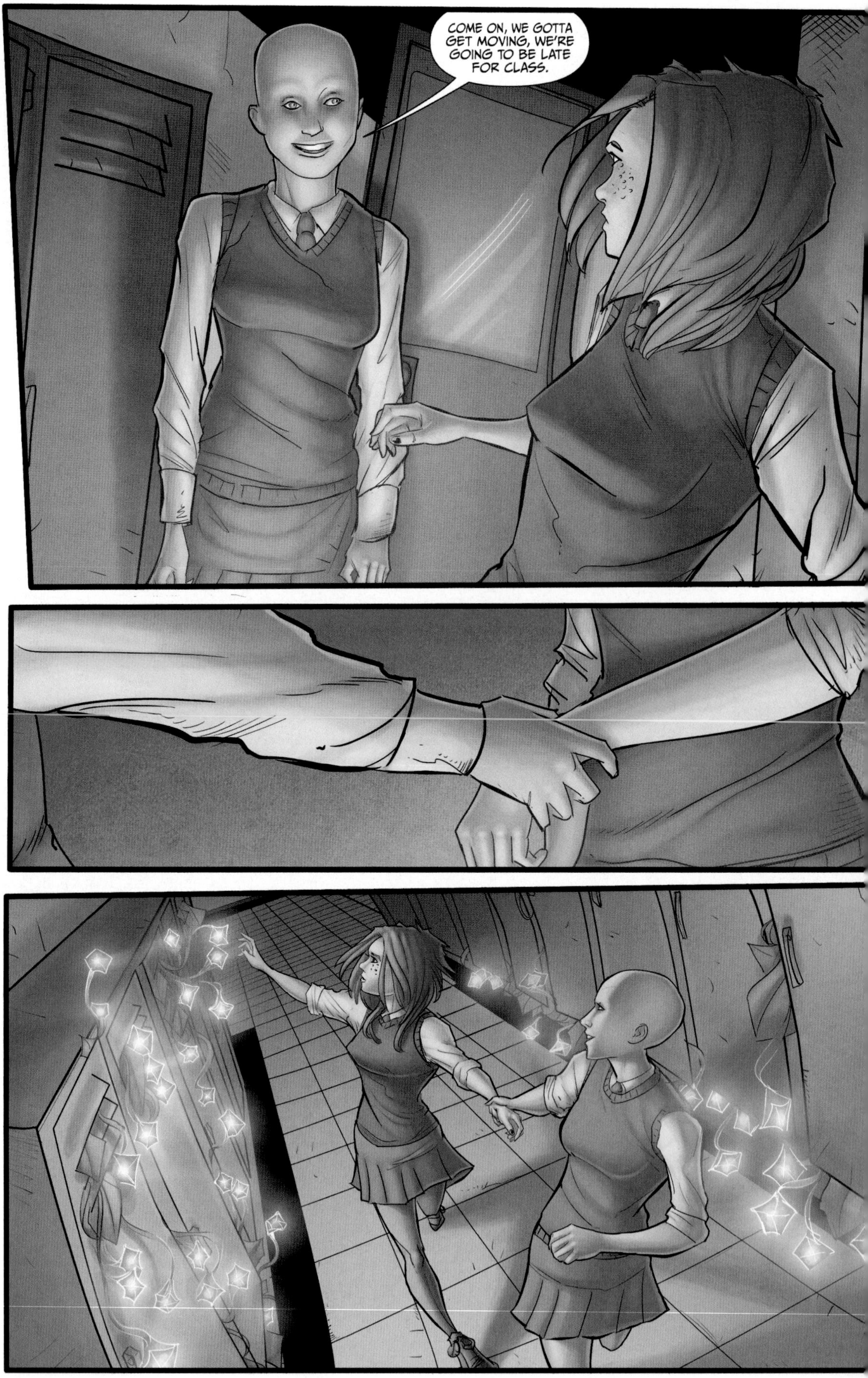
COME ON, WE GOTTA GET MOVING, WE'RE GOING TO BE LATE FOR CLASS.

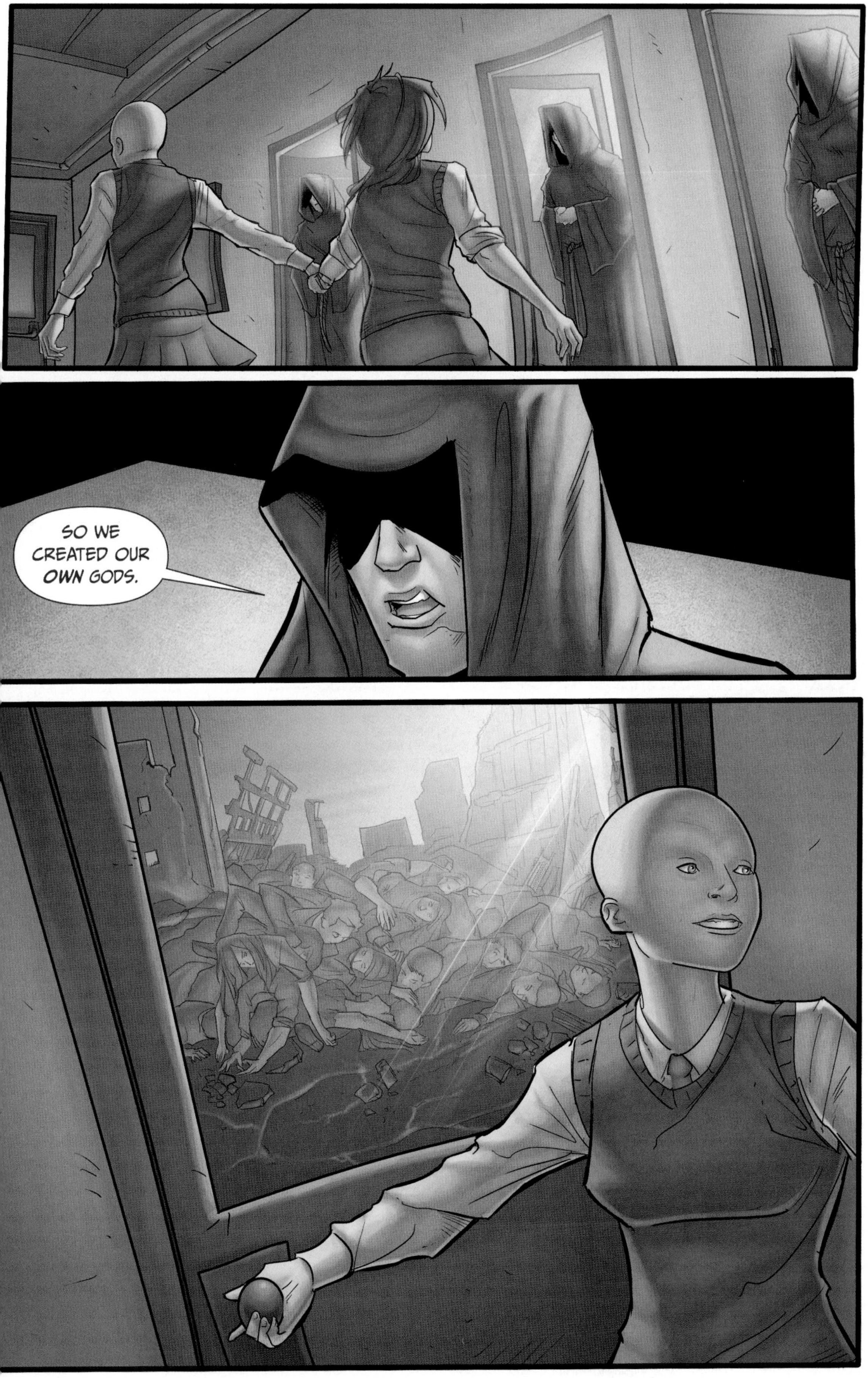
SO WE CREATED OUR OWN GODS.

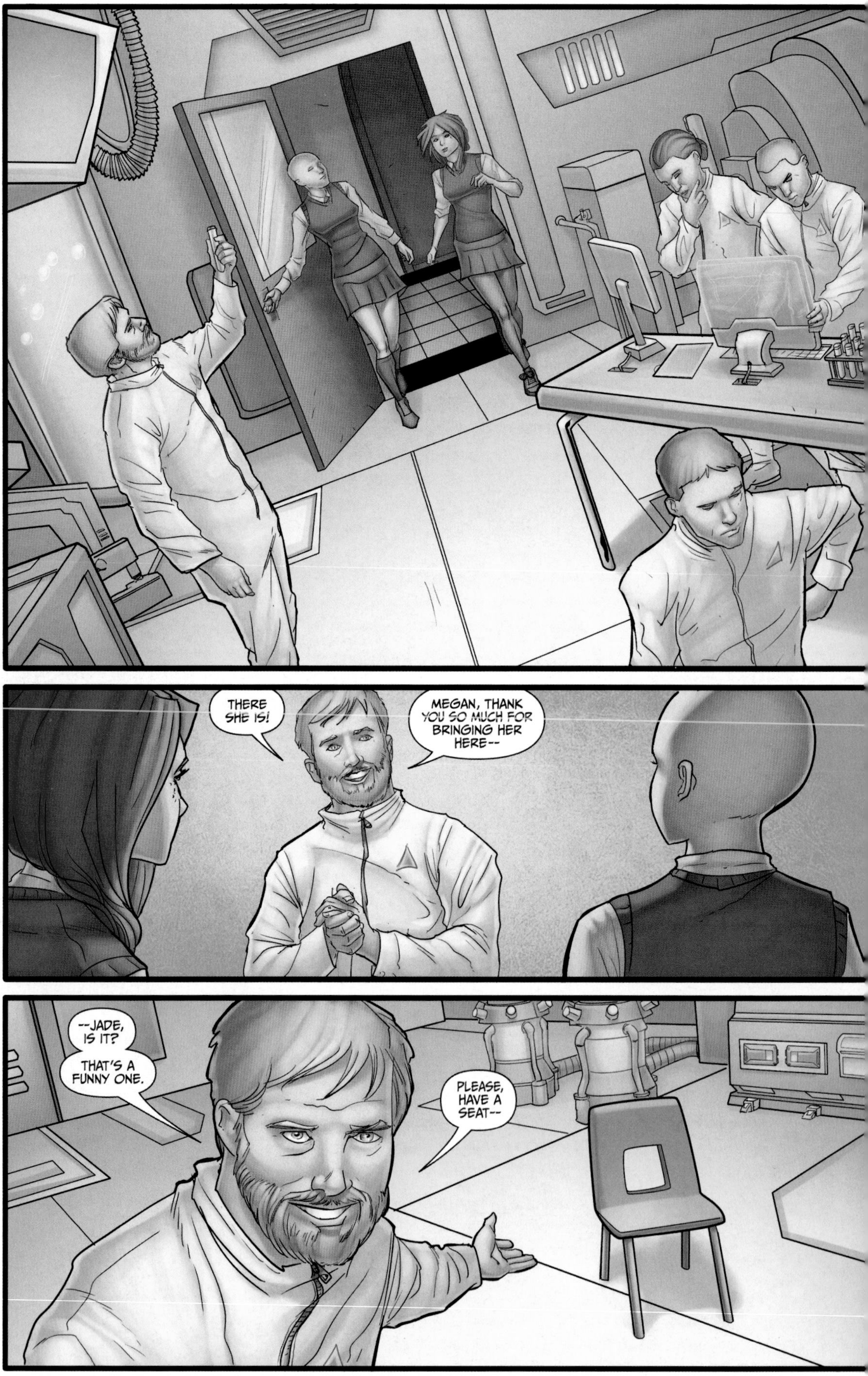
THERE SHE IS!
MEGAN, THANK YOU SO MUCH FOR BRINGING HER HERE--
--JADE, IS IT?
THAT'S A FUNNY ONE.
PLEASE, HAVE A SEAT--

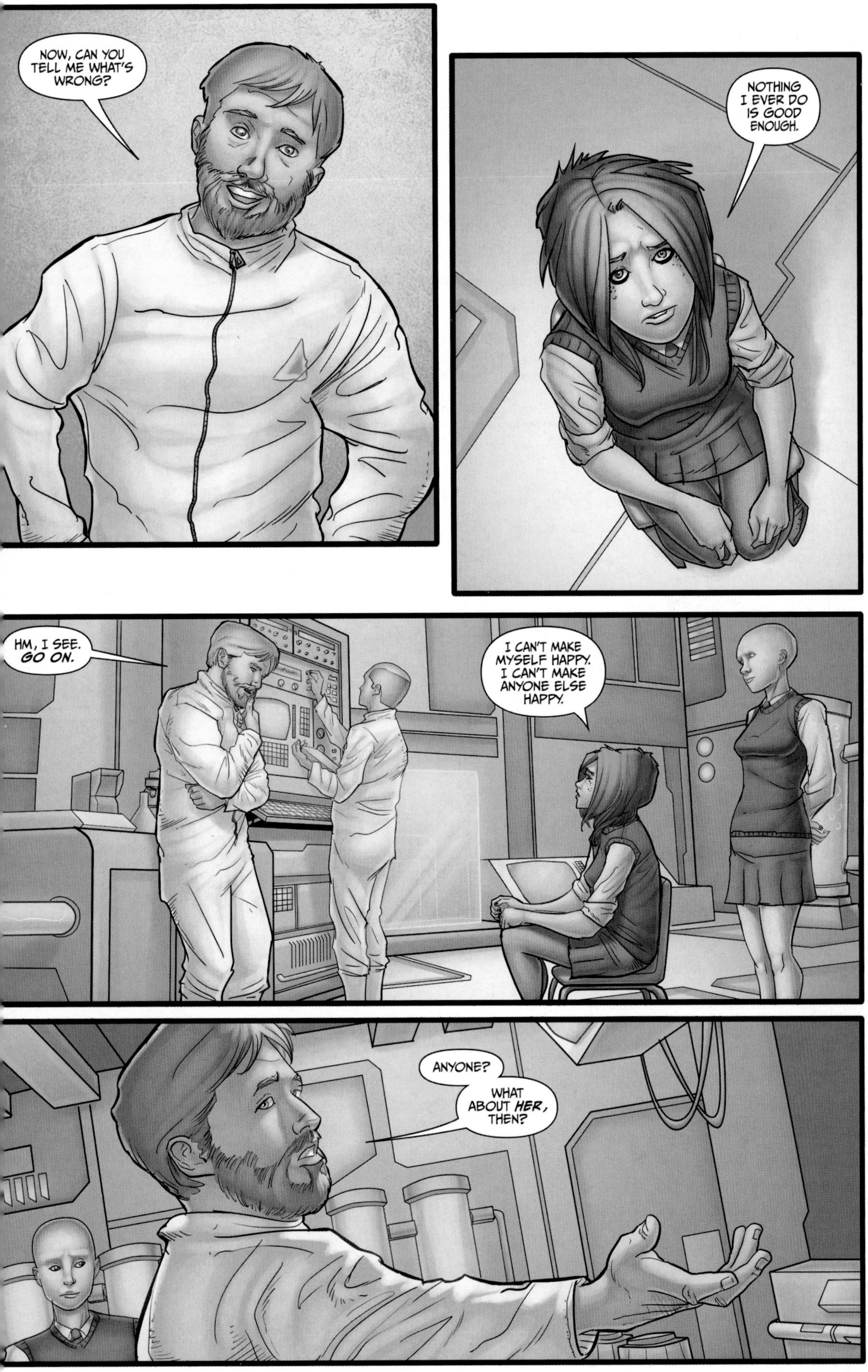
NOW, CAN YOU TELL ME WHAT'S WRONG?
NOTHING I EVER DO IS GOOD ENOUGH.
HM, I SEE. *GO ON.*
I CAN'T MAKE MYSELF HAPPY. I CAN'T MAKE ANYONE ELSE HAPPY.
ANYONE?
WHAT ABOUT *HER*, THEN?

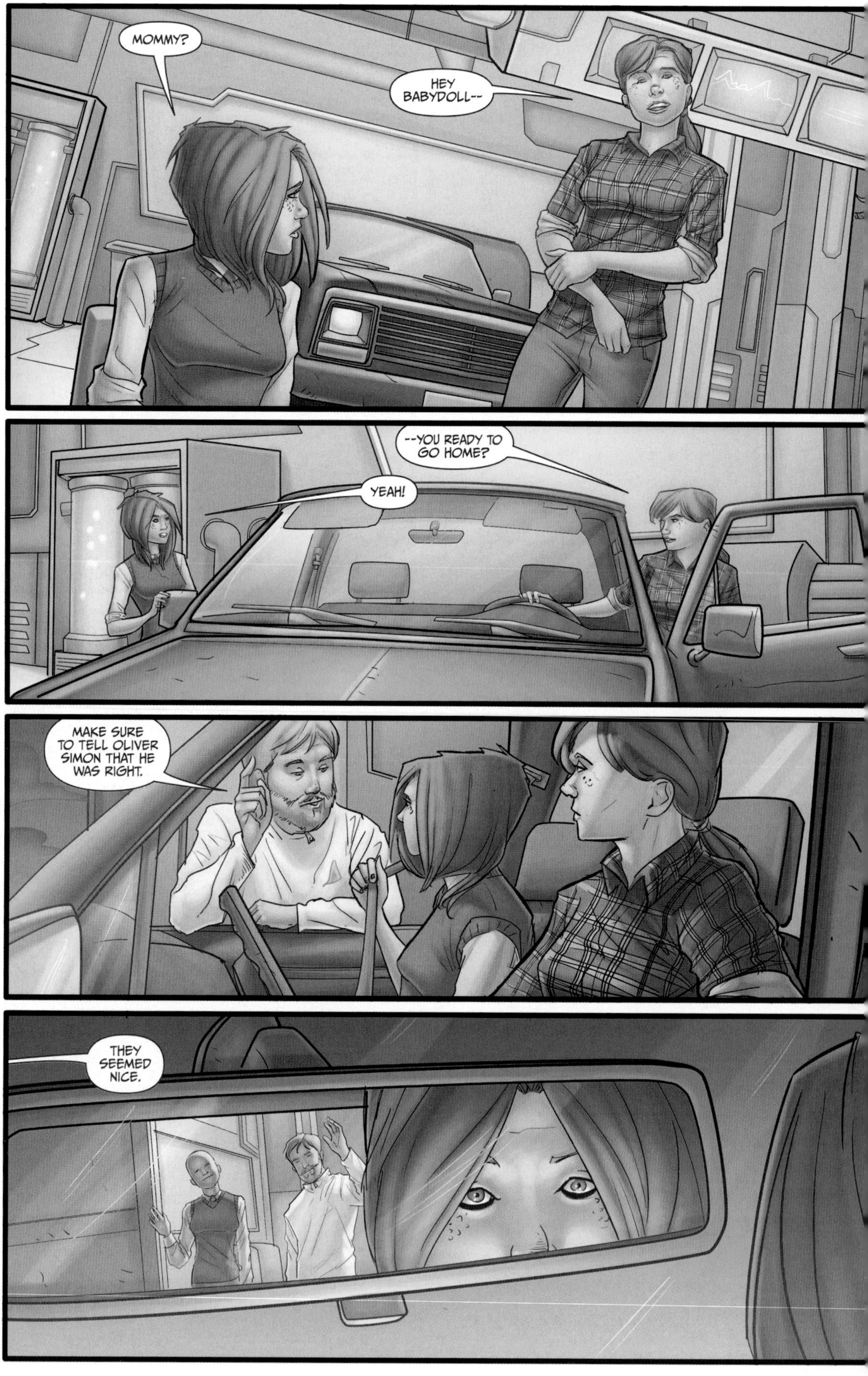
MOMMY?
HEY BABYDOLL--
--YOU READY TO GO HOME?
YEAH!
MAKE SURE TO TELL OLIVER SIMON THAT HE WAS RIGHT.
THEY SEEMED NICE.

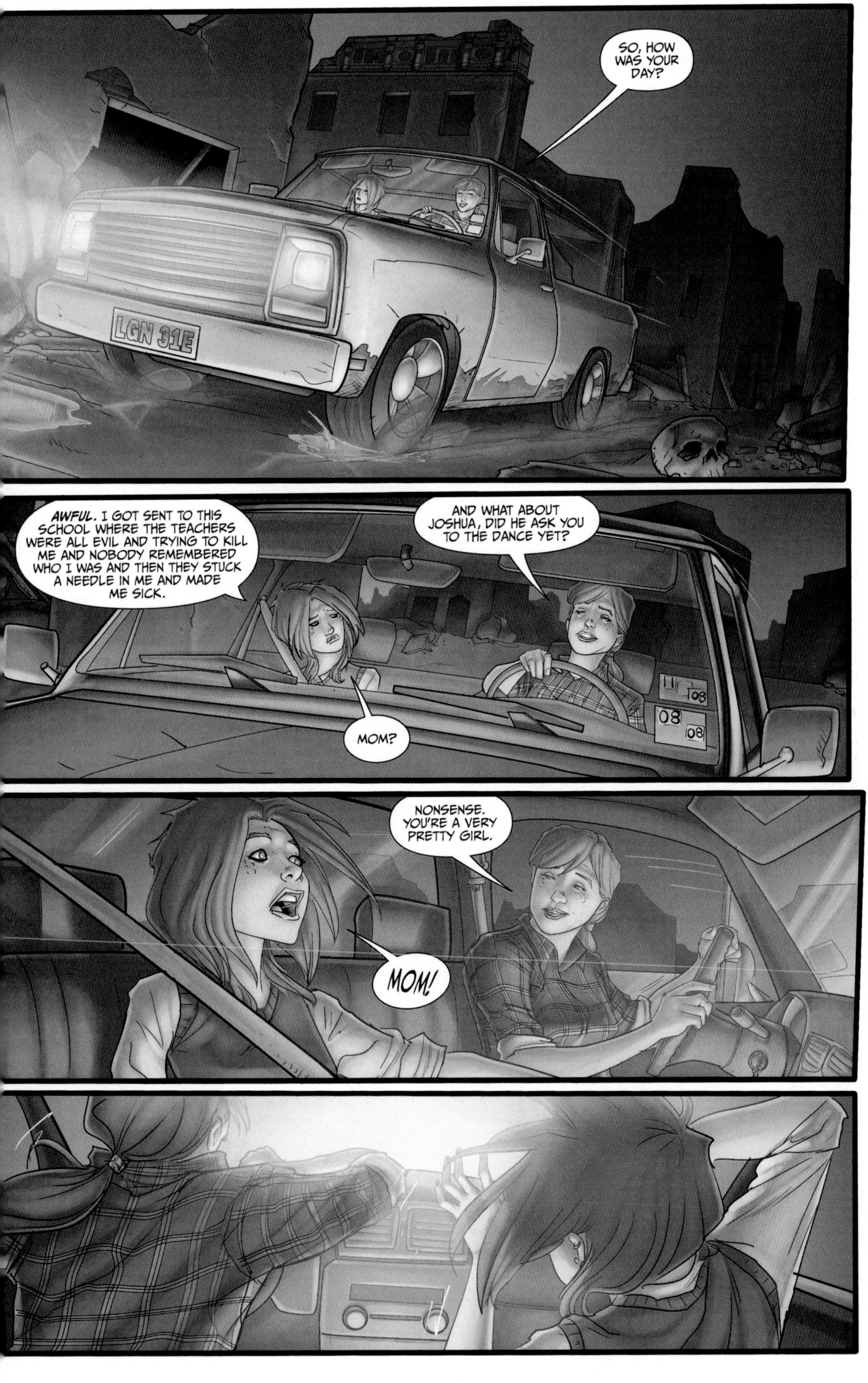

LGN 31E
SO, HOW WAS YOUR DAY?
AWFUL. I GOT SENT TO THIS SCHOOL WHERE THE TEACHERS WERE ALL EVIL AND TRYING TO KILL ME AND NOBODY REMEMBERED WHO I WAS AND THEN THEY STUCK A NEEDLE IN ME AND MADE ME SICK.
AND WHAT ABOUT JOSHUA, DID HE ASK YOU TO THE DANCE YET?
MOM?
NONSENSE. YOU'RE A VERY PRETTY GIRL.
MOM!

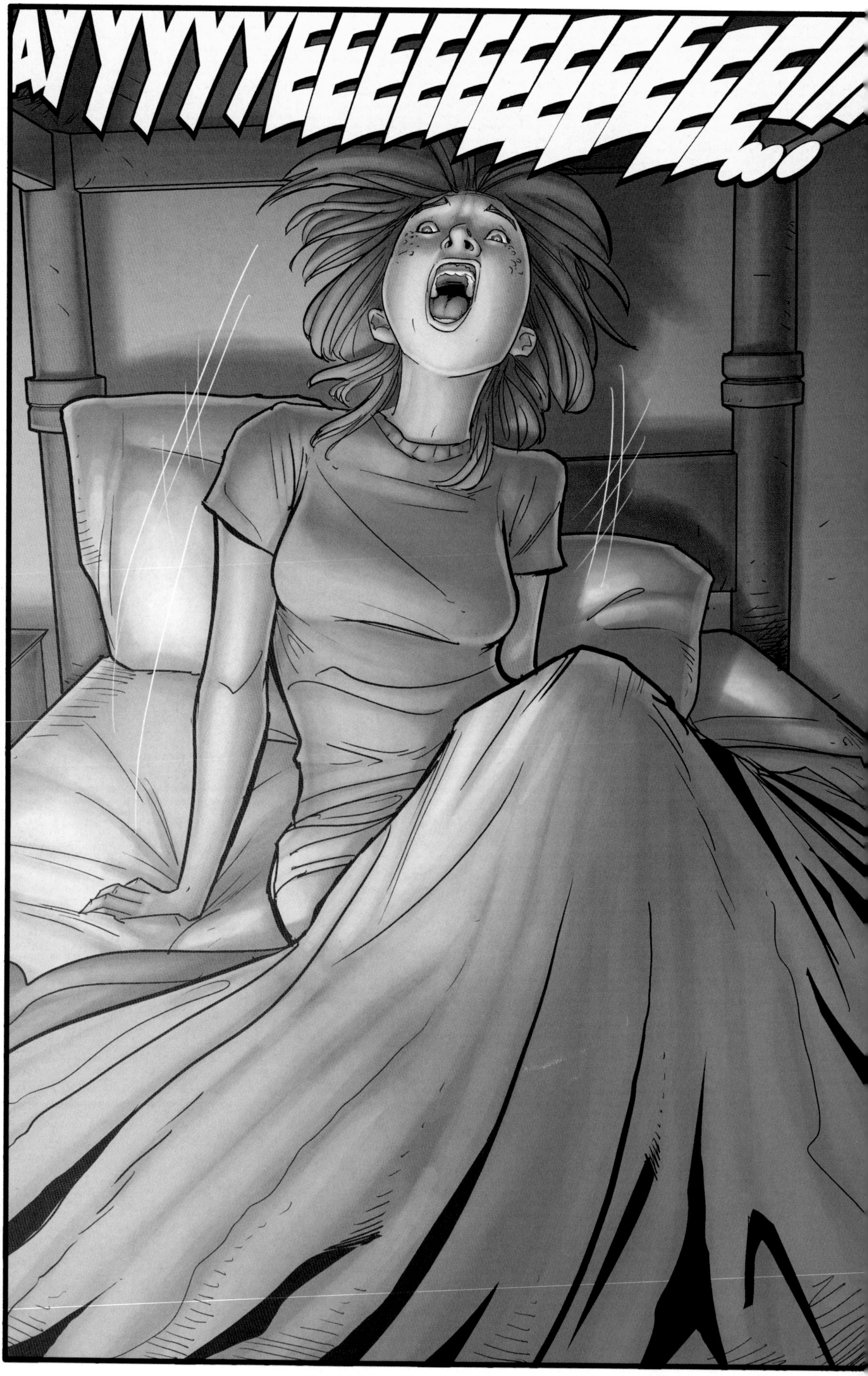
AYYYYEEEEEEEEEEE!!..

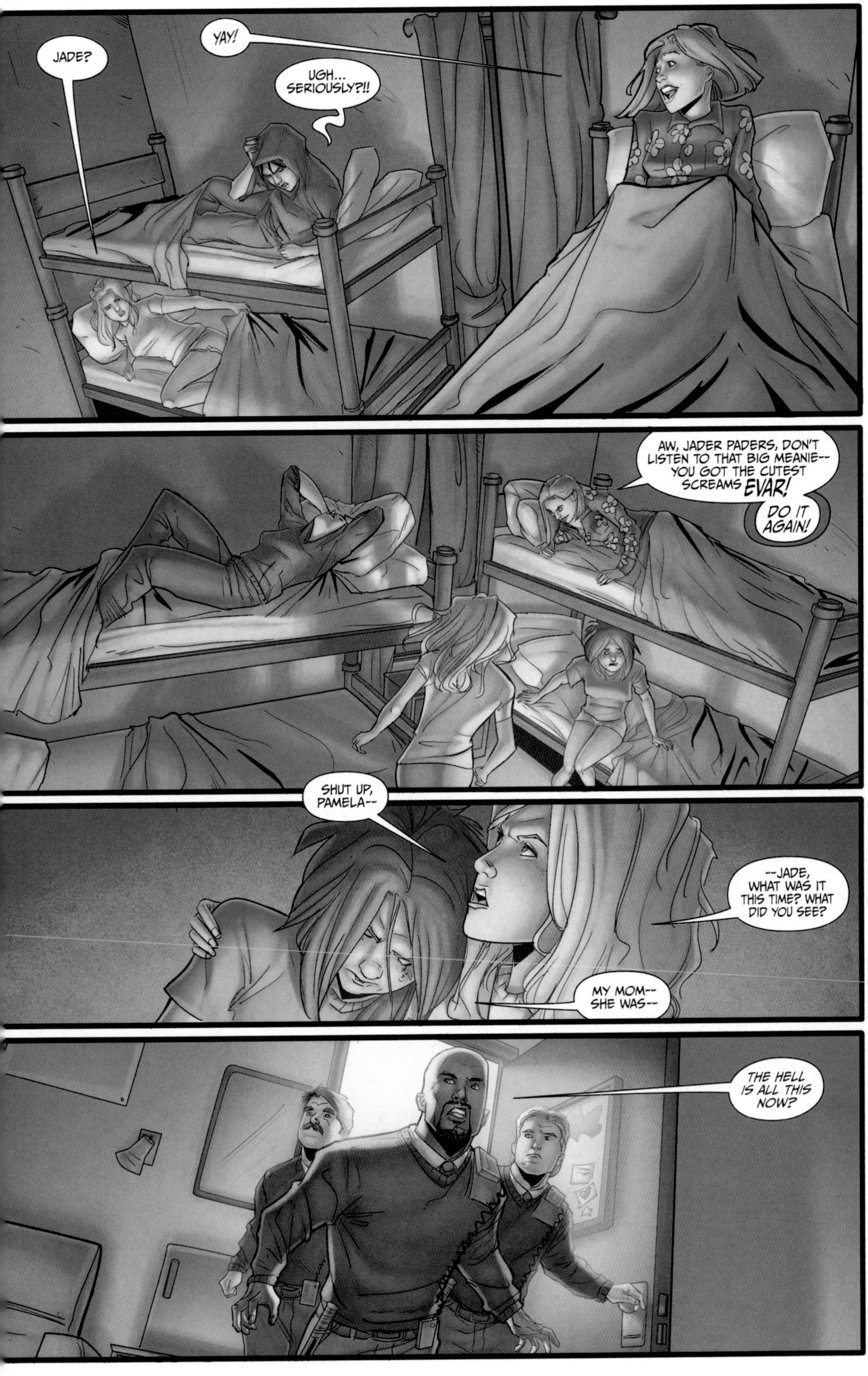
JADE?
YAY!
UGH... SERIOUSLY?!!
AW, JADER PADERS, DON'T LISTEN TO THAT BIG MEANIE-- YOU GOT THE CUTEST SCREAMS EVAR!
DO IT AGAIN!
SHUT UP, PAMELA--
--JADE, WHAT WAS IT THIS TIME? WHAT DID YOU SEE?
MY MOM-- SHE WAS--
THE HELL IS ALL THIS NOW?

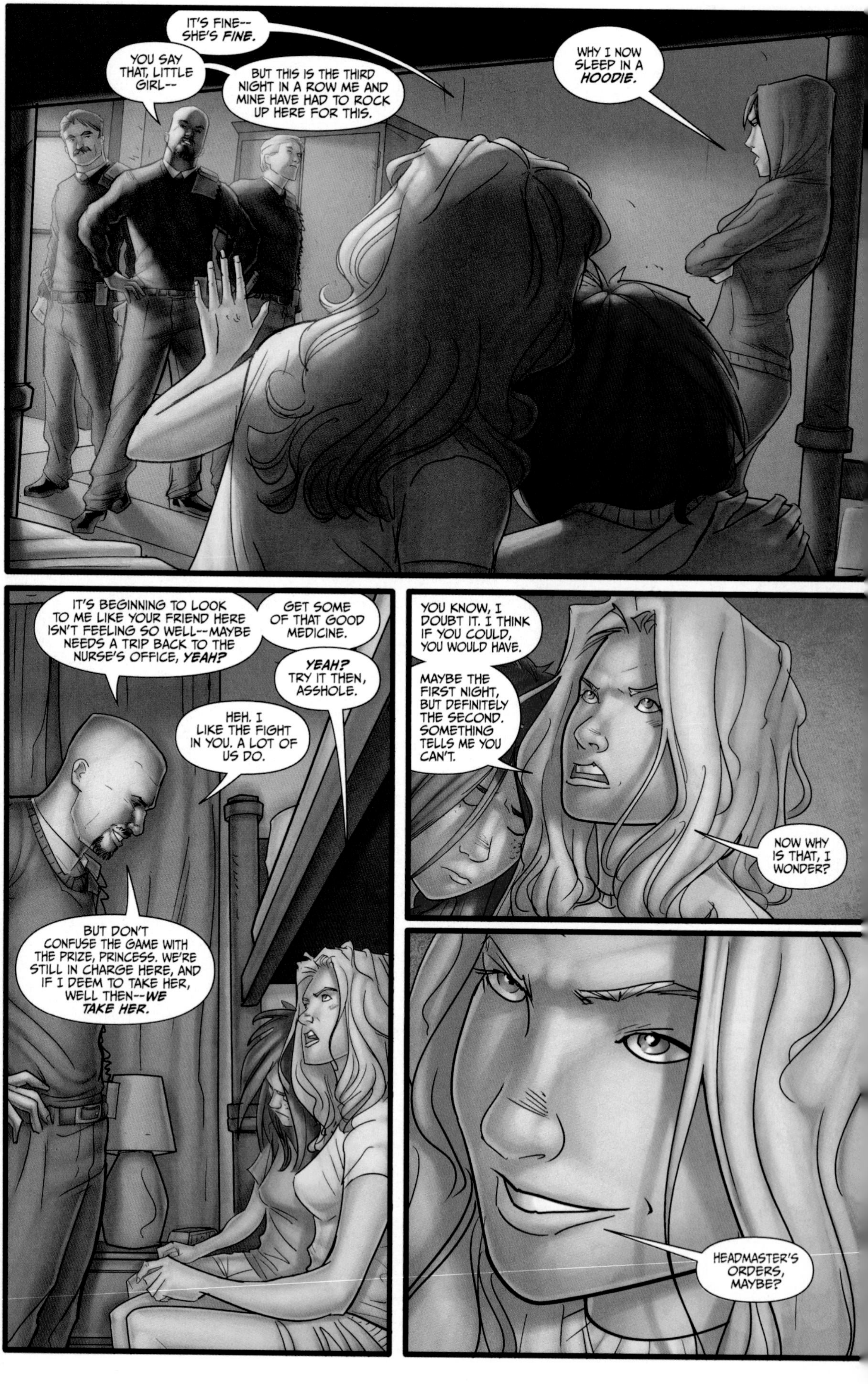
IT'S FINE--
SHE'S *FINE.*
YOU SAY THAT, LITTLE GIRL--
BUT THIS IS THE THIRD NIGHT IN A ROW ME AND MINE HAVE HAD TO ROCK UP HERE FOR THIS.
WHY I NOW SLEEP IN A *HOODIE.*
IT'S BEGINNING TO LOOK TO ME LIKE YOUR FRIEND HERE ISN'T FEELING SO WELL--MAYBE NEEDS A TRIP BACK TO THE NURSE'S OFFICE, *YEAH?*
GET SOME OF THAT GOOD MEDICINE.
YEAH? TRY IT THEN, ASSHOLE.
HEH. I LIKE THE FIGHT IN YOU. A LOT OF US DO.
BUT DON'T CONFUSE THE GAME WITH THE PRIZE, PRINCESS. WE'RE STILL IN CHARGE HERE, AND IF I DEEM TO TAKE HER, WELL THEN--*WE TAKE HER.*
YOU KNOW, I DOUBT IT. I THINK IF YOU COULD, YOU WOULD HAVE.
MAYBE THE FIRST NIGHT, BUT DEFINITELY THE SECOND. SOMETHING TELLS ME YOU CAN'T.
NOW WHY IS THAT, I WONDER?
HEADMASTER'S ORDERS, MAYBE?

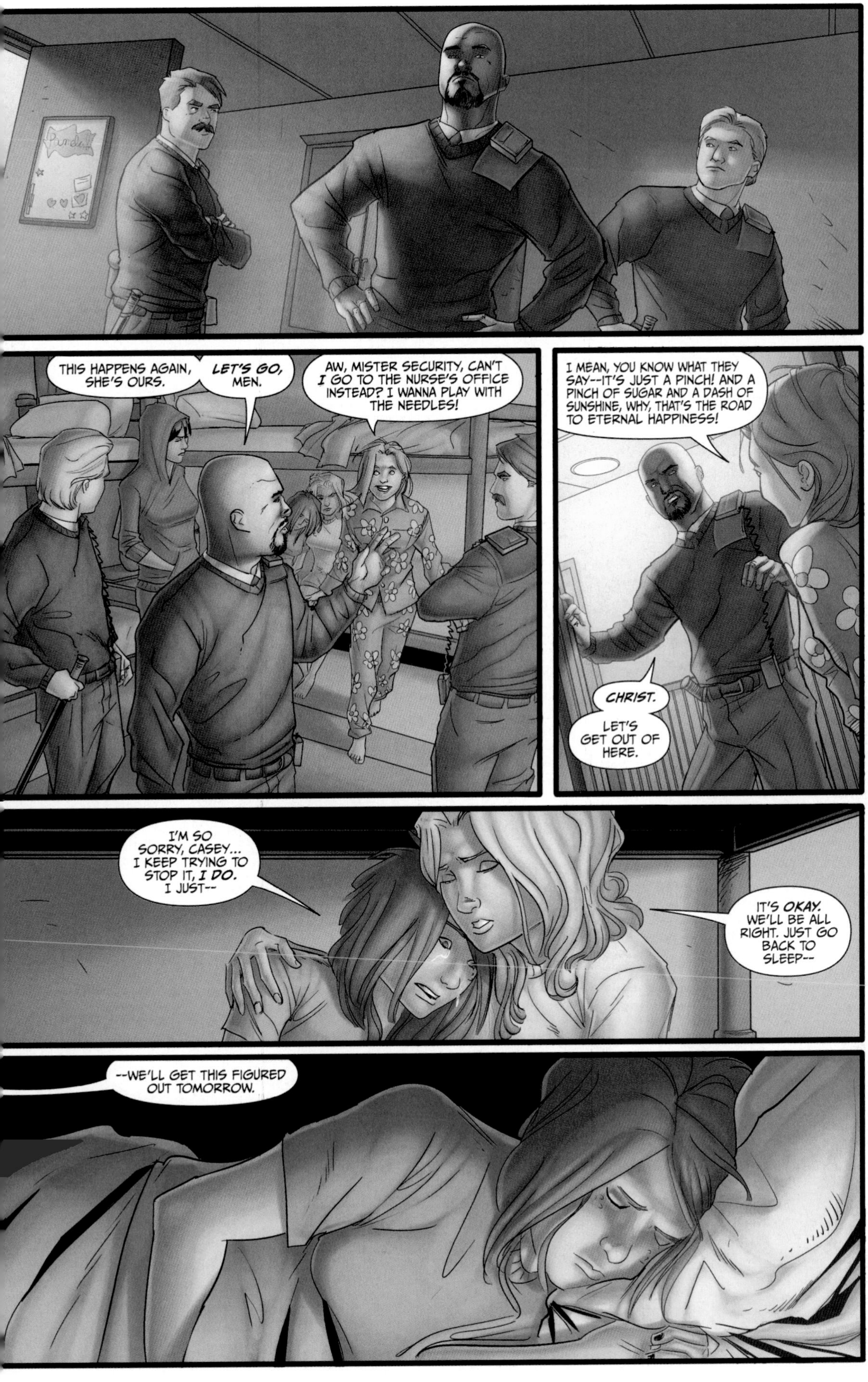

THIS HAPPENS AGAIN, SHE'S OURS.
LET'S GO, MEN.
AW, MISTER SECURITY, CAN'T I GO TO THE NURSE'S OFFICE INSTEAD? I WANNA PLAY WITH THE NEEDLES!
I MEAN, YOU KNOW WHAT THEY SAY--IT'S JUST A PINCH! AND A PINCH OF SUGAR AND A DASH OF SUNSHINE, WHY, THAT'S THE ROAD TO ETERNAL HAPPINESS!
CHRIST.
LET'S GET OUT OF HERE.
I'M SO SORRY, CASEY... I KEEP TRYING TO STOP IT, I DO. I JUST--
IT'S OKAY. WE'LL BE ALL RIGHT. JUST GO BACK TO SLEEP--
--WE'LL GET THIS FIGURED OUT TOMORROW.

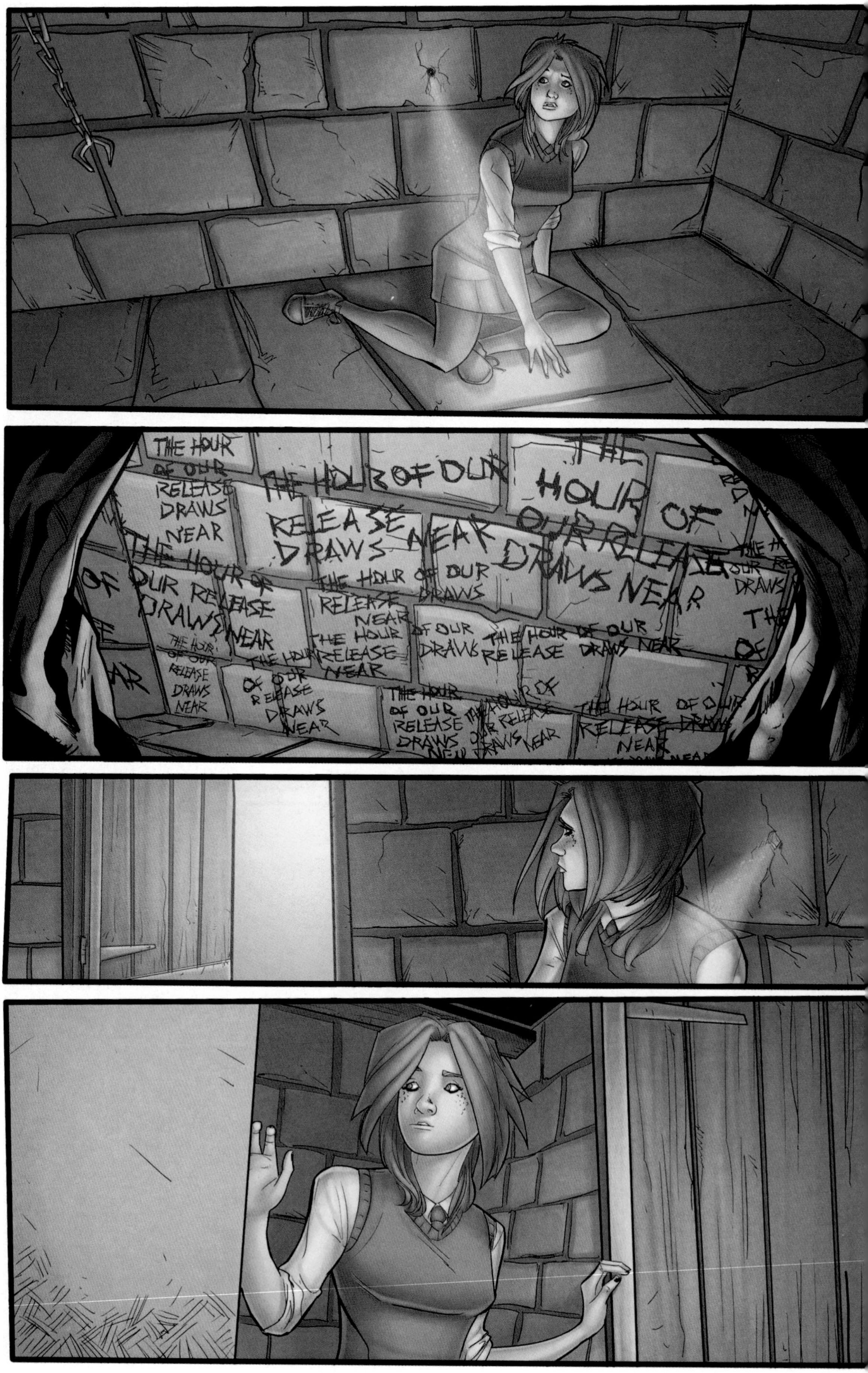
THE HOUR OF OUR RELEASE DRAWS NEAR
THE HOUR OF OUR RELEASE DRAWS NEAR
THE HOUR OF OUR RELEASE DRAWS NEAR
THE HOUR OF OUR RELEASE DRAWS NEAR
THE HOUR OF OUR RELEASE DRAWS NEAR

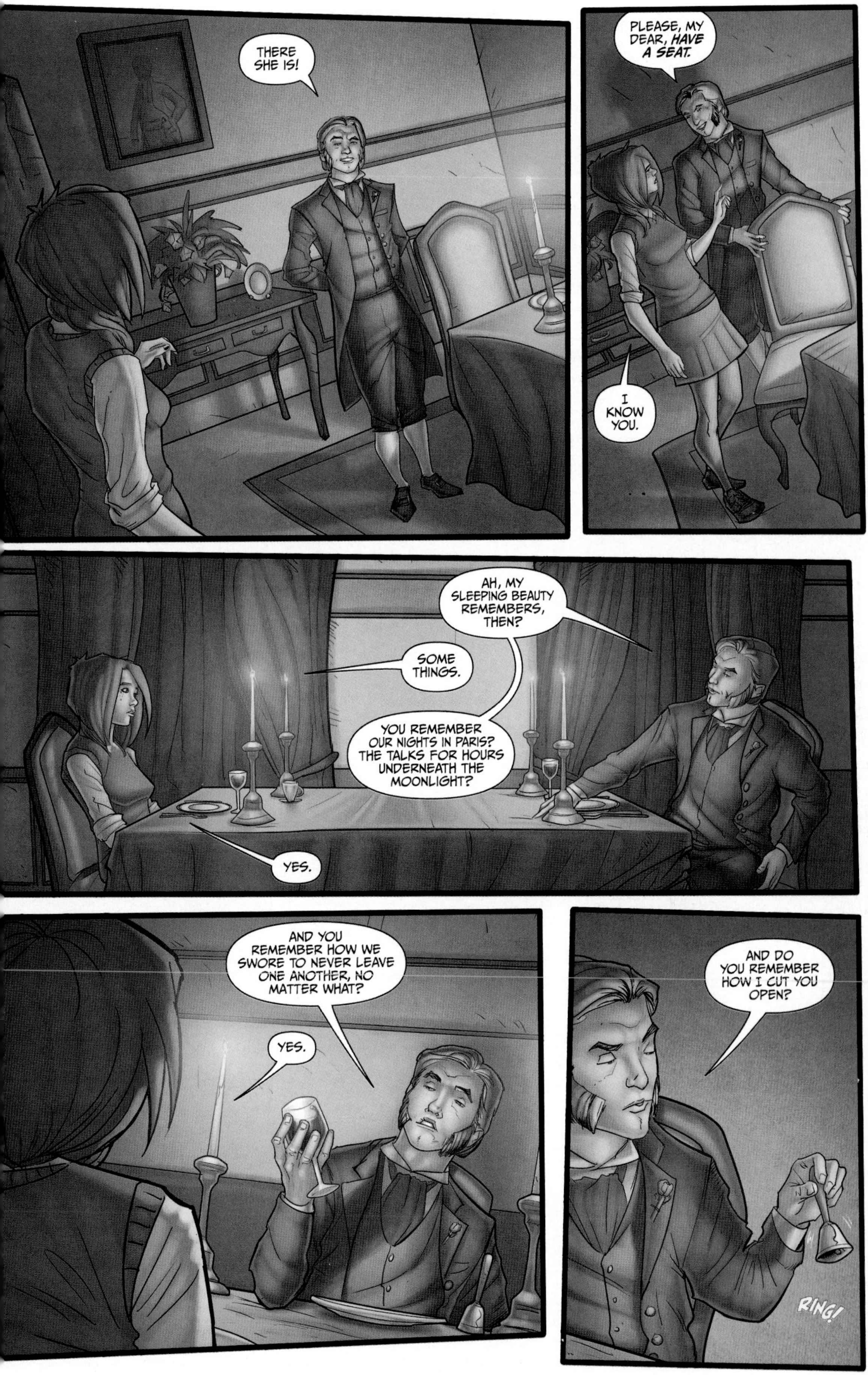
THERE SHE IS!
PLEASE, MY DEAR, **HAVE A SEAT.**
I KNOW YOU.
AH, MY SLEEPING BEAUTY REMEMBERS, THEN?
SOME THINGS.
YOU REMEMBER OUR NIGHTS IN PARIS? THE TALKS FOR HOURS UNDERNEATH THE MOONLIGHT?
YES.
AND YOU REMEMBER HOW WE SWORE TO NEVER LEAVE ONE ANOTHER, NO MATTER WHAT?
YES.
AND DO YOU REMEMBER HOW I CUT YOU OPEN?
RING!

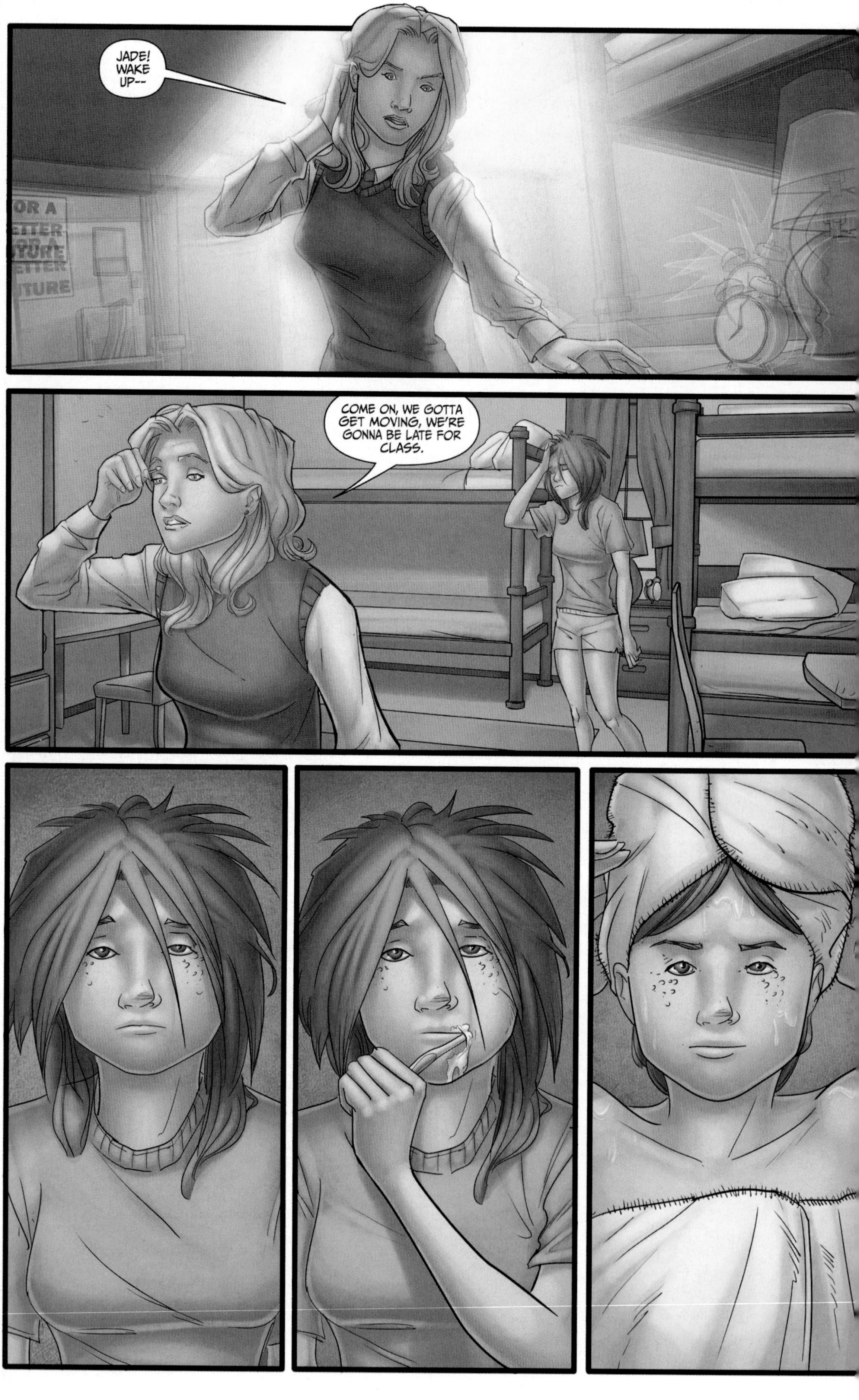
JADE! WAKE UP--
OR A
ETTER
OR A
UTURE
ETTER
UTURE
COME ON, WE GOTTA GET MOVING, WE'RE GONNA BE LATE FOR CLASS.

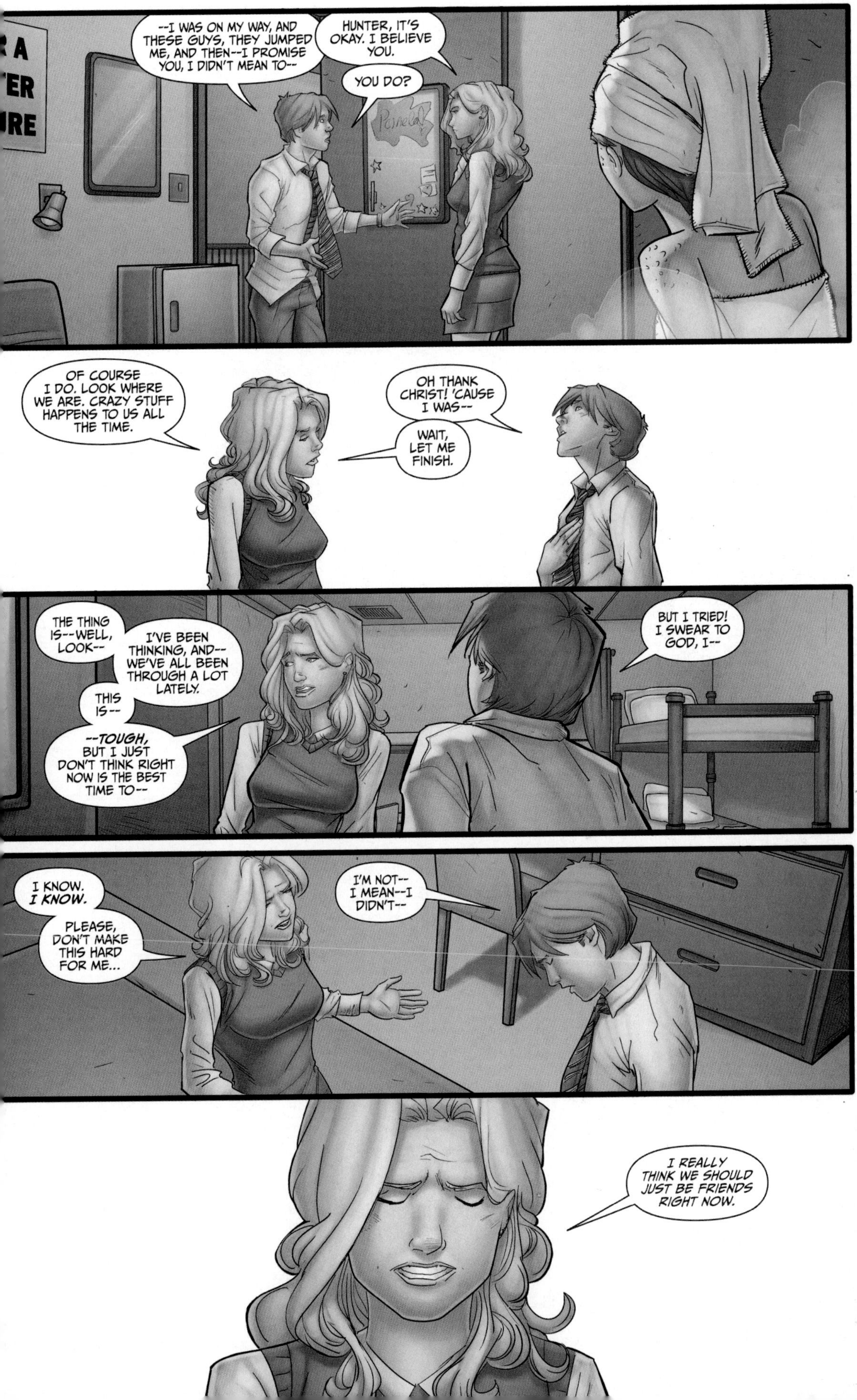

--I WAS ON MY WAY, AND THESE GUYS, THEY JUMPED ME, AND THEN--I PROMISE YOU, I DIDN'T MEAN TO--
HUNTER, IT'S OKAY. I BELIEVE YOU.
YOU DO?
OF COURSE I DO. LOOK WHERE WE ARE. CRAZY STUFF HAPPENS TO US ALL THE TIME.
OH THANK CHRIST! 'CAUSE I WAS--
WAIT, LET ME FINISH.
THE THING IS--WELL, LOOK--
I'VE BEEN THINKING, AND--WE'VE ALL BEEN THROUGH A LOT LATELY.
THIS IS--
--TOUGH, BUT I JUST DON'T THINK RIGHT NOW IS THE BEST TIME TO--
BUT I TRIED! I SWEAR TO GOD, I--
I KNOW. *I KNOW.*
PLEASE, DON'T MAKE THIS HARD FOR ME...
I'M NOT--I MEAN--I DIDN'T--
I REALLY THINK WE SHOULD JUST BE FRIENDS RIGHT NOW.

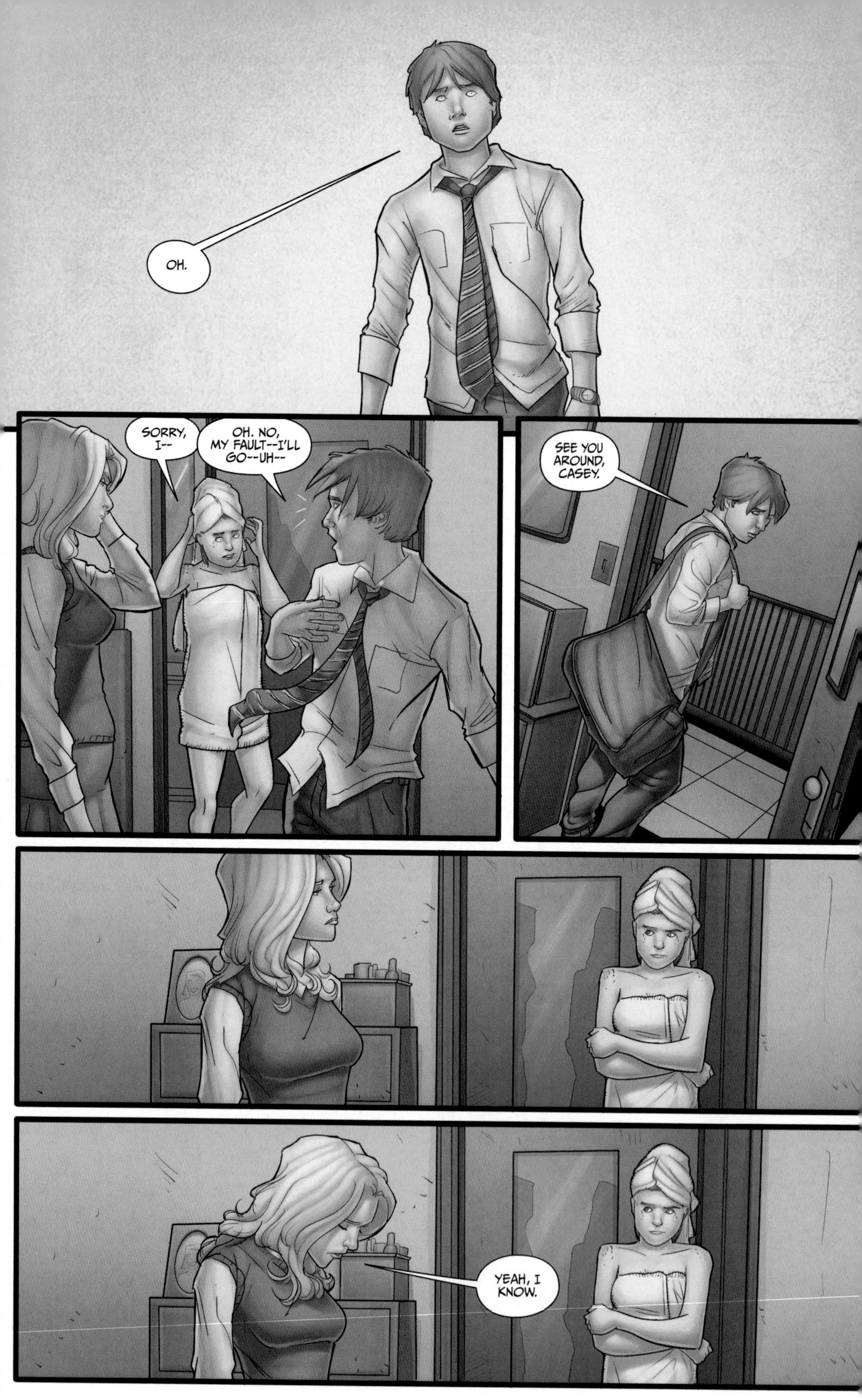
OH.
SORRY, I--
OH. NO, MY FAULT--I'LL GO--UH--
SEE YOU AROUND, CASEY.
YEAH, I KNOW.

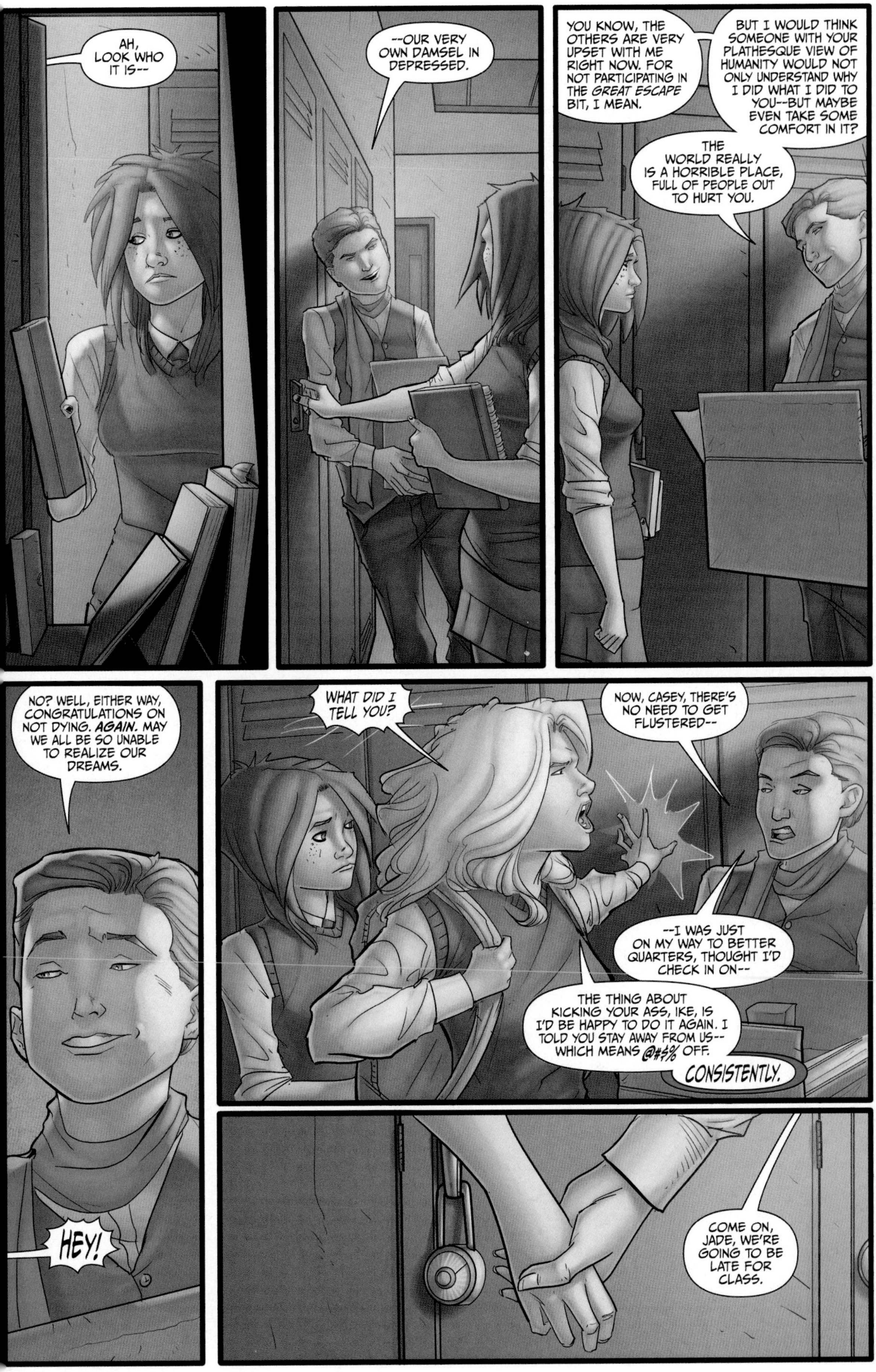
AH, LOOK WHO IT IS--
--OUR VERY OWN DAMSEL IN DEPRESSED.
YOU KNOW, THE OTHERS ARE VERY UPSET WITH ME RIGHT NOW. FOR NOT PARTICIPATING IN THE *GREAT ESCAPE* BIT, I MEAN.
BUT I WOULD THINK SOMEONE WITH YOUR PLATHESQUE VIEW OF HUMANITY WOULD NOT ONLY UNDERSTAND WHY I DID WHAT I DID TO YOU--BUT MAYBE EVEN TAKE SOME COMFORT IN IT?
THE WORLD REALLY IS A HORRIBLE PLACE, FULL OF PEOPLE OUT TO HURT YOU.
NO? WELL, EITHER WAY, CONGRATULATIONS ON NOT DYING. **AGAIN.** MAY WE ALL BE SO UNABLE TO REALIZE OUR DREAMS.
HEY!
WHAT DID I TELL YOU?
NOW, CASEY, THERE'S NO NEED TO GET FLUSTERED--
--I WAS JUST ON MY WAY TO BETTER QUARTERS, THOUGHT I'D CHECK IN ON--
THE THING ABOUT KICKING YOUR ASS, IKE, IS I'D BE HAPPY TO DO IT AGAIN. I TOLD YOU STAY AWAY FROM US--WHICH MEANS @#$% OFF.
CONSISTENTLY.
COME ON, JADE, WE'RE GOING TO BE LATE FOR CLASS.

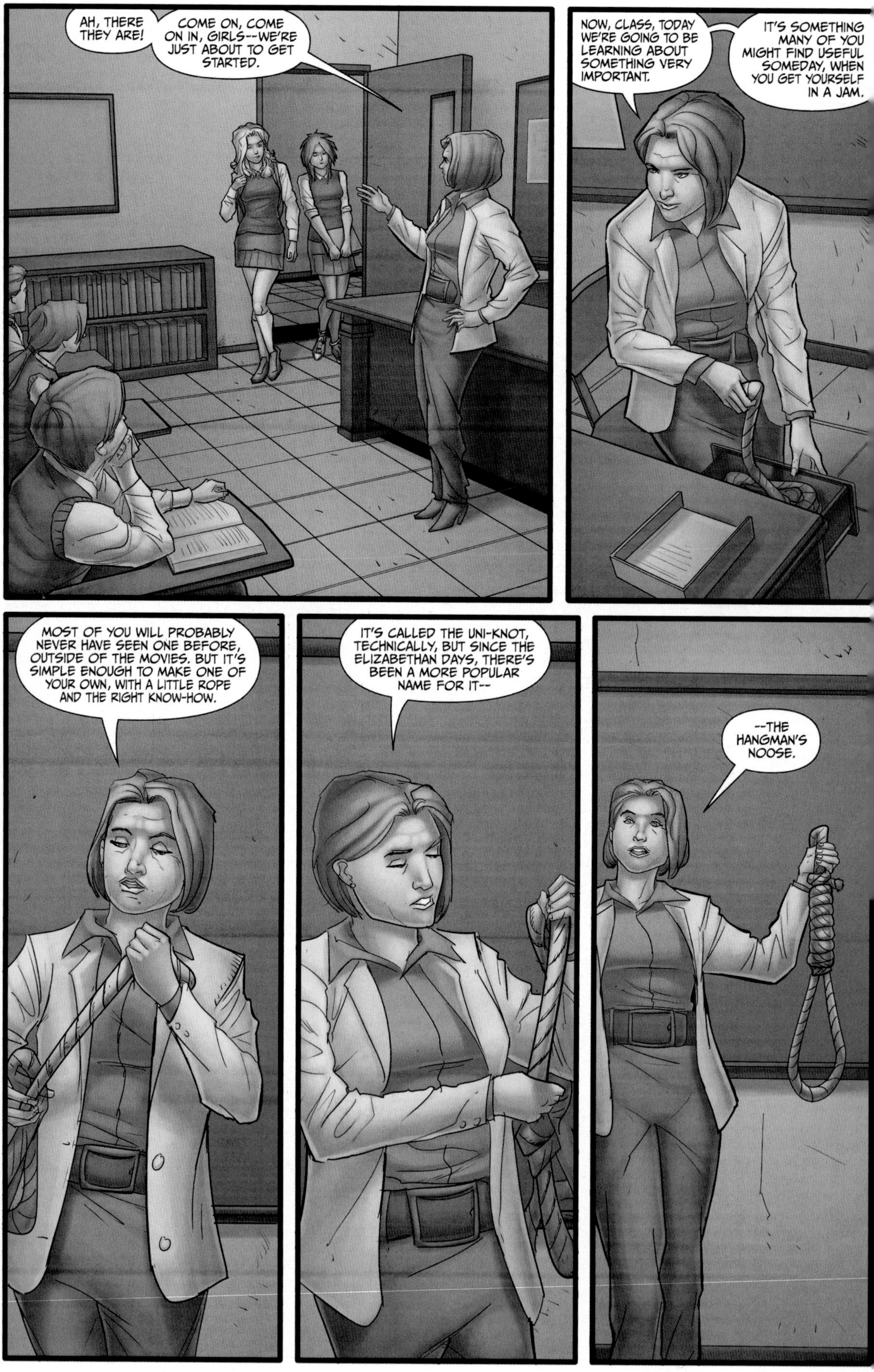

AH, THERE THEY ARE!
COME ON, COME ON IN, GIRLS--WE'RE JUST ABOUT TO GET STARTED.
NOW, CLASS, TODAY WE'RE GOING TO BE LEARNING ABOUT SOMETHING VERY IMPORTANT.
IT'S SOMETHING MANY OF YOU MIGHT FIND USEFUL SOMEDAY, WHEN YOU GET YOURSELF IN A JAM.
MOST OF YOU WILL PROBABLY NEVER HAVE SEEN ONE BEFORE, OUTSIDE OF THE MOVIES. BUT IT'S SIMPLE ENOUGH TO MAKE ONE OF YOUR OWN, WITH A LITTLE ROPE AND THE RIGHT KNOW-HOW.
IT'S CALLED THE UNI-KNOT, TECHNICALLY, BUT SINCE THE ELIZABETHAN DAYS, THERE'S BEEN A MORE POPULAR NAME FOR IT--
--THE HANGMAN'S NOOSE.

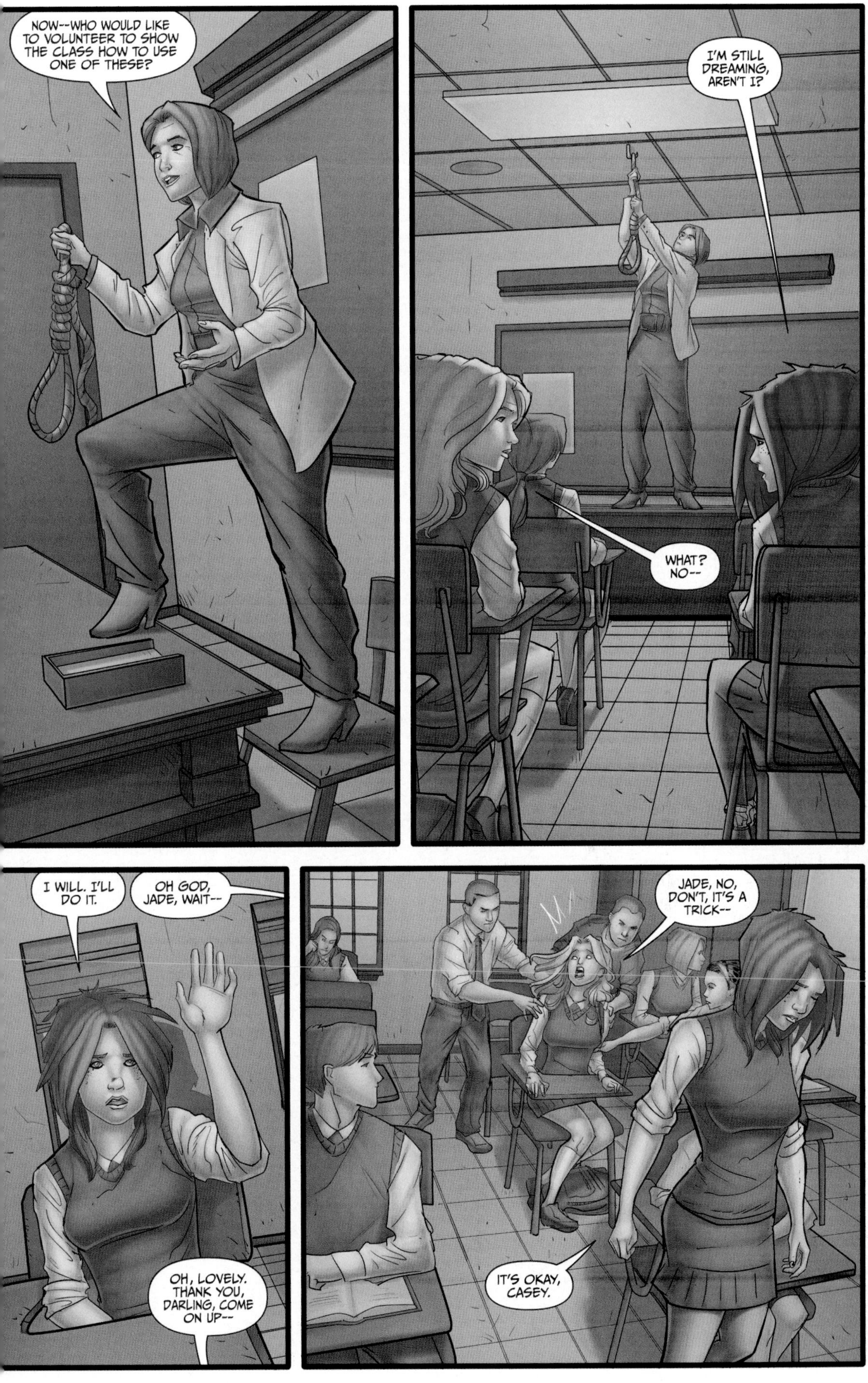
NOW--WHO WOULD LIKE TO VOLUNTEER TO SHOW THE CLASS HOW TO USE ONE OF THESE?
I'M STILL DREAMING, AREN'T I?
WHAT? NO--
I WILL. I'LL DO IT.
OH GOD, JADE, WAIT--
OH, LOVELY. THANK YOU, DARLING, COME ON UP--
JADE, NO, DON'T, IT'S A TRICK--
IT'S OKAY, CASEY.

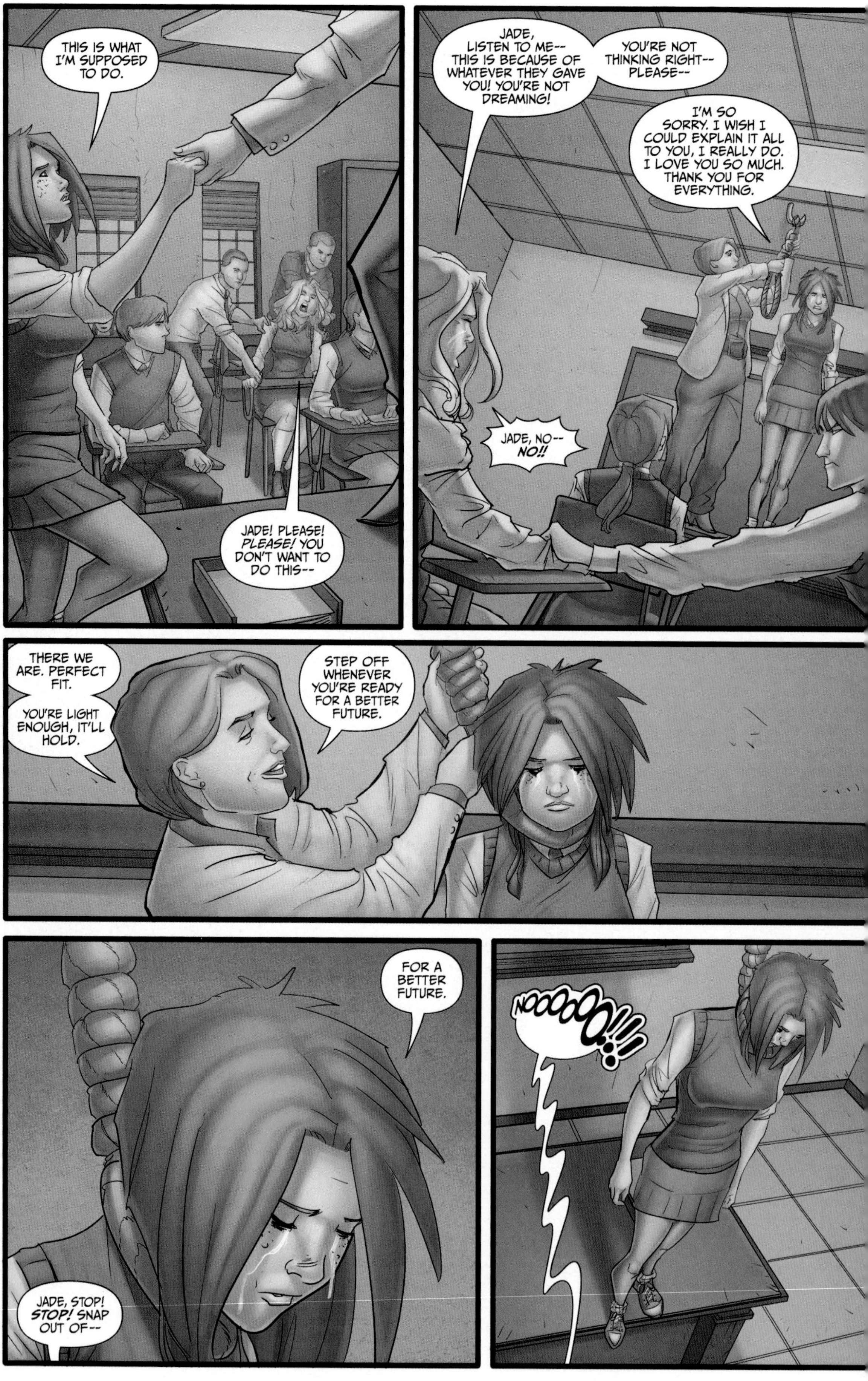
THIS IS WHAT I'M SUPPOSED TO DO.
JADE! PLEASE! PLEASE! YOU DON'T WANT TO DO THIS--
JADE, LISTEN TO ME-- THIS IS BECAUSE OF WHATEVER THEY GAVE YOU! YOU'RE NOT DREAMING!
YOU'RE NOT THINKING RIGHT-- PLEASE--
I'M SO SORRY. I WISH I COULD EXPLAIN IT ALL TO YOU, I REALLY DO. I LOVE YOU SO MUCH. THANK YOU FOR EVERYTHING.
JADE, NO-- NO!!
THERE WE ARE. PERFECT FIT.
YOU'RE LIGHT ENOUGH, IT'LL HOLD.
STEP OFF WHENEVER YOU'RE READY FOR A BETTER FUTURE.
FOR A BETTER FUTURE.
JADE, STOP! STOP! SNAP OUT OF--
NOOOOOO!!!

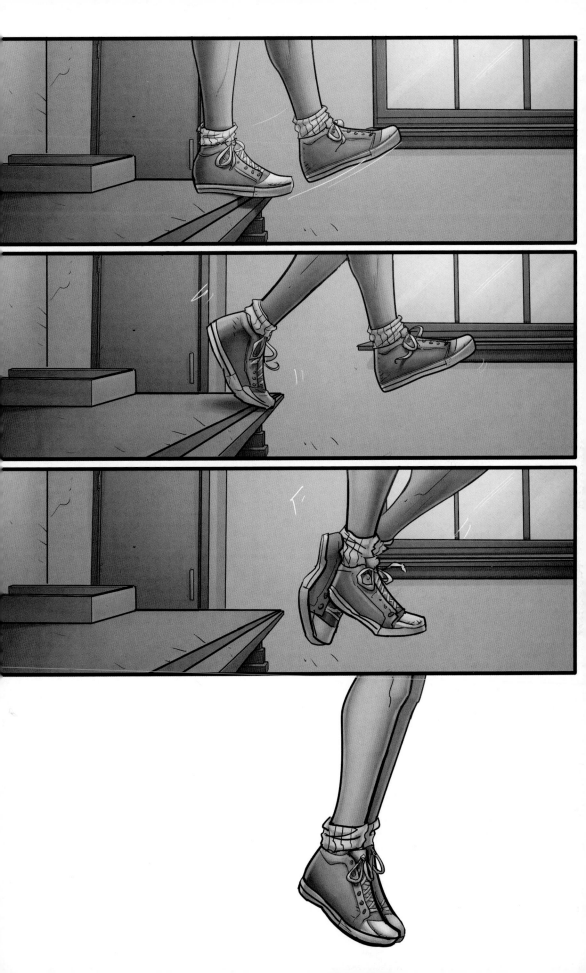

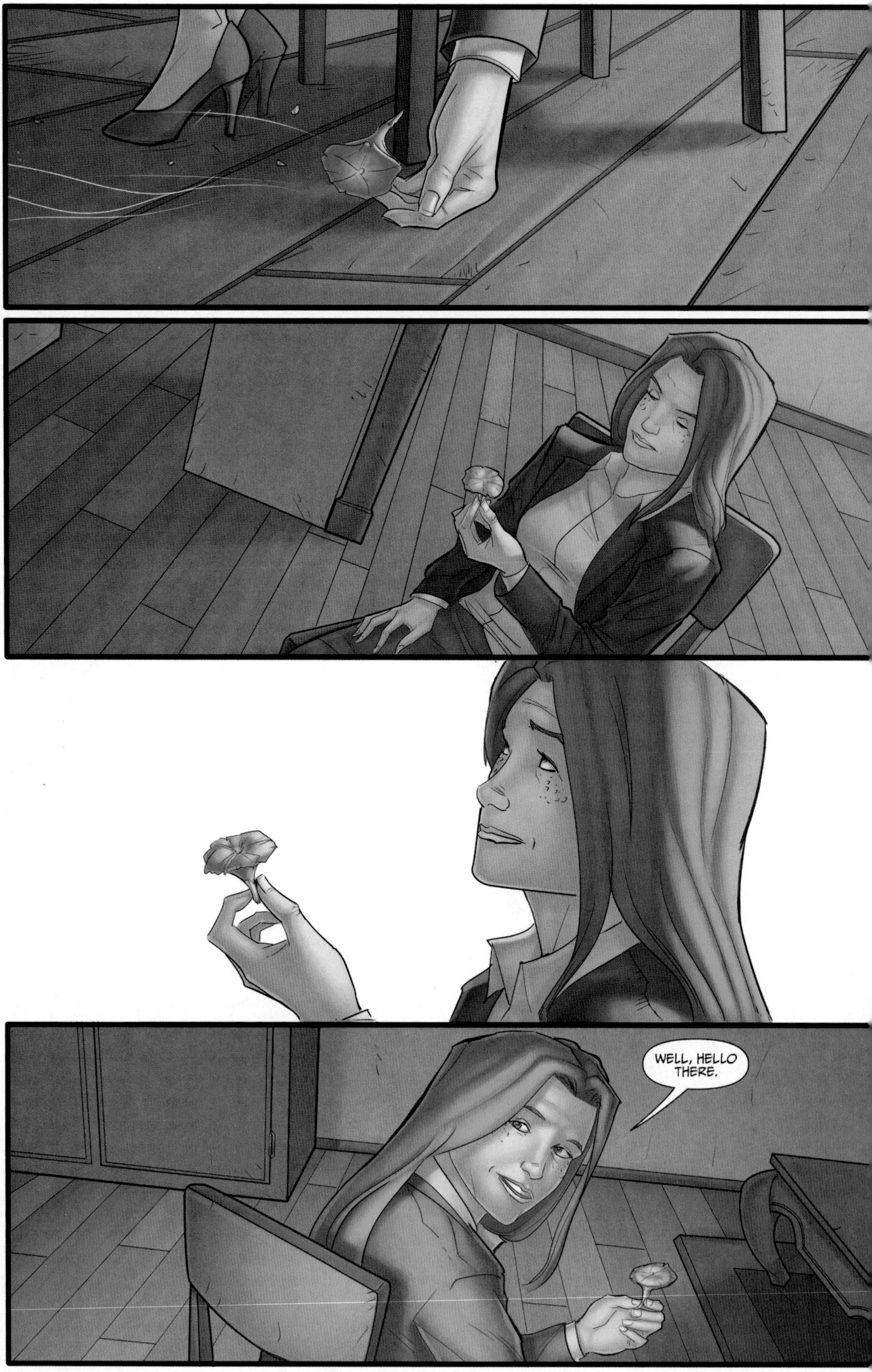
WELL, HELLO THERE.

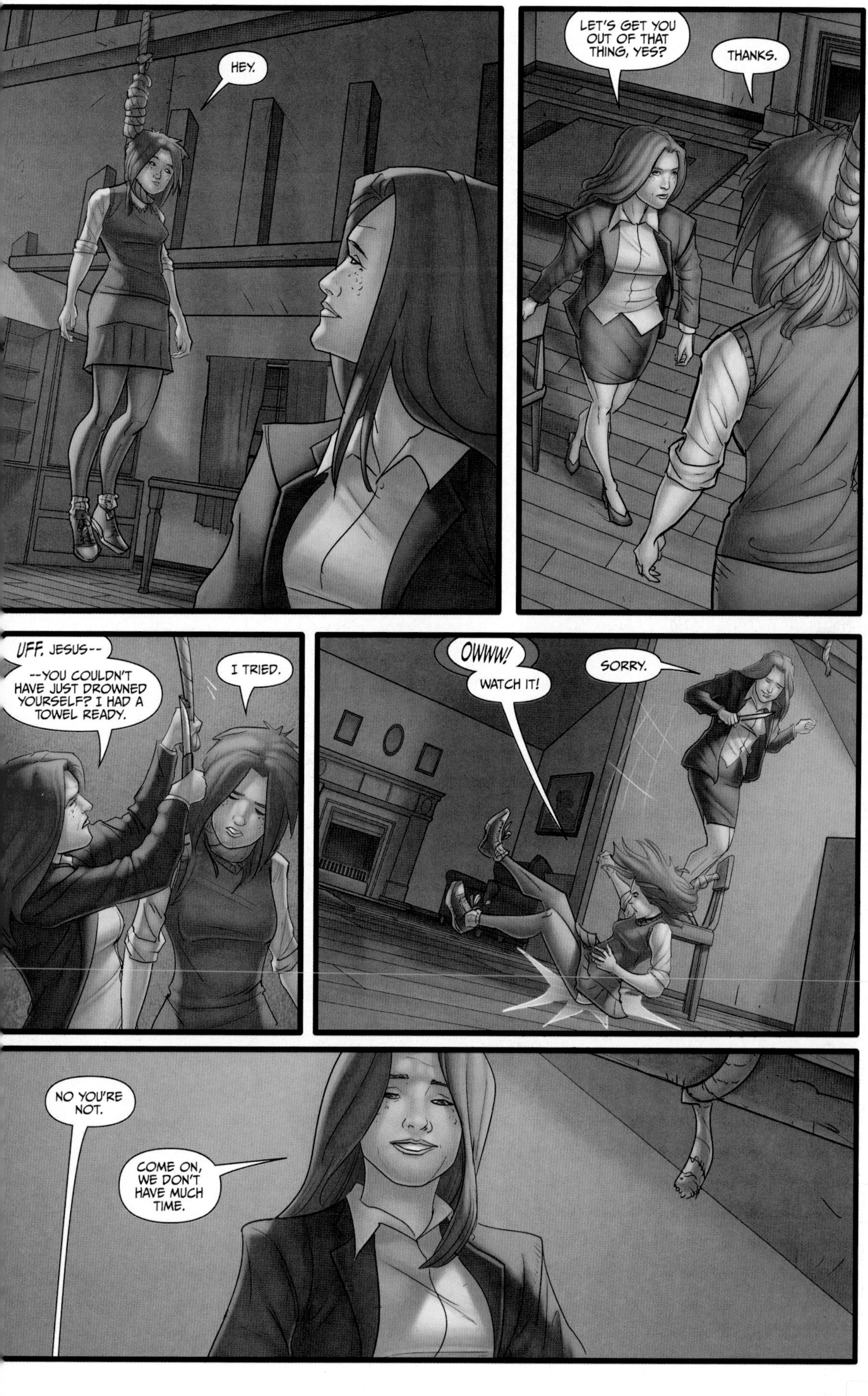
HEY.
LET'S GET YOU OUT OF THAT THING, YES?
THANKS.
UFF. JESUS--
--YOU COULDN'T HAVE JUST DROWNED YOURSELF? I HAD A TOWEL READY.
I TRIED.
OWWW!
WATCH IT!
SORRY.
NO YOU'RE NOT.
COME ON, WE DON'T HAVE MUCH TIME.

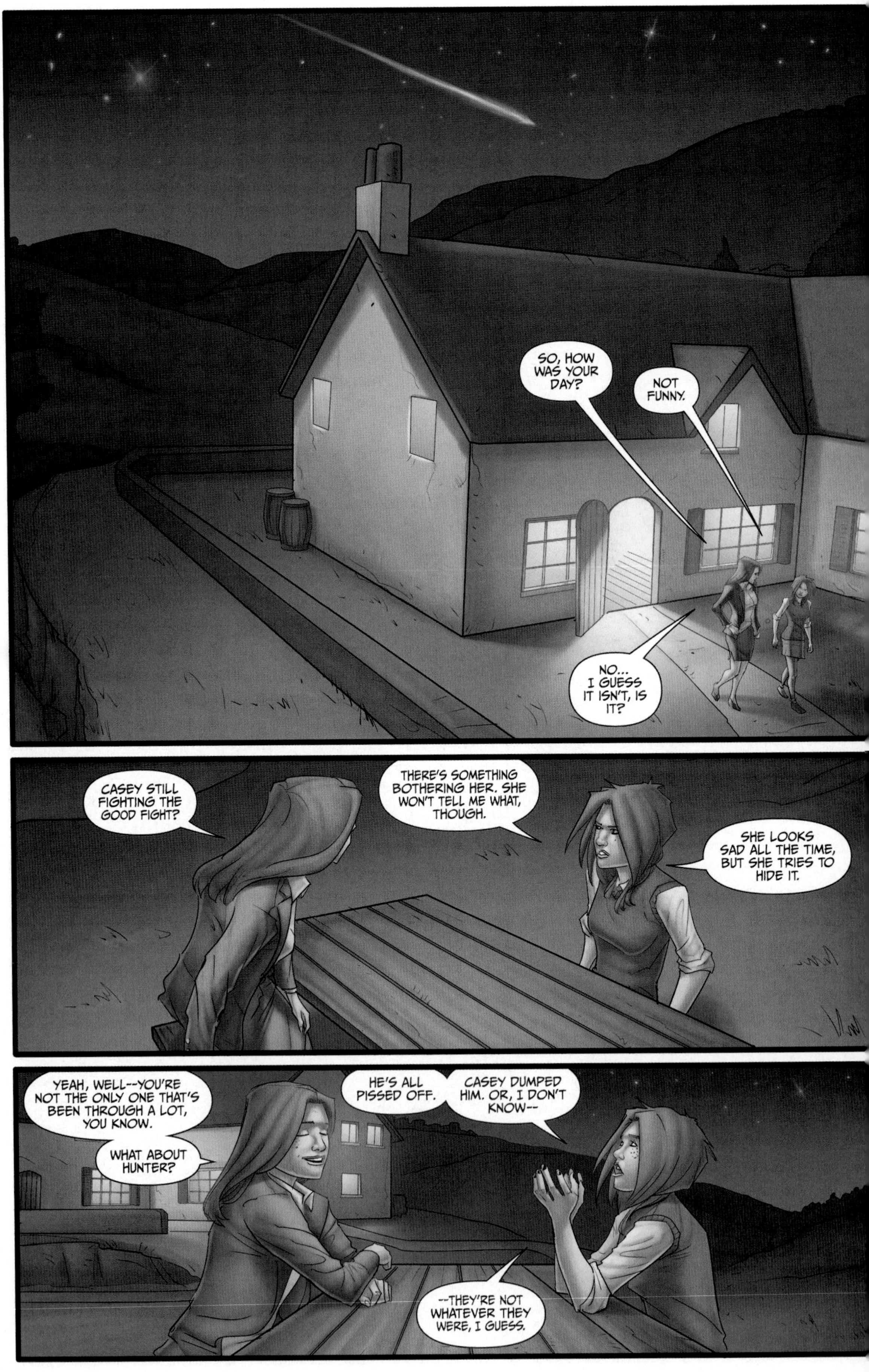
SO, HOW WAS YOUR DAY?
NOT FUNNY.
NO... I GUESS IT ISN'T, IS IT?
CASEY STILL FIGHTING THE GOOD FIGHT?
THERE'S SOMETHING BOTHERING HER. SHE WON'T TELL ME WHAT, THOUGH.
SHE LOOKS SAD ALL THE TIME, BUT SHE TRIES TO HIDE IT.
YEAH, WELL--YOU'RE NOT THE ONLY ONE THAT'S BEEN THROUGH A LOT, YOU KNOW.
WHAT ABOUT HUNTER?
HE'S ALL PISSED OFF.
CASEY DUMPED HIM. OR, I DON'T KNOW--
--THEY'RE NOT WHATEVER THEY WERE, I GUESS.

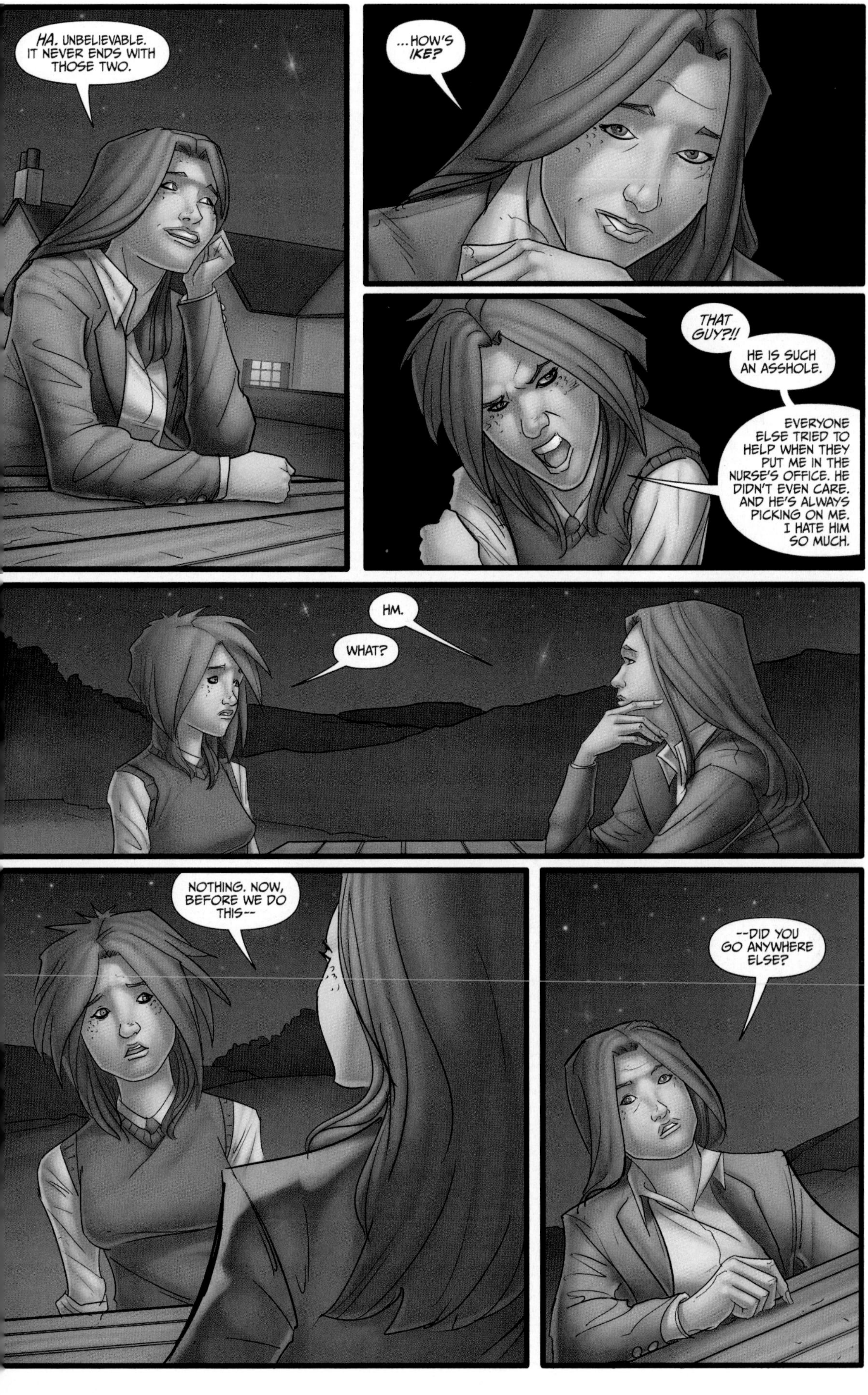
HA. UNBELIEVABLE. IT NEVER ENDS WITH THOSE TWO.
...HOW'S IKE?
THAT GUY?!!
HE IS SUCH AN ASSHOLE.
EVERYONE ELSE TRIED TO HELP WHEN THEY PUT ME IN THE NURSE'S OFFICE. HE DIDN'T EVEN CARE. AND HE'S ALWAYS PICKING ON ME. I HATE HIM SO MUCH.
HM.
WHAT?
NOTHING. NOW, BEFORE WE DO THIS--
--DID YOU GO ANYWHERE ELSE?

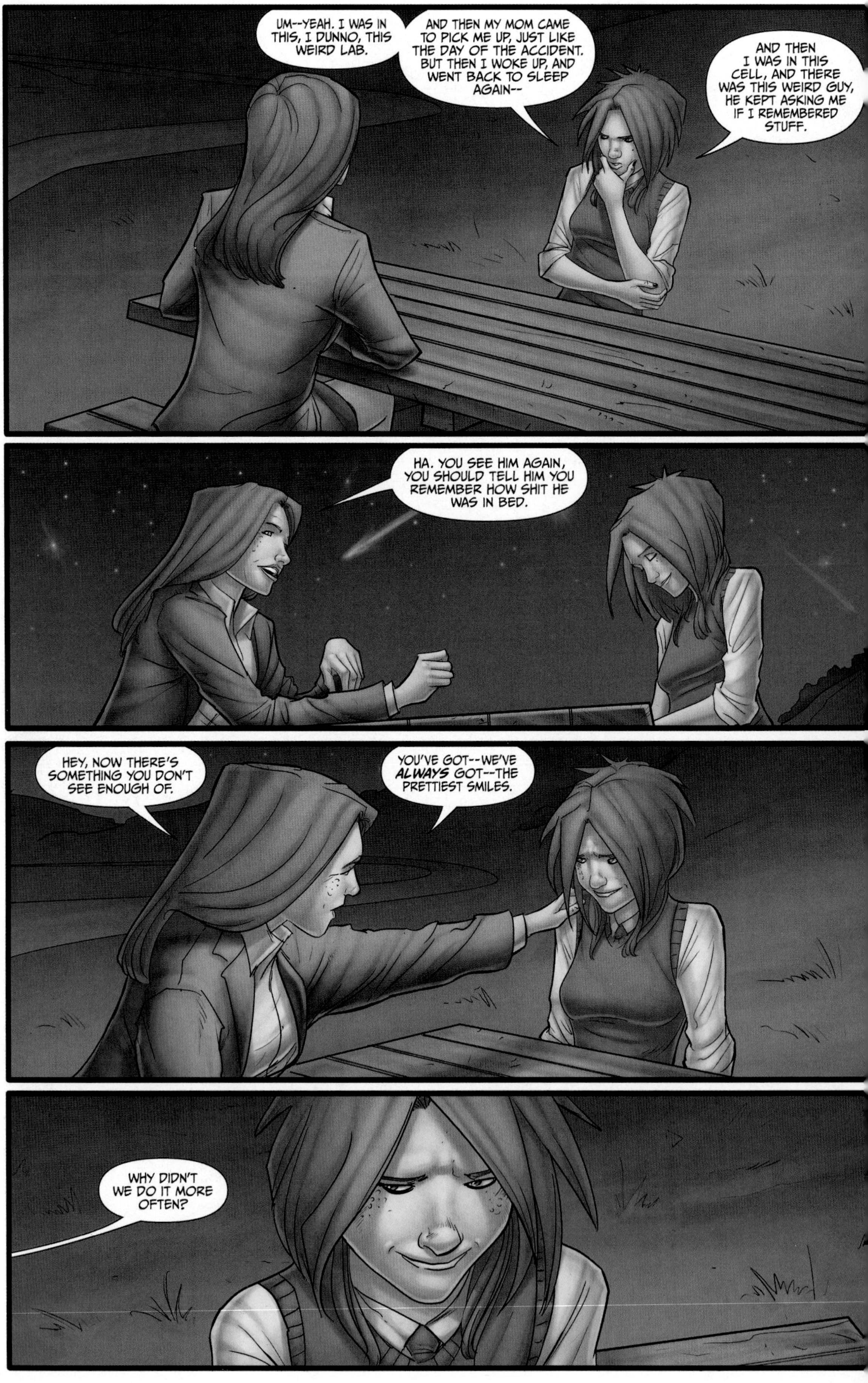
UM--YEAH. I WAS IN THIS, I DUNNO, THIS WEIRD LAB.
AND THEN MY MOM CAME TO PICK ME UP, JUST LIKE THE DAY OF THE ACCIDENT. BUT THEN I WOKE UP, AND WENT BACK TO SLEEP AGAIN--
AND THEN I WAS IN THIS CELL, AND THERE WAS THIS WEIRD GUY, HE KEPT ASKING ME IF I REMEMBERED STUFF.
HA. YOU SEE HIM AGAIN, YOU SHOULD TELL HIM YOU REMEMBER HOW SHIT HE WAS IN BED.
HEY, NOW THERE'S SOMETHING YOU DON'T SEE ENOUGH OF.
YOU'VE GOT--WE'VE ALWAYS GOT--THE PRETTIEST SMILES.
WHY DIDN'T WE DO IT MORE OFTEN?

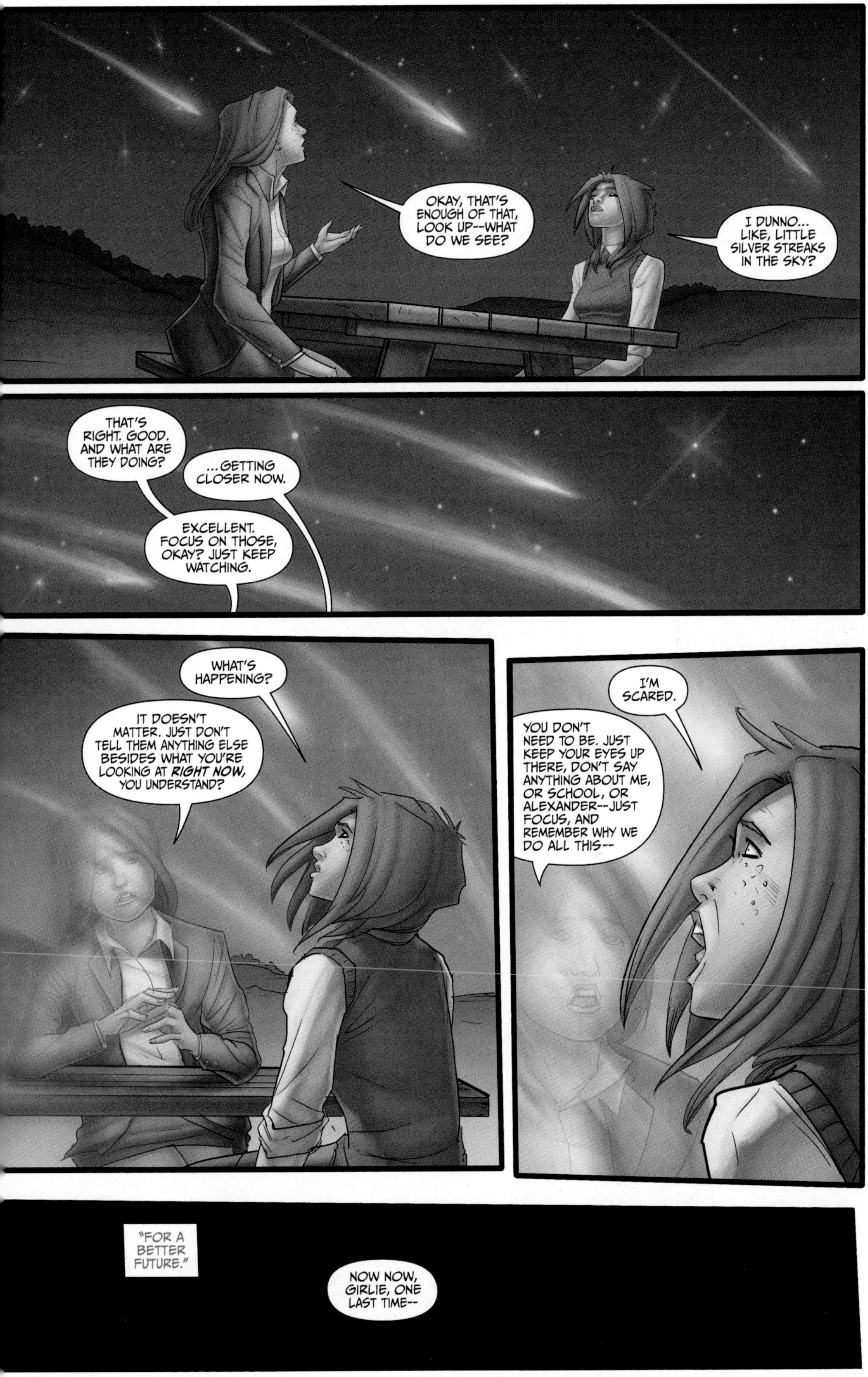

OKAY, THAT'S ENOUGH OF THAT, LOOK UP--WHAT DO WE SEE?
I DUNNO... LIKE, LITTLE SILVER STREAKS IN THE SKY?
THAT'S RIGHT. GOOD. AND WHAT ARE THEY DOING?
...GETTING CLOSER NOW.
EXCELLENT. FOCUS ON THOSE, OKAY? JUST KEEP WATCHING.
WHAT'S HAPPENING?
IT DOESN'T MATTER. JUST DON'T TELL THEM ANYTHING ELSE BESIDES WHAT YOU'RE LOOKING AT *RIGHT NOW,* YOU UNDERSTAND?
I'M SCARED.
YOU DON'T NEED TO BE. JUST KEEP YOUR EYES UP THERE, DON'T SAY ANYTHING ABOUT ME, OR SCHOOL, OR ALEXANDER--JUST FOCUS, AND REMEMBER WHY WE DO ALL THIS--
"FOR A BETTER FUTURE."
NOW NOW, GIRLIE, ONE LAST TIME--

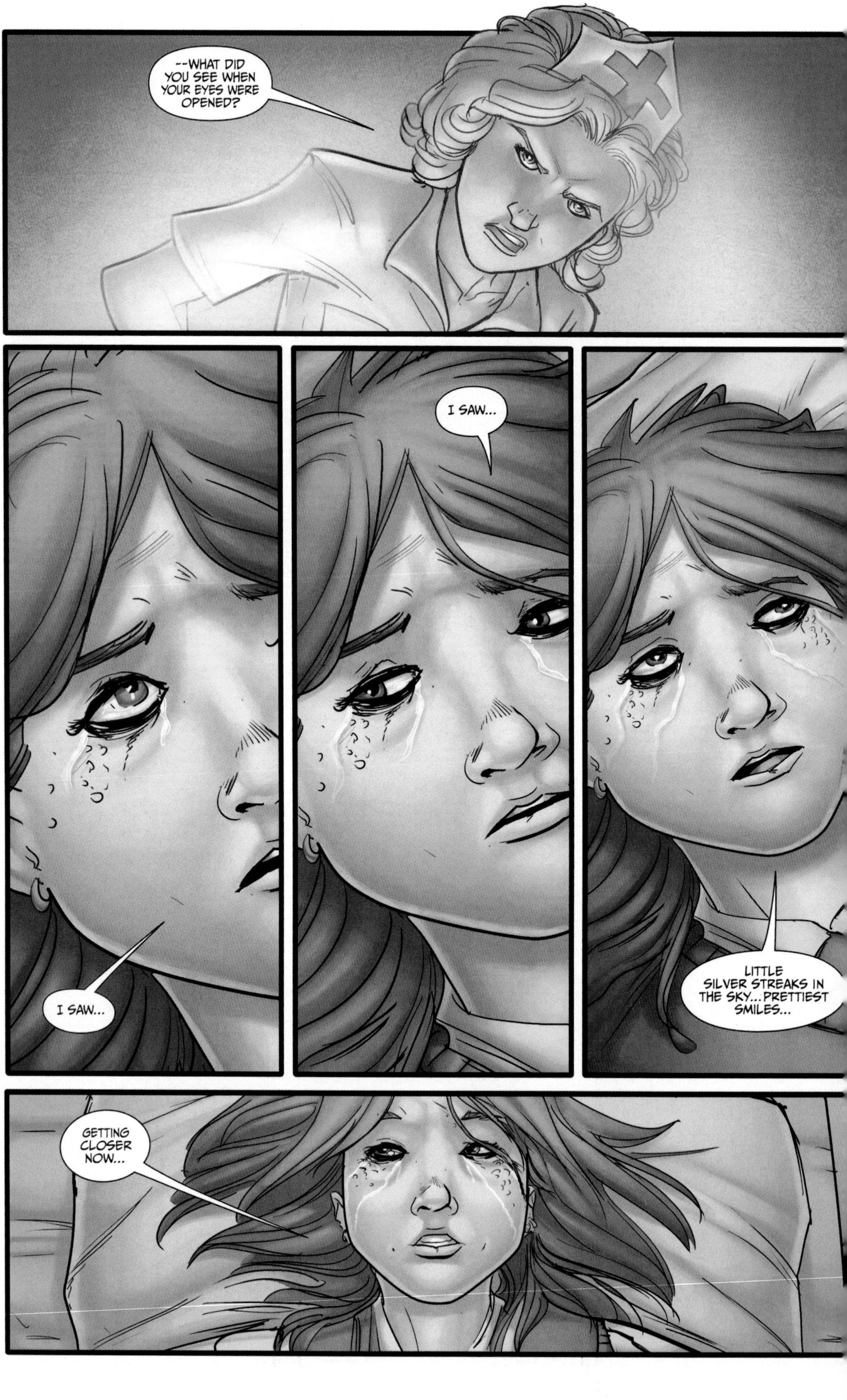
--WHAT DID YOU SEE WHEN YOUR EYES WERE OPENED?
I SAW...
I SAW...
LITTLE SILVER STREAKS IN THE SKY...PRETTIEST SMILES...
GETTING CLOSER NOW...

eleven

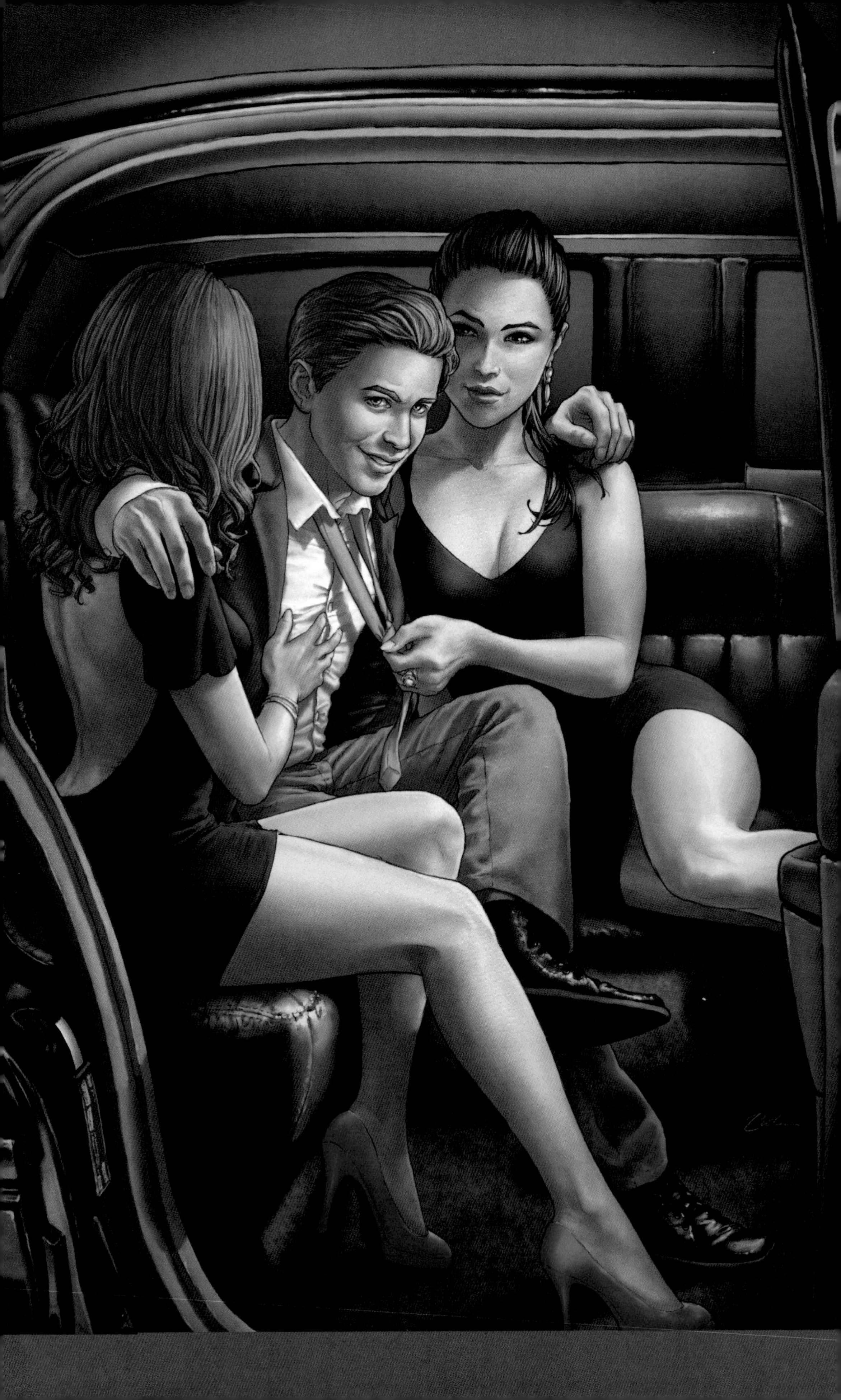

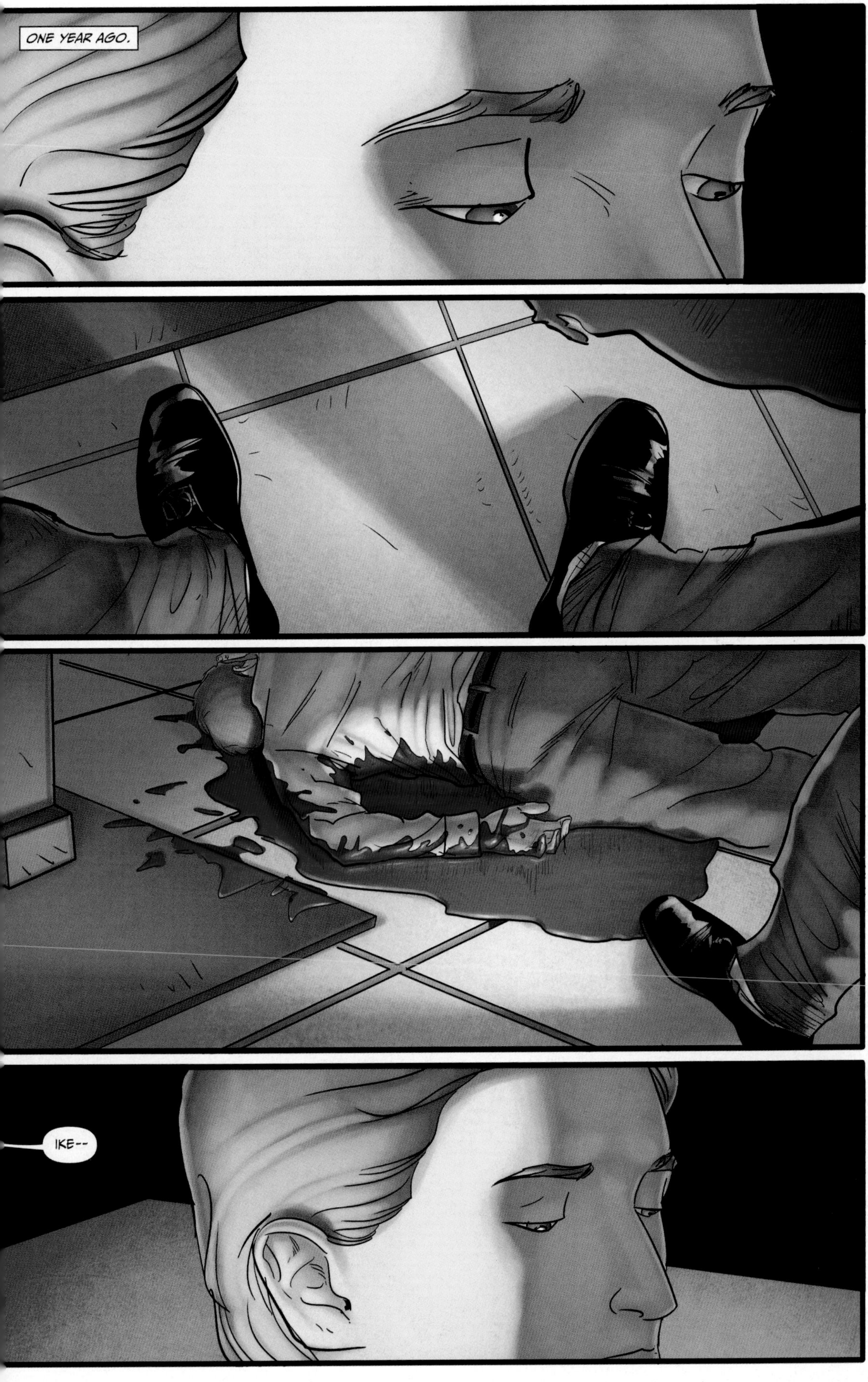
ONE YEAR AGO.
IKE--

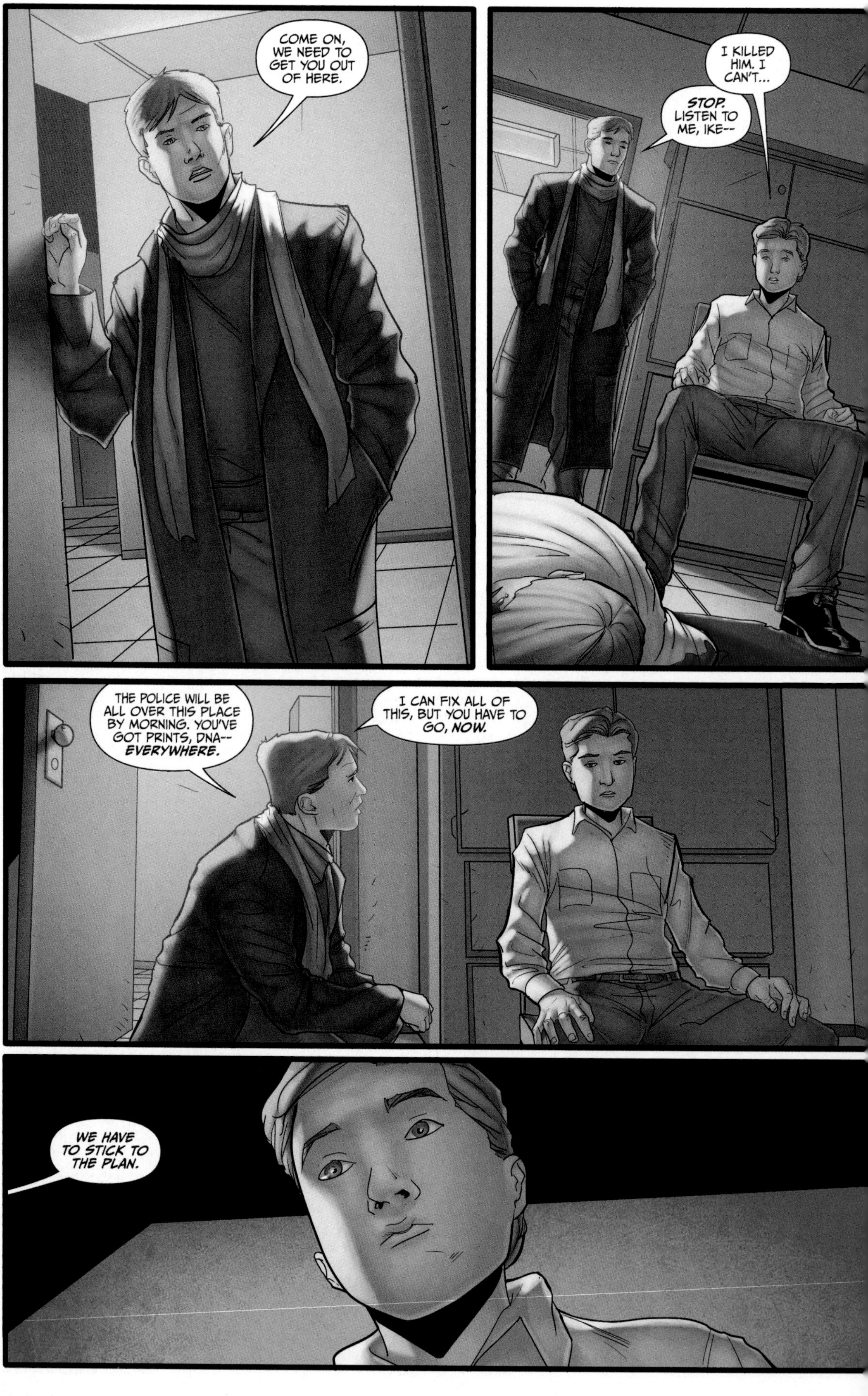
COME ON, WE NEED TO GET YOU OUT OF HERE.
I KILLED HIM. I CAN'T...
STOP. LISTEN TO ME, IKE--
THE POLICE WILL BE ALL OVER THIS PLACE BY MORNING. YOU'VE GOT PRINTS, DNA-- EVERYWHERE.
I CAN FIX ALL OF THIS, BUT YOU HAVE TO GO, NOW.
WE HAVE TO STICK TO THE PLAN.

WHAT ABOUT MOTHER? HOW WILL I--

DON'T WORRY ABOUT ANY OF THAT, YOU'VE GOT BIGGER THINGS TO CONCERN YOURSELF WITH.

IT'S ALL *YOURS* NOW, YOU KNOW. *THE COMPANY, THE FOUNDATION...* SOON AS YOU TURN EIGHTEEN, THEY'LL ALL BE WAITING FOR YOU. FROM THERE, WELL--

--YOU KNOW WHAT TO DO.

NOW *GO.*

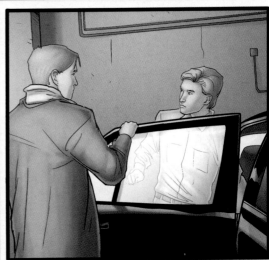

ABRAHAM...

THANK YOU.

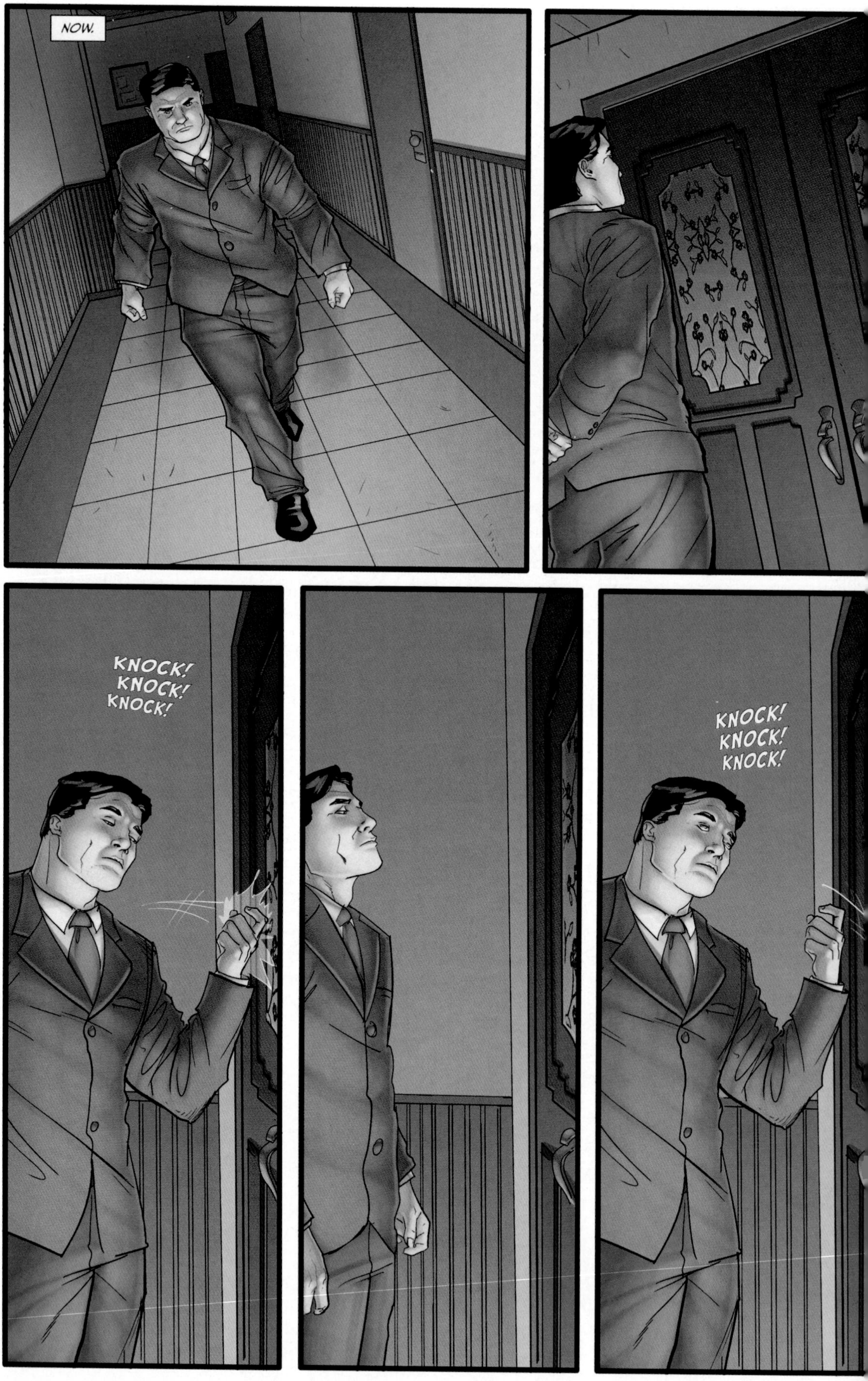
NOW.
KNOCK! KNOCK! KNOCK!
KNOCK! KNOCK! KNOCK!

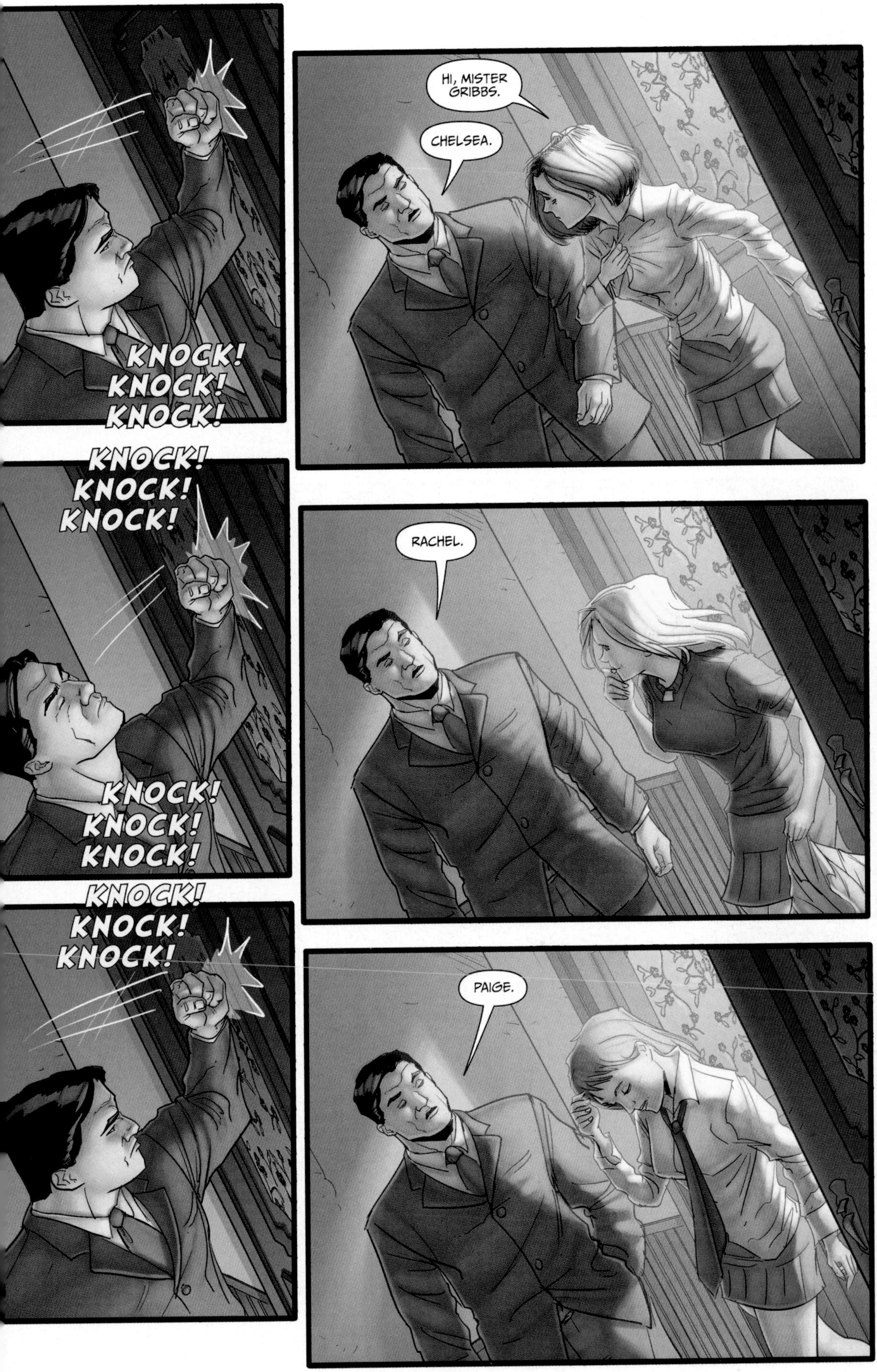
KNOCK! KNOCK! KNOCK!
HI, MISTER GRIBBS.
CHELSEA.
KNOCK! KNOCK! KNOCK!
KNOCK! KNOCK! KNOCK!
RACHEL.
KNOCK! KNOCK! KNOCK!
PAIGE.

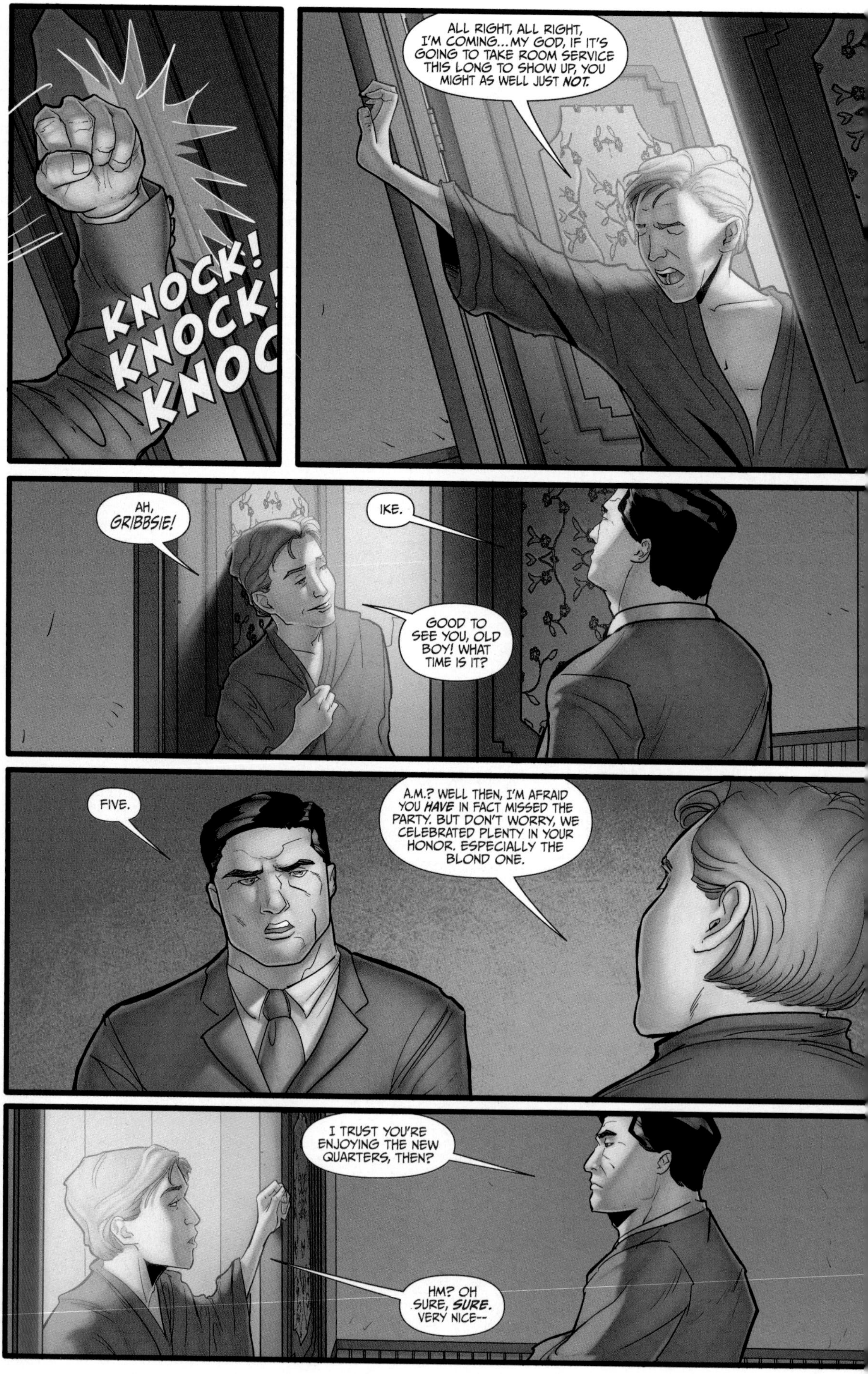
KNOCK! KNOCK! KNOC
ALL RIGHT, ALL RIGHT, I'M COMING...MY GOD, IF IT'S GOING TO TAKE ROOM SERVICE THIS LONG TO SHOW UP, YOU MIGHT AS WELL JUST NOT.
AH, GRIBBSIE!
IKE.
GOOD TO SEE YOU, OLD BOY! WHAT TIME IS IT?
FIVE.
A.M.? WELL THEN, I'M AFRAID YOU HAVE IN FACT MISSED THE PARTY. BUT DON'T WORRY, WE CELEBRATED PLENTY IN YOUR HONOR. ESPECIALLY THE BLOND ONE.
I TRUST YOU'RE ENJOYING THE NEW QUARTERS, THEN?
HM? OH SURE, SURE. VERY NICE--

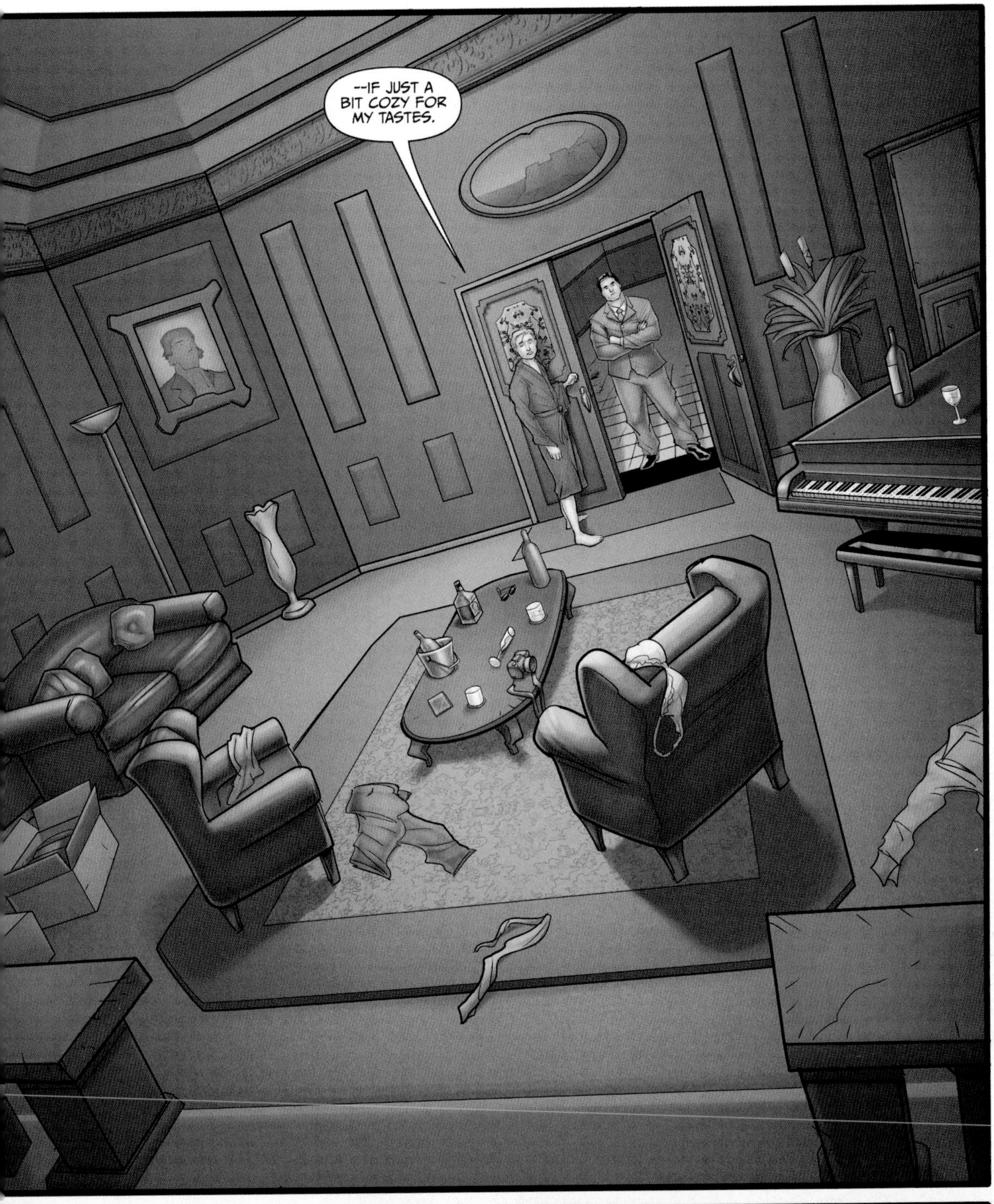
--IF JUST A BIT COZY FOR MY TASTES.

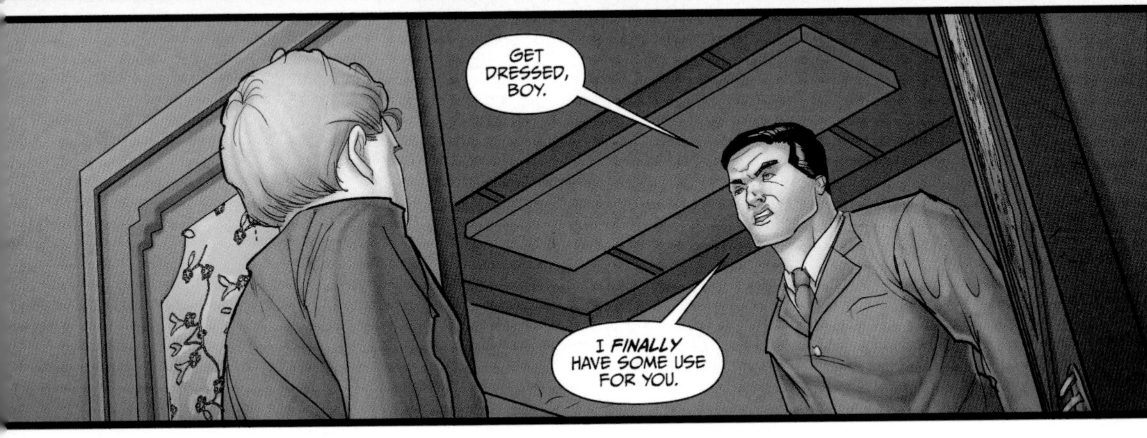
GET DRESSED, BOY.
I *FINALLY* HAVE SOME USE FOR YOU.

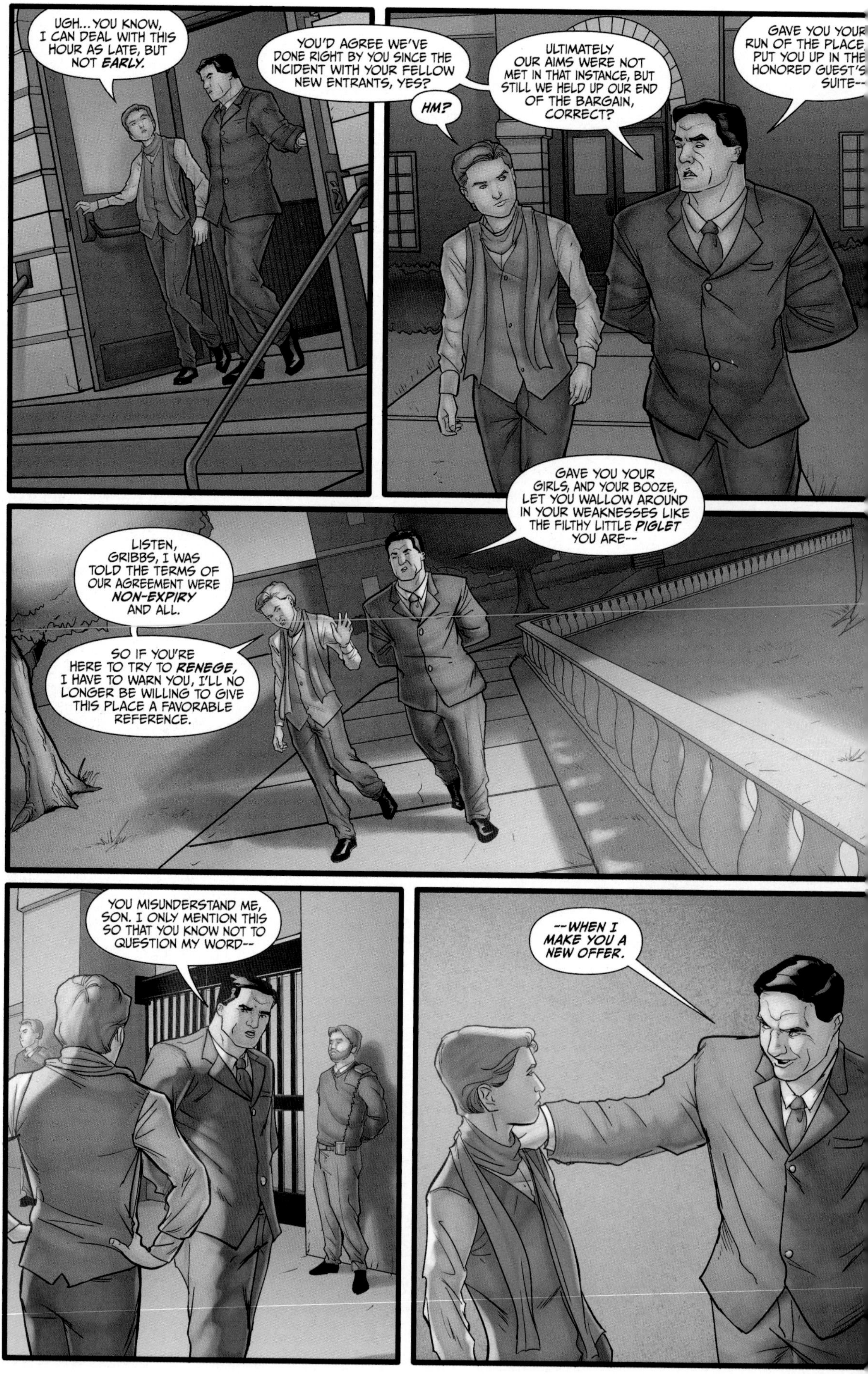
UGH...YOU KNOW, I CAN DEAL WITH THIS HOUR AS LATE, BUT NOT EARLY.
YOU'D AGREE WE'VE DONE RIGHT BY YOU SINCE THE INCIDENT WITH YOUR FELLOW NEW ENTRANTS, YES?
HM?
ULTIMATELY OUR AIMS WERE NOT MET IN THAT INSTANCE, BUT STILL WE HELD UP OUR END OF THE BARGAIN, CORRECT?
GAVE YOU YOUR RUN OF THE PLACE PUT YOU UP IN THE HONORED GUEST'S SUITE--
GAVE YOU YOUR GIRLS, AND YOUR BOOZE, LET YOU WALLOW AROUND IN YOUR WEAKNESSES LIKE THE FILTHY LITTLE PIGLET YOU ARE--
LISTEN, GRIBBS, I WAS TOLD THE TERMS OF OUR AGREEMENT WERE NON-EXPIRY AND ALL.
SO IF YOU'RE HERE TO TRY TO RENEGE, I HAVE TO WARN YOU, I'LL NO LONGER BE WILLING TO GIVE THIS PLACE A FAVORABLE REFERENCE.
YOU MISUNDERSTAND ME, SON. I ONLY MENTION THIS SO THAT YOU KNOW NOT TO QUESTION MY WORD--
--WHEN I MAKE YOU A NEW OFFER.

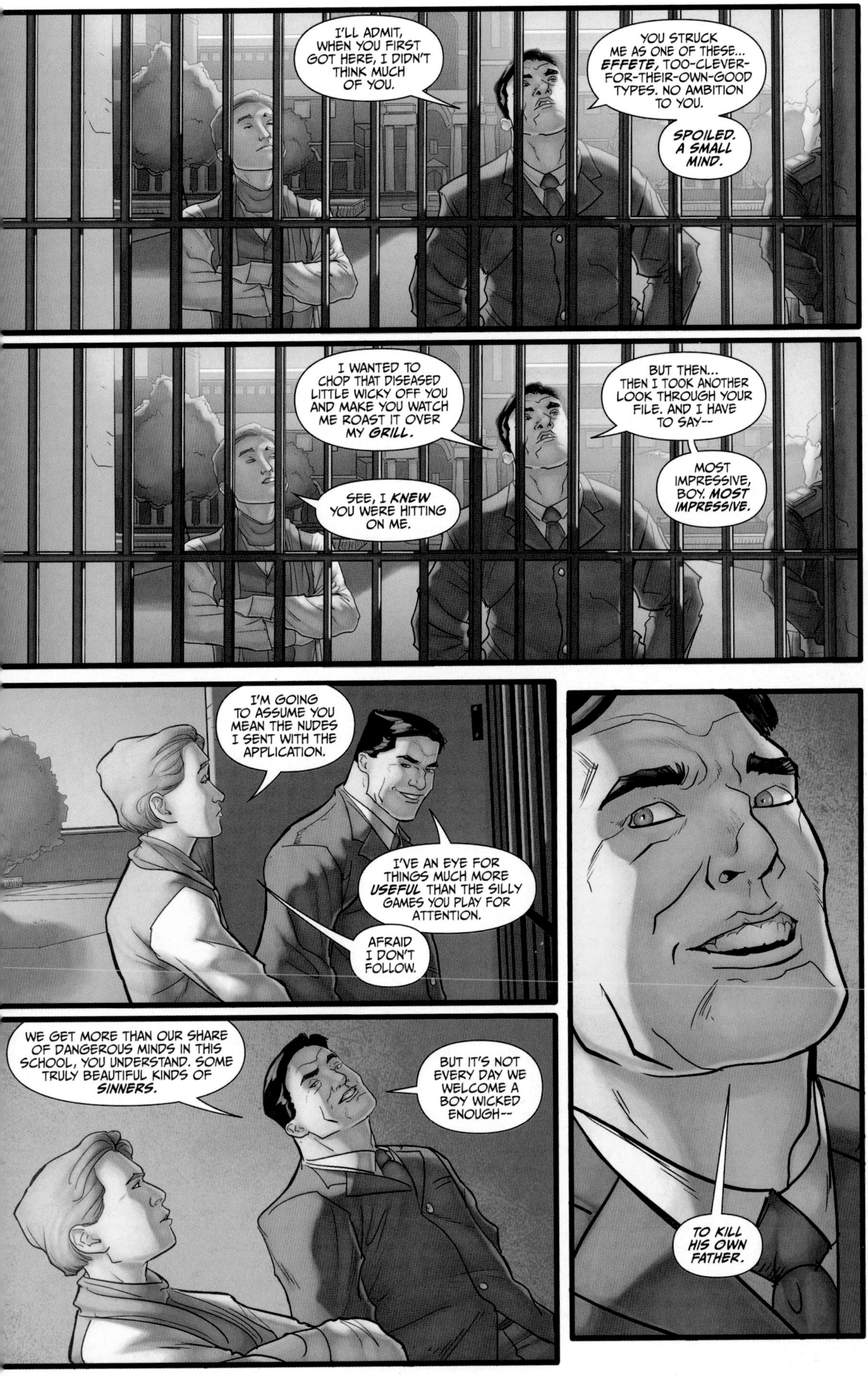
I'LL ADMIT, WHEN YOU FIRST GOT HERE, I DIDN'T THINK MUCH OF YOU.
YOU STRUCK ME AS ONE OF THESE... EFFETE, TOO-CLEVER-FOR-THEIR-OWN-GOOD TYPES. NO AMBITION TO YOU.
SPOILED. A SMALL MIND.
I WANTED TO CHOP THAT DISEASED LITTLE WICKY OFF YOU AND MAKE YOU WATCH ME ROAST IT OVER MY GRILL.
SEE, I KNEW YOU WERE HITTING ON ME.
BUT THEN... THEN I TOOK ANOTHER LOOK THROUGH YOUR FILE. AND I HAVE TO SAY--
MOST IMPRESSIVE, BOY. MOST IMPRESSIVE.
I'M GOING TO ASSUME YOU MEAN THE NUDES I SENT WITH THE APPLICATION.
I'VE AN EYE FOR THINGS MUCH MORE USEFUL THAN THE SILLY GAMES YOU PLAY FOR ATTENTION.
AFRAID I DON'T FOLLOW.
WE GET MORE THAN OUR SHARE OF DANGEROUS MINDS IN THIS SCHOOL, YOU UNDERSTAND. SOME TRULY BEAUTIFUL KINDS OF SINNERS.
BUT IT'S NOT EVERY DAY WE WELCOME A BOY WICKED ENOUGH--
TO KILL HIS OWN FATHER.

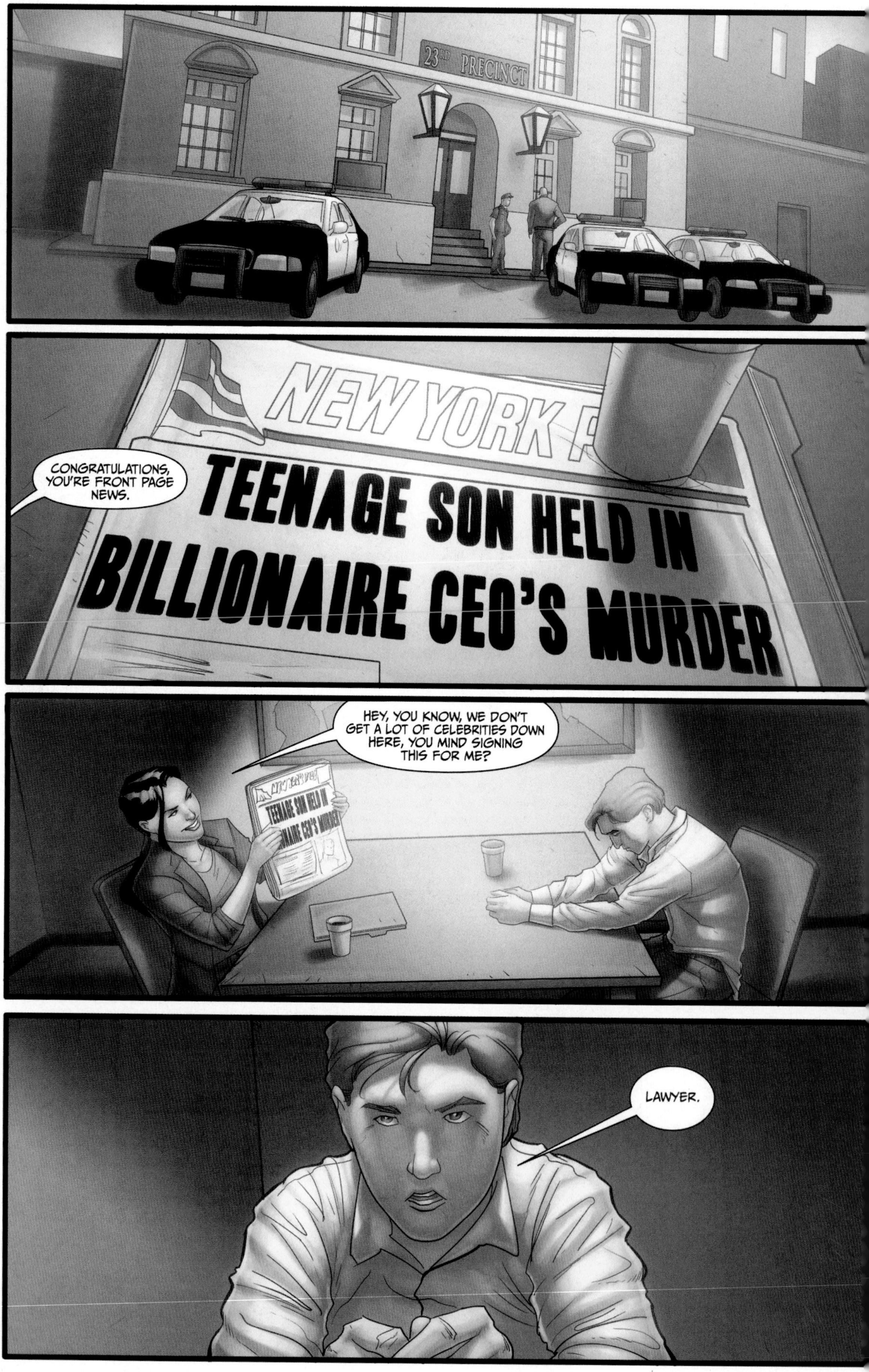
23RD PRECINCT
NEW YORK P
CONGRATULATIONS, YOU'RE FRONT PAGE NEWS.
TEENAGE SON HELD IN BILLIONAIRE CEO'S MURDER
HEY, YOU KNOW, WE DON'T GET A LOT OF CELEBRITIES DOWN HERE, YOU MIND SIGNING THIS FOR ME?
LAWYER.

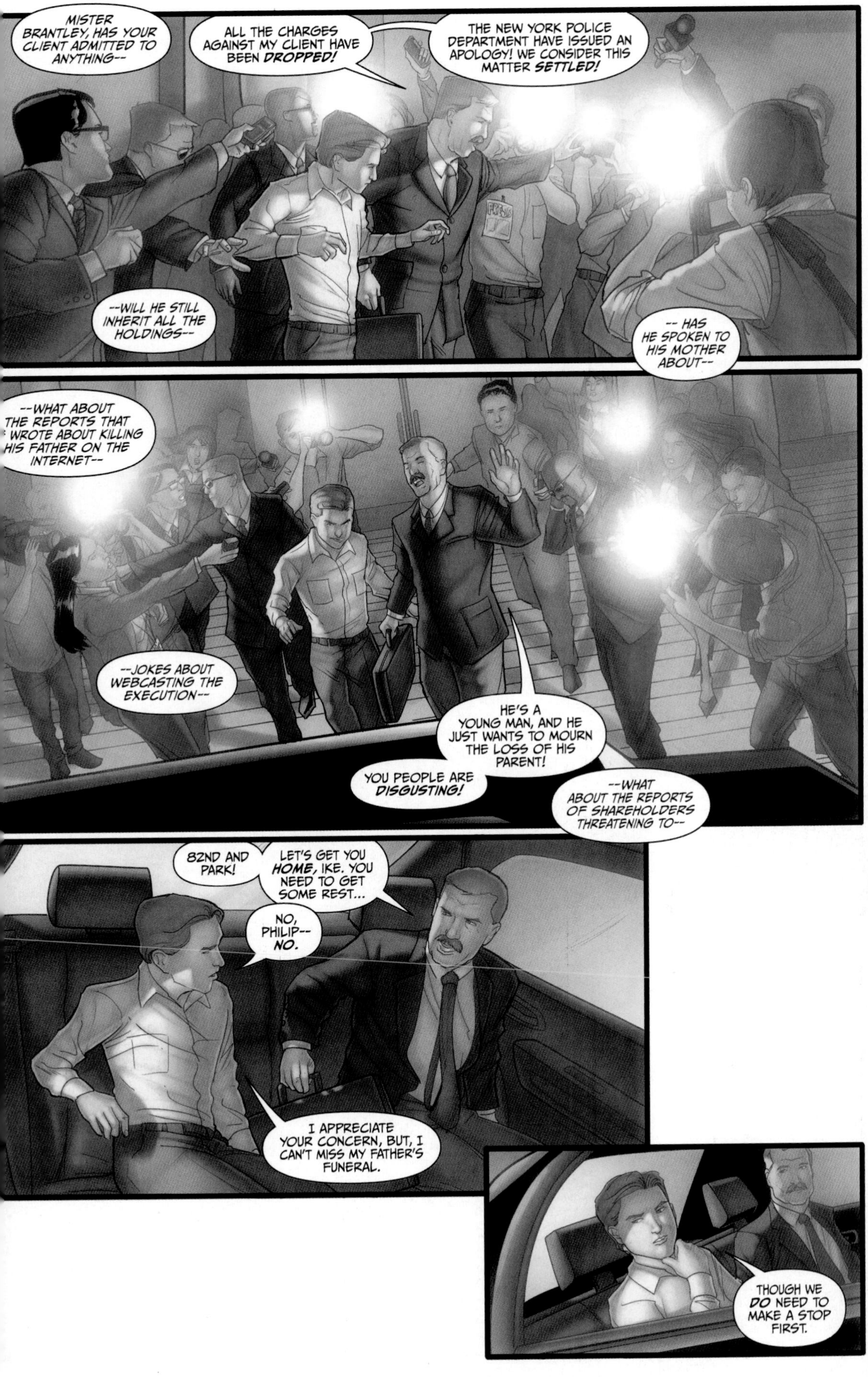

MISTER BRANTLEY, HAS YOUR CLIENT ADMITTED TO ANYTHING--
ALL THE CHARGES AGAINST MY CLIENT HAVE BEEN DROPPED!
THE NEW YORK POLICE DEPARTMENT HAVE ISSUED AN APOLOGY! WE CONSIDER THIS MATTER SETTLED!
--WILL HE STILL INHERIT ALL THE HOLDINGS--
-- HAS HE SPOKEN TO HIS MOTHER ABOUT--
--WHAT ABOUT THE REPORTS THAT HE WROTE ABOUT KILLING HIS FATHER ON THE INTERNET--
--JOKES ABOUT WEBCASTING THE EXECUTION--
HE'S A YOUNG MAN, AND HE JUST WANTS TO MOURN THE LOSS OF HIS PARENT!
YOU PEOPLE ARE DISGUSTING!
--WHAT ABOUT THE REPORTS OF SHAREHOLDERS THREATENING TO--
82ND AND PARK!
LET'S GET YOU HOME, IKE. YOU NEED TO GET SOME REST...
NO, PHILIP-- NO.
I APPRECIATE YOUR CONCERN, BUT, I CAN'T MISS MY FATHER'S FUNERAL.
THOUGH WE DO NEED TO MAKE A STOP FIRST.

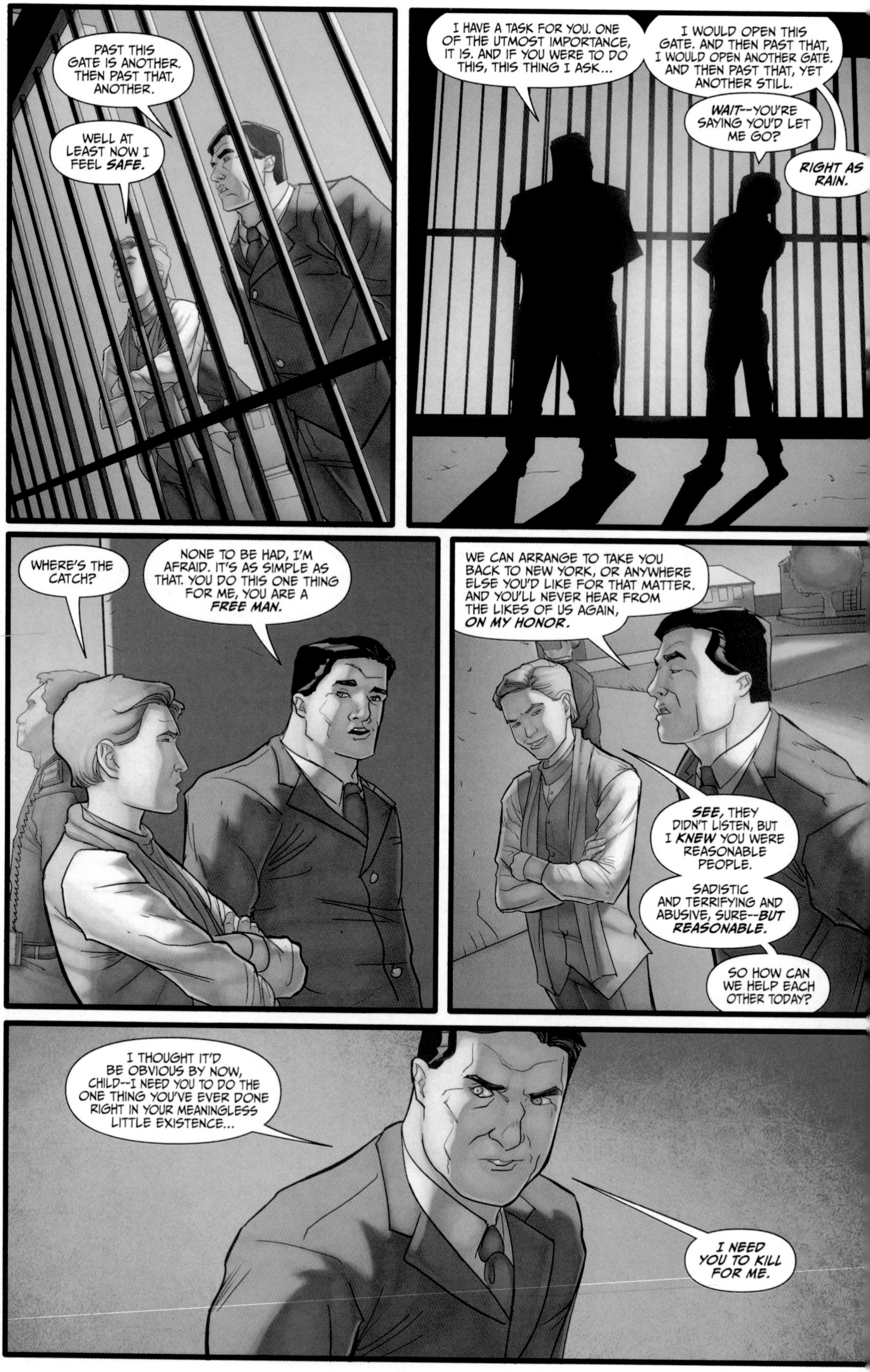
PAST THIS GATE IS ANOTHER. THEN PAST THAT, ANOTHER.
WELL AT LEAST NOW I FEEL ***SAFE.***
I HAVE A TASK FOR YOU. ONE OF THE UTMOST IMPORTANCE, IT IS. AND IF YOU WERE TO DO THIS, THIS THING I ASK...
I WOULD OPEN THIS GATE. AND THEN PAST THAT, I WOULD OPEN ANOTHER GATE. AND THEN PAST THAT, YET ANOTHER STILL.
WAIT--YOU'RE SAYING YOU'D LET ME GO?
RIGHT AS RAIN.
WHERE'S THE CATCH?
NONE TO BE HAD, I'M AFRAID. IT'S AS SIMPLE AS THAT. YOU DO THIS ONE THING FOR ME, YOU ARE A ***FREE MAN.***
WE CAN ARRANGE TO TAKE YOU BACK TO NEW YORK, OR ANYWHERE ELSE YOU'D LIKE FOR THAT MATTER. AND YOU'LL NEVER HEAR FROM THE LIKES OF US AGAIN, ***ON MY HONOR.***
SEE, THEY DIDN'T LISTEN, BUT I ***KNEW*** YOU WERE REASONABLE PEOPLE.
SADISTIC AND TERRIFYING AND ABUSIVE, SURE--***BUT REASONABLE.***
SO HOW CAN WE HELP EACH OTHER TODAY?
I THOUGHT IT'D BE OBVIOUS BY NOW, CHILD--I NEED YOU TO DO THE ONE THING YOU'VE EVER DONE RIGHT IN YOUR MEANINGLESS LITTLE EXISTENCE...
I NEED YOU TO KILL FOR ME.

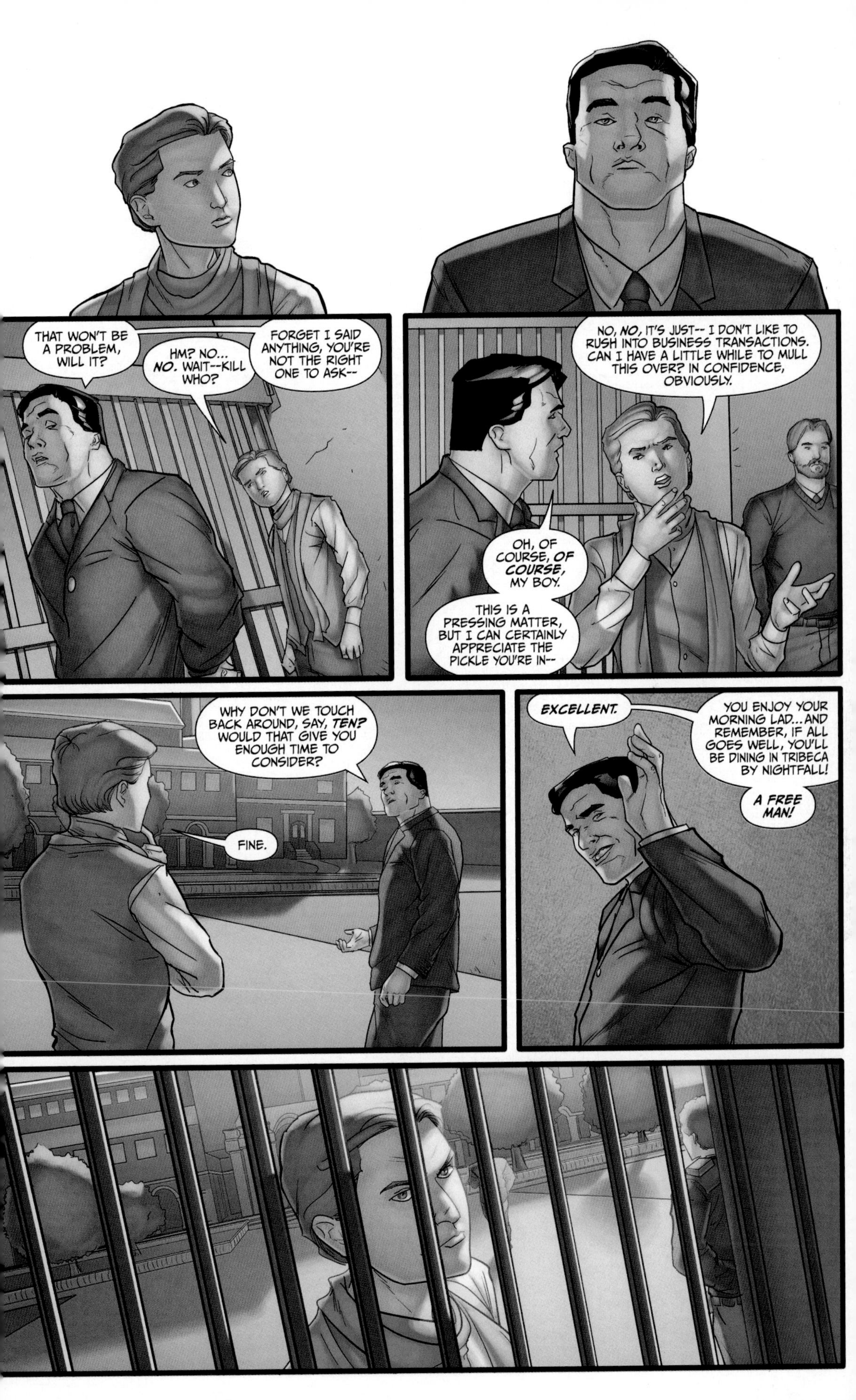
THAT WON'T BE A PROBLEM, WILL IT?
HM? NO... NO. WAIT--KILL WHO?
FORGET I SAID ANYTHING, YOU'RE NOT THE RIGHT ONE TO ASK--
NO, NO, IT'S JUST-- I DON'T LIKE TO RUSH INTO BUSINESS TRANSACTIONS. CAN I HAVE A LITTLE WHILE TO MULL THIS OVER? IN CONFIDENCE, OBVIOUSLY.
OH, OF COURSE, OF COURSE, MY BOY.
THIS IS A PRESSING MATTER, BUT I CAN CERTAINLY APPRECIATE THE PICKLE YOU'RE IN--
WHY DON'T WE TOUCH BACK AROUND, SAY, TEN? WOULD THAT GIVE YOU ENOUGH TIME TO CONSIDER?
FINE.
EXCELLENT.
YOU ENJOY YOUR MORNING LAD...AND REMEMBER, IF ALL GOES WELL, YOU'LL BE DINING IN TRIBECA BY NIGHTFALL!
A FREE MAN!

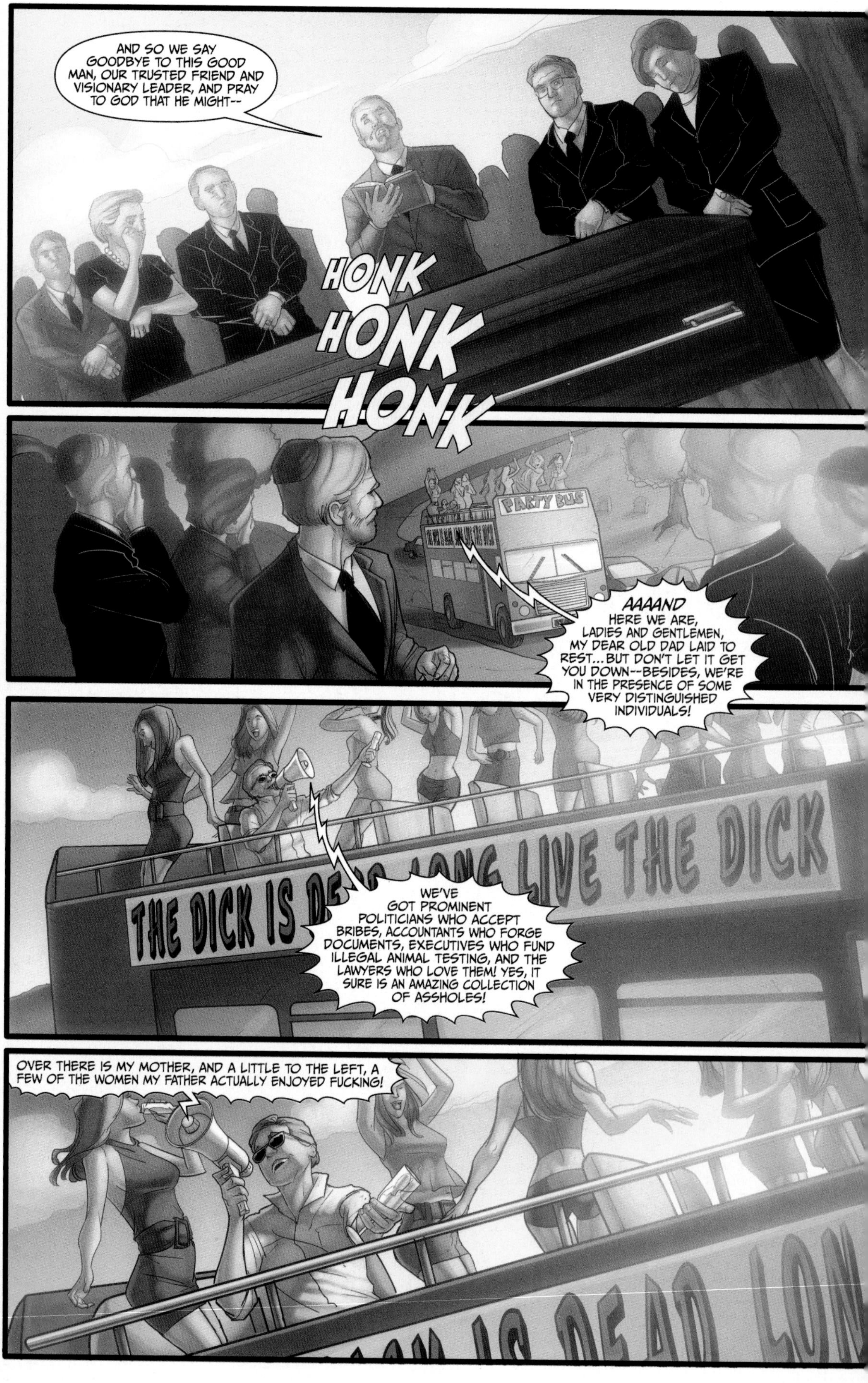
AND SO WE SAY GOODBYE TO THIS GOOD MAN, OUR TRUSTED FRIEND AND VISIONARY LEADER, AND PRAY TO GOD THAT HE MIGHT--
HONK HONK HONK
PARTY BUS
AAAAND HERE WE ARE, LADIES AND GENTLEMEN, MY DEAR OLD DAD LAID TO REST... BUT DON'T LET IT GET YOU DOWN--BESIDES, WE'RE IN THE PRESENCE OF SOME VERY DISTINGUISHED INDIVIDUALS!
LIVE THE DICK
THE DICK IS
WE'VE GOT PROMINENT POLITICIANS WHO ACCEPT BRIBES, ACCOUNTANTS WHO FORGE DOCUMENTS, EXECUTIVES WHO FUND ILLEGAL ANIMAL TESTING, AND THE LAWYERS WHO LOVE THEM! YES, IT SURE IS AN AMAZING COLLECTION OF ASSHOLES!
OVER THERE IS MY MOTHER, AND A LITTLE TO THE LEFT, A FEW OF THE WOMEN MY FATHER ACTUALLY ENJOYED FUCKING!

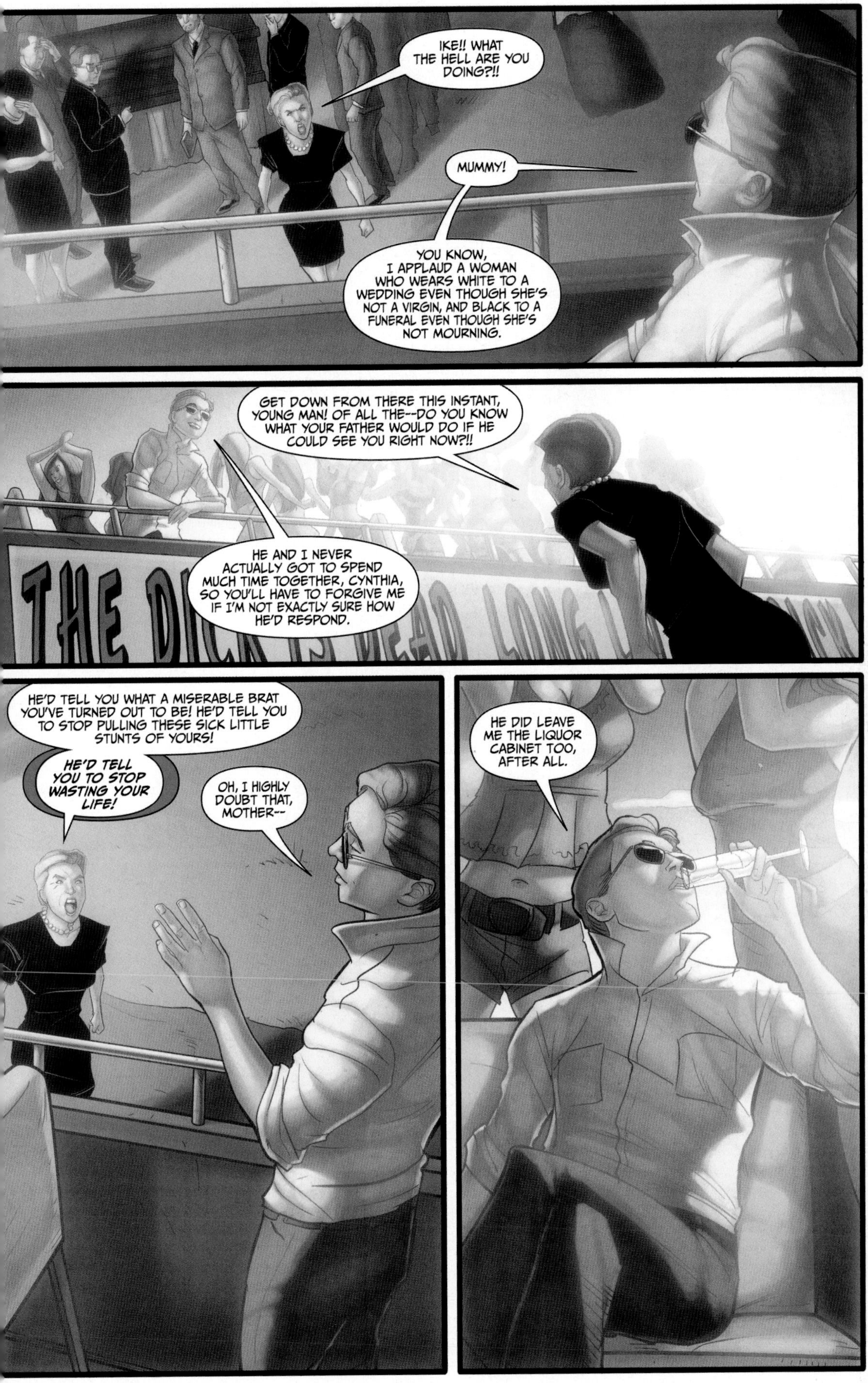
IKE!! WHAT THE HELL ARE YOU DOING?!!
MUMMY!
YOU KNOW, I APPLAUD A WOMAN WHO WEARS WHITE TO A WEDDING EVEN THOUGH SHE'S NOT A VIRGIN, AND BLACK TO A FUNERAL EVEN THOUGH SHE'S NOT MOURNING.
GET DOWN FROM THERE THIS INSTANT, YOUNG MAN! OF ALL THE--DO YOU KNOW WHAT YOUR FATHER WOULD DO IF HE COULD SEE YOU RIGHT NOW?!!
HE AND I NEVER ACTUALLY GOT TO SPEND MUCH TIME TOGETHER, CYNTHIA, SO YOU'LL HAVE TO FORGIVE ME IF I'M NOT EXACTLY SURE HOW HE'D RESPOND.
HE'D TELL YOU WHAT A MISERABLE BRAT YOU'VE TURNED OUT TO BE! HE'D TELL YOU TO STOP PULLING THESE SICK LITTLE STUNTS OF YOURS!
HE'D TELL YOU TO STOP WASTING YOUR LIFE!
OH, I HIGHLY DOUBT THAT, MOTHER--
HE DID LEAVE ME THE LIQUOR CABINET TOO, AFTER ALL.

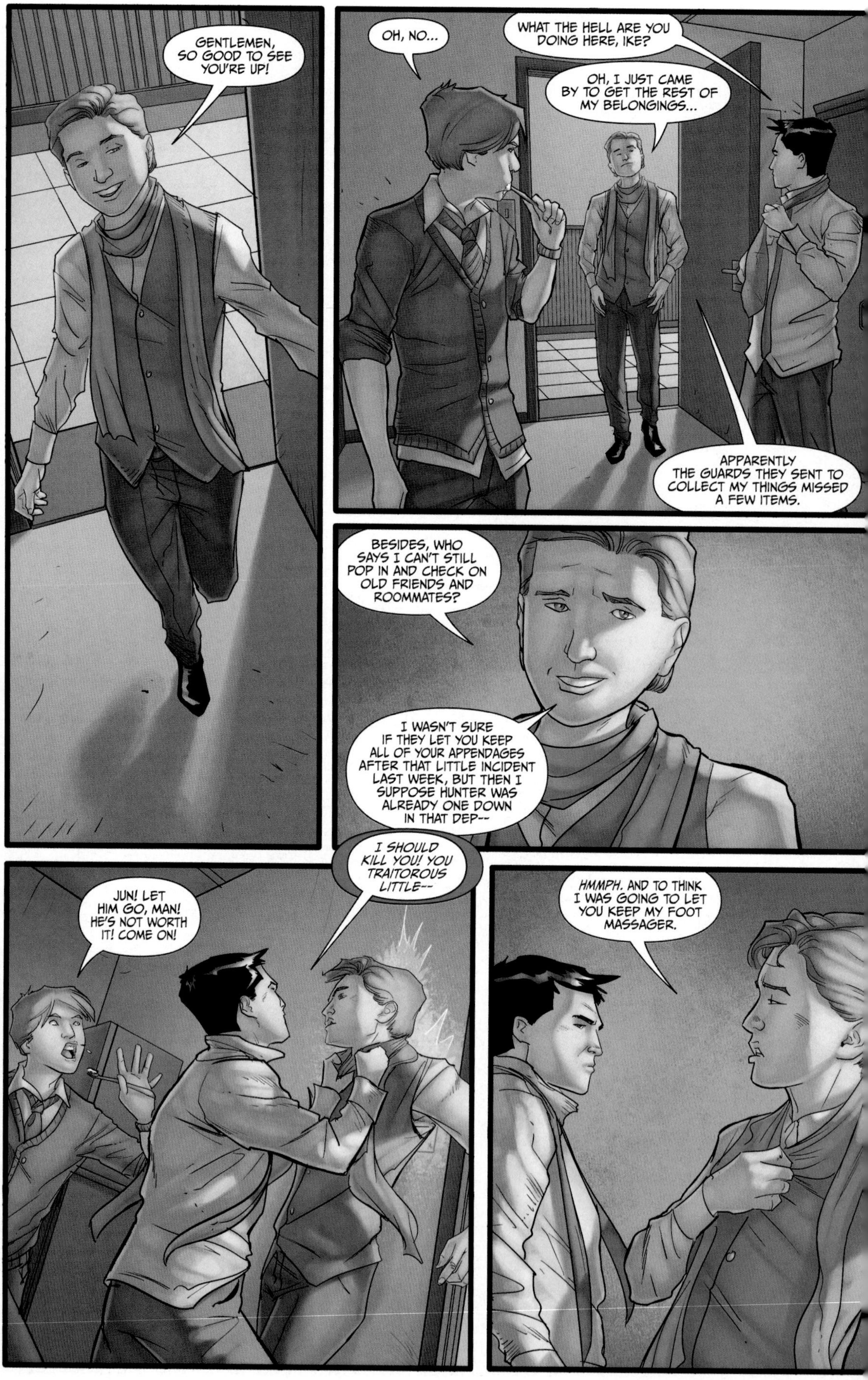
GENTLEMEN, SO GOOD TO SEE YOU'RE UP!
OH, NO...
WHAT THE HELL ARE YOU DOING HERE, IKE?
OH, I JUST CAME BY TO GET THE REST OF MY BELONGINGS...
APPARENTLY THE GUARDS THEY SENT TO COLLECT MY THINGS MISSED A FEW ITEMS.
BESIDES, WHO SAYS I CAN'T STILL POP IN AND CHECK ON OLD FRIENDS AND ROOMMATES?
I WASN'T SURE IF THEY LET YOU KEEP ALL OF YOUR APPENDAGES AFTER THAT LITTLE INCIDENT LAST WEEK, BUT THEN I SUPPOSE HUNTER WAS ALREADY ONE DOWN IN THAT DEP--
JUN! LET HIM GO, MAN! HE'S NOT WORTH IT! COME ON!
I SHOULD KILL YOU! YOU TRAITOROUS LITTLE--
HMMPH. AND TO THINK I WAS GOING TO LET YOU KEEP MY FOOT MASSAGER.

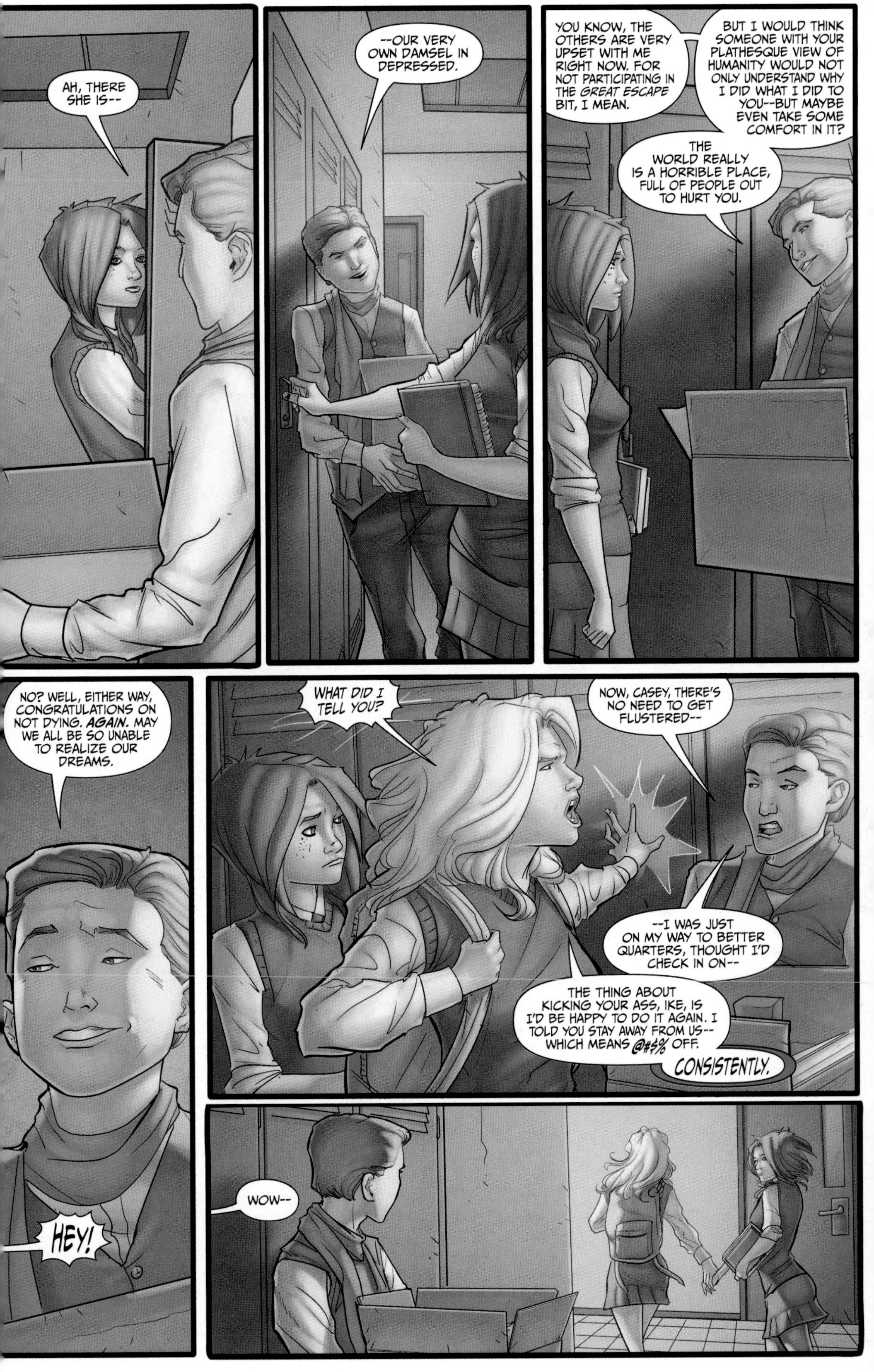
AH, THERE SHE IS--
--OUR VERY OWN DAMSEL IN DEPRESSED.
YOU KNOW, THE OTHERS ARE VERY UPSET WITH ME RIGHT NOW. FOR NOT PARTICIPATING IN THE GREAT ESCAPE BIT, I MEAN.
BUT I WOULD THINK SOMEONE WITH YOUR PLATHESQUE VIEW OF HUMANITY WOULD NOT ONLY UNDERSTAND WHY I DID WHAT I DID TO YOU--BUT MAYBE EVEN TAKE SOME COMFORT IN IT?
THE WORLD REALLY IS A HORRIBLE PLACE, FULL OF PEOPLE OUT TO HURT YOU.
NO? WELL, EITHER WAY, CONGRATULATIONS ON NOT DYING. AGAIN. MAY WE ALL BE SO UNABLE TO REALIZE OUR DREAMS.
HEY!
WHAT DID I TELL YOU?
NOW, CASEY, THERE'S NO NEED TO GET FLUSTERED--
--I WAS JUST ON MY WAY TO BETTER QUARTERS, THOUGHT I'D CHECK IN ON--
THE THING ABOUT KICKING YOUR ASS, IKE, IS I'D BE HAPPY TO DO IT AGAIN. I TOLD YOU STAY AWAY FROM US-- WHICH MEANS @#$% OFF.
CONSISTENTLY.
WOW--

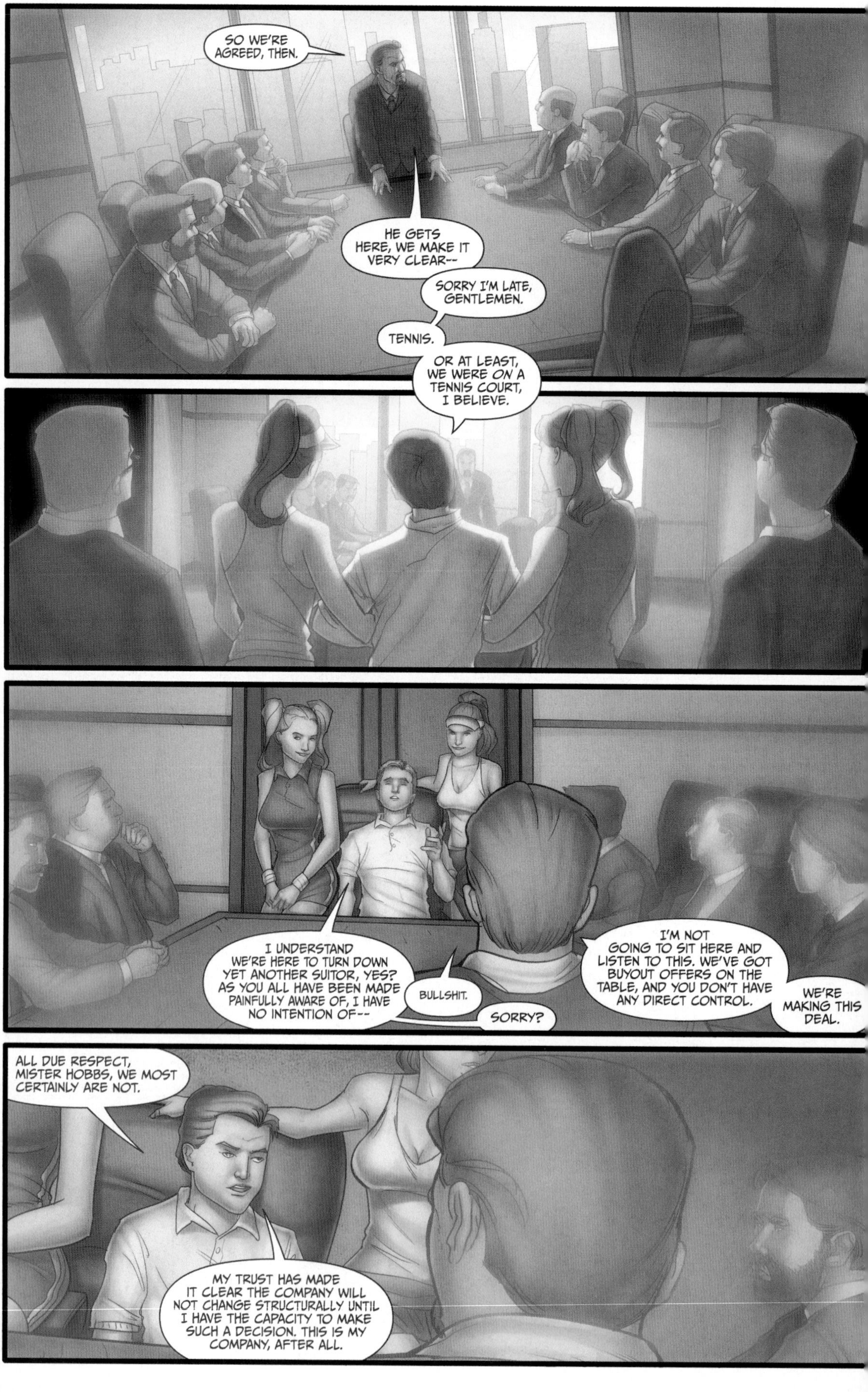
SO WE'RE AGREED, THEN.
HE GETS HERE, WE MAKE IT VERY CLEAR--
SORRY I'M LATE, GENTLEMEN.
TENNIS.
OR AT LEAST, WE WERE ON A TENNIS COURT, I BELIEVE.
I UNDERSTAND WE'RE HERE TO TURN DOWN YET ANOTHER SUITOR, YES? AS YOU ALL HAVE BEEN MADE PAINFULLY AWARE OF, I HAVE NO INTENTION OF--
BULLSHIT.
SORRY?
I'M NOT GOING TO SIT HERE AND LISTEN TO THIS. WE'VE GOT BUYOUT OFFERS ON THE TABLE, AND YOU DON'T HAVE ANY DIRECT CONTROL.
WE'RE MAKING THIS DEAL.
ALL DUE RESPECT, MISTER HOBBS, WE MOST CERTAINLY ARE NOT.
MY TRUST HAS MADE IT CLEAR THE COMPANY WILL NOT CHANGE STRUCTURALLY UNTIL I HAVE THE CAPACITY TO MAKE SUCH A DECISION. THIS IS MY COMPANY, AFTER ALL.

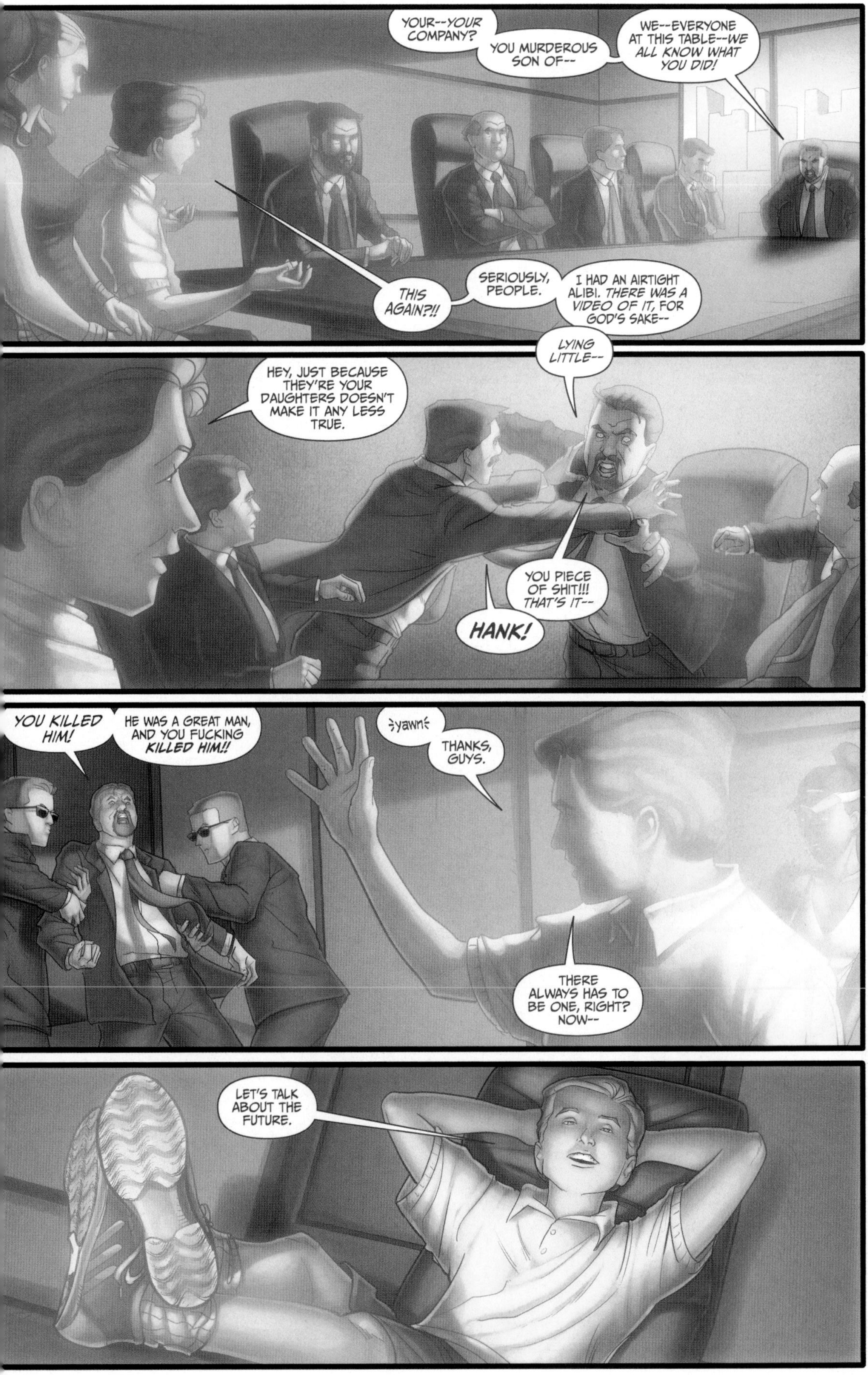

YOUR--*YOUR* COMPANY?
YOU MURDEROUS SON OF--
WE--EVERYONE AT THIS TABLE--*WE ALL KNOW WHAT YOU DID!*
THIS AGAIN?!!
SERIOUSLY, PEOPLE.
I HAD AN AIRTIGHT ALIBI. *THERE WAS A VIDEO OF IT,* FOR GOD'S SAKE--
LYING LITTLE--
HEY, JUST BECAUSE THEY'RE YOUR DAUGHTERS DOESN'T MAKE IT ANY LESS TRUE.
YOU PIECE OF SHIT!!! *THAT'S IT--*
HANK!
YOU KILLED HIM!
HE WAS A GREAT MAN, AND YOU FUCKING ***KILLED HIM!!***
yawn
THANKS, GUYS.
THERE ALWAYS HAS TO BE ONE, RIGHT? NOW--
LET'S TALK ABOUT THE FUTURE.

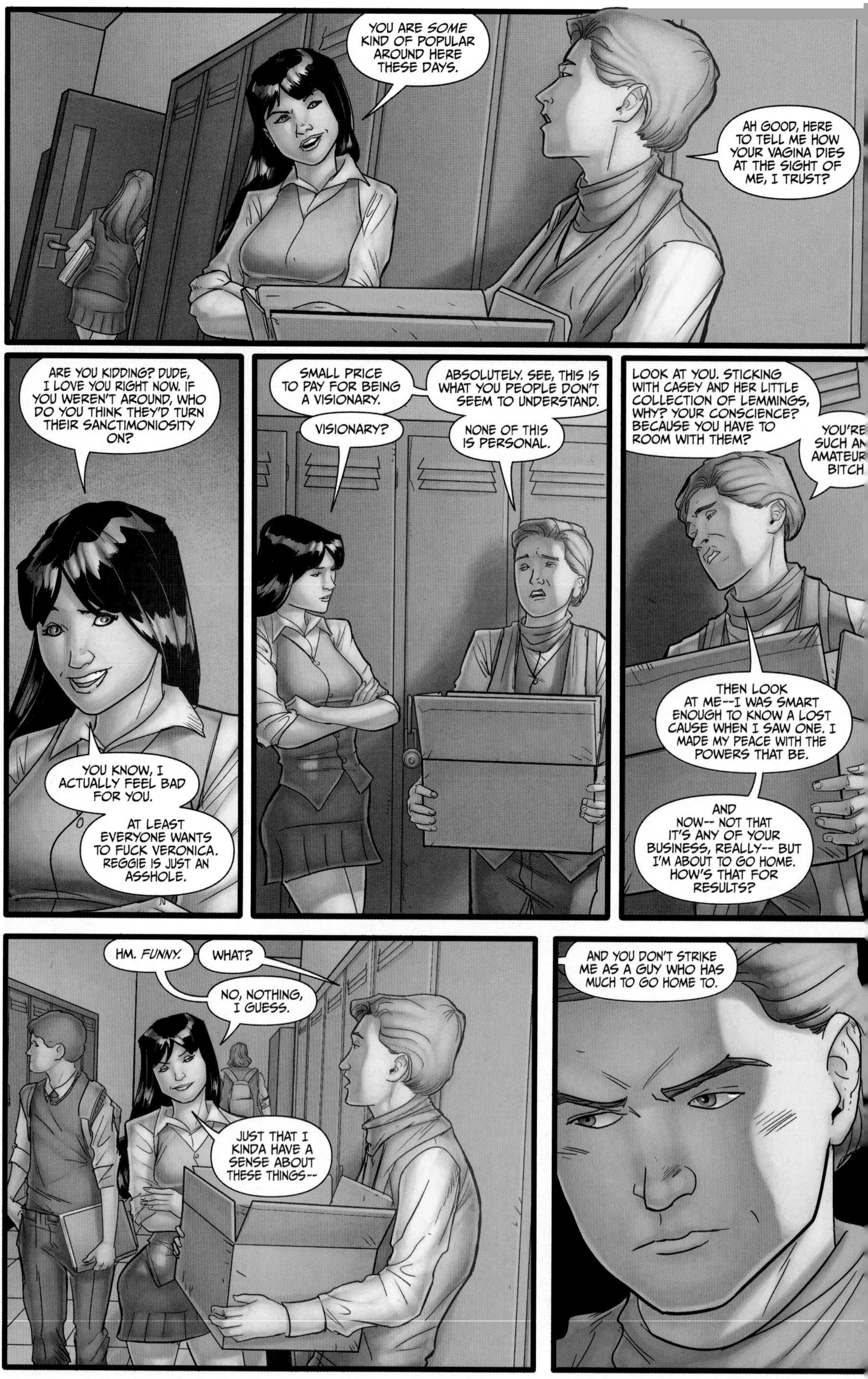
YOU ARE *SOME* KIND OF POPULAR AROUND HERE THESE DAYS.
AH GOOD, HERE TO TELL ME HOW YOUR VAGINA DIES AT THE SIGHT OF ME, I TRUST?
ARE YOU KIDDING? DUDE, I LOVE YOU RIGHT NOW. IF YOU WEREN'T AROUND, WHO DO YOU THINK THEY'D TURN THEIR SANCTIMONIOSITY ON?
YOU KNOW, I ACTUALLY FEEL BAD FOR YOU.
AT LEAST EVERYONE WANTS TO FUCK VERONICA. REGGIE IS JUST AN ASSHOLE.
SMALL PRICE TO PAY FOR BEING A VISIONARY.
VISIONARY?
ABSOLUTELY. SEE, THIS IS WHAT YOU PEOPLE DON'T SEEM TO UNDERSTAND.
NONE OF THIS IS PERSONAL.
LOOK AT YOU. STICKING WITH CASEY AND HER LITTLE COLLECTION OF LEMMINGS, WHY? YOUR CONSCIENCE? BECAUSE YOU HAVE TO ROOM WITH THEM?
YOU'RE SUCH AN AMATEUR BITCH.
THEN LOOK AT ME--I WAS SMART ENOUGH TO KNOW A LOST CAUSE WHEN I SAW ONE. I MADE MY PEACE WITH THE POWERS THAT BE.
AND NOW-- NOT THAT IT'S ANY OF YOUR BUSINESS, REALLY-- BUT I'M ABOUT TO GO HOME. HOW'S THAT FOR RESULTS?
HM. *FUNNY.*
WHAT?
NO, NOTHING, I GUESS.
JUST THAT I KINDA HAVE A SENSE ABOUT THESE THINGS--
AND YOU DON'T STRIKE ME AS A GUY WHO HAS MUCH TO GO HOME TO.

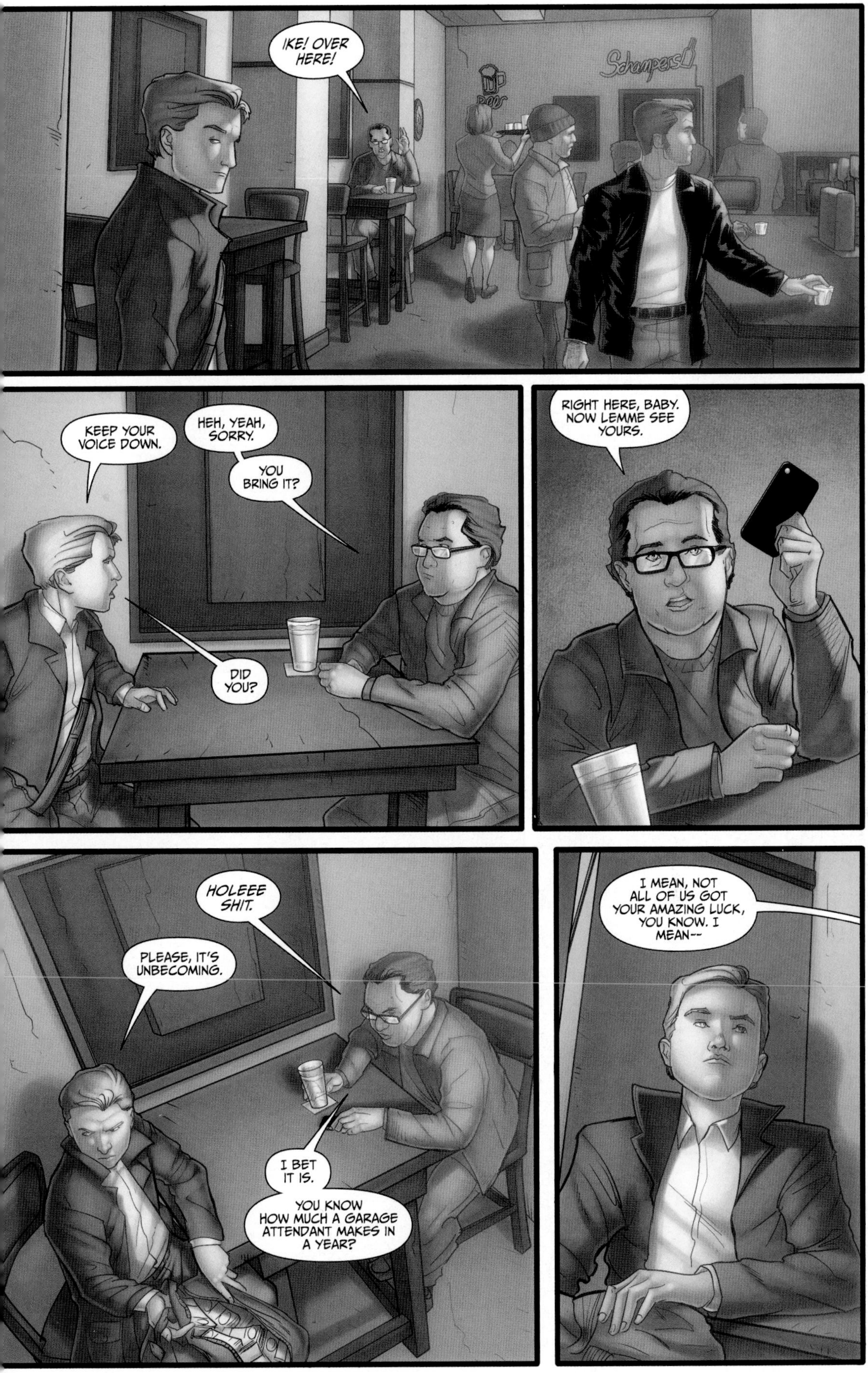
IKE! OVER HERE!
KEEP YOUR VOICE DOWN.
HEH, YEAH, SORRY.
YOU BRING IT?
DID YOU?
RIGHT HERE, BABY. NOW LEMME SEE YOURS.
HOLEEE SHIT.
PLEASE, IT'S UNBECOMING.
I BET IT IS.
YOU KNOW HOW MUCH A GARAGE ATTENDANT MAKES IN A YEAR?
I MEAN, NOT ALL OF US GOT YOUR AMAZING LUCK, YOU KNOW. I MEAN--

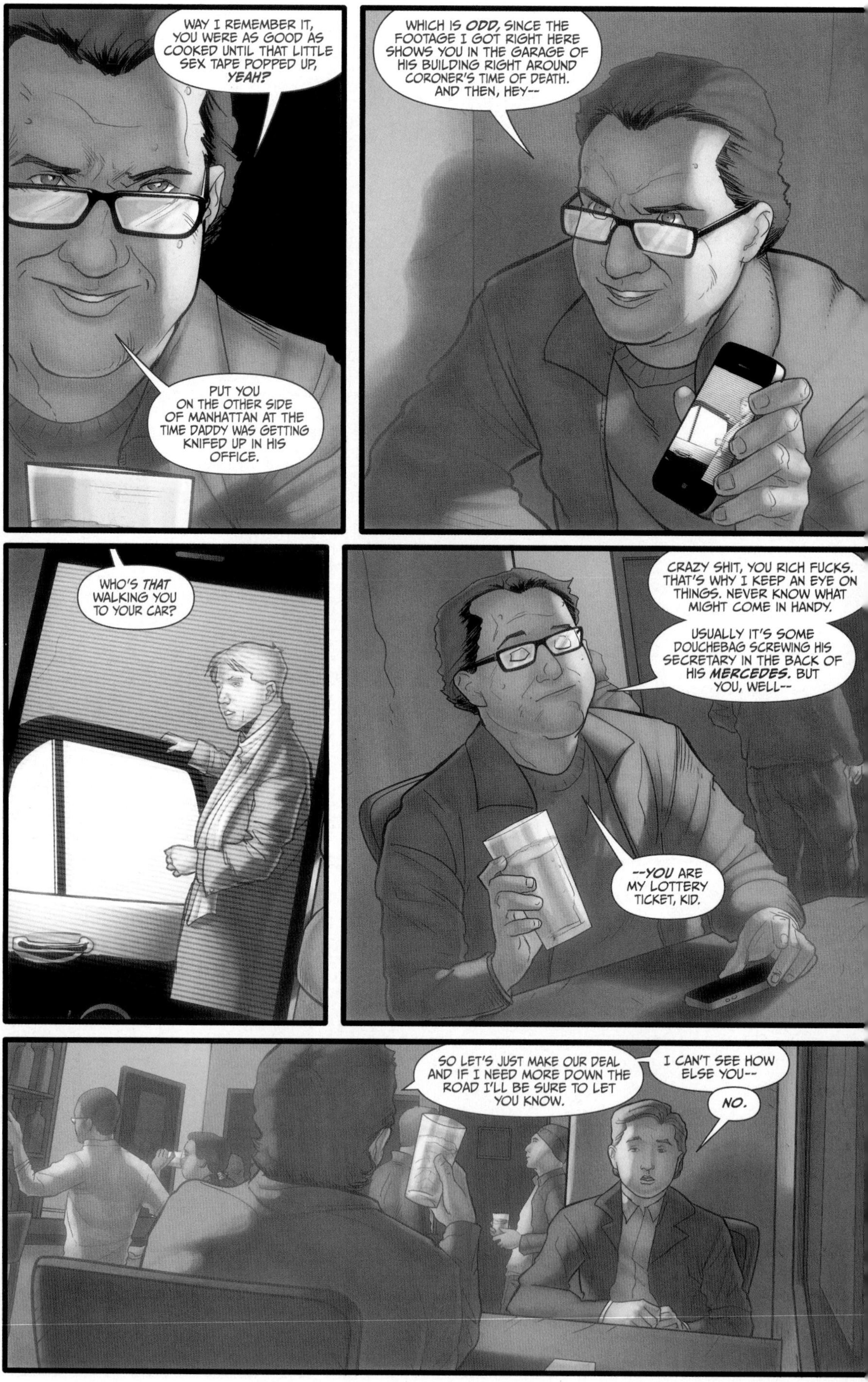
WAY I REMEMBER IT, YOU WERE AS GOOD AS COOKED UNTIL THAT LITTLE SEX TAPE POPPED UP, YEAH?
PUT YOU ON THE OTHER SIDE OF MANHATTAN AT THE TIME DADDY WAS GETTING KNIFED UP IN HIS OFFICE.
WHICH IS ODD, SINCE THE FOOTAGE I GOT RIGHT HERE SHOWS YOU IN THE GARAGE OF HIS BUILDING RIGHT AROUND CORONER'S TIME OF DEATH. AND THEN, HEY--
WHO'S THAT WALKING YOU TO YOUR CAR?
CRAZY SHIT, YOU RICH FUCKS. THAT'S WHY I KEEP AN EYE ON THINGS. NEVER KNOW WHAT MIGHT COME IN HANDY.
USUALLY IT'S SOME DOUCHEBAG SCREWING HIS SECRETARY IN THE BACK OF HIS MERCEDES. BUT YOU, WELL--
--YOU ARE MY LOTTERY TICKET, KID.
SO LET'S JUST MAKE OUR DEAL AND IF I NEED MORE DOWN THE ROAD I'LL BE SURE TO LET YOU KNOW.
I CAN'T SEE HOW ELSE YOU--
NO.

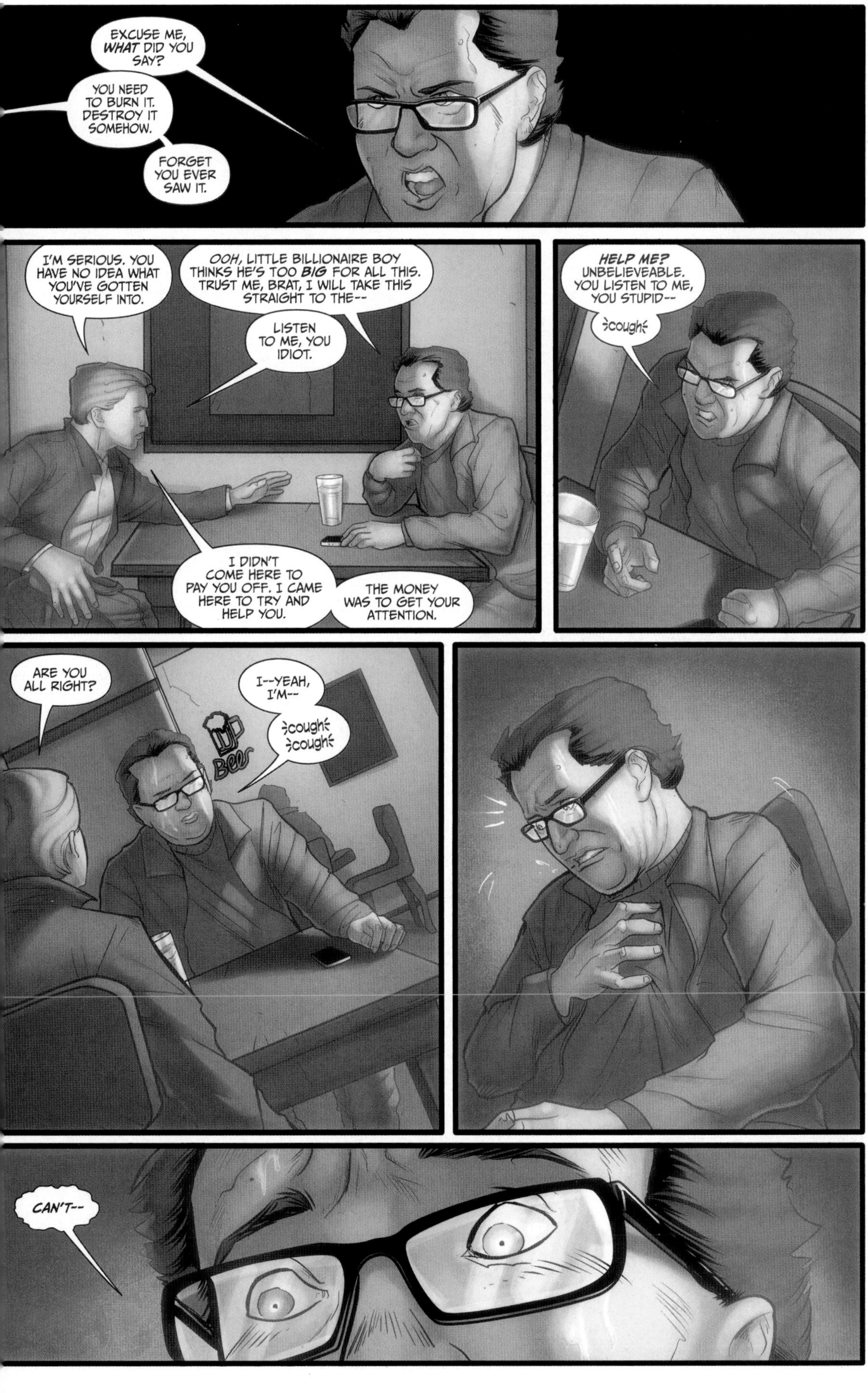
EXCUSE ME, WHAT DID YOU SAY?
YOU NEED TO BURN IT. DESTROY IT SOMEHOW.
FORGET YOU EVER SAW IT.
I'M SERIOUS. YOU HAVE NO IDEA WHAT YOU'VE GOTTEN YOURSELF INTO.
OOH, LITTLE BILLIONAIRE BOY THINKS HE'S TOO BIG FOR ALL THIS. TRUST ME, BRAT, I WILL TAKE THIS STRAIGHT TO THE--
LISTEN TO ME, YOU IDIOT.
I DIDN'T COME HERE TO PAY YOU OFF. I CAME HERE TO TRY AND HELP YOU.
THE MONEY WAS TO GET YOUR ATTENTION.
HELP ME? UNBELIEVEABLE. YOU LISTEN TO ME, YOU STUPID--
cough
ARE YOU ALL RIGHT?
I--YEAH, I'M--
cough cough
CAN'T--

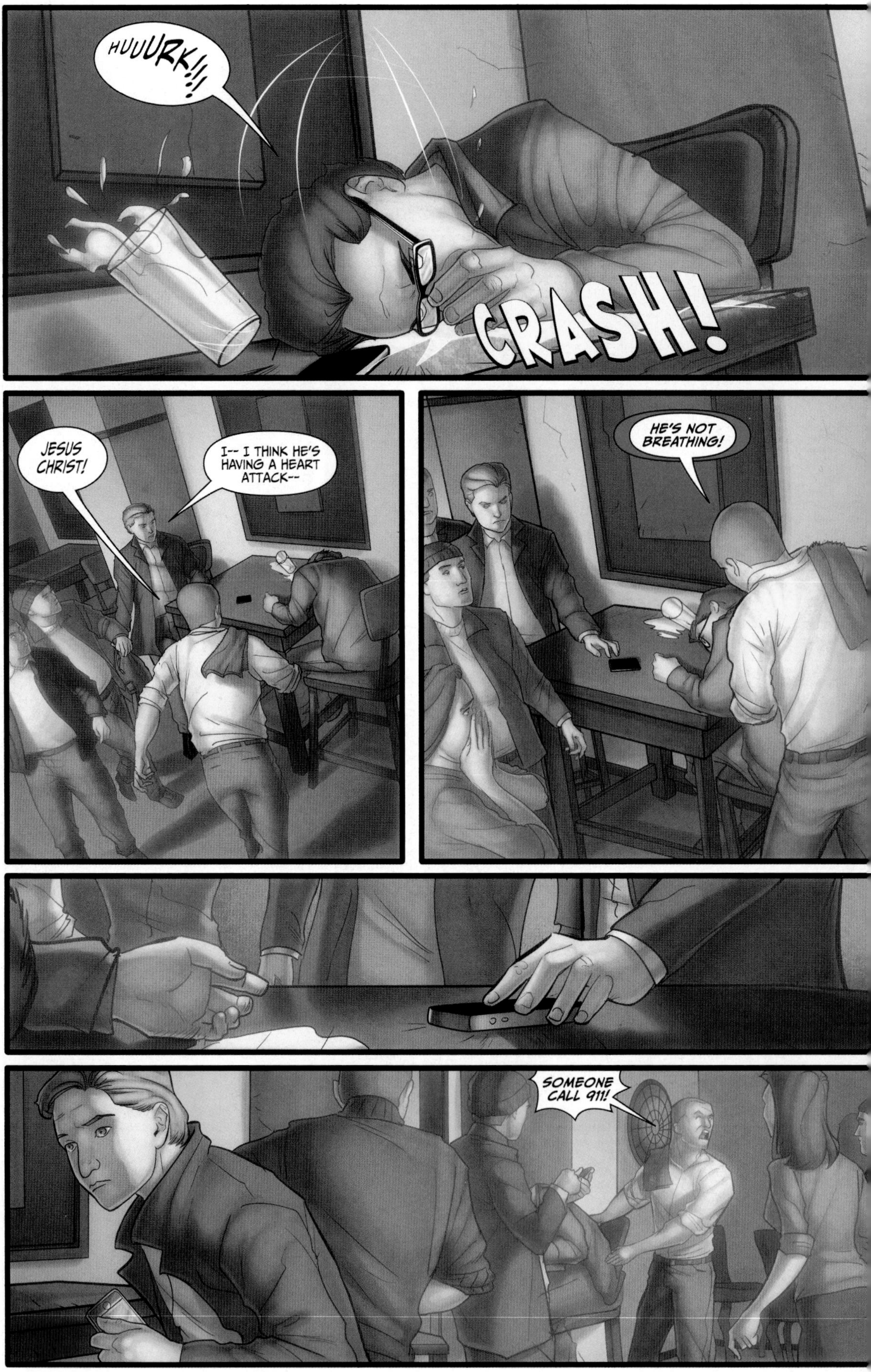
HUUURK!!!
CRASH!
JESUS CHRIST!
I-- I THINK HE'S HAVING A HEART ATTACK--
HE'S NOT BREATHING!
SOMEONE CALL 911!

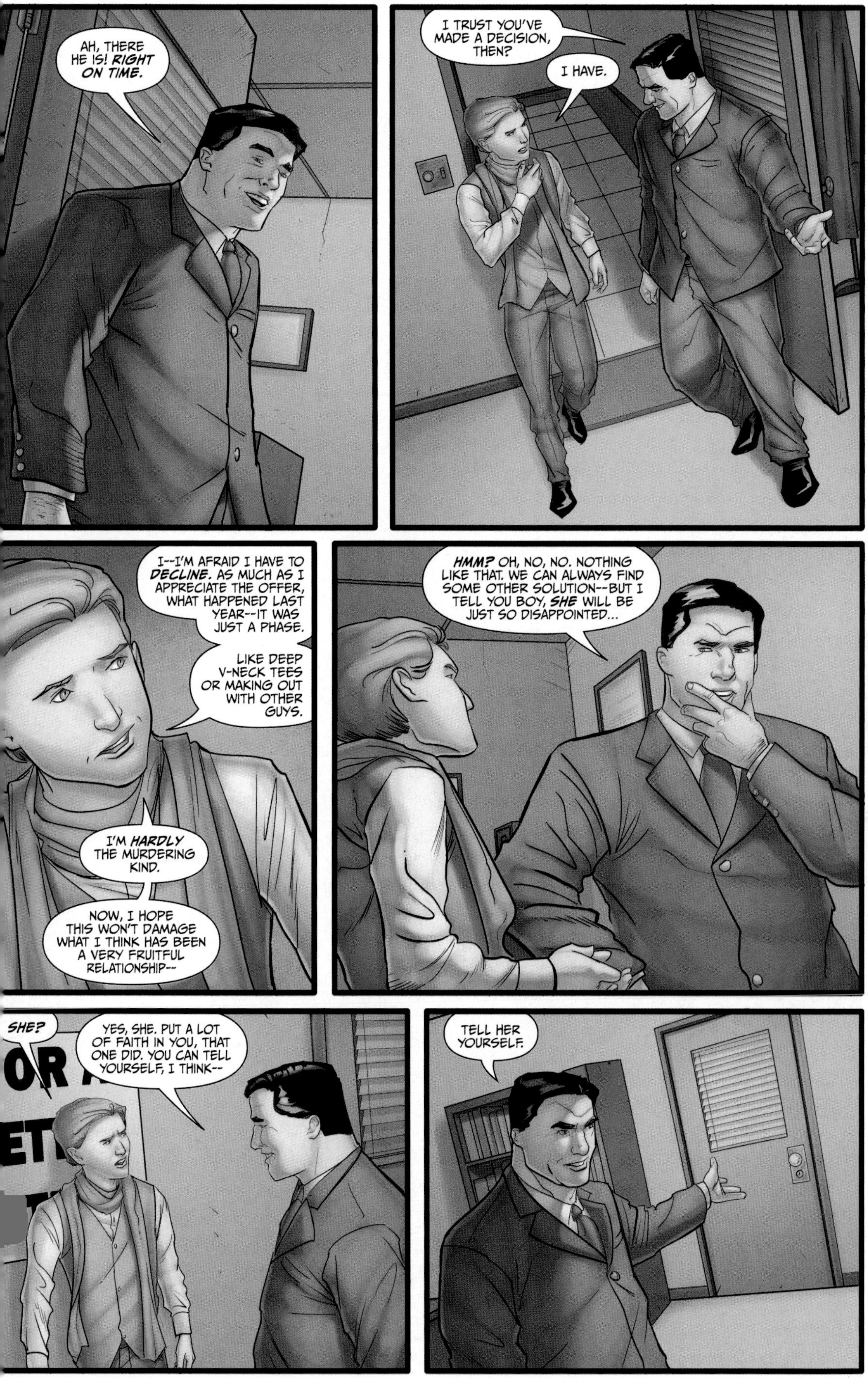
AH, THERE HE IS! *RIGHT ON TIME.*
I TRUST YOU'VE MADE A DECISION, THEN?
I HAVE.
I--I'M AFRAID I HAVE TO *DECLINE.* AS MUCH AS I APPRECIATE THE OFFER, WHAT HAPPENED LAST YEAR--IT WAS JUST A PHASE.
LIKE DEEP V-NECK TEES OR MAKING OUT WITH OTHER GUYS.
I'M *HARDLY* THE MURDERING KIND.
NOW, I HOPE THIS WON'T DAMAGE WHAT I THINK HAS BEEN A VERY FRUITFUL RELATIONSHIP--
HMM? OH, NO, NO. NOTHING LIKE THAT. WE CAN ALWAYS FIND SOME OTHER SOLUTION--BUT I TELL YOU BOY, *SHE* WILL BE JUST SO DISAPPOINTED...
SHE?
YES, SHE. PUT A LOT OF FAITH IN YOU, THAT ONE DID. YOU CAN TELL YOURSELF, I THINK--
TELL HER YOURSELF.

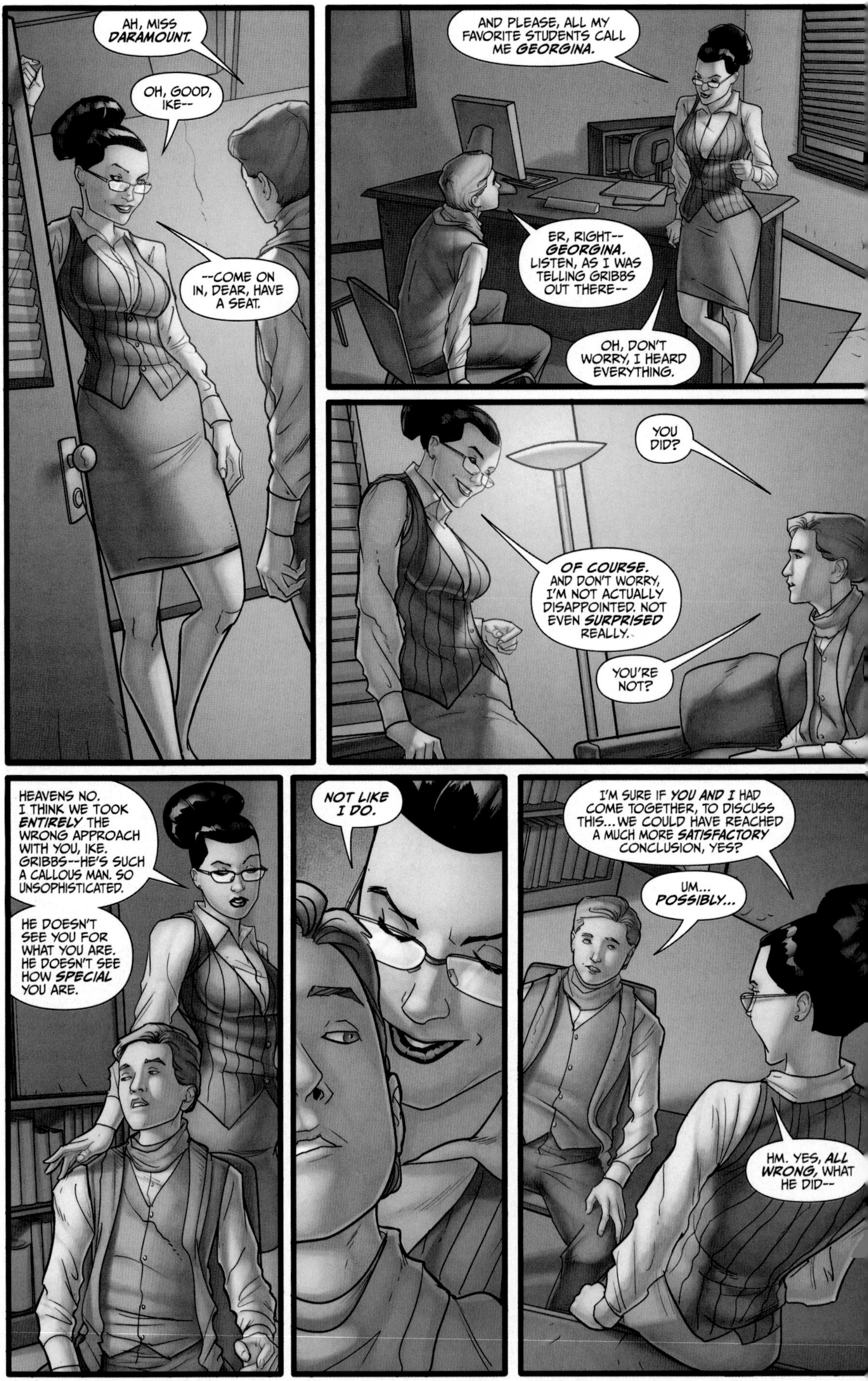
AH, MISS DARAMOUNT.
OH, GOOD, IKE--
--COME ON IN, DEAR, HAVE A SEAT.
AND PLEASE, ALL MY FAVORITE STUDENTS CALL ME GEORGINA.
ER, RIGHT-- GEORGINA. LISTEN, AS I WAS TELLING GRIBBS OUT THERE--
OH, DON'T WORRY, I HEARD EVERYTHING.
YOU DID?
OF COURSE. AND DON'T WORRY, I'M NOT ACTUALLY DISAPPOINTED. NOT EVEN SURPRISED REALLY.
YOU'RE NOT?
HEAVENS NO. I THINK WE TOOK ENTIRELY THE WRONG APPROACH WITH YOU, IKE. GRIBBS--HE'S SUCH A CALLOUS MAN. SO UNSOPHISTICATED.
HE DOESN'T SEE YOU FOR WHAT YOU ARE. HE DOESN'T SEE HOW SPECIAL YOU ARE.
NOT LIKE I DO.
I'M SURE IF YOU AND I HAD COME TOGETHER, TO DISCUSS THIS...WE COULD HAVE REACHED A MUCH MORE SATISFACTORY CONCLUSION, YES?
UM... POSSIBLY...
HM. YES, ALL WRONG, WHAT HE DID--

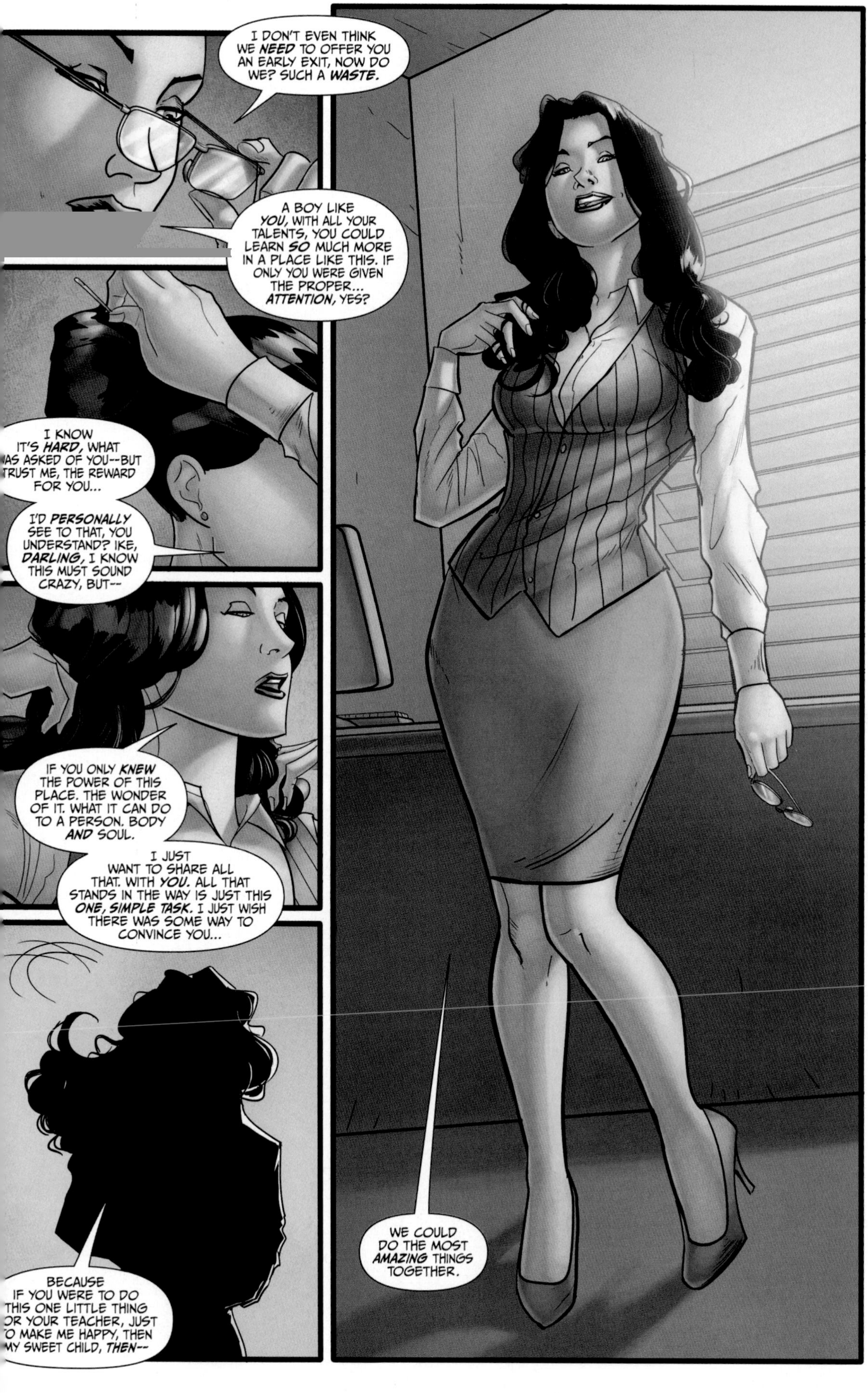

I DON'T EVEN THINK WE NEED TO OFFER YOU AN EARLY EXIT, NOW DO WE? SUCH A WASTE.
A BOY LIKE YOU, WITH ALL YOUR TALENTS, YOU COULD LEARN SO MUCH MORE IN A PLACE LIKE THIS. IF ONLY YOU WERE GIVEN THE PROPER... ATTENTION, YES?
I KNOW IT'S HARD, WHAT WAS ASKED OF YOU--BUT TRUST ME, THE REWARD FOR YOU...
I'D PERSONALLY SEE TO THAT, YOU UNDERSTAND? IKE, DARLING, I KNOW THIS MUST SOUND CRAZY, BUT--
IF YOU ONLY KNEW THE POWER OF THIS PLACE. THE WONDER OF IT. WHAT IT CAN DO TO A PERSON. BODY AND SOUL.
I JUST WANT TO SHARE ALL THAT. WITH YOU. ALL THAT STANDS IN THE WAY IS JUST THIS ONE, SIMPLE TASK. I JUST WISH THERE WAS SOME WAY TO CONVINCE YOU...
BECAUSE IF YOU WERE TO DO THIS ONE LITTLE THING FOR YOUR TEACHER, JUST TO MAKE ME HAPPY, THEN MY SWEET CHILD, THEN--
WE COULD DO THE MOST AMAZING THINGS TOGETHER.

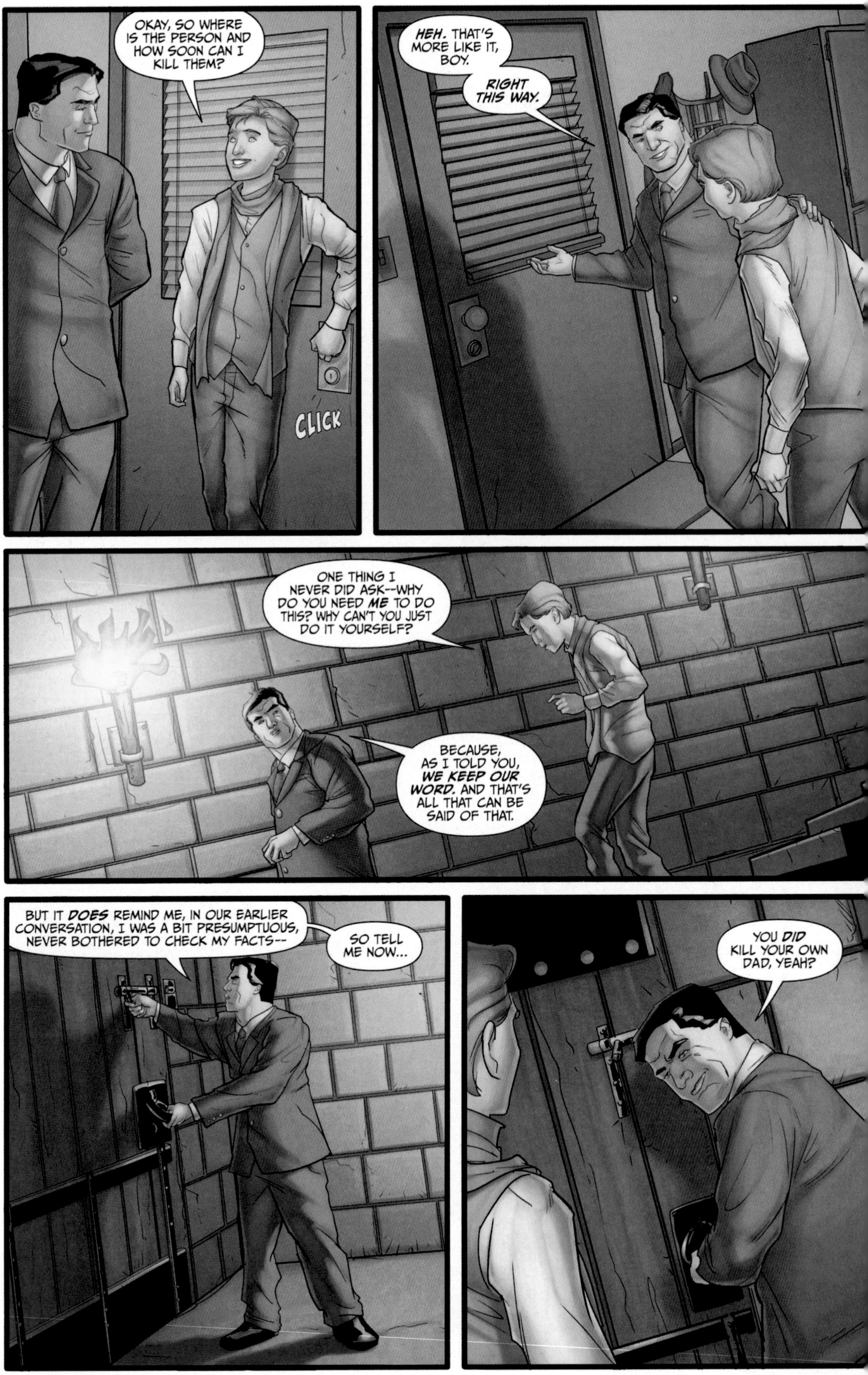
OKAY, SO WHERE IS THE PERSON AND HOW SOON CAN I KILL THEM?
CLICK
HEH. THAT'S MORE LIKE IT, BOY.
RIGHT THIS WAY.
ONE THING I NEVER DID ASK--WHY DO YOU NEED ME TO DO THIS? WHY CAN'T YOU JUST DO IT YOURSELF?
BECAUSE, AS I TOLD YOU, WE KEEP OUR WORD. AND THAT'S ALL THAT CAN BE SAID OF THAT.
BUT IT DOES REMIND ME, IN OUR EARLIER CONVERSATION, I WAS A BIT PRESUMPTUOUS, NEVER BOTHERED TO CHECK MY FACTS--
SO TELL ME NOW...
YOU DID KILL YOUR OWN DAD, YEAH?

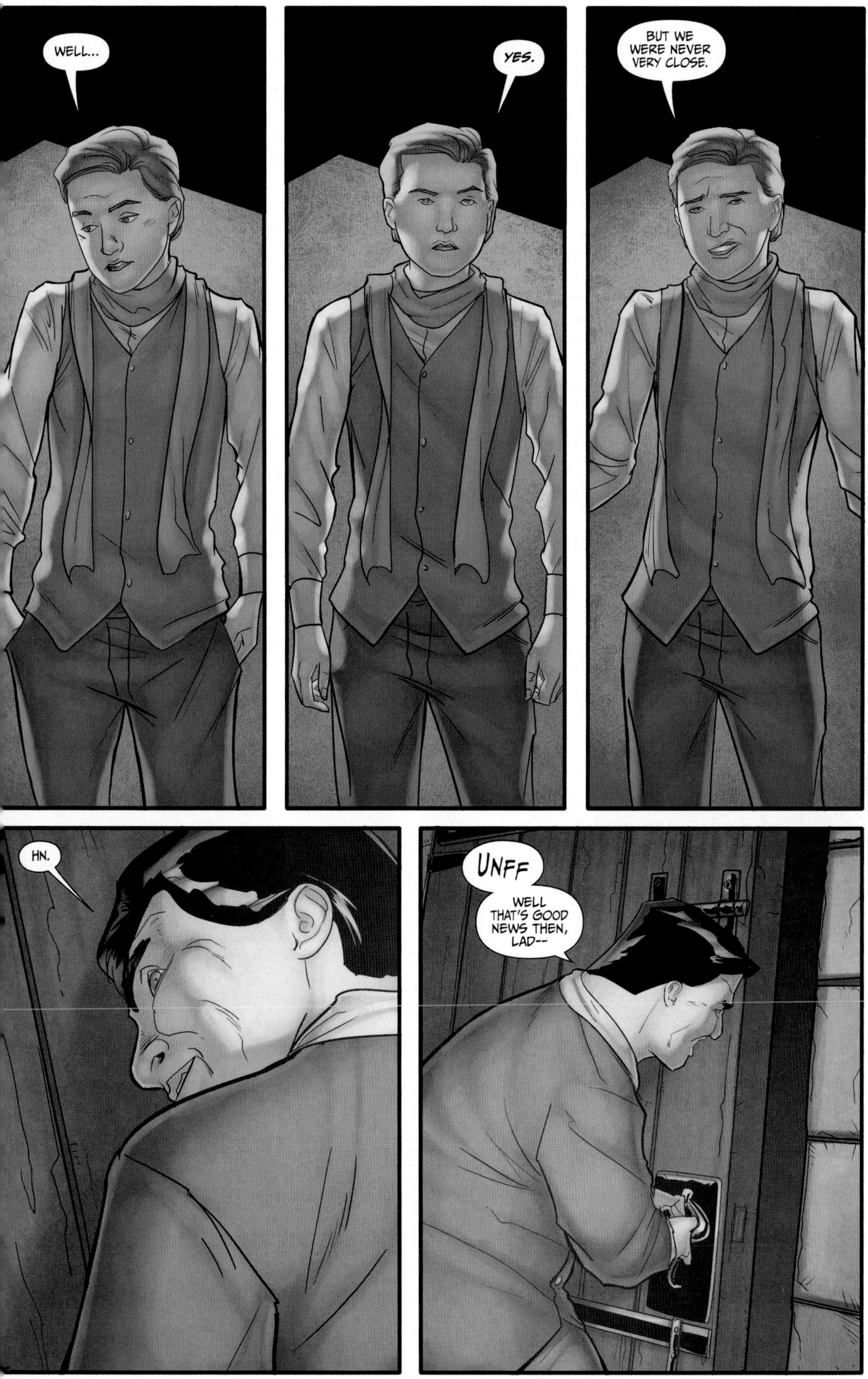
WELL...
YES.
BUT WE WERE NEVER VERY CLOSE.
HN.
UNFF
WELL THAT'S GOOD NEWS THEN, LAD--

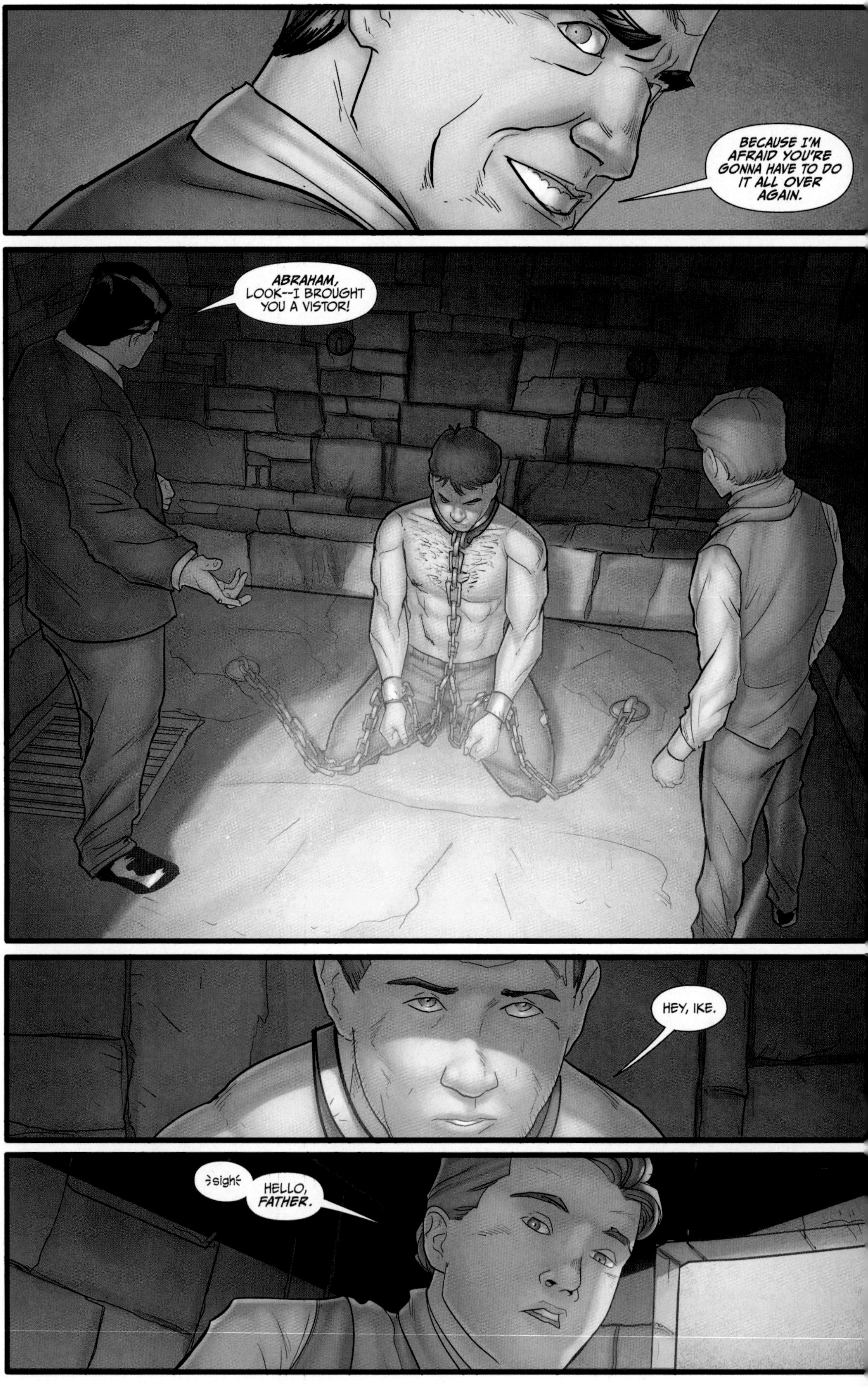
BECAUSE I'M AFRAID YOU'RE GONNA HAVE TO DO IT ALL OVER AGAIN.
ABRAHAM, LOOK--I BROUGHT YOU A VISTOR!
HEY, IKE.
sigh
HELLO, FATHER.

twelve

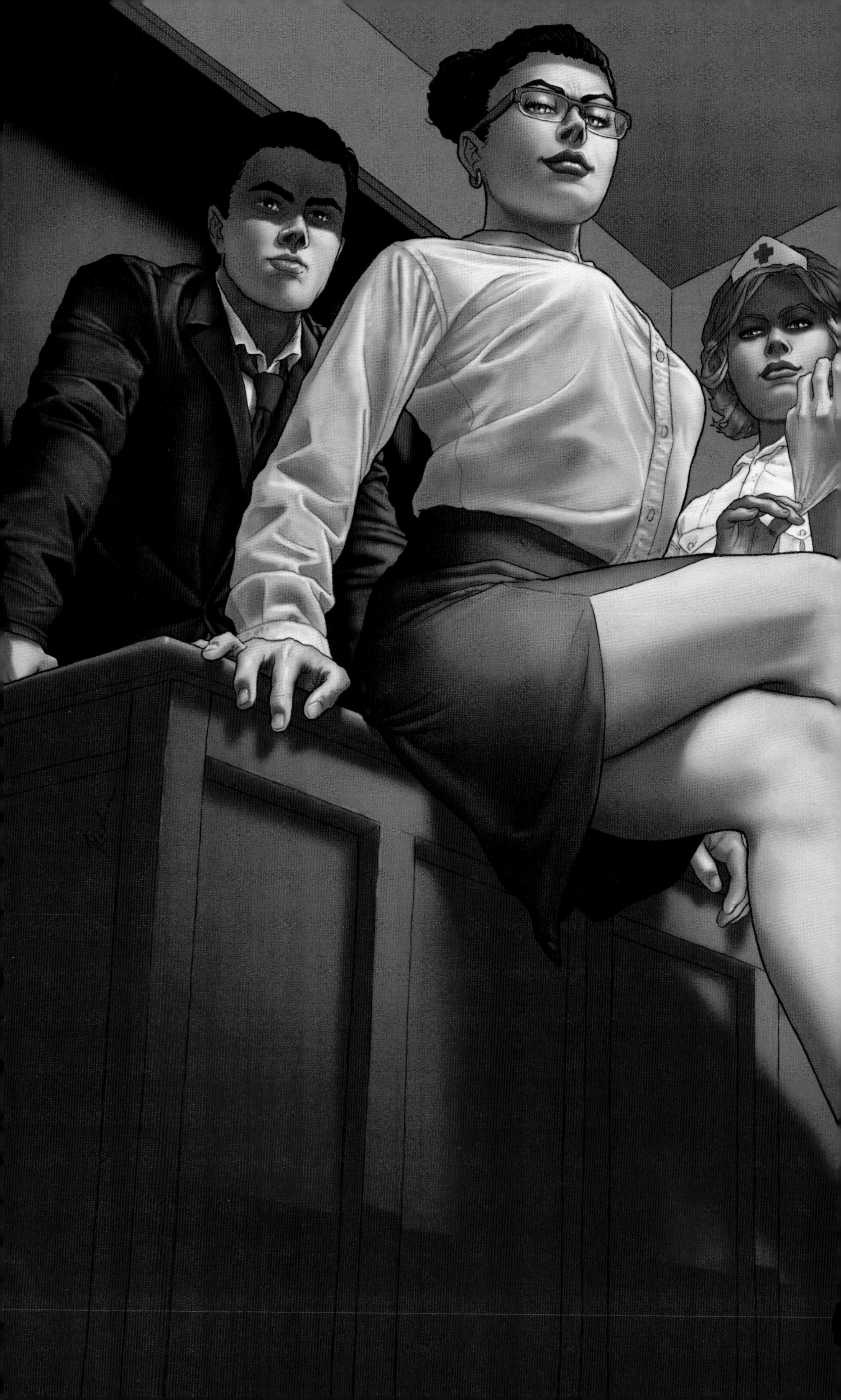

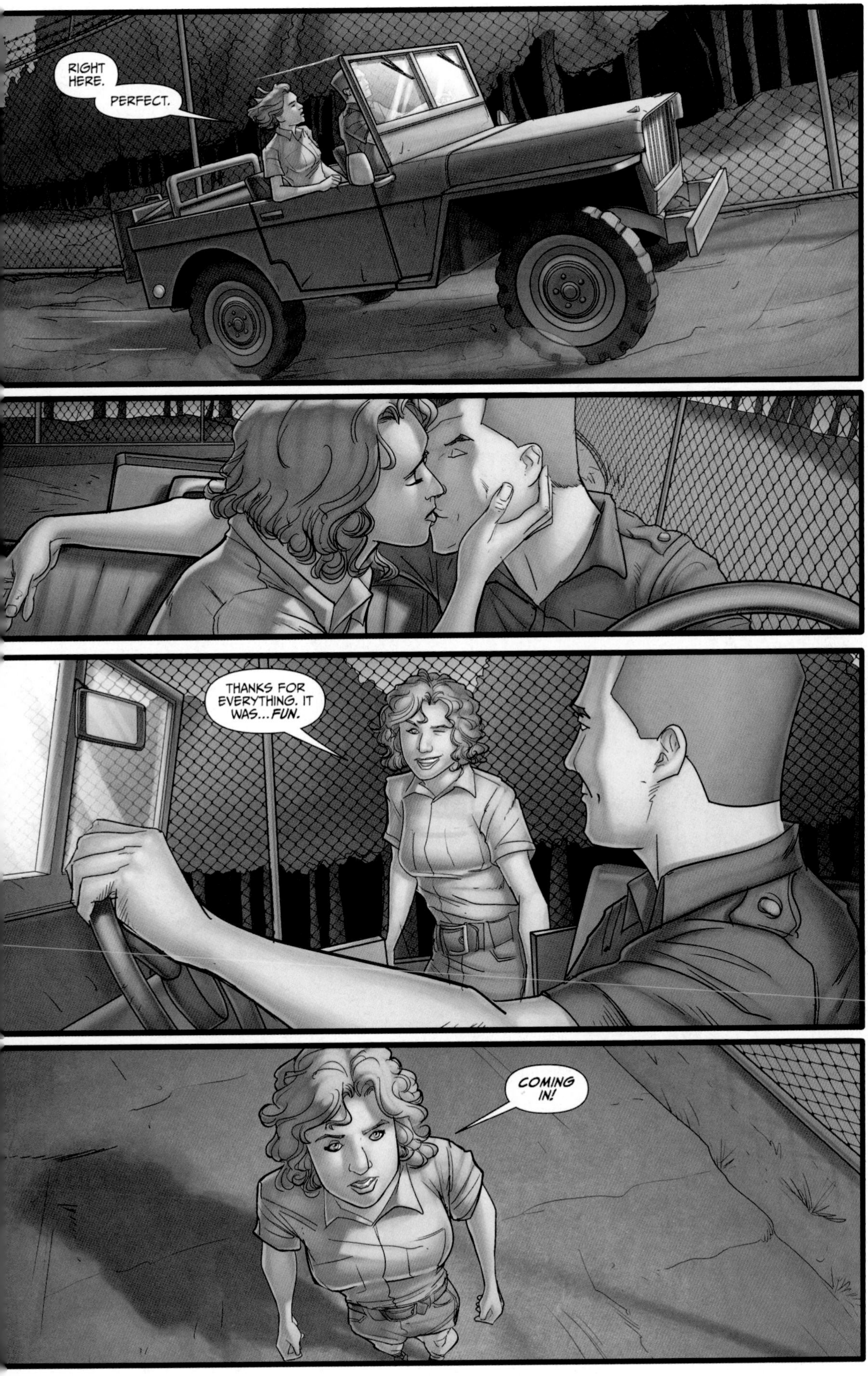
RIGHT HERE.
PERFECT.
THANKS FOR EVERYTHING. IT WAS... FUN.
COMING IN!

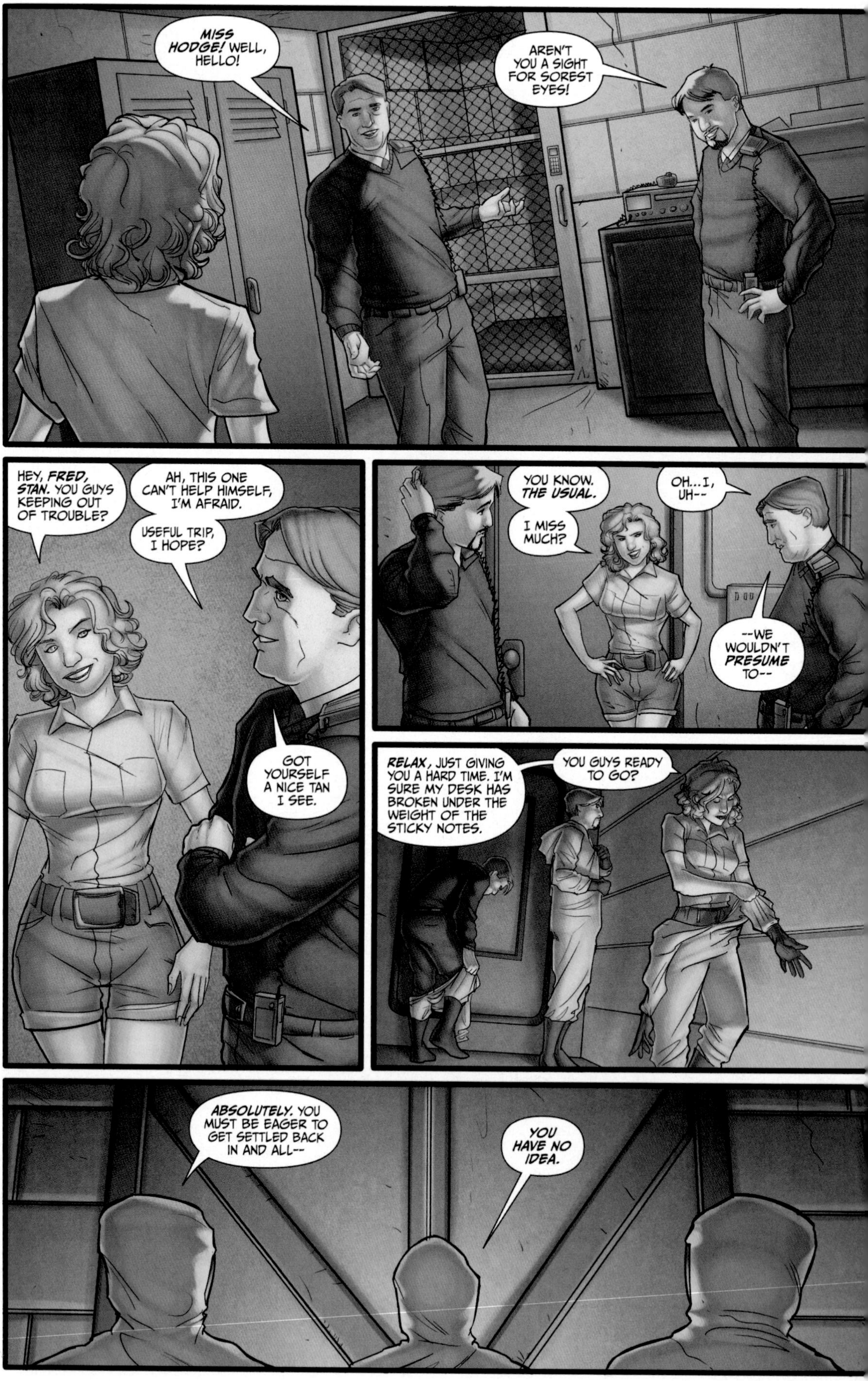
MISS HODGE! WELL, HELLO!
AREN'T YOU A SIGHT FOR SOREST EYES!
HEY, FRED, STAN. YOU GUYS KEEPING OUT OF TROUBLE?
AH, THIS ONE CAN'T HELP HIMSELF, I'M AFRAID.
USEFUL TRIP, I HOPE?
GOT YOURSELF A NICE TAN I SEE.
YOU KNOW. THE USUAL.
I MISS MUCH?
OH...I, UH--
--WE WOULDN'T PRESUME TO--
RELAX, JUST GIVING YOU A HARD TIME. I'M SURE MY DESK HAS BROKEN UNDER THE WEIGHT OF THE STICKY NOTES.
YOU GUYS READY TO GO?
ABSOLUTELY. YOU MUST BE EAGER TO GET SETTLED BACK IN AND ALL--
YOU HAVE NO IDEA.

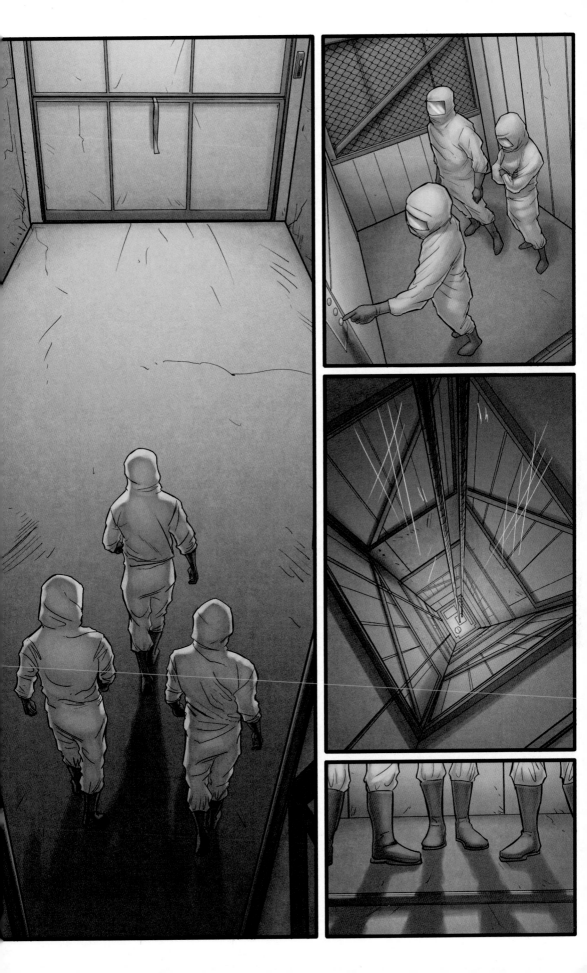

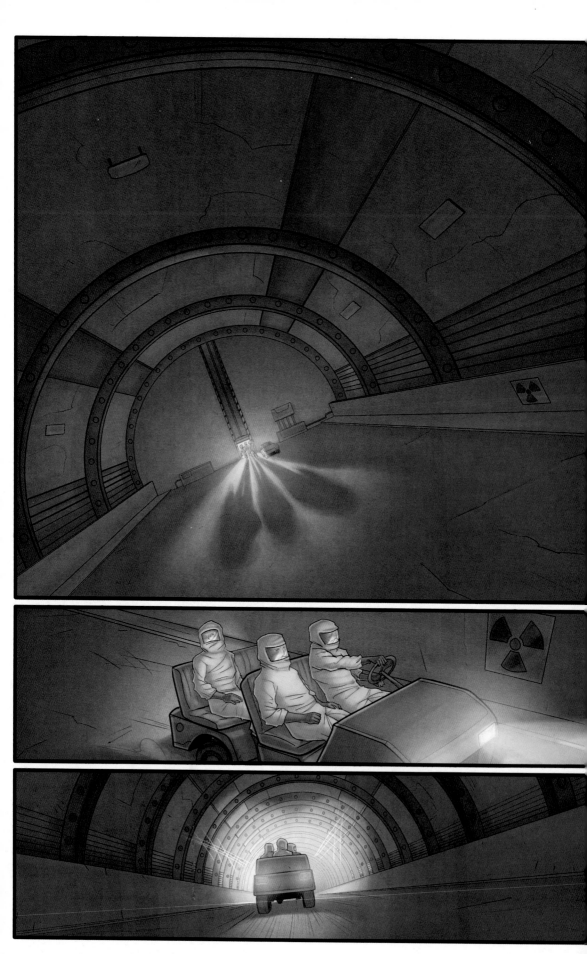

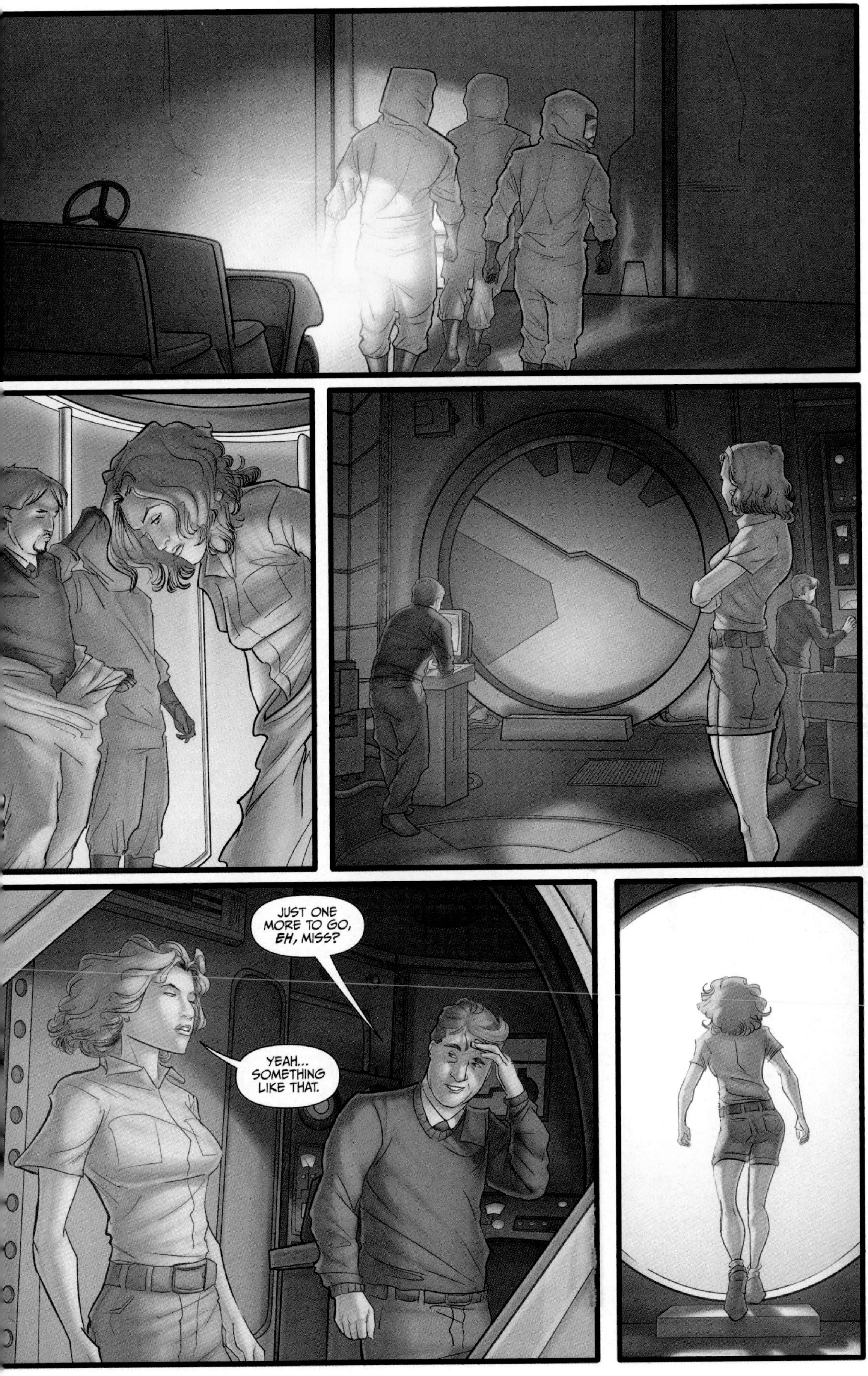
JUST ONE MORE TO GO, EH, MISS?
YEAH... SOMETHING LIKE THAT.

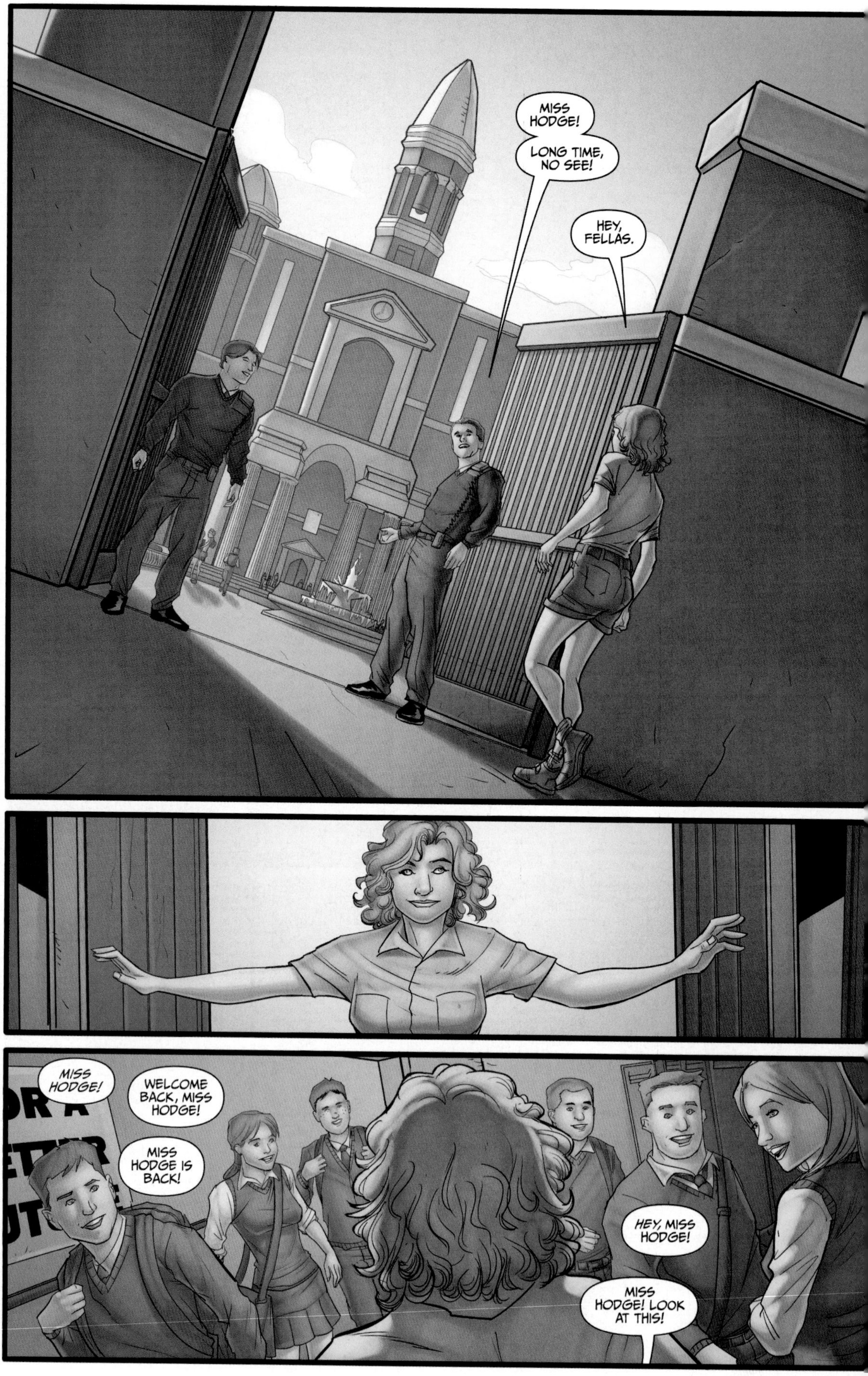
MISS HODGE!
LONG TIME, NO SEE!
HEY, FELLAS.
MISS HODGE!
WELCOME BACK, MISS HODGE!
MISS HODGE IS BACK!
HEY, MISS HODGE!
MISS HODGE! LOOK AT THIS!

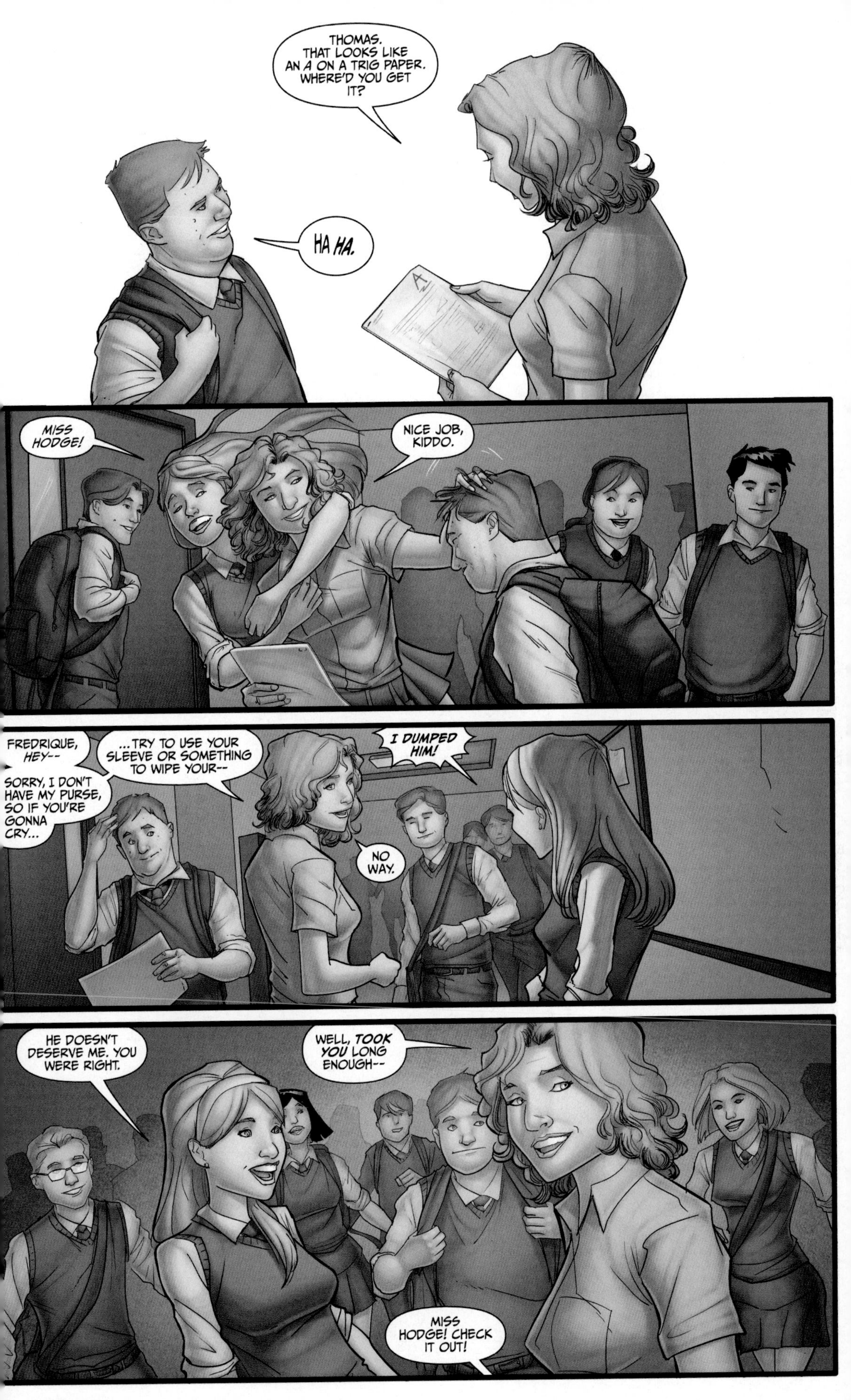
THOMAS. THAT LOOKS LIKE AN A ON A TRIG PAPER. WHERE'D YOU GET IT?
HA HA.
MISS HODGE!
NICE JOB, KIDDO.
FREDRIQUE, HEY--
SORRY, I DON'T HAVE MY PURSE, SO IF YOU'RE GONNA CRY...
...TRY TO USE YOUR SLEEVE OR SOMETHING TO WIPE YOUR--
I DUMPED HIM!
NO WAY.
HE DOESN'T DESERVE ME. YOU WERE RIGHT.
WELL, TOOK YOU LONG ENOUGH--
MISS HODGE! CHECK IT OUT!

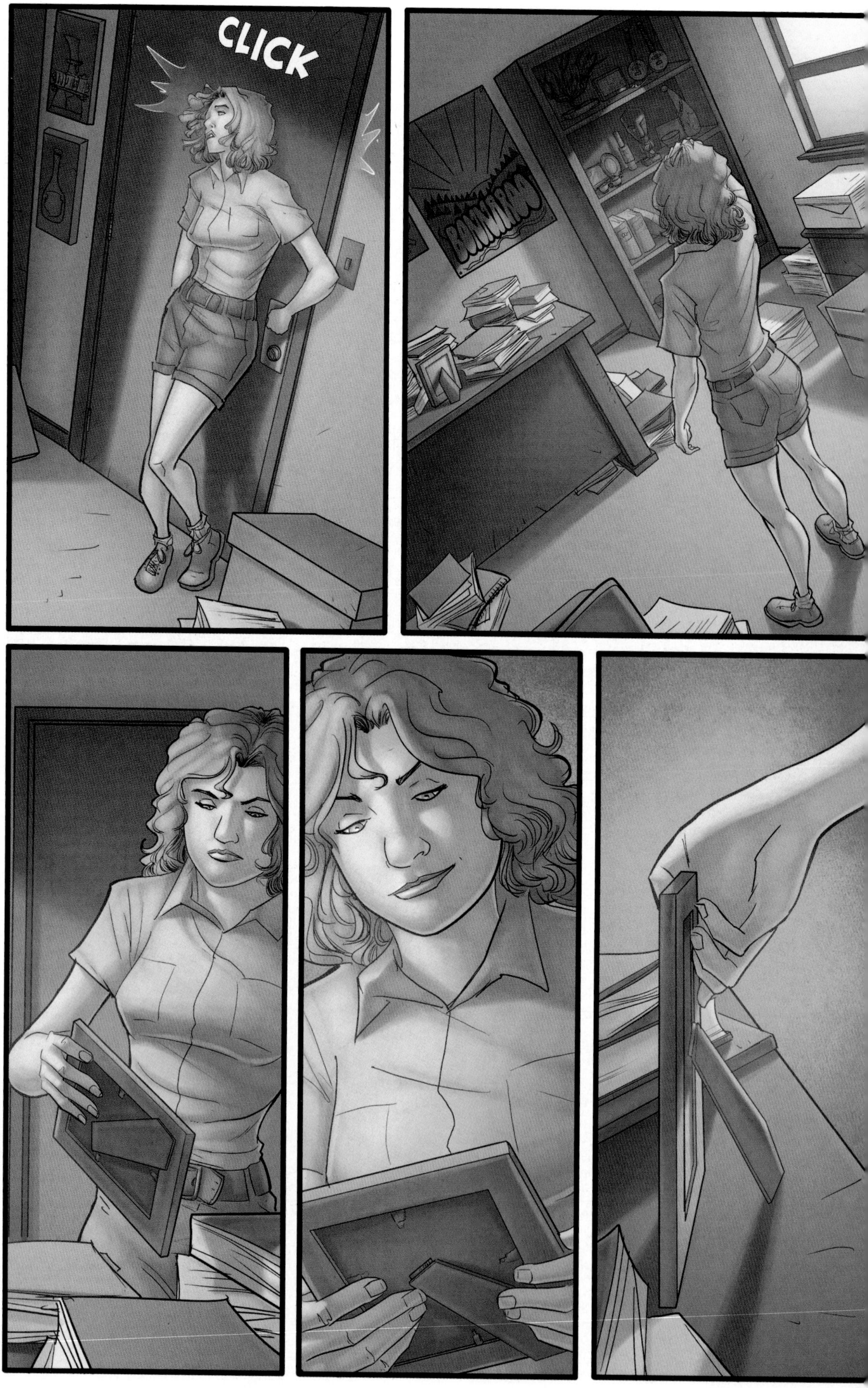
CLICK

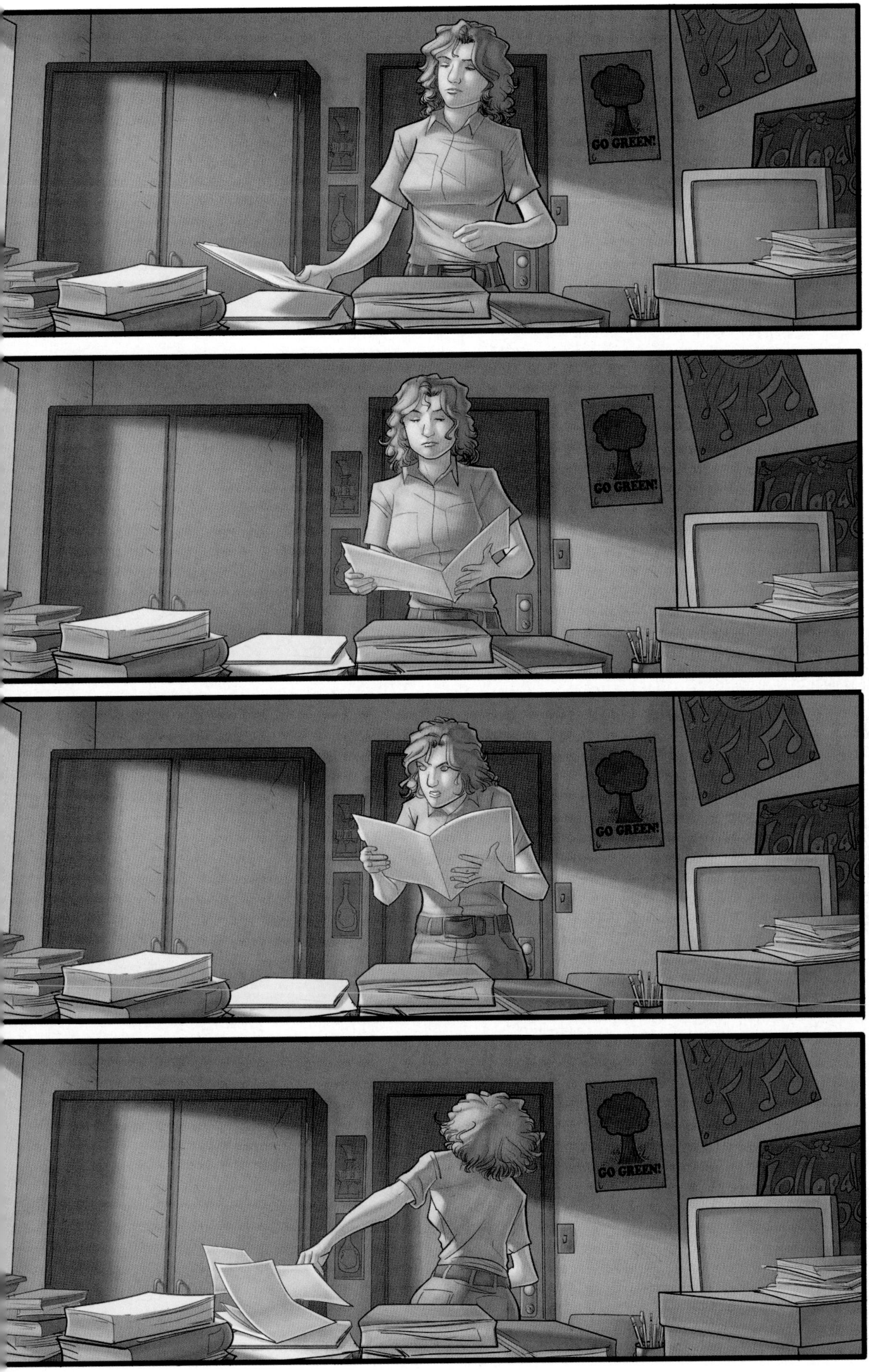
GO GREEN!
GO GREEN!
GO GREEN!
GO GREEN!

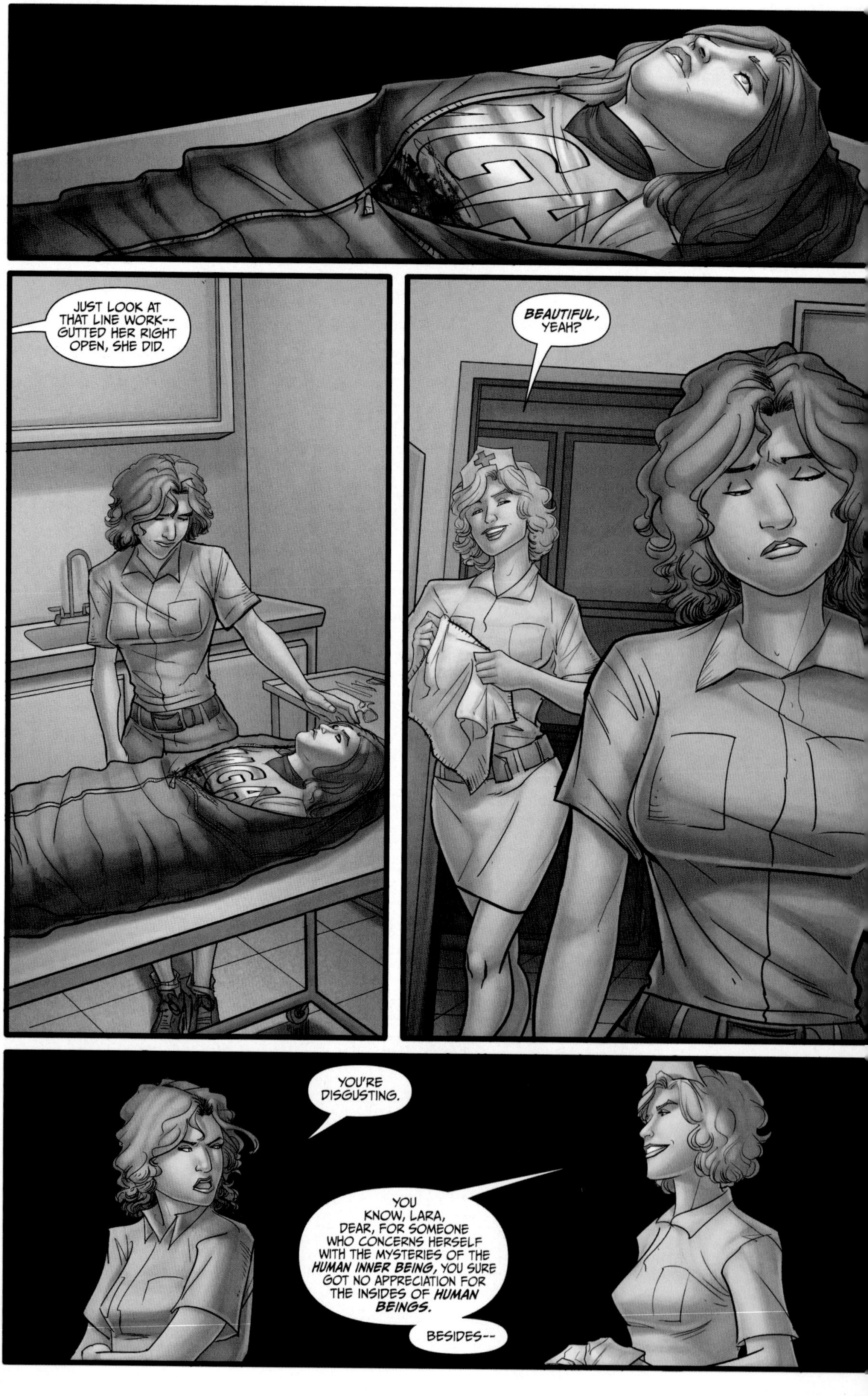
JUST LOOK AT THAT LINE WORK-- GUTTED HER RIGHT OPEN, SHE DID.
BEAUTIFUL, YEAH?
YOU'RE DISGUSTING.
YOU KNOW, LARA, DEAR, FOR SOMEONE WHO CONCERNS HERSELF WITH THE MYSTERIES OF THE HUMAN INNER BEING, YOU SURE GOT NO APPRECIATION FOR THE INSIDES OF HUMAN BEINGS.
BESIDES--

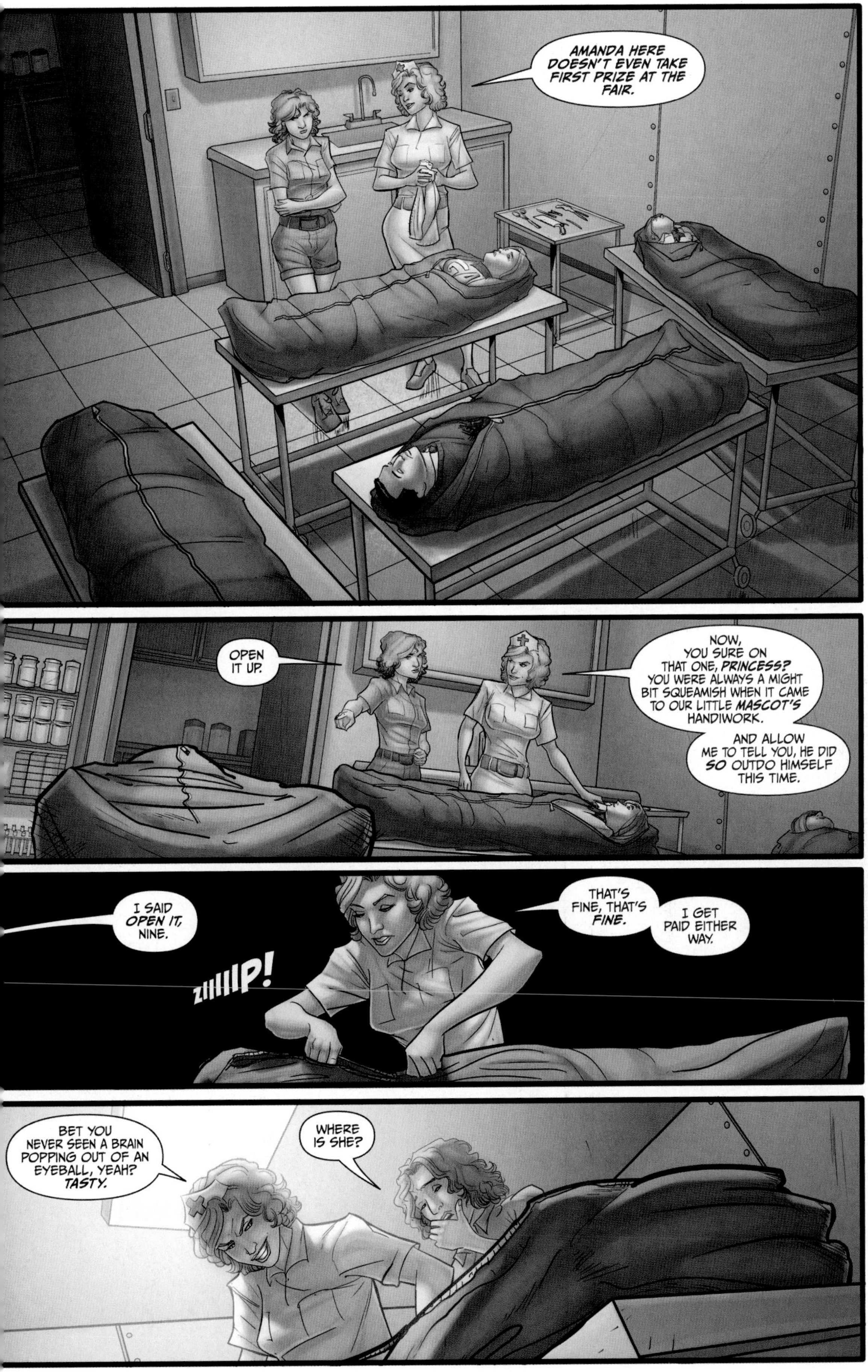
AMANDA HERE DOESN'T EVEN TAKE FIRST PRIZE AT THE FAIR.
OPEN IT UP.
NOW, YOU SURE ON THAT ONE, PRINCESS? YOU WERE ALWAYS A MIGHT BIT SQUEAMISH WHEN IT CAME TO OUR LITTLE MASCOT'S HANDIWORK.
AND ALLOW ME TO TELL YOU, HE DID SO OUTDO HIMSELF THIS TIME.
I SAID OPEN IT, NINE.
THAT'S FINE, THAT'S FINE.
I GET PAID EITHER WAY.
ZIIIIIP!
BET YOU NEVER SEEN A BRAIN POPPING OUT OF AN EYEBALL, YEAH? TASTY.
WHERE IS SHE?

AND SO, CLASS, WE COME UPON A MOST INTERESTING LITTLE ANECDOTE FROM HISTORY--HOW A CHANDELIER CAME TO DETERMINE THE SPEED OF LIGHT. WE ALL KNOW THAT--

AHEM--

AH, MISS HODGE!

STUDENTS, LOOK, THE PRODIGAL DAUGHTER RETURNS!

WHAT CAN WE DO FOR YOU, LARA?

MISS DARAMOUNT. MAY I SPEAK WITH YOU FOR A MOMENT IN THE HALL?

MM, WELL-- I'M AFRAID NOW IS A BAD TIME. WHATEVER IT IS, IT WILL HAVE TO WAIT UNTIL AFTER MY LESSON HAS--

GALILEO.

SHE DOES THIS WHOLE BIG RUNAROUND FOR AN HOUR, BUT BASICALLY, GALILEO SEES A CHANDELIER SWINGING AS A TEENAGER DURING THE 1581 EARTHQUAKE.

IT GETS HIM INTERESTED IN PHYSICS, HE EVENTUALLY CREATES AN EXPERIMENT TO MEASURE THE SPEED OF LIGHT, BLAH, BLAH, BLAH.

GALILEO.

NOW, MISS DARAMOUNT.

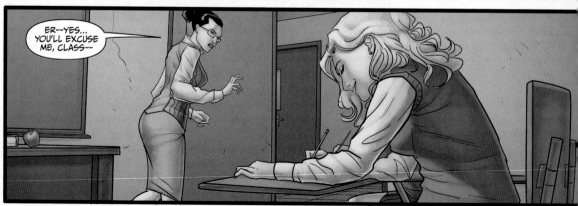

ER--YES... YOU'LL EXCUSE ME, CLASS--

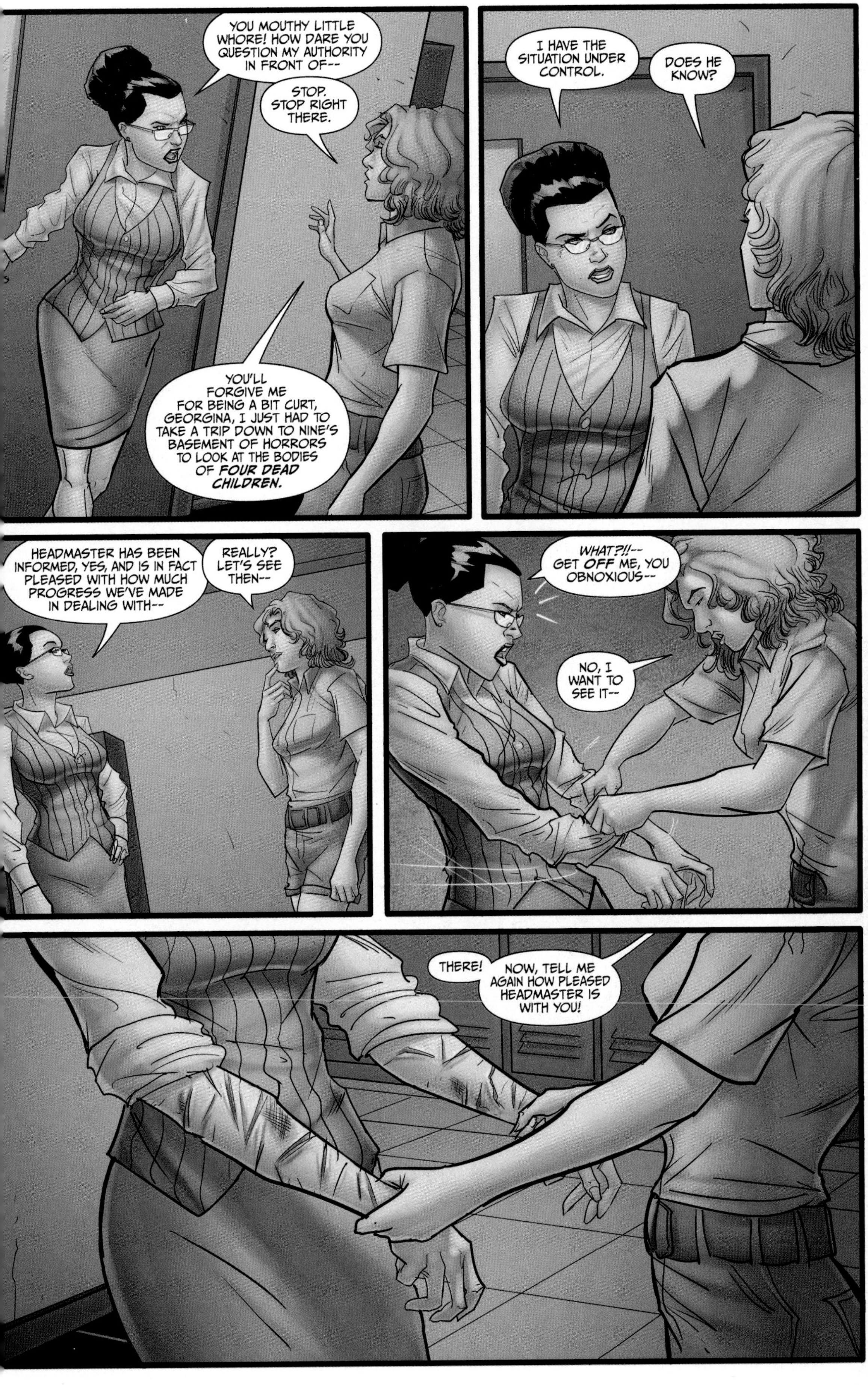

YOU MOUTHY LITTLE WHORE! HOW DARE YOU QUESTION MY AUTHORITY IN FRONT OF--
STOP. STOP RIGHT THERE.
YOU'LL FORGIVE ME FOR BEING A BIT CURT, GEORGINA, I JUST HAD TO TAKE A TRIP DOWN TO NINE'S BASEMENT OF HORRORS TO LOOK AT THE BODIES OF **FOUR DEAD CHILDREN.**
I HAVE THE SITUATION UNDER CONTROL.
DOES HE KNOW?
HEADMASTER HAS BEEN INFORMED, YES, AND IS IN FACT PLEASED WITH HOW MUCH PROGRESS WE'VE MADE IN DEALING WITH--
REALLY? LET'S SEE THEN--
WHAT?!!-- GET ***OFF*** ME, YOU OBNOXIOUS--
NO, I WANT TO SEE IT--
THERE!
NOW, TELL ME AGAIN HOW PLEASED HEADMASTER IS WITH YOU!

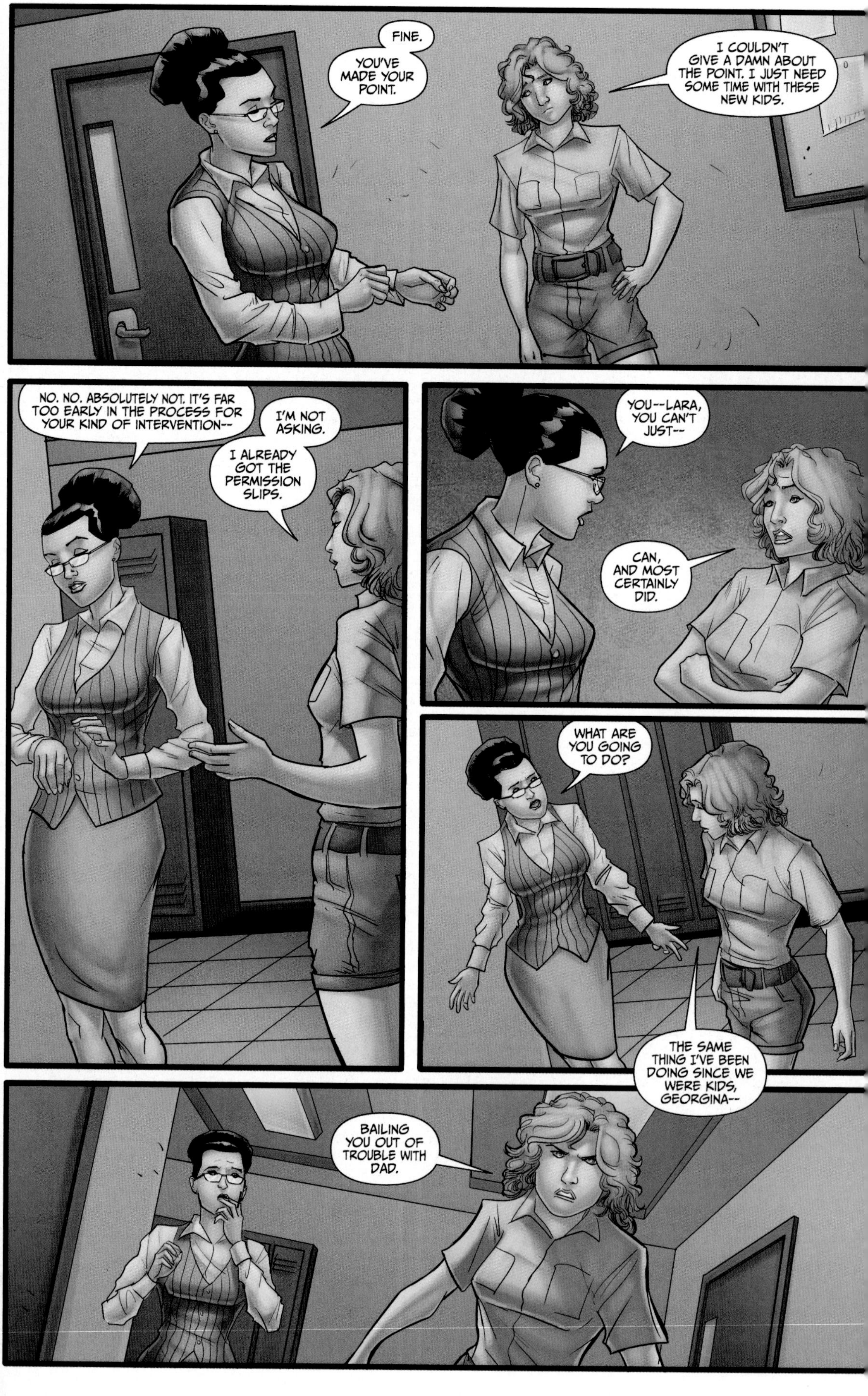
FINE.
YOU'VE MADE YOUR POINT.
I COULDN'T GIVE A DAMN ABOUT THE POINT. I JUST NEED SOME TIME WITH THESE NEW KIDS.
NO. NO. ABSOLUTELY NOT. IT'S FAR TOO EARLY IN THE PROCESS FOR YOUR KIND OF INTERVENTION--
I'M NOT ASKING.
I ALREADY GOT THE PERMISSION SLIPS.
YOU--LARA, YOU CAN'T JUST--
CAN, AND MOST CERTAINLY DID.
WHAT ARE YOU GOING TO DO?
THE SAME THING I'VE BEEN DOING SINCE WE WERE KIDS, GEORGINA--
BAILING YOU OUT OF TROUBLE WITH DAD.

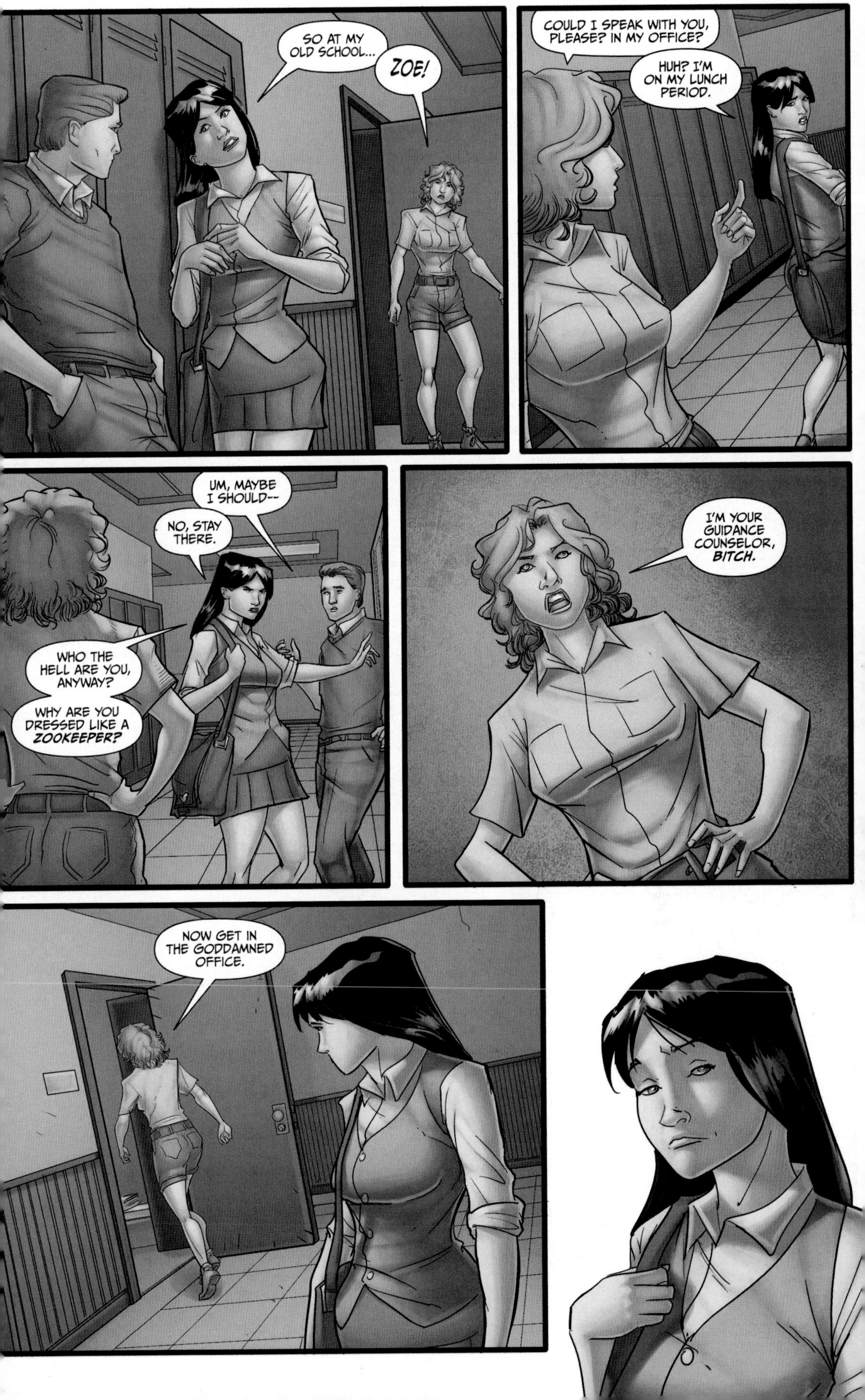
SO AT MY OLD SCHOOL...
ZOE!
COULD I SPEAK WITH YOU, PLEASE? IN MY OFFICE?
HUH? I'M ON MY LUNCH PERIOD.
UM, MAYBE I SHOULD--
NO, STAY THERE.
WHO THE HELL ARE YOU, ANYWAY?
WHY ARE YOU DRESSED LIKE A ZOOKEEPER?
I'M YOUR GUIDANCE COUNSELOR, BITCH.
NOW GET IN THE GODDAMNED OFFICE.

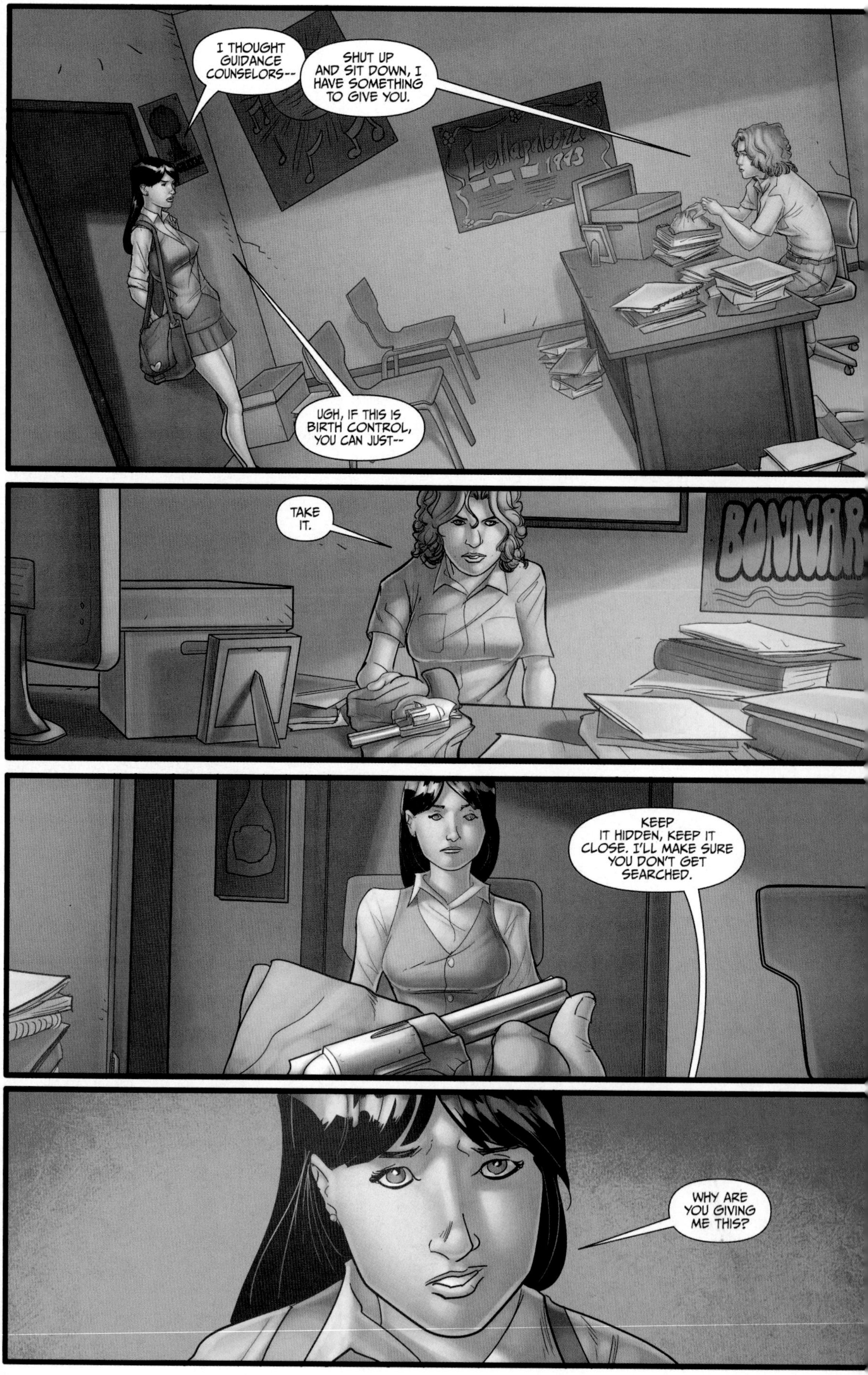
I THOUGHT GUIDANCE COUNSELORS--
SHUT UP AND SIT DOWN, I HAVE SOMETHING TO GIVE YOU.
UGH, IF THIS IS BIRTH CONTROL, YOU CAN JUST--
TAKE IT.
KEEP IT HIDDEN, KEEP IT CLOSE. I'LL MAKE SURE YOU DON'T GET SEARCHED.
WHY ARE YOU GIVING ME THIS?

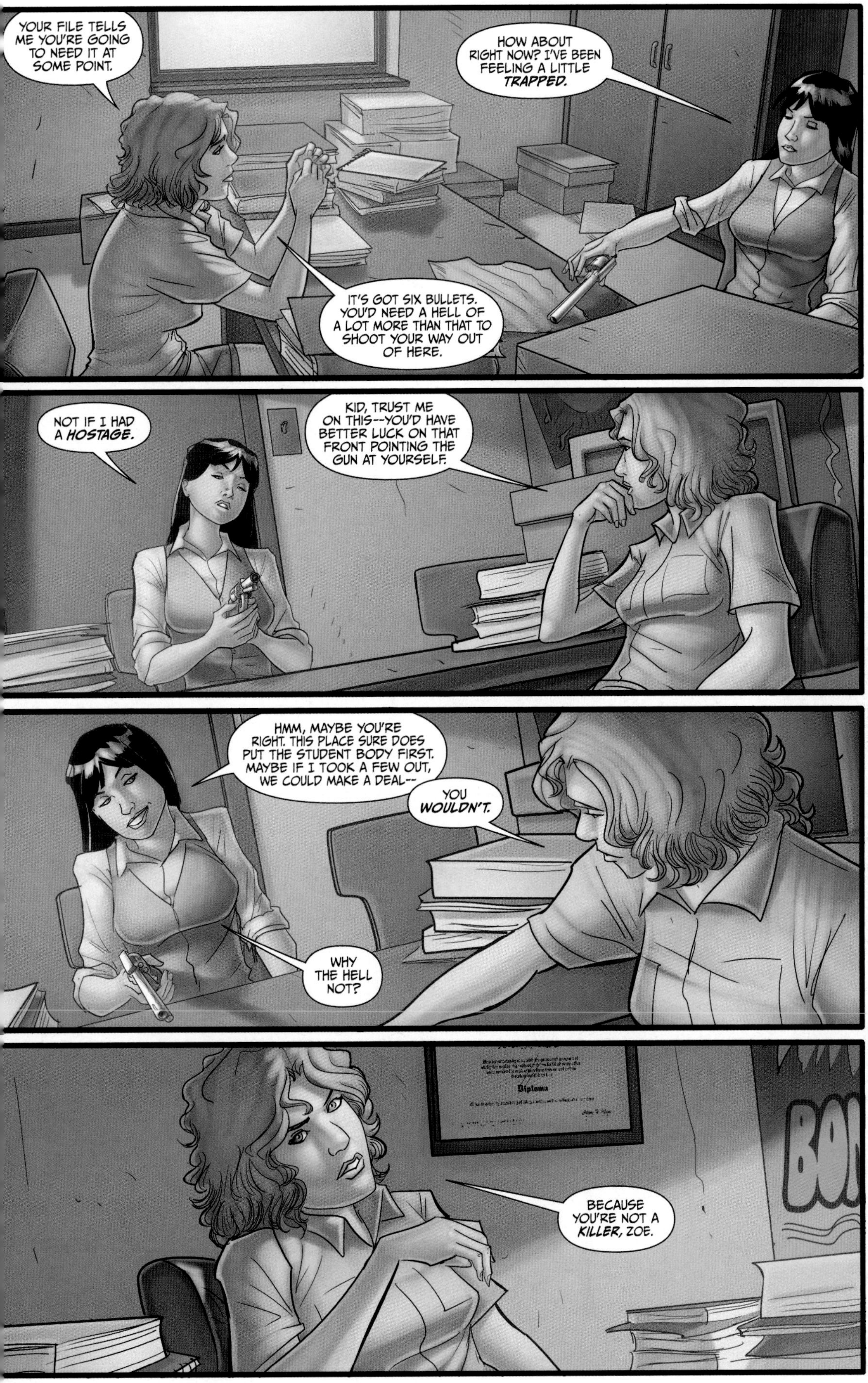
YOUR FILE TELLS ME YOU'RE GOING TO NEED IT AT SOME POINT.
HOW ABOUT RIGHT NOW? I'VE BEEN FEELING A LITTLE TRAPPED.
IT'S GOT SIX BULLETS. YOU'D NEED A HELL OF A LOT MORE THAN THAT TO SHOOT YOUR WAY OUT OF HERE.
NOT IF I HAD A HOSTAGE.
KID, TRUST ME ON THIS--YOU'D HAVE BETTER LUCK ON THAT FRONT POINTING THE GUN AT YOURSELF.
HMM, MAYBE YOU'RE RIGHT. THIS PLACE SURE DOES PUT THE STUDENT BODY FIRST. MAYBE IF I TOOK A FEW OUT, WE COULD MAKE A DEAL--
YOU WOULDN'T.
WHY THE HELL NOT?
Diploma
BECAUSE YOU'RE NOT A KILLER, ZOE.

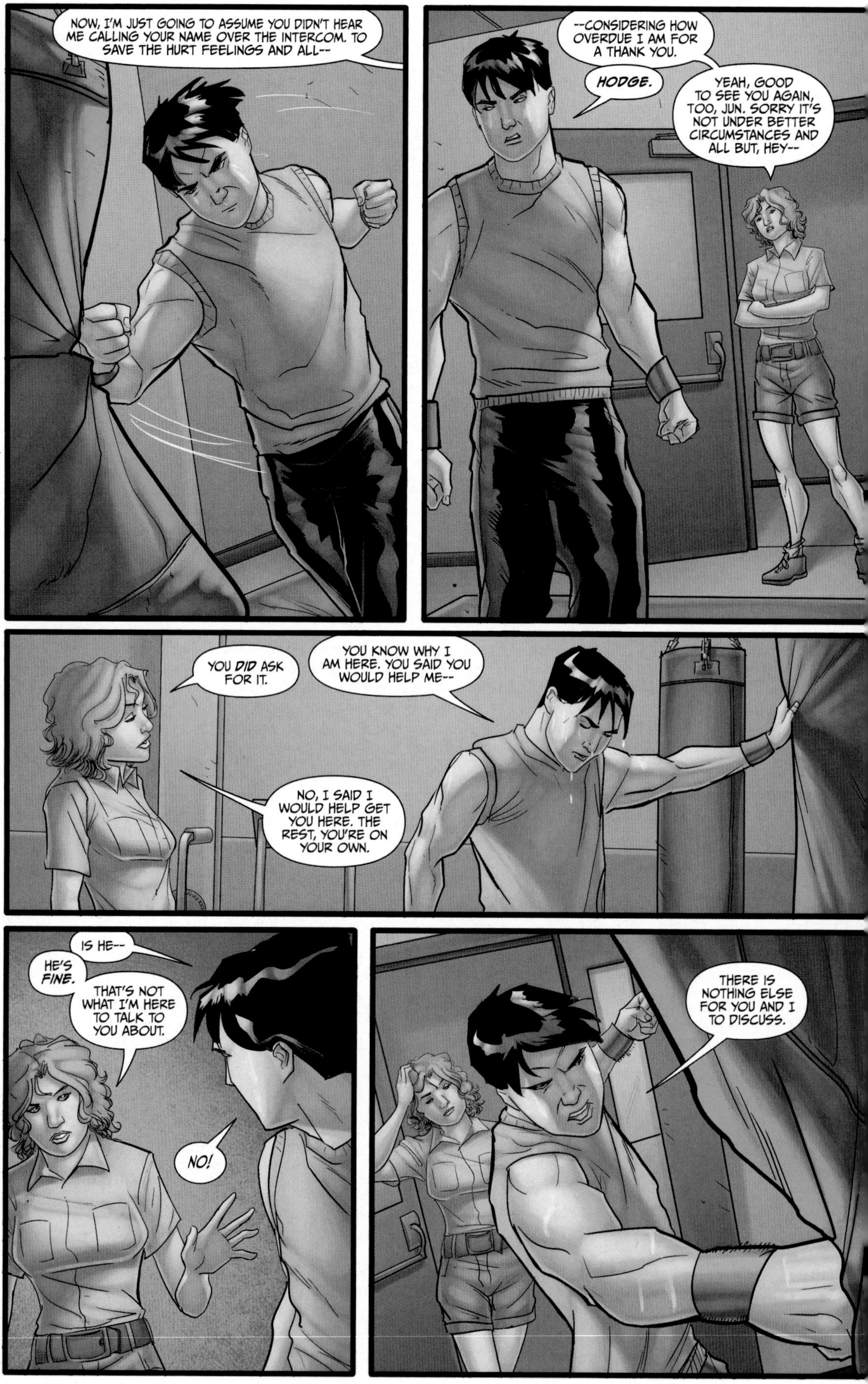
NOW, I'M JUST GOING TO ASSUME YOU DIDN'T HEAR ME CALLING YOUR NAME OVER THE INTERCOM. TO SAVE THE HURT FEELINGS AND ALL--
--CONSIDERING HOW OVERDUE I AM FOR A THANK YOU.
HODGE.
YEAH, GOOD TO SEE YOU AGAIN, TOO, JUN. SORRY IT'S NOT UNDER BETTER CIRCUMSTANCES AND ALL BUT, HEY--
YOU DID ASK FOR IT.
YOU KNOW WHY I AM HERE. YOU SAID YOU WOULD HELP ME--
NO, I SAID I WOULD HELP GET YOU HERE. THE REST, YOU'RE ON YOUR OWN.
IS HE--
HE'S FINE.
THAT'S NOT WHAT I'M HERE TO TALK TO YOU ABOUT.
NO!
THERE IS NOTHING ELSE FOR YOU AND I TO DISCUSS.

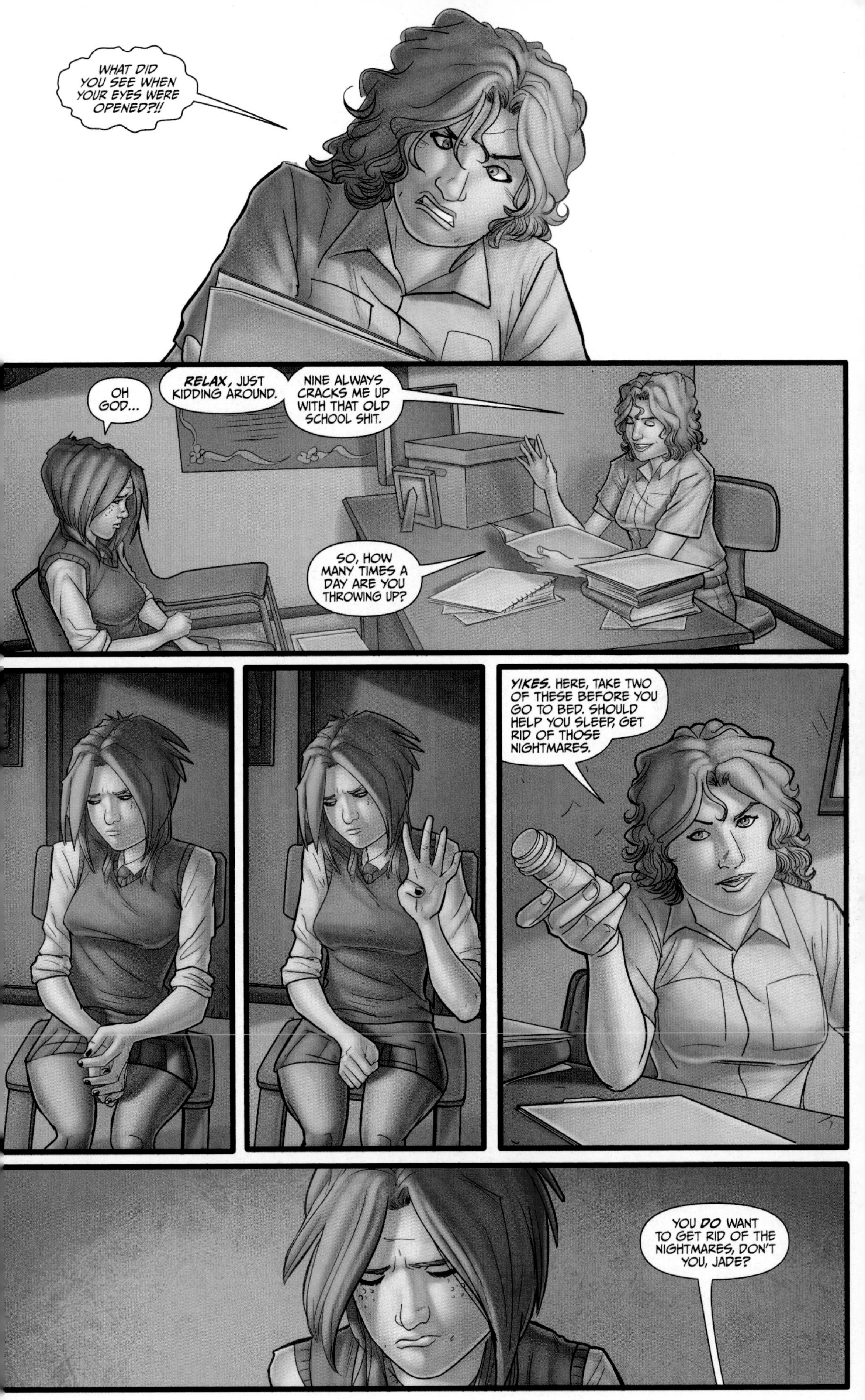

WHAT DID YOU SEE WHEN YOUR EYES WERE OPENED?!!
OH GOD...
RELAX, JUST KIDDING AROUND.
NINE ALWAYS CRACKS ME UP WITH THAT OLD SCHOOL SHIT.
SO, HOW MANY TIMES A DAY ARE YOU THROWING UP?
YIKES. HERE, TAKE TWO OF THESE BEFORE YOU GO TO BED. SHOULD HELP YOU SLEEP, GET RID OF THOSE NIGHTMARES.
YOU DO WANT TO GET RID OF THE NIGHTMARES, DON'T YOU, JADE?

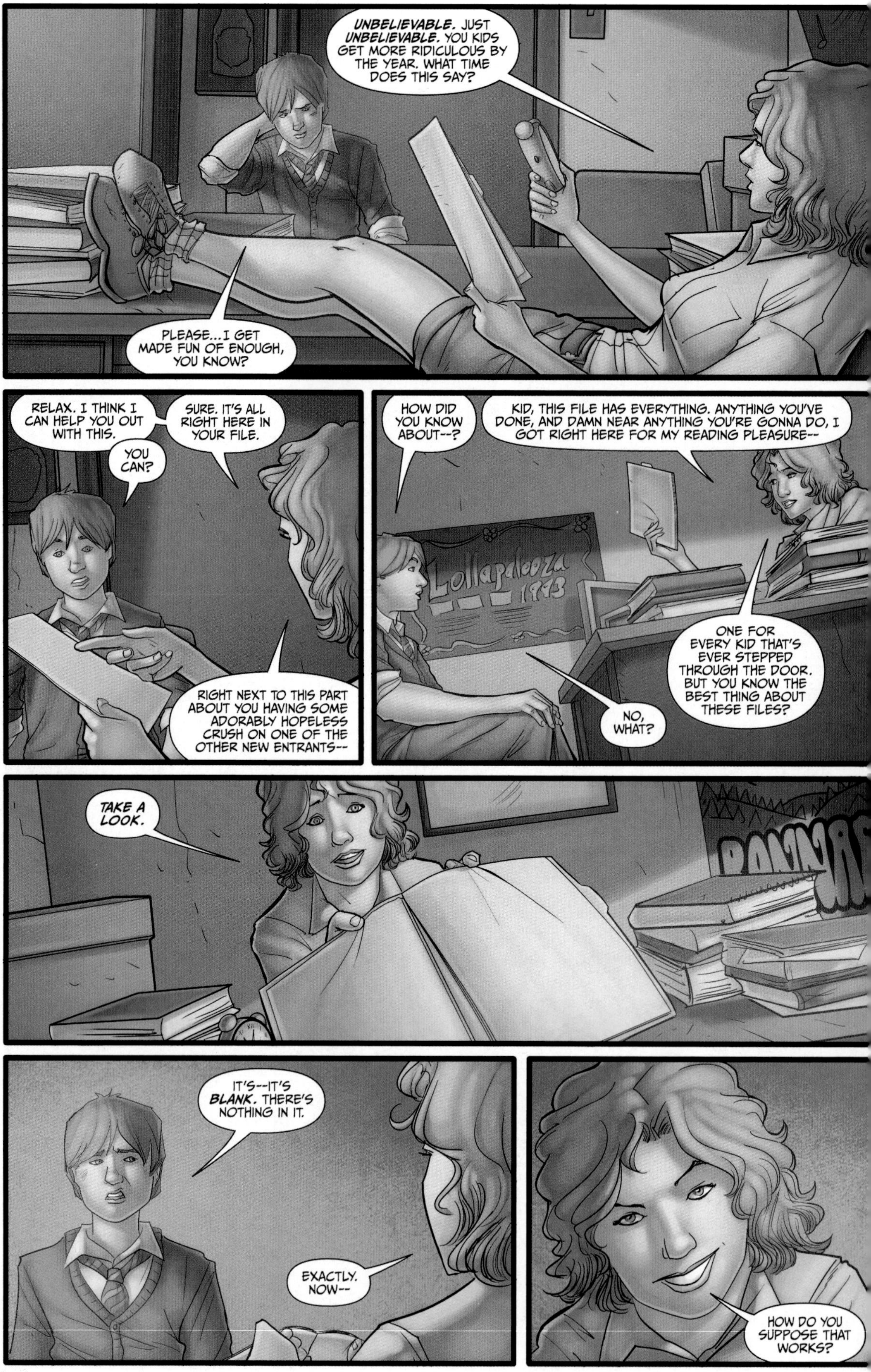

UNBELIEVABLE. JUST *UNBELIEVABLE.* YOU KIDS GET MORE RIDICULOUS BY THE YEAR. WHAT TIME DOES THIS SAY?
PLEASE...I GET MADE FUN OF ENOUGH, YOU KNOW?
RELAX. I THINK I CAN HELP YOU OUT WITH THIS.
YOU CAN?
SURE. IT'S ALL RIGHT HERE IN YOUR FILE.
RIGHT NEXT TO THIS PART ABOUT YOU HAVING SOME ADORABLY HOPELESS CRUSH ON ONE OF THE OTHER NEW ENTRANTS--
HOW DID YOU KNOW ABOUT--?
KID, THIS FILE HAS EVERYTHING. ANYTHING YOU'VE DONE, AND DAMN NEAR ANYTHING YOU'RE GONNA DO, I GOT RIGHT HERE FOR MY READING PLEASURE--
Lollapalooza 1993
ONE FOR EVERY KID THAT'S EVER STEPPED THROUGH THE DOOR. BUT YOU KNOW THE BEST THING ABOUT THESE FILES?
NO, WHAT?
TAKE A LOOK.
IT'S--IT'S *BLANK.* THERE'S NOTHING IN IT.
EXACTLY. NOW--
HOW DO YOU SUPPOSE THAT WORKS?

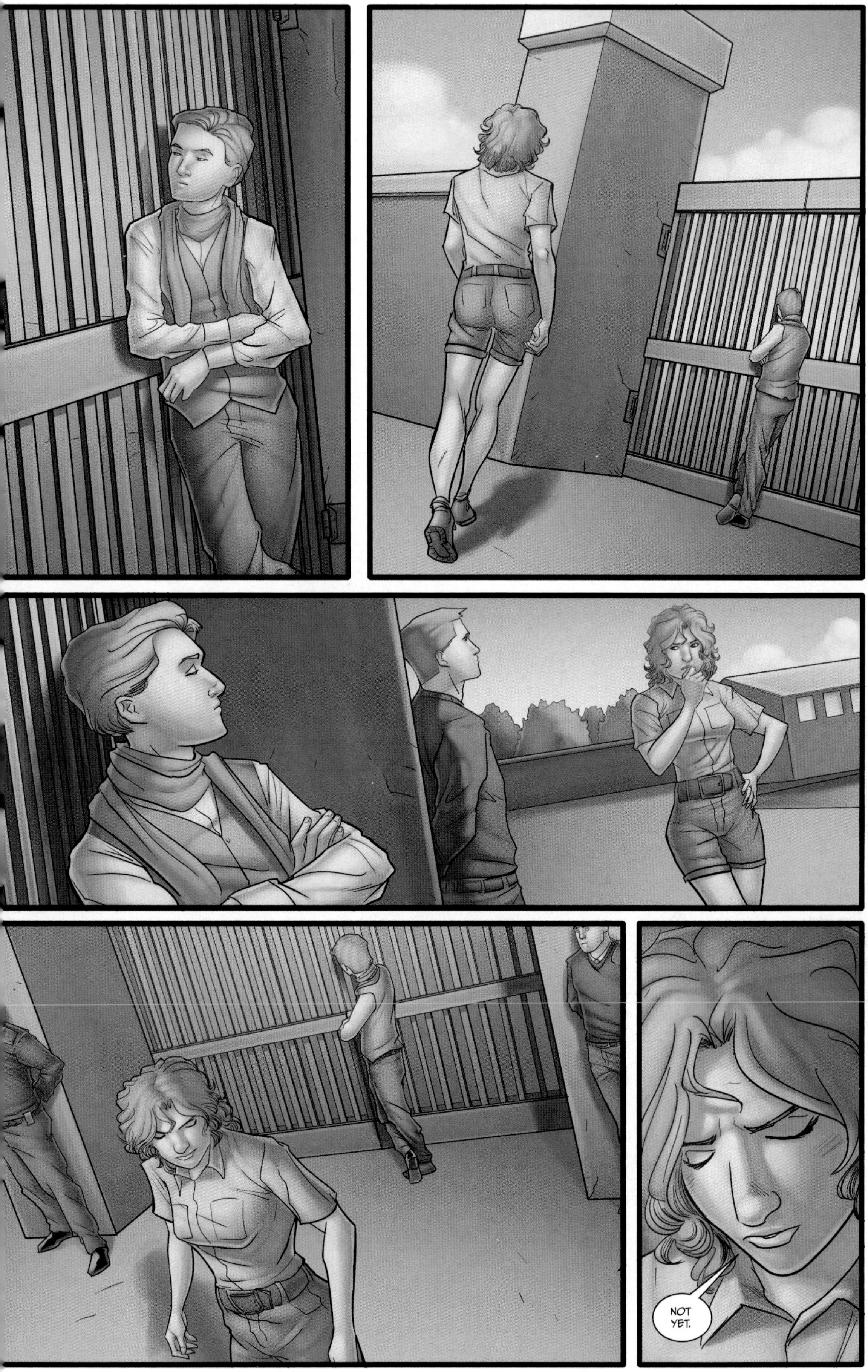
NOT YET.

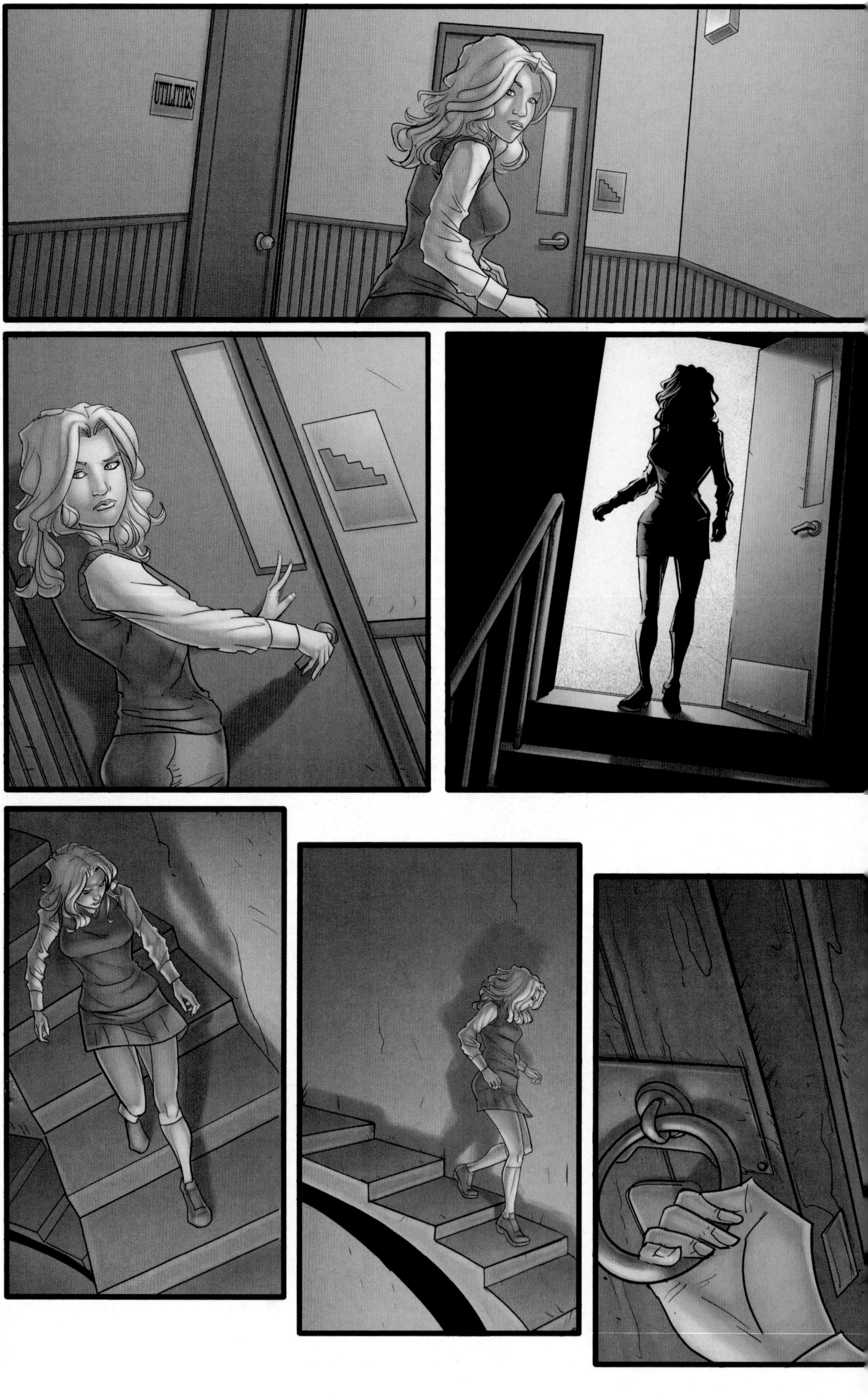
UTILITIES

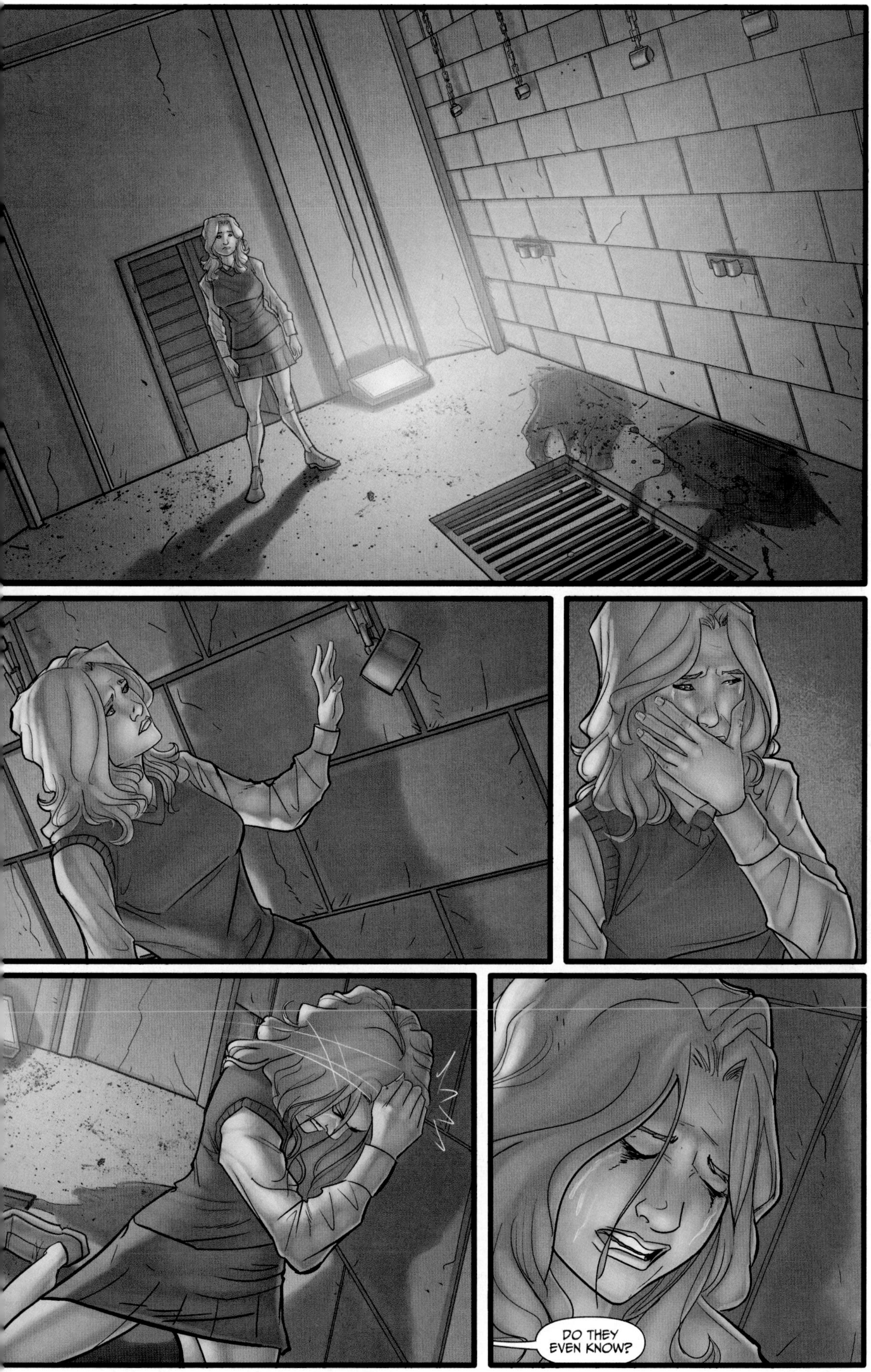
DO THEY EVEN KNOW?

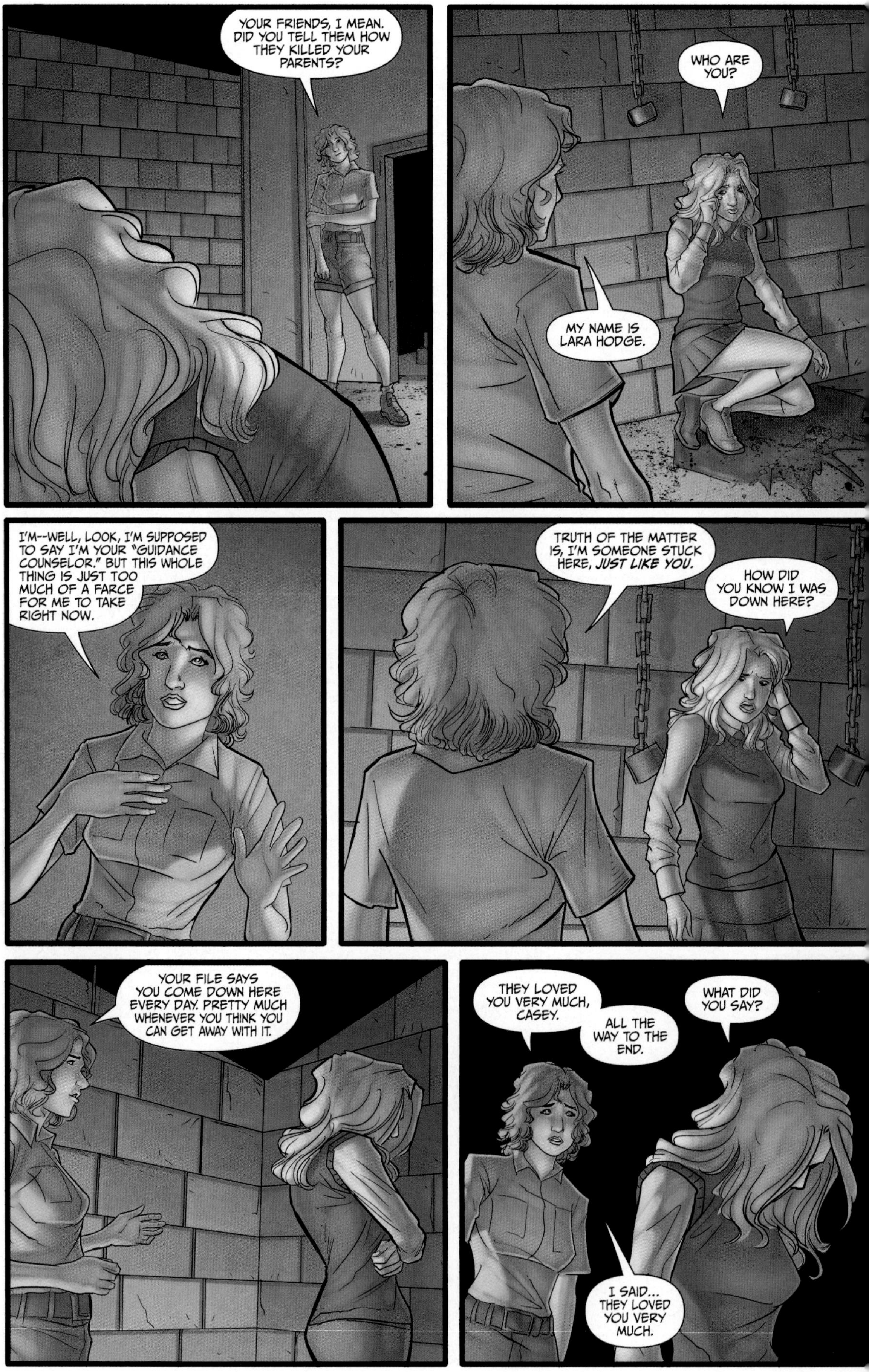
YOUR FRIENDS, I MEAN. DID YOU TELL THEM HOW THEY KILLED YOUR PARENTS?
WHO ARE YOU?
MY NAME IS LARA HODGE.
I'M--WELL, LOOK, I'M SUPPOSED TO SAY I'M YOUR "GUIDANCE COUNSELOR." BUT THIS WHOLE THING IS JUST TOO MUCH OF A FARCE FOR ME TO TAKE RIGHT NOW.
TRUTH OF THE MATTER IS, I'M SOMEONE STUCK HERE, JUST LIKE YOU.
HOW DID YOU KNOW I WAS DOWN HERE?
YOUR FILE SAYS YOU COME DOWN HERE EVERY DAY. PRETTY MUCH WHENEVER YOU THINK YOU CAN GET AWAY WITH IT.
THEY LOVED YOU VERY MUCH, CASEY.
ALL THE WAY TO THE END.
WHAT DID YOU SAY?
I SAID... THEY LOVED YOU VERY MUCH.

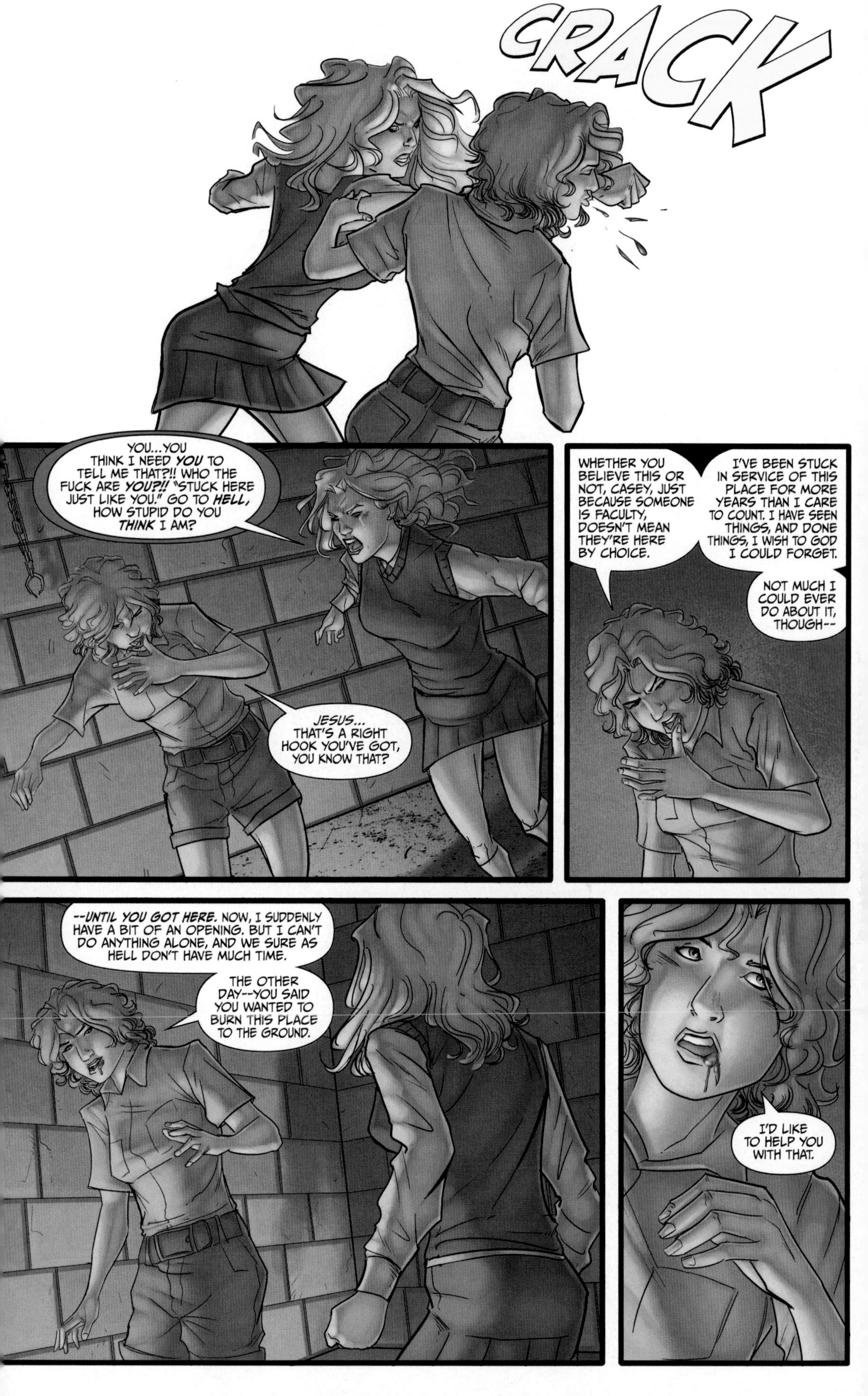
CRACK
YOU...YOU THINK I NEED YOU TO TELL ME THAT?!! WHO THE FUCK ARE YOU?!! "STUCK HERE JUST LIKE YOU." GO TO HELL, HOW STUPID DO YOU THINK I AM?
JESUS... THAT'S A RIGHT HOOK YOU'VE GOT, YOU KNOW THAT?
WHETHER YOU BELIEVE THIS OR NOT, CASEY, JUST BECAUSE SOMEONE IS FACULTY, DOESN'T MEAN THEY'RE HERE BY CHOICE.
I'VE BEEN STUCK IN SERVICE OF THIS PLACE FOR MORE YEARS THAN I CARE TO COUNT. I HAVE SEEN THINGS, AND DONE THINGS, I WISH TO GOD I COULD FORGET.
NOT MUCH I COULD EVER DO ABOUT IT, THOUGH--
--UNTIL YOU GOT HERE. NOW, I SUDDENLY HAVE A BIT OF AN OPENING. BUT I CAN'T DO ANYTHING ALONE, AND WE SURE AS HELL DON'T HAVE MUCH TIME.
THE OTHER DAY--YOU SAID YOU WANTED TO BURN THIS PLACE TO THE GROUND.
I'D LIKE TO HELP YOU WITH THAT.

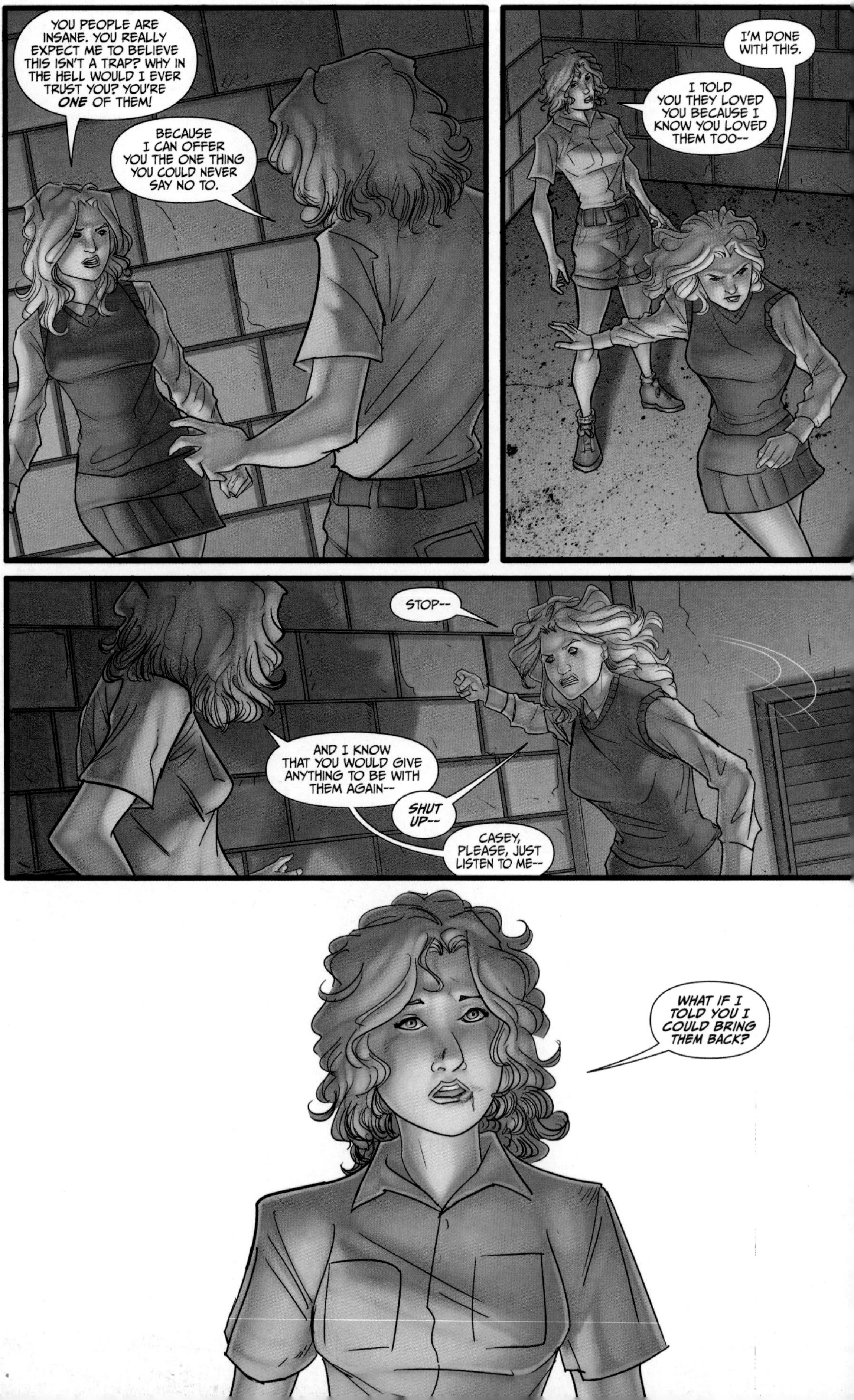
YOU PEOPLE ARE INSANE. YOU REALLY EXPECT ME TO BELIEVE THIS ISN'T A TRAP? WHY IN THE HELL WOULD I EVER TRUST YOU? YOU'RE *ONE* OF THEM!
BECAUSE I CAN OFFER YOU THE ONE THING YOU COULD NEVER SAY NO TO.
I'M DONE WITH THIS.
I TOLD YOU THEY LOVED YOU BECAUSE I KNOW YOU LOVED THEM TOO--
STOP--
AND I KNOW THAT YOU WOULD GIVE ANYTHING TO BE WITH THEM AGAIN--
SHUT UP--
CASEY, PLEASE, JUST LISTEN TO ME--
WHAT IF I TOLD YOU I COULD BRING THEM BACK?

7

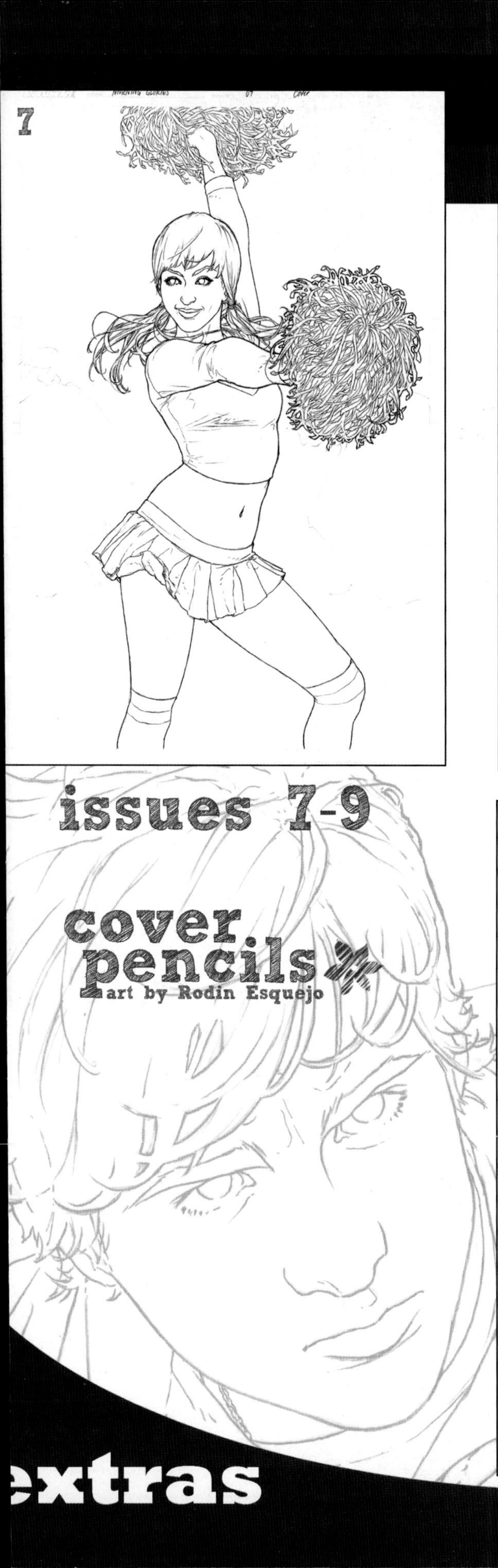
MORNING GLORIES
09
Cover

8

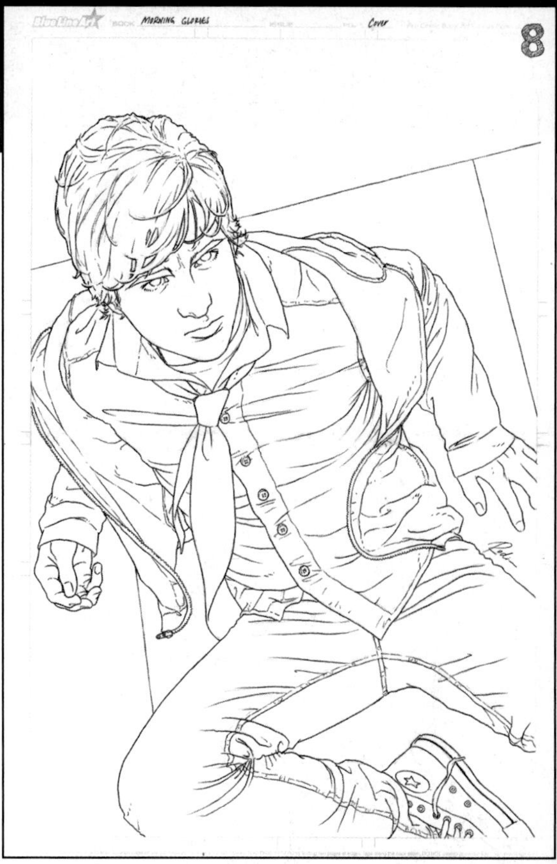
MORNING GLORIES
Cover

issues 7-9

cover pencils

art by Rodin Esquejo

9

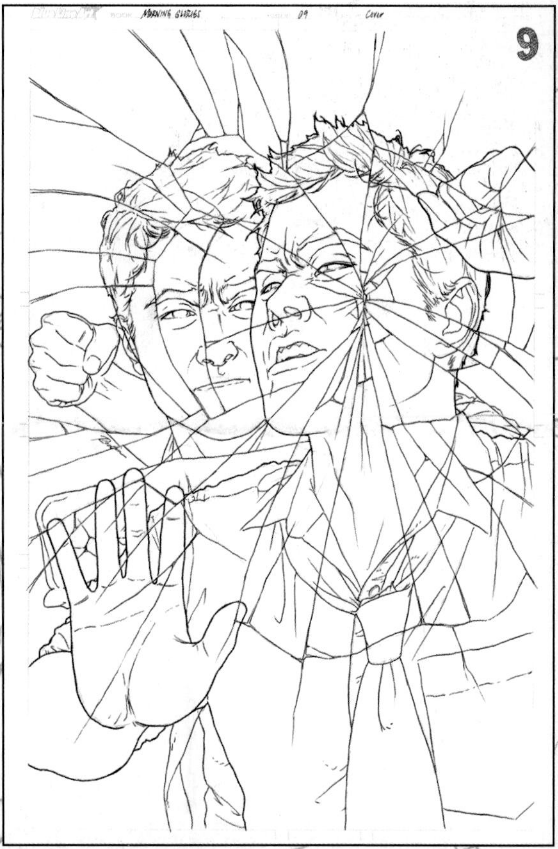
MORNING GLORIES
09
Cover

extras

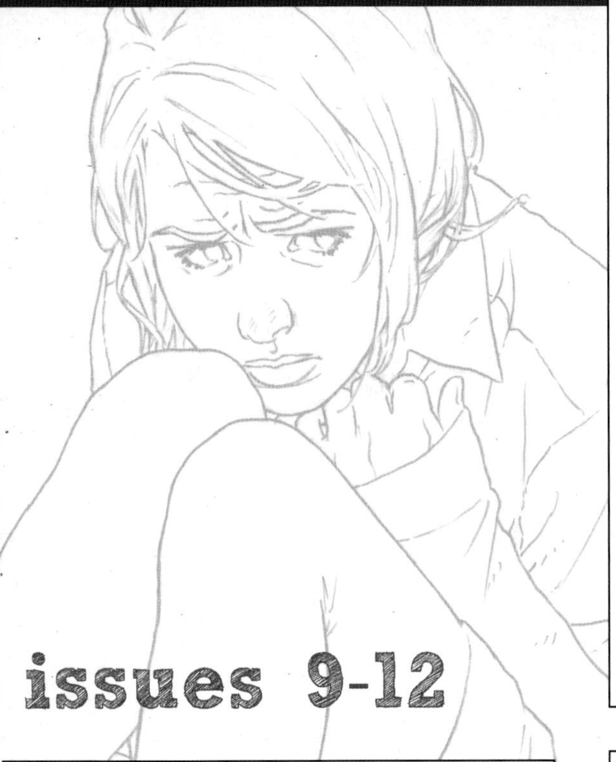

issues 9-12

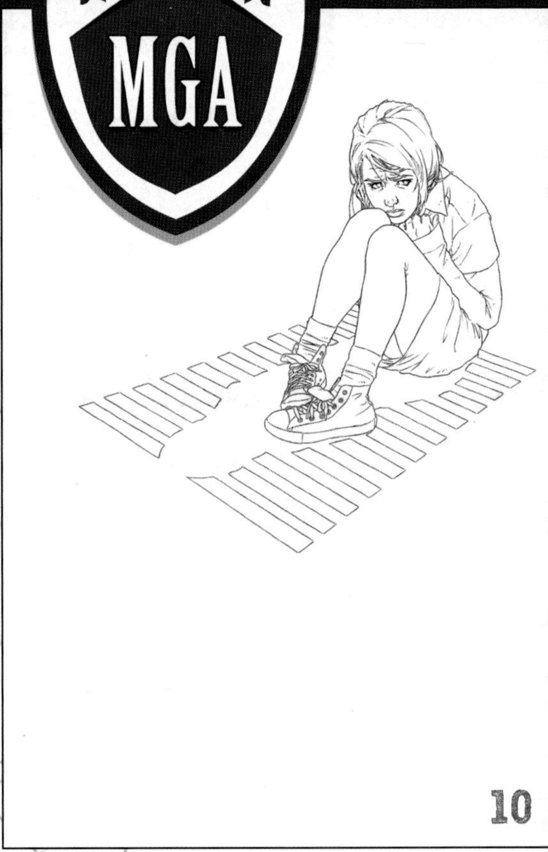

10

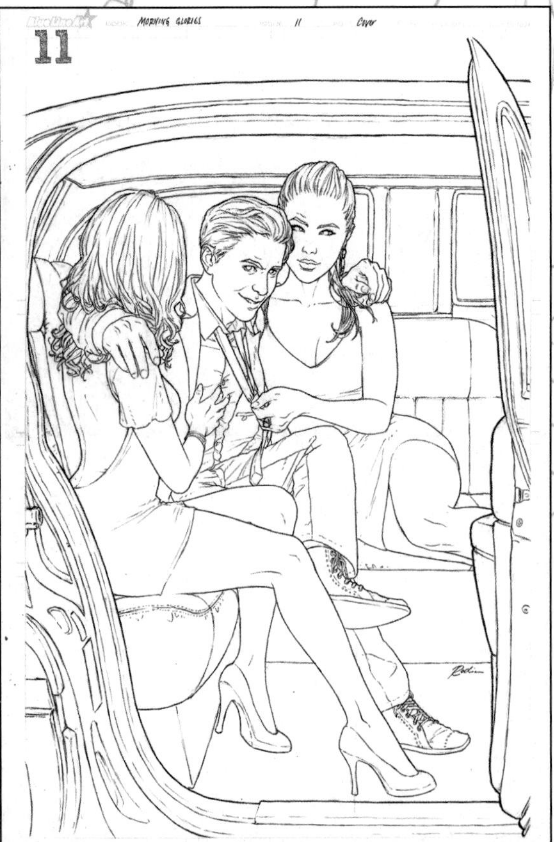

11

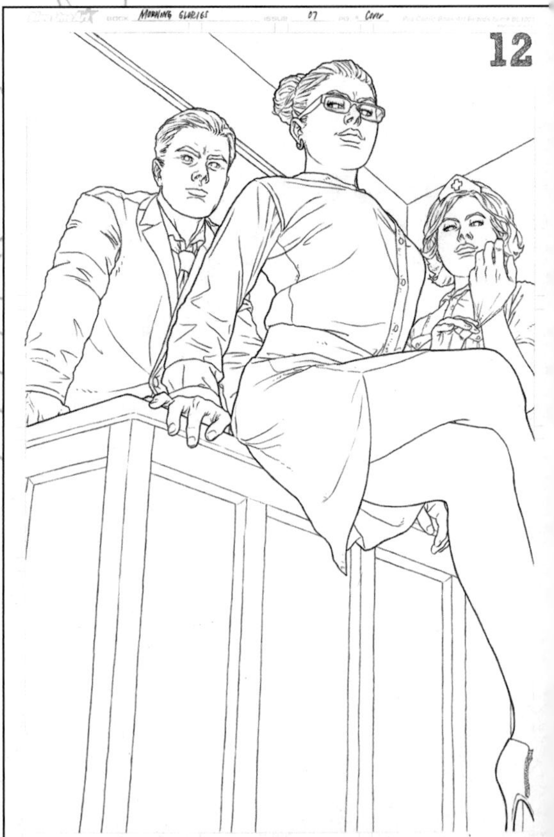

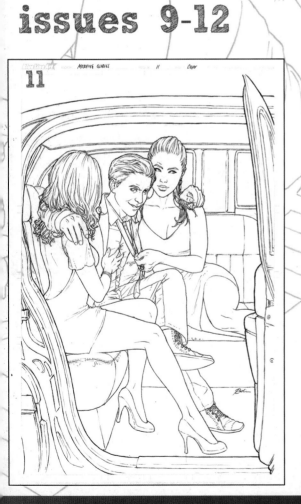

12